LIFE Story

LIFE Story

The Education of an American Journalist

GERALD MOORE

University of New Mexico Press | Albuquerque

Library of Congress
Cataloging-in-Publication Data

Moore, Gerald, 1938–
  LIFE story : the education of an
American journalist /
Gerald Moore. — First edition.
  pages cm
ISBN 978-0-8263-5677-2
(pbk. : alk. paper) —
ISBN 978-0-8263-5678-9
(electronic)
  1. Moore, Gerald, 1938–
2. Journalists—United States—
Biography. I. Title.
  PN4874.M5832A3 2016
  070.92—dc23
  [B]

2015026522

Cover photograph courtesy of the
  author.
Designed by Lisa Tremaine
Composed in Frutiger, Meridien
  and Franklin Gothic

*This book is dedicated to Joyce Nereaux with love and admiration,
and to Catherine, Benjamin, and Andrew.*

CHAPTER ONE

In May 1963, feeling both despair and panic about all the life decisions ahead, I sold my beautiful pale-green Volkswagen bug and used the proceeds to finance a summer program at the National University in Mexico City. I wanted to learn Spanish and Mexican history, and I yearned to be in a foreign place, but mostly I needed time to decide how to spend the rest of my life. I had no job-winning credentials, no degree in engineering or business or education. I had no intention of returning to my job with the Albuquerque Police Department. I was twenty-four, and any pretense that I was not yet an adult would end abruptly in July when I turned twenty-five.

When classes ended in late August and the fateful birthday had passed, I was still without an answer. I set out to explore Acapulco and San Miguel de Allende with a friend, carefully preserving my little cache of cash. We ate cheap, stayed in local hotels—places with curtains for doors and toilets without seats. The intrinsic pleasures of traveling and the comfort of hanging out with other students were clouded by the constant worry of what I would do when I got back to the States. Very soon I would cross the border at El Paso without a nickel and arrive back in Albuquerque homeless, jobless, and without any real notion of how I might survive. I had pushed all my chips onto the table without any solid prospect of winning a jackpot. None of the part-time work I had done as a student appealed to me as a possible profession. Writing, a pursuit utterly without hope of any financial success, was the only thing that really appealed to me, and it had been very much on my mind since that May when I passed through Juárez on the way to Mexico City. Waiting to change buses that afternoon, I put aside my American training in food hygiene and stopped a street vendor to buy a lump of spicy meat wrapped in a fresh tortilla.

Completely engrossed in the pleasure of eating after seven hours on the bus from Albuquerque, juices running down the back of my hand, I looked up and saw poverty of a kind I had never seen before. Several Tarahumara Indian women—tiny, frail things wrapped in rags—nursing infants and trailing small children, appeared on the dusty street to beg. A few years later I would accompany a group of doctors flying deep into the hinterlands of Chihuahua to treat these virtually Stone Age people. I would learn about their amazing ability as long-distance runners and more about their ancient customs, but this was my first encounter with them and with poverty at the level of near starvation. It was shocking. While I studied a woman holding out a dirty hand no larger than that of a four-year-old, I was suddenly, inexplicably, and powerfully struck by the notion that here but for the grace of Providence was I. A deep fear seized my stomach, and I found myself wondering not how to help this woman but how to prevent myself from ever being in her situation. Instinctively, even then, I did not fully trust the institutions of civilization upon which I relied every day. I was able to imagine a series of events that would leave me as poor as this woman for whom a peso, or even a few centavos, would determine if she and her children ate that night. It is almost impossible to write about this kind of poverty and a tourist's reaction to it without falling into cliché and sentimentalism, but it is true, nonetheless, that I found myself rooted to that dusty sidewalk for several minutes as I considered the fate of this hungry woman and my own circumstances. Then it occurred to me, in a moment of great and memorable relief, that I had one thing that she did not have, a skill that would forever protect me from her condition. I was literate.

It had never before entered my mind that this ability, acquired almost effortlessly, was precious and permanent. It could not be taken from me by political action, greed, dire circumstances, or anything else short of brain damage. It was mine and it was safe, and it set me apart from all the people of the world who could not read and write. I could be poor and desperate, but I would never be as helpless as this poor woman who had come to town in a wretched effort to feed herself and her kids.

This insight quieted my fear momentarily and led me to think about writing, about exercising the gift of literacy. I knew I was too young and inexperienced to have anything important to say. I also suspect I was more enamored of the idea of being a writer than with actually writing, but I wanted to try. Throughout the summer I considered getting a part-time job to allow time to write, but when I did the math I saw I would have to work full time at part-time wages to support myself. I had to get a real job.

I was sitting on a food-stained concrete bleacher beside an empty basketball court looking out at Acapulco Bay, feeling forlorn in my dilemma, scribbling in a flimsy student notebook, a *cuaderno*, when the notion hit me that reporters spend their days writing. Suddenly I remembered Orwell and Hersey and a host of other writers I admired who began as journalists. The more I thought about reporting, the more I liked the idea. I liked the possibility of being paid to find out things. I liked the idea of having access to places and events where the public is not welcome, an opportunity to learn how things really work, and a license to ask questions. I liked the idea of writing about things that were actually happening rather than things I made up. The desire to be a reporter flamed into an obsession. By the time I left San Miguel and headed back to the United States, I had made a firm commitment to apply for a reporting job at both Albuquerque newspapers. If they turned me down, I would go to Arizona and then to California. I would continue banging on newsroom doors until someone hired me. I was filled with fresh determination and a lot of anxiety, but a distinctly different kind of anxiety from what I had felt three or four months earlier.

Crossing the border into El Paso with all my possessions in one ratty backpack, without money, a car, or a place to live, I dreaded the difficulty of trying to reenter commercial society without a place to bathe, dress, or receive a phone call. I was on my own without material resources. My sister would let me use her phone, but there had been disagreements with my parents over money and the direction of my education, so I knew better than to ask them for a loan. Most of my friends were scraping by, and in any case, lending money to the unemployed was not considered a sound financial practice.

The friend who accompanied me on the Mexican adventure offered to let me sleep a few nights on his screened-in porch, temporarily sparing me the indignity of a park bench. Maurice, a laid-back man of modest passions, had not drawn down his resources quite so recklessly as I had. When we returned from Mexico he was able with his older brother to rent a small house near the University of New Mexico. Feeling deeply grateful for his generosity, I arranged a surplus army cot and one disreputable green satin comforter in a corner of his porch. I lay down to consider whether I could stay there until cold weather. Then Maurice appeared to tell me that he was sorry, but his brother, a man who affected bohemian values, thought it was uncool to have a squatter on the porch. I would have to move on.

I negotiated for a few more days on the porch and the next morning called Michael Hopkins at the *Albuquerque Tribune*, a thriving Scripps Howard paper published every afternoon but Sunday. The *Tribune* exists no longer. Though I did not know it that October morning, I was about to dedicate the next decade of my life to a form of journalism that was already becoming obsolete. It may seem a distant connection, but that December, during the Army-Navy game, CBS broadcast the first instant replay ever shown on TV. Who was watching? Not I. Television, as far as I was concerned, was strictly an entertainment medium. I just did not understand how broad the meaning of "entertainment" would become. The Internet and personal computers were still so far beyond our reality as to be virtually unimaginable. It is a mark of the time more than any measure of my powers of destruction that every publication where I would work during the next twenty years would fold or become so monstrously deformed as to be unrecognizable. The application of electronics, mathematics, and capitalist enterprise to journalism was my nemesis.

Michael received my call with all the cordiality one might expect from an old and dear friend. When I told him why I was calling, he missed a beat, but only one.

"You're not in the police department anymore?"

"No, I resigned six or eight months ago. I just spent the summer in Mexico trying to learn Spanish, but right now I need a job and I really want to be a reporter."

"You are actually calling at a very good time," he said. "I know they're looking for someone. When do you want to come down?"

"As soon as possible."

"Let me talk to the editor, and I'll call you back." He paused, then added thoughtfully, "I hope you understand that this is not the *Los Angeles Times* or the *New York Times* or even the *Denver Post*. This is pretty mundane stuff, day to day."

"It must not be too bad," I said. "You came back here to work."

"Only because I love New Mexico," he said. Then he added for emphasis, "There isn't any glamour here. There is no place for a young Hemingway—or Ben Hecht or Charlie MacArthur."

I was surprised that he would think I was looking for something glamorous, but I understood the conversation perfectly: admitting to any ambition beyond a staff position at the *Tribune* would disqualify me. I reinforced my understanding. "I just want an opportunity to be a really good reporter," I said. "I know the *Tribune* is not perfect, but neither am I." I probably laid it on a bit too thick with the remark about my own imperfection, but Michael didn't seem to notice.

"OK, I'll call you as soon as I can speak to Mr. Burrows."

CHAPTER TWO

I didn't know Michael Hopkins well, but I had known him for a very long time. We grew up in houses facing in opposite directions, divided at the rear by an alley. My family's house was a single-story white clapboard of a vaguely Arts and Crafts cottage style. The Hopkins house was a grand three-story edifice painted a tasteful soft green. Gardens surrounded the Hopkins property. A struggling, sporadically watered lawn separated my house from the street. Behind our house, nearly bare dirt nurtured goathead vines with thorns so sharp they could easily puncture a bike tire or inflict excruciating pain on an unshod foot. Still, once or twice every summer I would take a chance that I could retrieve a stray ball on bare feet. My failures to spot the thorns would send me into a hopping, howling frenzy that often resulted in my hurtling into another patch for another round of pain. These failures taught me how to stand still in spite of great pain and gave me a special pleasure in hoeing weeds that I still enjoy.

We had no garage. The Hopkins house had a three-bay affair where the current year's Cadillac always joined a new Buick and a somewhat older Chevrolet pickup truck. In a larger city we would not have shared a neighborhood and chances are good that I would never have met Michael, but in Tucumcari most white Protestants lived together, regardless of their wealth. The other half of town was occupied by Hispanics, or Spanish Americans as we were taught to call them, and they were without exception Roman Catholic. There were three Jewish families. Then, after *Brown v. Board of Education* began to desegregate schools, I discovered there were also black people—African Americans—living in Tucumcari. They were relegated to a small area north of the railroad tracks where they attended their own schools and churches, drank in their own bars, and kept their own company. Until six black students joined my high school senior class in the fall of 1955, seeming to appear from nowhere, they had been, in the ways Ralph Ellison described in *Invisible Man*, entirely outside the consciousness of our community. Years later I would read a bitter recollection by one of these briefly "fellow" students, a woman now a PhD working in Washington, DC, for the Department of Education. Her memories of our little eastern New Mexico town are very different from mine.

I came to Tucumcari, age eight, after my parents sold our ranch in 1946. My mother, sick of the isolation and danger of living on a remote patch halfway between Albuquerque and Roswell with two small children and lots of venomous snakes, carried on a more or less constant campaign to move to town. My father resisted throughout World War II, arguing that because ranching was considered a vital industry, his status as a rancher took him out of the pool of men eligible for the draft. Anyway, he was also too old, in his midthirties, and he had two small children, but it served his purpose to argue that ranching kept him close to home. With the war over and his draft argument gone, he might have held out a bit longer if the rains had ever come, but they didn't. Our pastures grew browner and more sparse each year. So when a doctor from Texas—who just had to have a ranch—happened by, we sold out and moved to Tucumcari.

During the Great Depression, the Army Corps of Engineers built a dam at the confluence of the Canadian and Conchas Rivers about thirty miles northwest of Tucumcari in east-central New Mexico. Ostensibly the dam was part of the Upper Mississippi Valley Flood Control Project. In fact, it was simply another New Deal scheme to create jobs where there were none. After World War II, the US Soil Conservation Service decided, with encouragement from our congressman, that the dammed-up waters could be used to irrigate the prairie around Tucumcari. Thus began another job-producing construction project that also tremendously increased the value of rangeland, soon to be turned into irrigated farmland. As pasture, land might be worth a few dollars an acre. Irrigated farmland was worth several hundred. With the money we received from selling the ranch, my mother got a house in town and my father got eighty acres of prairie a short drive east of Tucumcari. The ranch had been fifteen thousand acres with little water. Now we had eighty acres and what looked like an unlimited supply of water. In 1946 optimism was everywhere. The area around Tucumcari was destined to become another Central Valley of California, feeding the world. Eventually the irrigation project would prove to be an economic and agricultural failure. Had it prospered, I might have been a farmer.

My father made the transition from rancher to industrial cog with dignity and some success, but he never gave up the idea that one day he would reclaim his independent rural heritage and move us back to a successful "cattle operation." Once the land was plowed, the sod broken, he worked at the farm seven days a week, before and after his regular job as a self-trained engineer at the local power plant, often leaving the house before dawn to get in a few hours before his shift began and going out again in the evening to work until after dark. I sometimes wondered if his work ethic was not partly inspired by a desire to be away from the house. He was not especially fond of children, and my mother, whom he loved very much, could be difficult when she was in "one of her moods." As she got older and the mood swings grew greater, sometimes compounded by alcohol, I came to suspect that she was borderline bipolar. But as a child I found her behavior simply mysterious—and sometimes painful and confusing. My father's best advice to my sister and me was to "just stay out of the way when she's like that." Of course, he had the farm as a refuge. We had only the backyard with the goathead vines, until I got a bike.

I think my father also fell victim to that common human delusion that a past, always remembered as glorious, can be reclaimed. The right effort will restore the plantation, the ranch, the kingdom, the big house on the hill, or the hegemony of "men like us." Many American families subscribe to a mythology that blames the loss of fortunes and high social standing on the Civil War, the Great Depression, or some other national calamity. In my father's family the great loss was a hardscrabble Texas ranch sold a decade before it became an oil field.

Before I was ten, my father enlisted me in his efforts to become a cattleman. In some of my earliest memories I sit half-frozen on a tractor surrounded by late-evening gloom. I can still hear the big two-cylinder engine banging in my ears as dim yellow headlights lead the John Deere tractor pulling a plow inexorably through our dense clay soil.

Michael Hopkins was simultaneously occupied with piano lessons. This is not to list a complaint about our different circumstances. I was given piano lessons for a time and hated them. Given a choice between driving a tractor and practicing scales, I would always choose the tractor. I still drive a tractor—a small one, in the garden—and I am grateful that I can, but on balance I would much prefer to play the piano.

Because our houses faced different streets, his on South Second and mine on South Third, and because Michael was five years ahead of me in school, we never saw each other during the week. The Presbyterian church was our nexus. While he was still in high school, he became the organist for the church and continued to play there when he returned home from college during summers and on vacations. I was curious about him, partly, I am sure, because he was the only person under thirty who had anything to do with the church service, and partly because the organ struck me as a thing of immense complexity. The semicircular console bristling with knobs and handles and foot pedals seemed more like the control room of a spaceship or an ocean liner than a musical instrument. I found it hard to imagine learning to play anything so complex. When I made excuses to talk to Michael after services, he was always friendly. Standing under the heavy southwestern sun, wearing the wool suits and ties we kept for church, funerals, and graduation, we stood on the sidewalk and made small talk. I had little to offer him but admiration and curiosity, which was not a bad combination, come to think of it. He was always generous with his time.

I lost track of Michael after I left for college in Albuquerque. Then, one night as I was discharging my duty as jail officer for the Albuquerque Police Department, he appeared, notebook in hand, at the heavy steel bars separating the booking desk from the jail. I recovered after an instant of surprised confusion and grabbed a big ring of jail keys to let him in. I don't remember the exact dialogue that followed, but I remember the feelings and the subjects we spoke about. The scene went something like this:

"What on earth are you doing here?" he asked.

"I could ask you the same question."

"You could," he said, laughing. "But this is a joke, right?" He gestured toward my uniform. "You are not actually a cop?"

"I really am a cop." I gave him a look of resignation and shrugged my shoulders and locked the gate behind us. We shook hands, and I showed him to a chair beside the big rolltop desk that served as the jailer's office.

"Wow," he said, looking at me carefully. "I just can't wrap my mind around it."

"And you, why are you here?"

"I work at the *Trib*," he said, holding up his reporter's pad. "I thought you knew that."

"No, I didn't. I guess the Tucumcari grapevine broke down."

"I'm an editor, a copyeditor. The police beat reporter is on vacation. I thought it would be fun to see the seamy side of journalism, so I offered to fill in." He laughed. "But you . . ." He held out his hands in a gesture of regard and put on a quizzical look.

"I'll get some coffee," I offered. "There's a story."

"I can't wait to hear it."

I let myself into the jail kitchen and got two chipped mugs of lukewarm coffee. When we were settled in, I explained how, two years earlier, after a brief and unauthorized tour of London and Paris at my parents' expense, an unauthorized "junior month abroad," I suddenly found I was self-supporting.

"Mother told me you went to Europe," Michael said. "So what did you do? Just take your father's money and run away? We wondered how they could afford to send you."

The reference to my parents' financial resources was not malicious, but it reminded me of the difference in our circumstances. "Something like that," I said. "I had this grand idea that I would go to England and enroll in a great English university and become an academic star. Then I would come home a hero and lord it over all my friends."

"Really?" he said, ignoring my effort to be funny. "You just got on a boat or a plane or whatever and went to England expecting to enroll at Oxford or someplace like that?"

"I had a plan, or I thought I did." I had his full attention.

"So what happened?"

"Well, I showed up at the London School of Economics, where I had the name of a professor and a letter of introduction from my favorite history professor at UNM. I found the English professor's office, showed him Dr. Dabney's letter, and he immediately offered to take me to tea. I don't think I had ever gone to tea. I didn't know whether to take milk or sugar or lemon or all three."

Michael smiled indulgently.

"When we got the tea under control"—I drank it black, hoping to avoid a show of gaucherie—"he explained that I would have to go through a series of exams that would not be offered again until the following spring. I spent a few days touring London and then decided I'd go to Paris and learn French while I was waiting for the exams. I did. I mean, I went to Paris and enrolled at the Alliance Française. I was about a month into French when I came to and realized I had made a big mistake."

Michael shook his head in disbelief. "I don't know, but this sounds crazy. You couldn't just write to LSE and find out if they would let you in?"

The question annoyed me because it was the perfectly logical route to have taken. My actions were irrational. I simply felt compelled that fall to leave Albuquerque and go to England. In retrospect it sounds pretentious, but my liberal arts education had taken root and given me an almost religious regard for the culture of Western civilization: British and European civilization. Albuquerque was too far from the source. I needed to go to the source.

There was another possible motivation—more basic and perhaps closer to the truth—but it was not something I could tell Michael that night. My wife of eighteen months, Hellyn, had betrayed me during the summer with my closest friend and mentor, an attractive, energetic PhD candidate whom I had adopted as a role model. The betrayal was not without provocation, but equity in these matters never calms the heart. My discovery of their tryst so shocked my tender sensibilities that I had difficulty thinking clearly for several weeks. Conducting my life on the University of New Mexico campus as if nothing had changed, continuing to sleep with Hellyn and lose at chess to George, to act as if I didn't know their secret, seemed more and more impossible. I needed to make a dramatic gesture. I needed to get out of Dodge.

I explained to Michael how I had scraped together the initial price of my trip. Only a few days after the fall semester began in 1958, I discovered that if I withdrew before the end of October, my entire tuition and fees would be refunded. I had $500 saved from working in the campus bookstore. Taken together, there was enough money to survive four or five months. My parents had promised to fund my final two years at the university, and I now planned to apply this to my new endeavor. By the time I had done these things, Hellyn and I had forgiven each other. She added a few hundred dollars to the pot, and we booked economy-class tickets to Southampton on the *Queen Mary*. Then we drove home to tell our parents.

"They can't have been very happy," Michael said.

"I found mine on the living room couch having a glass of wine. When I told them what I was doing and that my ticket was not refundable, my father reached for the wine and said, 'I think I'll get drunk.' Mother was more supportive."

Michael laughed. I couldn't tell if he approved of my adventure or

11

thought I had lost my mind. My behavior was so completely transgressive of parental authority that I am sure he was shocked.

"A few weeks later, when we boarded the ship in New York City, I was in a dream."

New York had been a huge, complex, exciting place waiting to be explored. Sights that previously existed only in photographs or in my imagination became real. We walked past Radio City Music Hall, and I thought, There it is! It is real. When we found Carnegie Hall, I was surprised that such a seemingly small, unpretentious place loomed so large in my mind. Places I had read about appeared on every corner. I was even excited to see Macy's! What a rube I must have been—but an excited, infatuated rube. Hellyn had been to New York City before. She tried to appear blasé, but I knew that she too was excited and transported. In the two days we spent walking Manhattan as we waited for the *Queen* to sail, I felt a deep affinity building between the city and me, the beginning of a powerful and growing desire to be there and to be part of the wonderful things that I knew must be happening there. By the time we sailed past the Statue of Liberty, my life had changed profoundly, though I did not know it then.

In my excitement about leaving Albuquerque for England, apparently I had only imagined that my parents agreed to provide the same financial support they promised if I attended school in Albuquerque. Why should it matter to them where their money was spent if the results were the same? But after a few months, when my wired pleas for money went unanswered and my cash began to dwindle alarmingly, I understood that they had no intention of supporting my folly, although if they had supported it, it might not have been a folly.

On reflection, I am astonished that I would ever imagine that my father, profoundly skeptical of my need for anything beyond a high school diploma, would support such an elite undertaking as a European education. Explaining to Michael how I literally had been down and out in Paris became so ridiculous that eventually we were both laughing at the absurdity of my behavior.

Absurd or not, the behavior had consequences. In a moment of shame and regret for my reckless gesture, I wrote to my parents and renounced any claim to further financial help. To my shock and disappointment, they accepted my offer. Age twenty, still in need of three semesters of study to complete a degree, I was on my own. We had enough money to fly home from Paris and to buy a bus ticket from New York to

Albuquerque, where I came back to reality, dirty and sore from the long bus ride that ended my fabulous dream.

"So you decided to become a cop?" Michael asked, not able to connect the dots between needing a job and deciding to wear a uniform and carry a gun.

"Not exactly," I said. "It took a year or so. Looking for a job in Albuquerque that would allow me to attend classes taught me a few things. Then Cathy, our daughter, was born. That lit a fire under me."

In the late 1950s, Albuquerque was still a city of regional banking, insurance brokers, warehousing, real-estate speculation, small businesses, and education. Aside from government jobs, the University of New Mexico and the Albuquerque public schools were probably the largest employers in town. Tourism was booming all along Route 66, and Albuquerque's main thoroughfare was becoming an ugly forest of neon signs. But the real engine of the economy, the stimulus that allowed the city to grow from fifty thousand people in 1938—the year I was born there—to two hundred thousand by 1955, was a very large federal government payroll. Sandia Laboratory, linked to Los Alamos National Laboratories and the University of California at Berkeley, and Kirtland Air Force Base combined advanced nuclear weapons research with the means of storage and delivery. This produced a monthly infusion of federal money that splashed over into the civilian service industries: rental properties, bars, and all the other activities needed to support thousands of federal employees, some in uniform, many not. Regional offices for the US Forest Service, the US Geological Survey, the US Soil Conservation Service, and the US Department of Agriculture were there as well. All came with a steady professional payroll. In 1960 New Mexico received two dollars and change from the federal government for every dollar it paid in taxes. Albuquerque and Los Alamos were the most favored beneficiaries.

Politically, the state was profoundly backward in the way both power and corruption were exercised. The forms were crude, open, and accepted. The eastern urban states had long ago devised more refined, less visible methods for converting tax dollars into private money.

Writing in the introduction to Governor David Cargo's book *Lonesome Dave*, political observer Dennis Domrzalski described conditions in New Mexico in 1957:

Governors sold liquor licenses for campaign contributions,

state legislators gave themselves state contracts, county sheriffs campaigned for themselves in their squad cars; lobbyists bought lawmakers cars, trucks, liquor, and everything else; political candidates bought votes with whiskey, chickens, money, threats, and promises. When those incentives didn't suffice, ballot boxes were stuffed.

White conservative southern Democrats controlled the statehouse and kept Hispanics, blacks, Indians, women, and anyone else they held in contempt and viewed as inferior down and out of government. Public schools were segregated. Government employment was based on the spoils and winner-take-all patronage system. There was no Civil Service or merit system, so every time a different faction of the Democratic Party won the governorship or a majority on school boards or county commissions or city councils, thousands upon thousands of people were fired and cronies of the winners hired.

Organized labor was kept down. Legislators and local elected officials were in the pockets of corporations and mining companies. Some state employees were forced to work six days a week. Governors hired and promoted and demoted state police officers. Some governors took kickbacks from insurance company executives for making it mandatory that state employees buy insurance they didn't need. Large companies dodged taxes by making hefty contributions to governors. State government had no formal budget. . . .

Then there was the Republican Party—a nearly nonexistent organization that was never able to muster enough guts to confront and challenge the Democrats' corruption and their lock on government.

None of this was apparent to me, of course. As a college student I really had no idea what was going on in Santa Fe. I just needed a night job, and night jobs were rare. The military and the police worked three shifts. Almost everyone else slept at night. At first I found a job working evenings at the airport earning seventy cents an hour gassing private planes. I enjoyed being around aircraft. There is a romance about flying, especially about flying one's own plane, and I participated in it vicariously. Like a good boat, a plane held the promise of freedom, the capacity to simply go off in any direction without regard to roads or other restrictions. I never got into the pilot's seat of the planes I serviced, but I felt a special, mysterious thrill when I looked inside at the complex instrument display and imagined what flying must be like. At that stage of my life I had flown only once, back from Paris to New York on a TWA Constellation at the end of my aborted European education.

The sleek Beechcrafts and Cessnas, the clunky Pipers and Mooneys spoke of freedom and money. Some of the smaller planes were owned by men and women of ordinary means who simply loved to fly, but most were owned by people with money or by corporations, which allowed me to observe the behavior of a privileged class of Americans. Most of the people flying privately behaved as properly as one would expect them to behave, but I also saw memorable sights, like Mickey Mantle crawling out of an expensive plane wildly drunk and disorderly, standing on the wing to piss on the tarmac before demanding a blow job from no one in particular. I got to see big contractors flying elected officials on personal business. And because I was essentially a service station attendant for airplanes, I was invisible to the men using the pay phone in our office. I got a glimpse into male duplicity as they told wives about how pressing business would keep them away another day and girlfriends about coming right over. It made me wonder if that was the way all the Big Boys lived.

Then one morning I saw an ad in the *Albuquerque Journal* seeking recruits for an expanding police department. I couldn't imagine myself assuming authority as a cop. I felt irrationally afraid that if I appeared at the police station to apply for a job they would arrest me for a subversive attitude. But reading the ad, I understood that the job paid much more than seventy cents an hour, offered benefits, and held the possibility of working nights. I wrestled successfully with my fear and snobbery and went to city hall to apply. Within a few weeks I found myself with a shorn head in starched cotton fatigues in a police academy run by a tough Marine Reserve colonel, police lieutenant Don Daniels. I was about to begin an experience in ego reduction that compared in intensity to showing up at a formal wedding wearing a polyester leisure suit.

After four months of serious training, in the best physical condition of my life, I was called into Lieutenant Daniels's office and told that I was graduating first in the class. This produced a decidedly complex mix of emotions. Astonished that I had outperformed my twenty-eight fellow cadets, at least in the eyes of my instructors, I was pleased by the accomplishment but made uneasy by the idea that I somehow embodied the best "cop" qualities of the group. I could see by Lieutenant Daniels's manner that he expected good things of me when I joined the force. This created further conflict because my main goal was to find a slot on the department where I would be left alone to study. He saw a future police commander in perfect creases and shining leather. I saw a tweedy would-be intellectual impersonating a cop. I had to work the streets for a year before maneuvering myself into jail duty, midnight to eight, but then I was able to attend classes during the day, sleep through the afternoon and evening, and study four or five hours during my shift.

Michael thought my decision to become a cop was brilliant under the circumstances. I was relieved that he seemed willing to continue our friendship despite my uniform. Some of my friends were not so understanding. I had learned with some pain that one of the reasons cops are socially insular is that noncops tend to avoid them. As much as people may praise and admire cops publicly, as much as we may like to watch them on television or in movies, the truth I discovered is that people are uncomfortable with authority figures like cops and priests.

Poor Michael! His story was so dull by comparison. He told me that he had completed a degree in journalism at the University of Missouri, and when the time came to get a job he found he really wanted to be in New Mexico. The *Tribune* took him on as a copyeditor. Using family money, he bought a beautiful old adobe house in Corrales, a picturesque little village just north of town. There he lived alone with his music and his ambitions to be a playwright, socializing occasionally with a few hard-drinking, middle-aged couples who were neighbors.

As we talked, I noticed for the first time how tense Michael had become. He always had a nervous laugh, but now it seemed more frequent and more pronounced. I couldn't locate the source of the tension exactly, but I began to understand that he was lonely and socially inept. He seemed thinner too, although the Levi's and work shirt he wore that night tended to make him look slimmer than the wool suits I was used to seeing. He sat beside my rolltop desk until nearly 2:00 a.m. while we talked about teachers we had in common and possible news stories about the department. We were interrupted occasionally when I had to lock up a prisoner or two.

"What are you reading?" he asked eventually, pointing to the paperback lying on the rolltop.

"*Masochism in Sex and Society* . . . Reik," I said, holding it up. "It is actually *Masochism and Modern Man*, but they retitled it to get 'sex' in."

He laughed. "Lots of cops reading Reik these days?"

"Not Reik, but there are several guys in law school who work swing shift in records. That is a student's dream!"

"Really," he said. "I had no idea. This is more like a dorm than a police station?"

"For God's sake, don't write that we study here," I said, alarmed that a story might upset my applecart.

"Don't worry. I won't blow your cover."

We exchanged phone numbers, agreed to get together, and I let him out. In fact, we didn't see each other or talk again until I had escaped the police department and called him looking for a job.

CHAPTER THREE

I sensed intuitively from the beginning that there was moral danger in being a police officer. Aside from the human inclination to abuse power, and aside from the coarsening awareness that your directions can be backed by force, other bad things happen to a person who always sees others in their worst moments: grief, fear, rage, deception, intoxication. The change is subtle and insidious. It begins to harden the observer. I assume this is a natural process to protect against frequent exposure to people behaving badly, a kind of scarring over of the common sensibility of empathy. It is hard to remember that you are seeing folks who normally lead acceptable lives, but who are now—in this moment, this "police" moment—at their very worst: drunk, bloody, vicious, without dignity. The moral hazard is simple and dangerous: one comes to think that humans are base and that when they behave well, it is only temporary or they are pretending in order to hide their true nature. It follows that if one sees people as base, selfish, and dishonest, then that behavior becomes permitted in one's self. It leads to contempt and cynicism. Add contempt to power, the common mix for fascism or Stalinism, and the result is at worst murderous, at best soul killing. Of course, the naïve belief that people are basically good also leads to dangerously fallacious thinking. It is sometimes hard to accept, but the only credible view on this question is that people are complex, often unpredictable, cunning, cruel, and kind, but they are not basically anything but human.

I often recall my father, who grew up along the border with Mexico, philosophizing once about Mexicans: "They can be the kindest, most caring people on earth, and then at other times they can be really cruel sons of bitches." At the time I thought he was describing the people of Mexico. By the time I left the Albuquerque Police Department I knew he had described us all.

A second hazard for me, though not a moral one, was an overly developed sense of empathy. Seeing how badly someone had screwed up his life, often in a single moment of ill-considered behavior, elicited a great sense of pity in me. Many people breaking the law—not all, but many—made me want to scold them and send them home. Admittedly, there were times when I wanted to beat the crap out of an obnoxious, arrogant drunk, but more often than not I would have been more comfortable in the role of counselor or priest than arresting officer. I learned a lot about myself working as a cop. I also learned invaluable lessons about human behavior and society, the kind of lessons that are not available in a classroom.

I learned how corruption works, how subtle and clever it is and how it draws in people who are not inclined to be corrupt. I learned about simultaneously contradictory truths, which I have come to believe are the only ways to understand human beings. During our four months of training, Lieutenant Daniels and his cadre of instructors worked hard to create for us the image of a police officer as an upstanding, serious, ethical guardian of social values as expressed in law. Despite the personal experience of many of the cadets, Daniels succeeded in convincing me and most of the others that good cops were the rule and rogue cops the exception, and that bad cops were always to be resisted. In time I would learn that reality is always more complex than theory.

Fresh out of the academy, shoes still glistening with the military spit-shine required of cadets, the thought of taking advantage of my position was repellent. I paid for my coffee, and if a waiter refused to bring a check, I left the price as a tip. When another officer began to beat a man I caught burglarizing a pharmacy, I intervened to stop it. In truth, I felt self-righteous in those first few months. Then, one night just before Christmas, Johnny Johnson gave me my first lesson in how it works.

Johnny, the oldest cadet in our class, was an affable, beer-bellied, retired navy chief approaching forty. He was hired despite his age because special rules applied to veterans. Raised in a tough area of Boston and having enlisted in the navy at age seventeen, he was worldly, likable, and ultimately treacherous. He lived with his family not far from me, and during the academy we began swapping rides to work, a practice we continued after we graduated. I liked Johnny, but I sensed he was a man comfortable with behavior that I found unacceptable. He spoke often, happily and in too much detail, about brothel visits in the Philippines.

19

He seemed to admire the brutality of the Boston cops he feared as a kid. I sensed that he saw me as a person in need of instruction in the ways of the real world. I kept my guard up in his presence, and yet I felt that in a pinch I could probably count on him.

One evening on the way to work, I checked my holster and, in a moment of sinking horror, realized that I had left my gun locked up at home. There was no time to go back and get it without being late for the shift briefing, an unacceptable breach of discipline. I fell into a state of near panic. I told Johnson what I'd done. "Don't worry, kid," he said reassuringly. "Take mine. I'm working records tonight. I don't need a gun."

Tremendously relieved, feeling a deep sense of gratitude, I took his revolver and slipped it into my holster. When the shift briefing ended, I headed to my assigned patrol car. Johnson followed a few feet behind me, headed for the records desk. I looked up to see Lieutenant Smiley, the shift commander, approaching. He walked at a brisk pace, nodding as he passed by. Suddenly he planted his feet and held up his hand to stop Johnson. I turned around in time to hear Smiley demand, "Where the hell is your gun, Johnson?"

Johnny looked crestfallen. He glanced at me and then, looking at the floor in a sheepish attitude, said, "I forgot it, Lieutenant, but I'm working records."

"You forgot your gun?"

"I'm sorry, sir. I just walked out of the house without it."

"What the hell kind of cop are you, Johnson, coming to work unarmed? I don't give a fuck if you're working latrine duty!"

I couldn't watch in silence. My sense of honor was on the line. I stepped up. "Lieutenant, Johnny didn't forget his gun. I forgot mine. This is his gun. He loaned it to me."

Lieutenant Smiley glowered at me for an awful moment, and then he and Johnson burst into wild laughter. They had set me up.

I had passed the test for a stand-up guy, but the whole episode struck me as dangerous. I saw how easily I could be fooled and how quickly Johnson and Smiley bonded over my error. Johnny had done me a good turn lending me his gun. He had also turned me in by making Smiley aware of my failure and then papered the whole thing over by enticing Smiley to join him in the practical joke. It was masterful. Twenty years of navy life had not been wasted on the conniving Johnson.

"You're OK, Moore," Johnson said approvingly. Smiley slapped me on the shoulder, still amused by my leap to honor. He went on his way with a big smile on his face.

I suspect the lieutenant regarded me as a tight-ass from the very beginning, and it may be that he encouraged Johnson to bring me around for his own protection and the peace of mind of all concerned. In my virginal moral state I was dangerous. In any case, the mechanism of my deflowering was simple. Johnny had to involve me in some illegal or unethical act that would be kept secret but recorded in his little black book, the record kept by every officer of the transgressions of every other officer as insurance against any urge to bear witness. The blue wall of silence is not just a code. It is a method of survival. It is not possible for even the well intentioned to conduct active police work for any length of time without breaking a rule or a law, because police actions are often made quickly, based on an almost instinctual understanding of exactly what is happening. The decisions are subject to interpretation and review, and the assumptions an officer brings to the moment can turn out to be completely wrong. Early in my brief career I experienced misperception with potentially deadly consequences, and I have never forgotten how shocking it is to see that what you are sure is the truth is not the truth at all, like a good magic show.

I was alone in a police car in deserted downtown Albuquerque at 2:00 a.m. on a cold winter morning. Suddenly I heard the metallic clatter of a burglar alarm coming from an alley behind several jewelry stores and a bank. I gunned the car, racing to the alley entrance. A beat officer, a classmate in the academy, ran toward the alley from the opposite direction. I stopped to avoid hitting the beat man as he reached the alley entrance. Another man, dressed in work clothes, suddenly emerged from the dark alley with a pistol in his hand. He stopped and raised the pistol toward my partner. I drew my gun, leveled it across the now open car window, and took aim to shoot. Seeing my intentions, my target pointed his pistol up to the sky and yelled, "I'm a cop!" I eased off on the trigger and heard my heart thundering in my ears. The beat cop stood stark still, frozen by the sudden appearance of the gun. A moment of silence passed before any of us regained perspective. I released the hammer on my revolver, yelling for the mystery man to put his gun on the ground. He complied, and while the beat man got him against a wall, I waited, gun in hand, for a resolution.

The man was not a cop. He was a security guard employed elsewhere in the city. He had armed himself on his own initiative and was passing by when he heard the alarm. Like many people who wish they were policemen but can't qualify for one reason or another, he played policeman and took it upon himself to investigate. He ran to the back of the store to check the door. The door was secure. He ran down the alley toward the front of the store where he saw us. What in his mind identified him as a cop was his gun, which he showed us, not his security officer's badge, which would have sent us a very different message. In those days I was a very good shot. Chances are that with a car door for a rest I would have driven a .357 Magnum round through his chest. Then what? "Cop Kills Security Guard in Case of Mistaken Identity." Equally upsetting upon reflection was the knowledge that had the man intended to shoot my partner I would have been too late to prevent it. It was a nasty night. Only later did I summon gratitude for the fact that I had not killed the guard.

Another magic show: I was called to a bar fight in a very tough section of town. Skidding to a stop near the Four Corners Cafe, I saw a tall, powerful man getting the best of a smaller man in a fistfight on the sidewalk outside the bar. Coming across the street, another character headed for the melee carrying a tire iron he appeared to have pulled from a car parked nearby, the door now left open. I hit the pavement, nightstick in hand, and yelled for them to stop. When the fighters looked up, I recognized Sherman Nobel, another police academy classmate and the only African American officer then on the force. When I had control of the parties, I pulled Sherman aside.

"What happened?" I asked.

"The cracker called me a nigger, and I punched his fucking face in."

Sherman's opponent had clearly gotten the worst of the fray, judging from the blood on his face and clothing. I was surprised to find Sherman in such a low bar, but my immediate thought was to protect him from a possible charge of assault. Even if he proved to be in the right, which I suspected would not be the case, involvement in a bar brawl would hurt his standing. I approached the bleeding man and his helper (who had mysteriously made the tire iron disappear) and, after a brief conversation and noting their identification, suggested that he and his companion take a hike. They seemed more than happy to get in their car and leave.

"Thanks, man," Sherman said, flexing his aching hand.

I was about to bask in Sherman's gratitude when our shift sergeant arrived. He jumped out of his car and rushed over. "What happened?"

"Sherman and some barfly got in a scuffle," I said.

"Where is the guy?"

"I sent him on his way."

Disbelief transformed Sergeant Chappell's face. "A man assaulted a police officer and you allowed him to leave?"

"Well, yes. I did," I said, like a contrite schoolboy. "I thought it better if Sherman wasn't involved in anything official."

Sergeant Chappell looked at me as if I were a creature from another planet and got into his car and left.

For a time after that, I wondered if Chappell had wanted to teach a lesson about insulting off-duty police officers, even African American ones, or if he wanted the whole thing to be official to reveal that Sherman had been involved in a brawl. The answer seemed to come a few months later, after I was on jail duty. A black man was arrested for discharging a firearm in the city limits. The arresting officer booked the suspect under a city law that held the infraction to be a violation of city ordinance. I happened by Sergeant Chappell's office to find him browsing through the New Mexico Criminal Code. There he found the felony statute "discharging a firearm within a settlement," which covered the same offense. He handed me a note instructing the booking officer to change the charge from a city violation to a state felony.

Moments like these taught me the way things really are. I doubt that I was any more naïve than most twenty-two-year-olds raised in small towns and taught about "our way of life" in the idealized manner common to parents and the public schools of the 1950s. I wasn't backward enough to believe in Santa Claus or the tooth fairy, but I was shocked to learn that men gratuitously hurt other men because of their color. It would be a few years before I learned that society operates very much the same way at the lowest and highest levels.

Johnny and I were assigned to the same patrol car one night just before Christmas, and we had been on duty only about half an hour when he said, "Let's go see if any of the liquor stores are handing out Christmas presents."

"What do you mean?" I knew exactly what he meant, and I was very unhappy with the idea.

"Drive up to Okie Joe's. We'll see if they have a Christmas present for the cops on the beat."

"They aren't going to give us a Christmas present. They've never seen us before."

"Go on. Drive up there," he insisted.

Feeling distinctly uncomfortable, I drove the few blocks to Okie Joe's, a joint I sometimes frequented during my student days before I was a cop. Okie's was a big beer hall and package store that served students of the university and the various types who hung around the fringes of the university. I pulled up in front, and Johnny said, "Come on, let's go in."

"You go," I said. "I don't need any presents."

"What is this, Moore?" he asked in a voice of great irritation. "It's Christmastime. You give the mailman a buck or two right?"

"Actually, I don't," I said. "Should I?"

He looked at me for a moment, his blue eyes studying my face as if he was looking at a stranger and trying to understand what he saw. I held his gaze.

"Well, fuck me," he said. "I'll go."

I felt deeply unsettled. I didn't want to go in begging or threatening some startled clerk for a bottle or two of booze, but I didn't want to alienate Johnny either. I might need him to save my life—or lend me a pistol. I watched as he guided his beer belly through the liquor store door. Through the big plate-glass window I saw him speaking to the clerk and saw the clerk shake his head in a slow negative gesture. Johnny spoke some more, and the clerk went to the phone. He dialed and spoke briefly. He shook his head in a positive gesture and hung up. He walked around the counter and selected four bottles of cheap bourbon, bagged them, and handed them to Johnson.

Johnny rolled into the car with his paper bag, laughing. "They weren't so much in the holiday spirit," he said. "Let's hit the next place."

I felt dirty. It is against my nature to be offensive, but I was firm that I wasn't driving us to any more liquor stores. "You want to go to a liquor store, you can drive," I offered.

"No, no," he said, suddenly seeming satisfied and happy. "Let's go look for broken windows."

No more mention was made of the four bottles of booze on the back floorboard. When the shift ended he offered me two.

"No," I said. "That's fine. You keep them."

He shrugged. We walked to his car and got in for the ride home. As we neared my place, he pulled into a 7-Eleven and came out with a quart of eggnog. He drove to my place, and instead of dropping me off as usual, he parked. "Let's have a Christmas drink," he said in a most convivial, friendly way.

How could I refuse to have a Christmas drink with my patrol partner? "OK," I said.

Johnny brought the eggnog and two of the bottles he had collected at Okie's. We went to the kitchen, where he took charge, finding glasses in the cupboard. He poured out two huge drinks, topped them with eggnog, and, hoisting his glass, said, "Merry Christmas, partner."

I lifted my glass and we drank. The sweet, thick eggnog made the whiskey go down easy. I was hungry. I hadn't eaten since 3:00 a.m., and it was now approaching nine in the morning. He drank quickly, and I tried to keep up with him. We were soon, too soon, on a second drink. He was almost a cheerleader in his exuberance and friendliness.

In only minutes the bourbon bottle was nearly empty and my head was spinning. I realized that I had drunk far too much and far too fast. I was drunk and going to be a lot drunker before the day was over. I could hardly think. "I think I have to lie down," I said.

Johnny got up, shook my hand, patted me on the back, and said, "Have a merry Christmas, buddy. I'll see you tonight."

I hardly remember him leaving. I remember being in bed until evening and waking with a horrendous hangover. I remember thinking that I was far too sick to work and calling in to report that, a serious breach of responsibility so near the holiday. Sometime the next day I was able to walk from the bedroom to the kitchen, where I opened a can of chilled beef consommé and ate the jelled soup directly from the can, hoping it would stay down. On my way back to the bedroom, I saw the other, unopened bottle of bourbon on the kitchen table where Johnny left it.

By eleven that night, having missed the previous night's shift, I felt I should drive Johnny to work. I called him about 10:00 p.m. to say that I'd pick him up.

"What happened to you last night?" he asked.

"Oh, man, I was so sick," I said. "You got me knee-walking drunk, you and that fucking eggnog."

"Hey, the whiskey was free," he joked. "Why not drink a lot?"

So there I was. Johnny had gone in and browbeat the clerk to get a gallon of rotgut bourbon, and I had participated in consuming it. It didn't take a lot of imagination to script the dialogue: "So, Officer Moore, you waited in the car while Officer Johnson intimidated the young clerk at Oklahoma Joe's Package Store to procure four quarts of bourbon. And just hours later, you joined Officer Johnson in drinking said liquor."

25

One consequence of my Christmas drunk was that I was never again able to drink bourbon. After fifty years, the slightest smell of it makes my stomach curl. Now aware that Johnson had something on me, I felt more cautious in my behavior toward other officers.

About a month later I got a clear view of how it worked on a higher level. I stopped a man after he slowly drove several blocks the wrong way down a one-way street. Flashing red lights and a siren were required to get his attention. I asked him to step out of the car. He was actually quite pleasant and quickly complied, rolling off the car seat and falling on his face on the pavement. As he struggled to stand, I decided he was roughly as drunk as I had been the Christmas Eve morning Johnny left me at my kitchen table with the bottle of bourbon. I made the arrest, had his car towed, and drove him to the station for booking.

We were not strict about an arrestee's right to make a phone call. If they were vaguely coherent and seemed to need to make more than one call, we allowed it. My man made two calls: one to his attorney, whom he seemed to reach at home, and one to another person whose name I did not recognize. Within a few minutes of his last call, the phone rang at the booking desk. Lieutenant Smiley asked to speak to me.

"Send that man down here," he said. "I want to talk to him."

I escorted my arrestee to the shift commander's office, holding onto him to keep him from falling down the stairs. I returned to the booking desk to wait. A short time later, Lieutenant Smiley called. "I have interviewed this man and I don't believe he is drunk," he said.

I was astonished. "Sir, I found him—"

"Officer Moore," he said in full command voice, "I believe this man is not legally intoxicated. I'm sending him back up to collect his property. Have Sergeant Scully arrange a taxi to get him home. And don't worry about the towed car. He understands."

I looked at Scully, the booking officer who had overheard my conversation. He shrugged.

Scully, another worldly type who had worked in federal prisons before moving to Albuquerque for his wife's asthma, helped me get our new friend on the road, returning his wallet, belt, keys, cash, rings, and tie. When he was gone, Scully asked, "Know who he is?"

"Some drunk with clout?"

"He owns a bunch of liquor stores up in the Heights, four or five. He's been in here before."

"Enjoys his wares?"

"I guess."

By the purest chance I happened to be in the rear of the police station a few nights later and saw a van from a Heights liquor store off-loading cases of Chivas Regal into the trunk of Lieutenant Smiley's personal car. Was there anything amiss? I didn't know for certain. Perhaps the lieutenant was planning a party and had the booze delivered to his car after he paid for it. But without further investigation, it appeared to me that the delivery was somehow connected to the aborted arrest.

A few cases of booze, a man gets away with driving drunk—perhaps with habitually driving drunk. If no one is killed or hurt in an accident, it seems like petty stuff. But once a police officer crosses the line, the territory on the other side is vast and tempting. Tell certain police officers who are speeding to watch out for cops, and they say, "I am the cops." Tell your shift commander you have located a truckload of untaxed cigarettes, and he might say, "Good work. I'll take care of it."

Two years after my observation in the rear of the police station, Lieutenant Smiley teamed up with a police captain to run for the offices of Bernalillo County sheriff and undersheriff. Simultaneously, a district attorney of like mind issued an indictment (soon dismissed) of the incumbent, more or less honest county sheriff, on a technical issue. In the confusion between the headlines the day before the election— "Sheriff Hay Indicted"—and the dismissal of the indictment two weeks later, Smiley and his buddy were elected.

It was a propitious time to be the chief law enforcement officer in Bernalillo County. A basically honest sheriff had kept the place relatively free of organized vice. It was virgin territory worth millions to those who wanted to improve the delivery of gambling, prostitution, and drugs. I was working at the *Tribune* when the paper began to expose one of the new sheriff's deals. Undersheriff Smiley stopped me in the courthouse corridor one evening to explain in the most gentle way how little it cost in Albuquerque to have someone killed. But I am getting ahead of my story.

On the day I went to resign, I was told that the chief himself would conduct the exit interview. I had been on the force two years and had an outstanding record of conduct and arrests. I graduated first in my class from the police academy. I was twenty-four years old, very close to a bachelor's degree, and by any measure the kind of person that the department wanted to retain. The chief seemed concerned that I was leaving.

"Is there anything wrong?" he asked. "Anything that I should know about?"

My first impulse was to say that he might want to look into the integrity of some of his shift commanders. Then I ran the numbers. He would have to defend the lieutenant, and I would have to make the prosecutor's case. Unless I wanted to devote the next year of my life to a campaign that might or might not succeed, and ultimately give me nothing but moral superiority, I was better off keeping my mouth shut, which is what I did. By that time I had seen Lieutenant Smiley operate in a variety of situations that seemed so questionable that I associated them with felonies. If the chief didn't know by then, I would not be able to adequately explain to him what was going on. It was just too much effort. I was polite, respectful, and vague. I was leaving, I said, simply to pursue other interests. "Other interests" turned out to be another semester of school and the trip to Mexico.

CHAPTER FOUR

While I was on the police force, Hellyn and I divorced, ending nearly six years of marriage—virtually a child marriage for both of us. Hellyn, Cathy, and I continued to live near one another and enjoyed regular and informal visiting arrangements. Hellyn and I traded holidays, and Cathy's grandparents all lived in the same small town, easing the strain of visits home. There was a kind of parallel pathway in our lives that served our needs in unusual ways. The summer I spent in Mexico, Hellyn took Cathy and attended an art institute in San Miguel de Allende. I was able to visit them and watch my graceful three-year-old trying to join in on an evening basketball game with local Mexican kids, yelling in Spanish for the ball.

When I returned from Mexico, broke and desperate for a job that would support me and cover my child-support commitment, no one, including my sister, was in a mood to accommodate my homeless state. Hanging around her house waiting for Michael's call was uncomfortable. When Sharron finally left for class I relaxed some, and an hour later the phone rang. I could come in the next afternoon, Michael said, when he would introduce me to the editor.

"There is a diner just across from the *Tribune* building," he said. "Meet me there at two, and I'll clue you in on a couple of things." He sounded happy, excited.

As I sat somewhat stunned by the suddenness of this good news, I realized that my bravado about marching on the halls of journalism until I found a job hid some deep doubts that anything would come of my desire. I felt a little disoriented, as if I had stepped into another reality or gotten high.

Beside the ratty backpack I carried to Mexico, all my worldly possessions were stored in a small trunk in my sister's basement. I set to work anxiously trying to pull together suitable clothes for the interview. There was a sport jacket and slacks stored from a more conventional life. With a lot of brushing they became presentable. One decent dress shirt, a high school graduation present made of fine Egyptian cotton, had been worn only half a dozen times because its lilac color struck me as too feminine. I had no choice now, and it had to be ironed. I set up my sister's ironing board in the kitchen, spread the delicate fabric across the board, and when the iron was hot, pressed it against the shirt. A small cloud of blue smoke rose instantly into my face. I looked in horror at the iron-shaped hole, realizing as my stomach turned that the smell of burning cotton is not unpleasant, a little like bread in the oven. I turned down the heat of the iron and finished the shirt, telling myself that as long as I didn't remove my jacket, the hole would not be visible. Then I went looking for shoes.

I was operating in a kind of high-speed, addled hysteria, trying to think of anything that might increase my chance of getting the job, imagining how the interview would go, guessing what Mr. Burrows might be like. I put together a package of essays and stories, including two that had been published in the student literary magazine, then tried to think what else I could offer the editor to show that I could write a news story. I headed back to Maurice's porch with my bundle. I wheeled an old bicycle out of the garage, wiped it down, and pumped up the balloon-style tires.

Just after 1:00 p.m. the following day, dressed in the best business attire I had, I left for downtown Albuquerque. On any other day the ride would have been supremely serene as it took me along streets shaded by mature Chinese elms and cottonwood trees. Autumn sunlight flashed through openings between the trunks, creating a hypnotic rhythm. The air was cool and dry and gave me a feeling of optimism. The ride calmed me and reminded me how tense I had become.

I didn't want Michael to know that I was reduced to a bicycle as my only transportation, so I parked the bike behind the diner and went inside to wait. In about ten minutes Michael appeared, looking very professional: tall and slender, he wore dark slacks and a perfectly pressed white shirt, a tie knotted firmly at his throat. The precision of his grooming gave him a vaguely military air, or the look of a young airline pilot. As he approached my table he seemed more mature than I remembered. He greeted me warmly, like an old friend. "What a small world," he said, laughing and shaking his head. "You wanting to work at the *Trib*."

We talked briefly about the man I was about to meet. Then, just before three o'clock, my burned shirt concealed by my jacket, Michael led me across the street to the second floor of the *Tribune* building. He opened a heavy steel fire door into a vast, brightly lit room. A wall of noise stopped us momentarily. Reporters beating on Royal Standard typewriters sat in long rows at green metal desks. Some were on the phone, talking above the noise. Teletype machines lining one wall chattered steadily, long tongues of white paper rolling out to lick the floor. Near the front of the room, half a dozen men in fierce concentration sat around the perimeter of a half-round desk larger than a pool table. In a slot cut into its center, a gray-haired man in big horned-rim glasses wielded a pair of giant shears as he cut and marked copy and stuffed it into a pneumatic tube behind him, where it was sucked down to the pressroom to be set in hot-lead type. The atmosphere conveyed urgency and seriousness. It cleared my mind the way a close ball game shuts out the rest of the world. What I saw that afternoon were paper and ink as the supreme medium. The noise, the excitement, the smell of fresh ink, and the physical labor loomed glorious in their tactile intensity. I felt a deep and piercing desire to be a part of this world.

Twenty-five years later I would be invited to tour the *Tribune*'s new city room and be shocked to enter a large, dimly lit space in an entirely new building where reporters stared into computer screens and worked in near silence. Temperature-controlled, quiet, almost dark but for the flickering screens, each reporter seemed isolated, subdued. The room smelled of paint rather than ink. The noisy, smoke-filled room where reporters literally battered out the news was gone, and with it the feeling of being at an exciting gathering each day where the events of the city appeared to collect and take form as they were written.

"Wait here," Michael said, indicating a chair outside Dan Burrows's office. I sat down. Michael returned in seconds and directed me into a large, tastefully furnished office where Burrows worked behind an impressive wooden desk. Antique rugs, mostly Navajo and Zuni, hung on the walls. A large window gave a clear view of activities in the city room. Mementos of various kinds—awards, plaques, inscribed clocks, the usual trinkets and trash of corporate life—were scattered about the place. Behind Burrows's desk hung two black-and-white photos of him with men I assumed to be owners of the paper, Mr. Scripps and Mr. Howard, perhaps. I was still too ignorant of the newspaper business to know that Scripps Howard was a huge corporation that had long ago

31

outgrown individual ownership. Burrows, in a brown three-piece suit that emphasized his modest middle-aged belly, appeared to be in his midsixties. His eyes were clear and alert. He smiled, making me feel more at ease, and invited me to sit down. Michael excused himself.

"You come highly recommended," Burrows said.

"Oh?" I was caught off guard by the remark.

"Michael seems to think highly of you."

"I'm flattered." I smiled politely.

"Michael says you want to be a reporter."

"Yes, sir, I do. Very much so."

"But you didn't study journalism?"

"No, sir. I felt I should get an education in a more traditional discipline: history, philosophy, literature. I felt I needed a broader education." In fact, I hadn't given a moment's thought to journalism as a profession until I decided in Mexico that I should be a reporter. I studied philosophy and history and literature because I liked them and they were easy for me.

"I agree with you," Burrows said, to my surprise. "We can teach people basic journalism out there." He gestured toward the window into the city room. "We can't teach perspective or judgment or clear thinking. That has to come from you."

"Yes, sir. I agree, emphatically."

"Do you type?"

"Yes, sir."

"Fast?"

"Pretty fast."

"Own a typewriter?"

"Yes."

"Have a driver's license?"

"Yes."

"Speak Spanish?"

"I do, but not as well as I would like."

"Michael said you were on the police force. So tell me about your time in the police department."

"Not a lot to tell. I needed a job to finish school. You know, there are not many places in Albuquerque where you can work at night. I had to take a semester off to go to the police academy, but that was actually good. I learned some very useful things there."

"Such as?"

"Some basic criminal law, legal procedure, investigative technique, report writing." I smiled, hoping what I said next would amuse him, "High-speed-pursuit driving, marksmanship."

He didn't react. "As a police officer you wrote a lot of reports?"

"Many, many reports. Hours of reports."

"Did you like writing reports?"

"Actually, I did. I felt they were important, you know, for the detectives and the lawyers and the people involved." This was not a lie. I had taken special pride in the quality and clarity of my reports.

"I happen to think that what police do and what reporters do is very similar," Burrows said, again to my surprise. "They both investigate things and write reports about it."

"That's true," I agreed. This had never occurred to me, but I liked the direction the discussion was going.

Burrows paused, distracted by something happening in the city room. I seized the moment. Pointing to a beautiful deep-red rug hanging behind him, I asked, "Is that a Germantown?"

"In fact, it is." I saw he was pleased by the question.

Fortune had favored me again. Just before I left for Mexico, I happened on a large exhibition of southwestern American Indian rugs at the anthropology department of the university. I remembered the story about Germantown rugs and how in the late nineteenth century the Navajos acquired the brightly dyed red yarn from Germantown near Philadelphia and wove these beautiful rugs, mostly for sale to tourists, some of them probably taken back to Pennsylvania where the yarn was made.

"Do you like rugs?" Burrows asked.

"I do. I saw a lot of Navajo rugs growing up. My grandfather used them for saddle blankets, and my grandmother had a lot on her floors. I don't think they considered them anything special at the time."

"Obviously, I collect them," he said, indicating the walls. "The good ones and the old ones are getting very rare, like that Germantown."

"Using them for saddle blankets didn't do them any good," I offered.

"They were made to be used." Burrows turned philosophical. "They were appreciated back then for their quality, their durability. Not their rarity."

I liked Burrows. My nervousness drained away.

"Who was your lieutenant when you left the police department?" he asked rather suddenly.

"Lieutenant Smiley, Jack Smiley."

I watched as he made the only note he had made during the interview. It occurred to me that he was going to call Smiley to ask about my performance. My scrotum tightened as I recalled how close I came to outing Smiley to the chief.

Burrows chatted with me for another few minutes, took the writing samples I offered without much apparent interest, and then rather abruptly got up from his desk and offered his hand. "I'll call you tomorrow and let you know my decision," he said. "Will you be home all day?"

"Yes, sir," I said. Hoping to convey my sense of urgency, I added, "I'll stay near the phone until I get your call."

Burrows returned to his desk and resumed work. I left for the city room to find Michael. "I'll meet you across the street," he said, pointing toward the diner.

As I left, I noticed a small, balding man sitting at an individual desk in front of the big circular desk. He struck me as highly stressed and uncomfortable and possibly unpleasant. He threw several pills into his mouth and washed them down with something from a large silver thermos. His gaze followed me across the room, seeming to study me. I guessed that his stomach was aflame with ulcers, then my thoughts returned to Lieutenant Smiley and what he might say. I reassured myself that he had never been aware of my feelings about him, nor known of my various observations of his behavior. As I negotiated the stairs, I thought of the irony that something I wanted and needed so badly might be in the hands of a man I judged to be so low.

Walking across Silver Avenue to the coffee shop, a feeling of being grossly unqualified suddenly invaded me. The activity in the city room undercut any belief that I could simply walk in and be an instant reporter. I badly wanted the job, but my hopes of getting it now weakened. When my coffee arrived, I noted that strange, vaguely sexual arousal that comes in the presence of high tension. I was scared.

Minutes later, I saw Michael rushing across the street. He settled in beside me, smiled happily, and ordered coffee. Without any comment on my interview, he took me completely by surprise when he asked, "Why don't you come out for dinner tonight?"

"What?"

"Come out to Corrales. I'll make some steaks. We can talk about all the people we used to know and the great place where we grew up. I can fill you in on some of the shoals at the *Trib*."

34

The bicycle I rode to the *Tribune* would not get me to Corrales and back. I wasn't prepared to reveal that I didn't have a car, let alone a place to live, so I lied.

"I would love to come, but I won't have transportation. I promised a friend that he could use my car tonight."

"Leave him the car. Ride out with me. I have lots of room. You can stay over. I'm not going to drive you home after dinner, but I can give you a good bed. I come in at seven."

After days of feeling very alone in the world, the offer of a nice meal and good company actually made me feel emotional. I had not realized how lonely I was.

"OK," I said. "You're on. We'll be back in plenty of time to get Mr. Burrows's call, right?"

"I'll have you here at seven. He doesn't come in until eight."

"You didn't hear anything, did you, about the interview?"

"No, not really," Michael said, looking down, stirring his coffee vigorously. "I should be honest with you about one thing, though."

I felt an immediate sense of dread. "Yes, please."

"There is a little . . ." Michael rocked his hand in the air to indicate something he couldn't quite express. Frustrated, he said, "I'll just be blunt. Ralph Looney, he's the city editor, the little guy you saw at the front desk. He wants an experienced, journeyman reporter. He is short staffed and always trying to dig out from a pile of work. He is not interested in training a cub. But an experienced reporter is going to cost them $115 to $135 a week. Burrows is not looking at Looney's workload; he is looking at the bottom line. He's the editor partly because he knows how to bring this beast in every year well in the black. He knows he can get you for a lot less than an experienced reporter would cost."

This was a whole line of reasoning that had never occurred to me. It was a little shocking that my future might be based not on ability, desire, or education, but on something as impersonal as a price difference, and not a very big difference at that. "I always like to be the low bidder," I joked, not happily.

"Burrows would like to fill the empty slot with a young, cheap reporter. Probably you. But if he does, Looney is going to be very pissed. I hate to tell you that it comes down to something like this, but there you are. You are the low bidder. Frankly, I think you have an advantage. The downside is, of course, that Looney will hate you and try to prove that he can't get by with someone so inexperienced. He will try to run you off. He is skilled at being nasty. It comes naturally to him. You saw him today, right?"

"I think so. He looks like his stomach is on fire?"

"That's him."

My world had just grown more complicated, but I was grateful for Michael's candor. I sensed even more strongly now that I had an ally. The idea of dinner with him delighted me. "Well, I want the job. I'll just have to wait and see," I said philosophically, without feeling at all philosophical.

"Yup."

"So isn't Corrales a long drive?"

"No."

"Half an hour?"

"Yes, but everybody lives half an hour from work," Michael said. "The difference is that I live in a wonderful place."

He was not exaggerating. The small Hispanic village north of Albuquerque had a reputation then as a sleepy village—area, really— where cool, artsy Anglos and eccentric PhDs from Sandia Corporation mixed easily with Spanish-speaking farmers and a few country gringos who loved horses. It was mostly adobe houses, many of them shaded by huge cottonwood trees growing dense and cool and beautiful in the shallow groundwater along the Rio Grande. There were orchards and chile fields and not very well concealed patches of local marijuana that may actually have been a native species. In spring, wild asparagus sprouted along the irrigation ditches. Nearly everyone kept horses, wore Levi's, drank a bit too much, and in thirty years would be seeking treatment for skin cancer.

A grocery store, an ethnic bar/restaurant, and one liquor store with a drive-up window made up much of the retail establishment. There, if you spoke Spanish and knew the owner, you could buy liquor on Sunday even though New Mexico still observed blue laws prohibiting liquor sales near churches and on Sundays. The Baptists and Methodists had to be protected from the temptation of liquor, even the sight of it, even on the Sabbath. The Catholics had made their uneasy peace with it centuries before.

We walked to Michael's car, a Chevrolet El Camino, that weird hybrid of a car and pickup truck that General Motors made in the fifties and sixties. I never understood its intended use, but Michael's father used it as an advertising vehicle. He drove it around Tucumcari with a big sandwich board in back advertising his movie theaters until, apparently, he passed it on to Michael.

"Cool car," I lied.

"Present from Father," he said. In my family, parents were "Dad" or "Papa." In the Hopkins family they were "Father." Hearing that word always reminded me of the difference in our backgrounds.

The drive north was quick and pleasant. We drove up Rio Grande Boulevard beyond the Albuquerque city limits and crossed the river, turning onto a little road that follows the river north along its western bank. Just outside Corrales, we headed down a dusty dirt road to Michael's house. Off to the east, behind us, the Sandia Mountains were taking on the deep watermelon glow that often comes to them at sunset. All around us, the low-angled, early-fall light enriched the natural colors, setting every object in high relief. Trees seemed outlined in black. Stones cast dark shadows. I saw Michael's house in the distance, nestled into a grove of mature cottonwoods and cedars. A few yards beyond, a little *acequia* carried water to the fields behind his property. The house had the low fluid lines of the old New Mexico adobes. Sharp, Brazilian blue trim set off the rich, nearly golden stucco now shimmering in the late afternoon light. As we got out of the car, a chill in the high-altitude evening hit me and I hunched my shoulders.

Inside the house, I saw that Michael, a man of essentially traditional values—a man who preferred Shakespeare over Beckett, Bach over the Beatles—had decorated the house in very traditional New Mexico style. Fine old Navajo rugs lay on polished stone floors. A well-used corner fireplace in virtually every room gave the place a sense of self-sufficiency. Small windows cut into thick walls added a sense of security. I turned a corner and found a huge new room that Michael had added to the old house. It was a long rectangle with brick floors and exposed vigas and hardly any furniture. An electric organ as large as the one I remembered from our church faced the room from the far end. Had Michael added rows of straight back chairs it would have been a small concert hall.

"You still play?"

"All the time," he said, smiling.

As I gawked at the place with all the amazement of a homeless man, Michael threw his keys on the kitchen counter and made a fire. Within minutes, the aroma of burning piñon wood filled me with a sense of autumn's impending arrival. I sat down to admire his carved woodwork and finely detailed door lentils and the old black-and-white photos displayed in antique frames, Kachina dolls, and Mimbres pottery. The Chevy was not the only present from Father. This was not anything a reporter could afford. "It's beautiful," I said, moved to a kind of awe by the exquisite arrangement of powerful New Mexico icons.

Remember that in 1963, what would come to be called "Santa Fe style" was not yet a cliché. It had not been marketed, advertised, exported, or much debased. The trapping of the old New Mexico culture—the agrarian, Spanish/Indian style that had been around for nearly four centuries—still resonated with mysterious cultural meaning.

Michael laughed nervously at my expression of reverence—the laugh I remembered from the night he visited me in the jail. "It's a little lonely out here at times," he said wistfully, "but I really like the area. Different from where we grew up, huh?"

The difference could hardly be overstated. The fact that eastern New Mexico and the Rio Grande Valley are in the same state is an accident of politics, not a reflection of culture. Corrales was a perfect expression of the old culture of New Mexico, where in the sixteenth century Spaniards with not a few Marranos among them made their way willy-nilly up the Rio Grande, conquering the native populations and settling in to form a kind of hybrid of Islamic-Hispanic and Native American culture. They were followed in the early nineteenth century by an assortment of Italian, Syrian, Jewish, and English merchants and traders who settled in Albuquerque and Santa Fe soon after the area was ceded to the United States by Mexico in 1847. A truly unique culture grew and flourished along the river and along all the little streams that formed its watershed from Colorado down to the Texas border near Las Cruces. At the same time, the area where Michael and I grew up was still buffalo pasture and Comanche hunting grounds. Sometime around 1900, Texans began to spill across the eastern border to establish towns like Clovis, Tucumcari, Portales, Roswell, Lovington, and Hobbs, bringing evangelical Protestantism, Confederate resentments, and big Easter hats to the Llano Estacado, the staked plains.

In 1541 Francisco Vásquez de Coronado, the first European to traverse this "sea of grass" where we were, described it this way: "I reached some plains so vast that I did not find their limit anywhere I went, although I traveled over them for more than 300 leagues . . . with no more landmarks than if we had been swallowed up by the sea. . . . There was not a stone, nor bit of rising ground, nor a tree, nor a shrub, nor anything to go by." Even the Comanche Indians, as tough as any people ever to walk the earth, avoided the Llano and only crossed it on carefully designated trails.

"I would say that this," I waved my hand to indicate the house and Corrales, "is about as different from where we grew up as San Francisco is from Bakersfield."

"True," Michael agreed. "But there were some good people there. I thought we had some great teachers."

"Absolutely. We did." I agreed. I had not fully understood how good they were until my first year at college when I discovered I already knew a lot of the material we were assigned. "Remember Mrs. Babcock, who carried a nickel-plated pistol in her purse?"

"I remember she said she had been a sheriff somewhere in Arizona, but I never believed that," Michael said.

"Me either, but she could teach physics to a golden retriever. And I adored the Chews. They saved me. My dad dislikes them. He thinks it was their influence that made me decide on liberal arts."

"Was it?"

"Of course. They helped me win a scholarship. He wasn't happy about that. He wanted me to go on a football scholarship, or not at all."

"Really? That was never an issue in our family. We were always going to college. It wasn't a decision."

Michael shook a batch of martinis, brought two frosty cocktail glasses from the freezer, and poured out the liquid, still milky from entrained air. He held his glass at eye level and watched as the liquor cleared. "Here's to your career in journalism. May you win a Pulitzer before you go bald!"

"I can drink to that," I said, hardly able to think of myself as anything other than a down-and-out student. Cold and smooth, the gin made me shudder.

I started to think again about my father's problem with the Chews, husband and wife, and their influence. I decided to tell Michael about my introduction to Henry James.

It was an August day before my senior year of high school, and I was working at our farm. The temperature was close to 100 degrees. It was so hot that one could hardly breathe. I worked until noon or one o'clock and decided I had to rest. Earlier that spring, Mr. Chew had said that I should read some Henry James, so a few days earlier, anticipating the start of school, I picked up a copy of *Daisy Miller* from the library and put it in my pickup truck. In the searing heat I found my copy of *Daisy* and crawled under the truck, into the only shade within miles. The clearance under the truck was about eighteen inches. My head nearly bumped the frame. I wallowed in that red clay dust we called soil. Sweat kept dripping on James's prose. It was difficult to imagine Daisy's problems in England, but I was trying hard when my father suddenly drove up. I had not heard him coming until he stopped beside my pickup. He got out. I watched his boots as he stood and then walked around the pickup. When he didn't see me, he started calling my name. There was nothing to do but reveal myself. I left Henry on the ground and crawled out. The old man was astonished. "What the hell were you doing under there?" he asked.

"I was reading," I said. If I had not been in a state of near panic I would have lied and said I was working on the truck.

"Reading what? One of those silly goddamned books?"

Michael wasn't laughing. "So what happened?"

"Nothing. He stomped around for a few minutes being disgusted. I guess if we had been Jewish he would have torn his clothes and thrown dust on his head. But being Scots Irish or whatever we are, he just cussed and gritted his teeth and then started to ask about the work I had done and to remind me what wasn't done."

"That is, actually, very funny," Michael said without laughing.

"It is funny now, but you know what was weird about him? He would sneak off and read. He told me once, in an unguarded moment, that the year he followed the wheat harvest as a laborer he read practically everything O. Henry wrote. Of course, O. Henry is more American than Henry James."

"Do as I say . . ." Michael quoted.

"I think he blamed the Chews for arousing an interest in literature. He has a kind of weird fear of anything intellectual. Ideas can lead you astray. In fact, I don't think he was really comfortable with anything but farming and raising cattle, and precision machine tools. The really contradictory thing is that he was actually interested in ideas. He was like the Grand Inquisitor in *The Brothers Karamazov*. It was acceptable for him to know things, but I was too weak and slow. Ideas could be dangerous to me."

"Really?"

"Well, he never encouraged anything that required any brains. I told him once that I was thinking of becoming a lawyer. He said, 'Lawyers all wear shiny pants.'"

40

"Meaning?"

"Meaning they spend all day sitting at a desk, reading abstracts or doing really boring stuff."

"A lot do," Michael agreed.

"Well, yes, maybe the lawyers in Tucumcari do, but what about the lawyers who become judges or go into court?"

"They have to be smart."

"Exactly. When I said I wanted to be a doctor, he said, 'You want to spend your life with sick people?'"

"What did you say?"

"I said no, that I'd be a psychiatrist. So he said, 'You want to spend your life with crazy people?'"

Michael laughed.

"I even told him once that I would be an engineer. I thought he would approve of that, right? He said he used to watch the engineer at a copper mill where he worked. He said the engineer's job was to take water samples every two hours and analyze them and write the results in a logbook. All those years in school to spend your day in a hot tin shack doing water samples."

"Did you suggest any other jobs?" Michael asked, amused by my plight.

"When I was about nine, my sister and I spent a rainy weekend painting with watercolors. When the old man got home I told him I had decided to be an artist. He said, quite simply, 'Artists are degenerates.'"

"Wow!" Michael threw his head back in mock surprise. "A lot of them are, you know," he said, pretending agreement.

"I had to ask my mother what 'degenerates' were. She didn't know how to explain it. She just said they were not people you'd want to be around."

"OK, but what's so great about farming?"

"Work outdoors. Work hard. You're your own boss. You answer to no man, except your banker. You actually feed people. He regarded feeding people as a nearly sacred endeavor."

"Well, yeah, it is, but man does not live by bread alone and all that stuff."

"I know. I know. But he's romantic about it. I went home from school once when I was about twenty, and we went out to the farm to feed his cattle. We had to go down to a neighboring farm to get the feed, and when we got down there I was shocked. When I was a kid, this man from Texas and his wife owned that farm. They had two little kids and great optimism. When they arrived, they built a two-car garage and moved into it until they could build a house. The day we went down there for feed, I saw the two-car garage was now a pigpen and there was no house. I hardly recognized the place. It was such a clear picture of someone's dashed dreams. I felt very sorry for them and kind of sad. I asked the old man, 'What ever happened to Tom and Becky?' He said rather casually, 'Oh, they starved out and went back to Texas.' I could just picture them living in that garage with two kids, working their butts off, baking in summer and freezing in winter, losing money every year until they just couldn't do it anymore. Then they had to go back to wherever they were from. Tom probably got a job as mechanic or a clerk in a feed store. Becky is probably driving a school bus."

"Yeah?" Michael seemed unsure of my point.

"Well, on the way back to town, referring to Tom and Becky, I said something like, 'Isn't it amazing what a man will put himself and his family through to realize a dream?' The old man got all misty and said, 'Oh, yeah, people will suffer terrible hardship to make a dream come true.'"

"And?"

"I couldn't help it. I had him in such a great position for a sucker punch. I said, 'When a farmer puts himself and his family through hell to establish a way of life, it is regarded as admirable, even if he fails. But when an artist or writer does the same thing it is thought selfish?' I saw his face turn red—not from embarrassment but from anger. He said, 'Nobody ever demonstrated that artists pull their own weight.' I said, 'Every farmer in this county is getting a check from the government for one thing or another. How's that pulling your own weight?' We didn't talk any more that day."

"The relationship is complicated."

"It is. He just makes all kind of excuses and exceptions for farmers that he can't make for other people. He believes that physical work is somehow sanctifying."

Michael seemed uncomfortable discussing father-son relationships. He never spoke of his own father except in the most formal terms and always with the highest respect.

"Did I tell you that I still see the Chews occasionally?" he asked, changing the subject.

"You were close to them?"

"I'm still close to Byron. I feel nothing but respect for Iris, but I never found her very accessible."

"Yeah, she's kind of stern, but she's one of the smartest people I ever met. My freshman English professor was astonished when I told him she had us reading Joyce in twelfth grade."

"He probably thought she was overreaching."

"She was overreaching, but she challenged us in the process."

"Which Joyce?"

"Ulysses."

"And how many kids in your class understood it?"

"None, including me. Are you kidding? I doubt that she really understood it, but that's not the point. By the end of the year, I understood there was something there to be understood. I understood that important things had been written after 1870."

"OK, but how many kids got that far?"

"Four or five, but you know what? I don't think teaching *Ulysses* took anything away from the others. And they loved the Molly Bloom business about 'Yes, yes, yes.' They thought that was downright dirty."

"'Yes' can be a very sexy word," Michael said.

The Chews were the teachers every lucky person encounters. In tenth grade I had no intentions of going to college. School bored me, and I began plotting to get through with the least possible effort. I just wanted it to be over. Each day dragged. I daydreamed endlessly. I spent hours watching sparrows pecking at gravel outside the schoolroom window. I thought I might become a farmer, except that farming required capital and I had none, so I made plans with my closest friend, Harry Heckendorn, to go to Alaska and become a trapper. I wanted to be away from people and all their silly concerns. Then I began Mr. Chew's junior English class, and suddenly, in a moment of true epiphany, I understood that *The Scarlet Letter* was more than just another story. As Mr. Chew led us by Socratic method through the moral tangle of Hawthorne's masterpiece, I was amazed that we could actually discuss whether a minister of the faith was also a hypocrite and whether passion was more forgivable than calculated harm. He led us into a world where moral positions were arrived at through reason—not by edict, not by simple reference to some verse in the Bible that could always be countered by another verse. I participated in deciding what was right and what was wrong. My mind came alive, and I was filled with enthusiasm. Excited, hungry, curious, I became a star.

The years in the academic doldrums put me behind in college preparation. I doubled up, taking two science courses and two math courses each year in an effort to catch up and prepare for college. Skeptical teachers became supporters. The following fall, in Mrs. Chew's senior English class, I found an even greater challenge and more stimulation. The intellectual fire rekindled my physical energy, and I rejoined the football team after dropping out in my sophomore year. I would be named to the all-state team that spring and get an invitation to play in the high school all-star game during the summer. This, of course, raised my father's hopes that I would be offered a football scholarship, relieving him of any pressure to send me to college at family expense.

One cannot entirely discount the role of hormones in all of this. The lethargy and depression that invaded me in ninth grade, at age fourteen, might have ended in my sixteenth year even if I had not met the Chews. What is certain in my mind is that, without the Chews, there would have been no framework for my new energy and curiosity and no one to encourage me to do more than play football and perhaps study physical education or range management, if I studied anything at all.

Iris Chew was a tall, graceful woman of such serious sternness that no one in her presence would remotely consider being anything but serious in return. Gray hair pulled back in a teacherly bun, she had done the course work for a doctorate in literature and then abandoned higher academia without completing a dissertation.

She moved us at a furious pace, pushing ideas at us and insisting we take a position on them. We read *The Odyssey*. She read to us from Joyce's *Ulysses*. We read *Macbeth* and *Hamlet* and *A Midsummer Night's Dream*. We discussed when, if ever, murder is justified or understandable. She moved us beyond the narrow confines of the peasant Christian morality that hitherto had constituted our moral education. This, of course, made her dangerous to the petty bourgeois society in which we lived and frequently brought the wrath of outraged parents down on her and Byron. They always survived their appearances before the school board to answer charges of teaching dangerous ideas, but they were treated as outsiders, as undesirables.

Sometime in February, Iris explained to me that the New Mexico Philosophical Society conducted an annual essay contest. She invited me to write and submit an essay on the assigned topic: "The Influence of the Idea in History." I had never thought about writing anything. Her faith that I could set me moving. I found myself leaping out of bed at night to write down notes for ideas that came to me as I was falling asleep. Mr. Chew typed my finished manuscript and drove me to the post office to mail it. Mother recognized that something good was going on, and while she did not openly voice admiration for the Chews, she encouraged my efforts and subtly let me know that she supported whatever it was they were doing.

In May, a simple envelope from the chairman of the Philosophy Department at the University of New Mexico arrived in our mailbox. In my haste to open the envelope, I ripped the top off the letter. Based on my essay, he wrote, the Philosophical Society wished to offer me four years of tuition to any school in New Mexico. Resident tuition was barely $100 per semester. Room and board were far more expensive in those halcyon days, but the offer of tuition was an affirmation that I was wanted. I think there were five four-year institutions in New Mexico then, so the choices were not vast. It didn't matter. The fact that someone outside of Tucumcari believed that I could go to college and wanted to help changed everything. The Chews had given me the courage to believe.

My father did not seem to share in my joy. He read the letter quietly. "Well, that's nice," he said, handing it back to me without further comment. I knew he favored my seeking a full football scholarship to a tiny college in southwestern New Mexico, in Silver City, where the recruiting coach who visited us that spring assured me that eventually I would decide to major in physical education, like all the other football players. My father didn't think it made much difference what I studied. His faith in my ability was minimal.

Michael and I sat near the fire and drank until it was dark outside. Then he lit kerosene lamps that cast a soft, intimate light across the room. When he went out into the walled patio to cook the steaks, I went along. In the clear country air without incidental light, I marveled at the star-hung autumn sky.

We had a Bordeaux with the steaks. I could not remember such an evening. Afterward Michael made stingers, a drink I had never heard of, and we stood in front of the fire listening to music and talking about life in the way that people do when they have had a lot to drink. I felt in an odd way that I had come home. The old New Mexico architecture, the traditional furnishings, talking about teachers and ideas in front of a piñon fire with a man who was quickly becoming a close friend—these things constituted just about everything I cared for.

It was just after daylight when I heard Michael in the kitchen and rolled out of bed to discover a fierce hangover living in my head and down my spine. I recognized it as the kind that goes on for at least a day or two. I would learn in time that brandy and I did not get along, and it would eventually be relegated, along with bourbon, to an ever-growing list of alcoholic drinks I could not tolerate.

After a shower, I joined Michael in the kitchen, where he was preparing to blend an egg, fruit, and milk into a smoothie-like breakfast. "Want one?" he asked, distracted by a sense of urgency. He gulped his down and grabbed a jacket and his keys. "Gotta go," he said. I followed him to the El Camino.

On the way back to Albuquerque I pondered the question of Michael's generosity. Did his motivation simply lie in the fact that we were from the same hometown? Was he a natural mentor who was interested in helping a younger man get started? Was he attracted to me? His generosity seemed too great to be motivated by simple friendship. There were times when his laughter struck me as too nervous, and I felt a tense undercurrent in his presence. Or was I imagining all this and somehow projecting some latent desire of my own into the relationship? The hangover didn't help me think clearly. I felt guilty and sick and tired. Michael didn't seem any the worse for wear.

He pulled into the *Tribune* parking lot and turned to me with a sprightly air. "You're welcome back tonight if you like," he said. "It's nice to have company."

"Thanks. Can I let you know later today?"

"Good luck with Burrows," he called over his shoulder as he hurried into the building. I walked to the bike. It was where I left it behind the diner. I stared at it, wondering if I could make it up the long climb from downtown to the university without throwing up.

My sister and her new boyfriend were asleep when I knocked on her door. Annoyed to be awakened, she let me in when I explained that I had to begin another vigil by her phone. A little before ten o'clock, I was nodding off when Burrows called. My heart raced.

"I spoke with Lieutenant Smiley," he began. "He said you were a good officer. I liked the stuff you gave me, though it's not journalism in any sense, but I'm calling to offer you a job anyway."

A jumble of elation, apprehension, and relief created a completely confusing emotional storm in my head and chest. I fought to stay focused on our conversation. "That is wonderful!" I said as evenly as possible.

"The starting pay is $70 a week. When do you want to begin?"

The number brought me to my senses. "Mr. Burrows, I have some old financial obligations that I have to meet. I absolutely want the job and I accept the job, but do you think you could give me a little more money?"

"All right," he said in an avuncular tone, "$72.50, but that's my best offer."

To keep things in perspective, one could buy a new Volkswagen at that time for $1,800. A modest one-bedroom apartment in Albuquerque rented for $75 a month. McDonald's still sold a basic burger (meat, bread, and sauce) for fifteen cents. But $72.50—roughly $290 a month before taxes and Social Security were taken out—was a very lean wage, especially since I was paying child support of $50 a month. Nevertheless, I was ecstatic, or nearly so. As good as the news was, it didn't cure the hangover.

I called Michael to share the good news and to thank him. When he repeated his invitation to stay at his house, I accepted.

The risk I ran by so totally depleting my resources was serious. The consequences could have been grave, certainly far more serious than they turned out to be. I never liked to think what another month without income would have meant, but the immediacy of the risk was brought home to me that afternoon when Maurice found me napping on my army cot, sleeping off the hangover, and reminded me that his pretentious brother was growing more impatient about my finding other quarters. It was a huge relief to tell him that I would be off his porch before sundown.

CHAPTER FIVE

Desperately needing a paycheck and excited beyond description by the prospect of being a reporter, I showed up for work at the *Tribune* two days after my conversation with Mr. Burrows. Ralph Looney, the *Tribune*'s city editor and now my direct supervisor, arranged for a reporter to show me to an empty desk and to the supply cabinet without actually acknowledging my presence. The snub was not subtle. Fortunately, Michael had warned me about Looney's problems and concerns, so I knew that he considered me a reminder that he had lost an argument. I set to work arranging my new desk, exploring the empty drawers that were strewn with lint, crumbs, ancient individual packs of mayonnaise, leaking ballpoint pens, paperclips, and bits of plastic that once had a function.

I looked up to see Looney standing in front of me with an enormous pile of press releases draped over his arm. He was a small, dark-haired man with a round, plain face and glasses. I looked at his nylon shirt and narrow black tie as he made a nasty chuckling sound. "Good morning!" he shouted. He threw the press releases on top of my typewriter with great force and turned and walked away like a satisfied child who had just thrown mud on an unsuspecting rival. I had no idea what to do. The sheets carried announcements: church events, club meetings, and corporate news about minor promotions. They were all two or three pages long, single spaced, and filled with tedious detail and open, long-winded self-promotion. Approaching Looney for help would prove my uselessness and confirm his petition to Burrows that he needed a journeyman reporter. Baffled and stalling for time, I rolled a sheet of paper into my typewriter, stacked the releases neatly beside the machine, and waited, hoping for inspiration.

Suddenly, Michael appeared beside my desk, a furtive look in his eyes.

Clearly he was fraternizing with the enemy in Looney's presence. "Edit them all down to two, at most three lines," he whispered hurriedly. "If they are pure garbage, throw them out. Watch for bigger, better stories buried in the releases: bankruptcy, local angles, that kind of stuff. Do it fast! Here is the formula." His hand trembled as he offered me a neatly typed sheet. I saw Looney scowling at us. Michael left quickly. I looked at what he had written.

"Name of organization, event, date (time of day, day of the week, month, day of the month), location, main attraction, e.g., 'The North Valley Lions' Club will hold its weekly luncheon at 12:00 p.m. on Thursday, October 22, at Lennie's Steak House, 2234 Rio Grande Blvd. Ima Bore will speak on 'Doing Well by Doing Good.'"

I studied the sheet for a moment and set to work. One by one the blather of the releases was reduced to two or three useful lines and the sheets were tossed. As the hours went by, my shoulders began to ache. By 10:00 a.m., I felt spacey but deeply grateful to Michael. Without his cheat sheet, the morning would have been a disaster.

At 12:30, the pile of press releases completed, I walked across the street for a tuna sandwich and glass of milk. Returning twenty minutes later, I found one of the notices I had written wadded and jammed violently into the top of my typewriter: a clear act of aggression, of vandalism. The copy paper was nearly destroyed by the wadding. The feeling that came to me was the same feeling when I see a cat or a raccoon freshly killed on a road. The violence is over, but something frightening and unpleasant lingers. Then I understood that this was not the act of a vandal but a message from the boss. It was a shocking moment.

I scanned the city room. All heads were down in an unusual show of concentration. Humiliation and anger took over as I pulled the paper out of the machine, smoothed it out on my desk, and saw that Looney had marked a misspelling by drawing a heavy circle around it with red grease pencil. It was a simple mistake. I had reversed an *i* and an *e*. I felt relief that the mistake was so minor. I sat down and rewrote the item and dropped the corrected sheet into the copy box. Looney didn't look up as I passed his desk. I acted as if nothing at all unusual had happened.

Only six or eight months earlier I had been a cop. Not very far below the surface of my unperturbed manner that afternoon was the old street instinct to grab him and jerk him over his desk and throw him on the floor. The adrenaline was there, and I was certainly strong enough to lift him, but I went back to my desk and let my pulse rate slow while I assessed the campaign to run me off. I had not counted on such open warfare.

Looney did not understand his terrible disadvantage in our struggle. He had no idea how much I wanted and needed the job. I was prepared to suffer almost any insult or humiliation. Short of assaulting me, which was unlikely, he could do almost nothing to provoke me to leave or to behave in a way that would justify my dismissal.

I also understood that I needed more allies. Michael was formidable, but if Looney was solely in charge of my work and the only judge of my performance, he could, I feared, do me in. He could keep me rewriting press releases until I couldn't stand the boredom. He could report to Burrows that my work was substandard, even for a novice. He could harass and humiliate me. I needed to take some action that would weaken his grip. I wasn't sure what that would be, but I knew I was too isolated. Instinctively I determined to reach out to other staff members.

At the end of the day I stepped outside into the crisp September air, breathed deeply, and walked to Michael's car as a sense of relief filled me. It had been a tense eight hours. I leaned against the El Camino, lit a cigarette, and thought about Michael.

My gratitude was limitless. He paved the way for me to get the job; he got me the job with the help of my old crooked police lieutenant. He pulled my butt out of the fire after Looney heaped the pile of press releases on my desk. Now he was providing shelter, food, and transportation. Without him, I would be a homeless, unemployed mess. It seemed bizarre, but I also sensed in the vaguest way that he might be falling in love with me. When I saw him headed for the car, I waved.

"You were a big hit," he said, smiling.

"Can't be. I rewrote some press releases and screwed up four of them."

"You stuck with it. You didn't let Looney get to you. Everyone thought you were great. Some people would have walked out or screamed at him. I think that's what he hoped for."

"Really?"

"Hey," Michael said, "you are the newest guy in the city room. What's more interesting than that?" He laughed his nervous laugh. "Want to stop at Al's for a drink?"

The place he suggested, Al Monte's Taos Bar, was a tastefully decorated, comfortable place, done in adobe style—quiet, softly lit, and clean. It was on Rio Grande Boulevard on the way to Michael's house.

In cooler weather, like late September, Al kept a fire burning in the fireplace at the back of the lounge. It was a good place to talk.

We drank beer and talked about the *Tribune*. When the waitress brought the second round, there was something in her manner that suggested she thought Michael and I were a couple. I was surprised and unsettled by the thought. This feeling had never before occurred to me, even when I traveled with male companions. It had, however, occurred to others. In Mexico that previous summer I picked up a woman at a party in San Miguel, and she told me later that she initially thought Maurice and I were "queers." The idea struck me as absurd. I laughed it off without bothering to consider why she might have thought so. On reflection, I suppose our matching straw-colored cords, white cotton shirts, and beige desert boots might have seemed coordinated by something more than bohemian collegiate style.

On the way to Corrales, still wondering if my observation about the waitress was some sort of homo paranoia, I confided my actual circumstances to Michael: I had no money and no place to live.

"Don't worry about it for a minute," he said with a carefree casualness. "You can stay with me as long as you need to."

"I am really embarrassed."

"Don't be. It can happen." This statement from a man who had never needed to worry about money.

"Well, I'd like to do something to repay you when I can."

Michael took his eyes off the road to look at me very directly for a moment, as if he was about to say something important. Then he changed his mind. "You realize that you won't get a check for two weeks," he said. "They hold back a week's pay."

"How can they do that? Can you stand me for two weeks?"

"I'm having a good time. Stop worrying."

Home in Corrales, Michael offered a house key, although it was unlikely I would be entering or leaving without him as I had no means of transportation. We then began what soon turned into a routine, with dinner, lots to drink, and much conversation.

I had been in residence two or three days when one evening, as I finished showering, Michael came into the bathroom carrying a larger towel than the one that hung on the rack. He handed me the towel, smiled gently, and settled into a little wicker chair that stood just inside the bathroom door. We talked, and he watched quite openly as I dried.

I made no effort to hide, and I did not object. His attention was strange and vaguely exciting: outré. I was shocked that I enjoyed it. He said nothing personal, nor did I. He just watched until I finished drying. As I wrapped the towel around my waist I understood that my dilemma was clear: to be a gracious houseguest without allowing the relationship to become physical. Feeling flattered by Michael's attention was acceptable. I was not prepared for anything more.

CHAPTER SIX

For the next several days I hammered out public notices without pause. I hardly looked up from the typewriter, ignoring Looney to the extent possible. In the evenings I read through Michael's basic journalism texts and listened as he gave me a crash course in style and structure. It wasn't too difficult to learn that a news story should tell the reader who, what, when, where, why, and how. It made perfect sense that a story should be written with all the most important information at the top, with the less important information at the bottom so that the story could be cut from the bottom up for fit, and to spare the reader any more reading time than necessary. The whole issue of sources became almost epistemological— how one should distinguish justified belief from opinion. Burrows had been right about the basics of journalism. The skills necessary to get started were rudimentary. Good judgment and clear thinking were another matter and ultimately vital and more difficult to achieve.

During the day I made an effort to meet my colleagues, especially a tall, perfectly dressed man of about thirty whom I often saw holding forth at the coffee station. He was there one day talking to another reporter, a woman in her midthirties whom I knew to be the Women's Page editor, and I decided to introduce myself. This was one of those moments that seem absolutely inconsequential at the time but that ultimately change the direction of one's life.

"Hello," he said, bowing extravagantly and offering his hand. "I am Fred Bonavita, and you are the newest member of our illustrious staff. Welcome to the *Albuquerque Post and Echo*." The woman smiled indulgently. I shook hands, not exactly sure what to make of Bonavita. "And this is our brilliant Women's Page editor, Barbara Taylor." Barbara, looking bemused, offered her hand, nodded, said "welcome" in a quiet voice, and then fell silent.

"So," Bonavita said, his tongue darting to the corners of his mouth, "what brings you to our rag?"

I decided to play his game. Imitating the cadence of a Southern Baptist preacher in full dramatic mode, I said, "A deep desire to set the world straight. To right the wrongs of our misguided leaders, to bring enlightenment and virtue to our readers so that my tiny, unworthy life will not have been in vain."

Bonavita laughed. "Please, call me Fred. I assure you, sir, you have come to the right place. Virtue and truth are our daily goals."

Barbara rolled her eyes at the silliness, raised her hand in a little good-bye wave, and went back to her desk.

"You have come here from the *New York Times*, no doubt, or the *St. Louis Post-Dispatch*," Bonavita continued in his role.

"My first newspaper job," I said, reverting to my normal voice. "My very first time pretending to be a journalist."

"I see," Bonavita said, suddenly growing serious. "Well, if I can be of help, let me know." He paused, "Are you married?"

An odd question, I thought. "No, divorced."

"Good. Then you might have time to have a beer one day."

Relieved, I said, "Sure, I'd like that."

As Bonavita walked away, I inspected his brown wingtip shoes shined to a perfect matte finish; the perfectly fitted wool slacks, pleated and cuffed; the white shirt of superior cotton; and a silk tie of a good weight. Either his daddy is rich, I thought, or he is making more than eighty dollars a week. In reality, neither was true. His father owned a fine men's store in Charlottesville, Virginia.

Unlike Bonavita, most of the men in the city room wore short-sleeved, translucent nylon wash-and-wear shirts with undershirts showing beneath. Several fat copy pencils usually rode jammed into the lead-stained shirt pocket. Pants were polyester or wool, baggy and threadbare. Shoes were scuffed or made of faux suede of some sort. There were exceptions. Pete Gentile, the wire editor, a young family man recently escaped from New York City, wore pants that fit and freshly ironed cotton shirts. But most of the men were modeled after Tony A. C. DeCola, the gruff political editor who chewed a cigar and could easily conceal a football in the baggy seat of his pants.

When I went across the street for a sandwich at lunch after meeting Bonavita, Michael showed up and took a seat next to me at the counter. "You OK?"

"I'm fine," I said. "I just met Fred Bonavita."

"Be careful. Looney hates him."

"Looney hates me."

"Not in the same way."

"Why does Looney hate him?"

"He is arrogant, and he makes it clear that he is slumming. He's worked for better papers."

"Why is he here?"

"Has something to do with a girlfriend back in Virginia."

"I see." I sensed that Michael was threatened by my interest in Bonavita.

"Burrows asked me this morning how you were doing."

"What did you say?"

"I said you were doing well. He said he took a chance because your old police lieutenant said you were a steady guy."

"I know. That is so strange I can hardly believe it."

"What?"

"That lieutenant is totally corrupt. He is one of the reasons I left the force when I did. I was sure he was going to try to suck me in to protect himself."

"That upset you?"

"It was a close call. When I went in to have my exit interview with the chief, he questioned me very closely about why I was leaving. He wanted to know if there was anything wrong or if I was unhappy about anything. I think he may have even suspected that I was leaving because I knew something. I came very close to turning in the lieutenant. I came within a second of saying, 'Maybe you ought to have a closer look at the conduct of some of your shift commanders.' Something told me to leave it alone. I just had a sense that nothing would change and I would be on his shit list. Well, you know what?"

"That is absolutely amazing," Michael said. "The irony is too heavy."

"It's scary. I would never have gotten this job. It is almost as if I owe my job to him, or to not being honest."

"I wouldn't dwell on it," Michael said.

I finished my standard tuna sandwich, pondering the possibility of a universal lesson contained in what I had just learned, and went back to see if Looney had jammed any more misspellings into my typewriter.

There were so many churches and service organizations! I looked at dozens of pictures of people recently appointed assistant sales manager at Brown Chevrolet or who had just completed training to become certified realtors. I hammered on, wading through the morass of paper until just before quitting time, when I saw a release announcing a whistle-stop visit by a high-ranking United Nations official. I thought it odd that a UN official would stop in Albuquerque. I wondered if he had a daughter or a mistress or an old friend in the city. For some reason, the guy wanted to stay overnight on his way to Los Angeles. A press release and a quick meeting with some local official would make that legitimate. I folded the release and stuck it in my jacket.

Just days earlier, Michael had delighted and surprised me with the information that a story did not have to be assigned to be written. Anyone in the city room could write a story about anything and dump it in the basket. Whether it was ever printed was a different matter. There were restrictions, of course. Certain areas had been assigned as beats, and poaching on a beat was discouraged. So, for example, if one came upon a story about city government, the correct approach was to send a note to the reporter covering city hall. Similarly, stories on education, the courts, or New Mexico history were spoken for. But it was a small paper, and many areas were not clearly assigned. Those were open for the entrepreneur, which, it would turn out, was one of the great advantages of starting a career at a small paper. There was simply more room to dig without working in another person's hole.

After deadline I called the hotel mentioned in the release and asked for the UN official. I heard myself say, "Gerald Moore from the *Albuquerque Tribune*," and I felt like an impostor. My man was surprised, and I think flattered, that someone so far from New York would regard him as worthy of an interview. He was open and cooperative. Indeed, it turned out that an old college friend taught political science at the university and was the main reason for the stopover. They were having dinner with other faculty members that evening.

Scribbling notes furiously, trying to remember to get the correct spelling of names and organizations, I understood instinctively that the *Tribune* editors would be interested in the local angle and not in any inside information on the workings of UNESCO. I wrote the story, imitating to the best of my ability the style I had been absorbing all week, and tossed my copy in the copy basket. At four o'clock I met Michael in the parking lot for our trip home.

My mind was completely preoccupied by the article. The entire process had been astonishingly simple, but I was wading the Rubicon.

Without invitation or permission I had offered an article for publication, and now I could not stop thinking how Looney might behave as a result.

"Martini?" Michael asked as he hung his suede jacket on a peg by the door. He tossed his car keys into a pottery bowl and hauled out the gin bottle.

"Sure." A martini would surely change my frame of mind.

I put on a Kingston Trio album and flopped down on the mission-style couch to wait for my drink. We rehashed the day without much interest, and when Michael made a second batch of martinis, I told him about the interview with the UN official.

"You should have told me," he said, looking distressed.

"Why?"

"I could have read it and maybe improved it. I hope you didn't make any mistakes."

A bad feeling came suddenly and powerfully. I was so dependent on Michael that I felt I should do anything he asked. But now I felt enclosed, confined by his concern and by the intensity of his care. For the first time I felt resentful. "You have to let me make some mistakes," I said lightly.

He walked to where I sat, put his drink on the floor, and kneeled down in front of me. Sitting on his calves, he placed a hand on each of my knees, looking up at me, moonstruck. "Do you know how much I care for you?" he said, his face a mask of desire.

Panic leaped in me. Even though I knew this was a moment bound to happen, I could not imagine where things went from here. "I think I do. I think I'm beginning to. And I care for you too. But this is very tricky for me."

"How?"

"I am so deeply indebted to you. I am deeply grateful to you. I wish I could give you something or repay you. But I don't think this is the way, maybe."

He smiled patiently. "I don't want to do anything to upset you." He didn't move.

"May I ask you a very personal question?" I almost blurted the question.

"Yes, of course."

"Do your parents know about this?" I was shocked by the childlike quality of my own question.

His head snapped back a little. "What an odd thing to ask! I mean, what an odd question at this moment."

"I know," I said. "It is. I can't help it. I can't help but think of them. And mine too."

He became pensive. "It would kill them. I think my mother may suspect something, but my father would never recover if he knew. It would just kill him. I worry all the time that he might find out." He stood up and took a step back.

"A heavy burden?"

"Very heavy. I love them so much. I considered going to California for that reason. But I really, really love it here, and I am very, very discreet. Why do you think I live out here?" He gestured to indicate the emptiness around us.

"So how did you find out? I mean, how did you first know that you felt this way?"

"I never felt any other way. When I was twelve I got excited in the locker room."

I was in trouble. This was not the common adolescent experience of masturbating in the same room with another boy. This had everything to do with powerful personal feelings. Michael was completely vulnerable, and I was conflicted—not by sexual desire but by my sense of duty and responsibility to another person. I could see that he was smitten. I was flattered. I felt desired in a very unmale way. At least I thought it was unmale, but I also felt like running away.

"I can't get into this in the way you're thinking," I said firmly. "It is not about you. It is just how I am. It wouldn't work, at least not for very long. You can understand?"

"Of course," he said, reaching for his drink. "Of course."

He looked away. I could see that he was hurt and disappointed.

"I'm happy just to be with you," he said, turning, looking down. "Having you here is really nice. It's enough, maybe."

I knew I would have to leave. I had no idea how, but I felt a powerful emotional force pushing me away.

We had a subdued dinner, and at nine or so we went to our separate bedrooms. I tried to read, but I have never been so aware of the presence of another person as I was that night. I could practically feel Michael breathing in the next room. I wasn't afraid. I just felt overwhelmed by the presence of his desire. I had done a lot of desiring in my life, but I was never aware of being desired until now. Surely there had been girls who felt an adolescent flush in my presence, but mostly I was too self-involved or insecure to notice. This was emotion on a different level of magnitude. Michael was not suggesting a one-night stand. He was suggesting that in some very fundamental way I give myself to him, possibly forever.

In the morning we rode to work in silence. I had been at my desk less than a minute when Looney appeared with my story in his hand. "Where did you get this?" he demanded.

"It was in one of the releases you gave me yesterday."

"And how did you interview this guy?"

"I called him at the number on the release."

"And he told you all this stuff about his friend, the professor?"

"Right."

Looney turned abruptly and walked to the next desk, where Jim Nelson, a senior political reporter, was arranging his desk and gulping his first cup of coffee. Looney shoved my copy against Nelson's chest and said, "Call this professor. Ask him if he knows this guy from the UN."

Startled, Nelson took the copy and started to read. Looney turned on his heel and walked back to his desk. Michael watched the encounter from his perch next to Looney. My phone rang. It was Bonavita, whispering into the phone.

"What was that all about?"

"I gave him a story. I guess he doesn't believe me."

"You gave him a story?"

I cupped my hand around the phone to muffle my voice. "Isn't that all right?"

"It is probably the only thing anyone has given him in a month. Be brave!" He hung up.

Nelson wasn't able to reach the professor right away. Trying to keep track of Nelson's progress made concentration on my press releases difficult. I should have called the professor after I interviewed the UN representative, but I hadn't thought ahead enough to confirm both ends of the story. This was probably something every student would learn in Journalism 101: if A tells you about B, you may want to hear what B has to say. Clearly, I had done only half the story.

Finally, Nelson hung up the phone and walked to the front desk, where he conferred briefly with Looney. He handed over the copy and returned to his desk without looking at me. Puzzled, ignored both by

Looney and Michael, I worked on through the morning. As deadline neared and the pace in the room grew more frantic, I tried to guess the meaning of what I had witnessed.

When the first run of papers arrived in the city room at 11:30, reporters rushed to the ink-stained printer's helper to grab a paper from the stack he carried, each one searching the paper for any story they had written, looking for typos that could still be corrected before the main press run. I had never been part of the ritual. I had no stories to check. I was still working on the releases when my phone rang.

"Good work," Bonavita whispered into the phone and hung up.

I grabbed a paper and paged through quickly until I spotted the headline: "UN Official: Good Times, Hard Times with UNM Prof." I was in print! I read the story over and over. It was the story I had written, unchanged. But in print, it didn't sound like my voice. It was mine, but it wasn't. It was not a big story, but it was of respectable length. It was well placed on the page, and somewhere, probably from the files, they had found a picture of the professor, a man I recognized from my recent days on campus. There was no byline. That didn't matter. I managed to get a story published. Feeling the need to celebrate, I looked around the room and saw that I was the only person there who thought this little story was in any way remarkable. The city room went about its routine business unaware of my triumph. I took a deep breath and walked slowly back to my desk, where I sat behind my typewriter holding the paper, sensing that this was the beginning of something wonderful.

The little story did not change our routine. Looney continued to pass my desk each morning, pausing just long enough to fling his thick stack of press releases at me before waddling off to annoy another reporter. I continued to dutifully gut and clean the mess of self-promotion until we had little fillets of information that might be useful to our readers. In batches of threes and fours, I dumped them into the copy basket and then repeated the process. Journalism as I had imagined it lay somewhere down the road. I had tasted it, and I knew that somehow I would break out of this purgatory where Looney kept me. The UN story demonstrated that I could get material into the paper in spite of Looney's quarantine.

I found Looney an interesting man, in spite of his early enmity toward me. He had been in Albuquerque for eleven years, but his voice still carried the long, open vowels of his old Kentucky home. He was ambitious and shrewd, both qualities that I would eventually admire.

He was also petty and vindictive and manipulative, as his daily behavior showed. As time passed, I would see him as a complex character, essentially an intelligent man crippled by the class and regional prejudices inherited from the worst of his native culture. He would eventually show himself to be a decent editor, and I would soon learn that he was an excellent photographer who made regular weekend trips to remote areas of the state, where he captured crisp images of ghost towns and New Mexico's majestic natural scenery. His perfectly exposed photos rarely included people, which I took as a sign of how little regard he had for mankind in general, a notion reinforced when I listened in shock to the occasional whispered racial slur. His attitude was that of many reactionaries: a mixture of resentment and self-righteousness. He would end a successful career with Scripps Howard as editor of the *Rocky Mountain News* in Denver, after he replaced Burrows as editor at the *Tribune*.

His politics and prejudices were unattractive enough, but when added to his utter obsequiousness in the presence of anyone with power, his demeanor bordered at times on being disgusting. The most immediate victim of his attitude was, quite predictably, the lining of his stomach. He gulped antacids and drank milk throughout the day in a vain effort to treat his seething resentments, to treat his spiritual maladjustment by physical means.

Having thus roundly condemned him, I need to add that in time he became a supporter of my efforts, and when I left Albuquerque he took me to dinner at the Albuquerque Elks' Club, where he had nice things to say about my work. Some were sincere. Some were meant to cement a relationship with someone going to work in the national media. Still, in those early weeks at the *Tribune*, the idea that I would ever hear an encouraging word from Looney was beyond imagination.

CHAPTER SEVEN

Michael calmed down considerably after our encounter. He seemed determined to have me in the house without pressing for anything more, but something sinister was happening at work. I noticed Bonavita and Looney taking an interest in my living arrangements.

Stopping by Looney's desk to drop off copy one morning, he looked up from his work, lifted his eyebrows, looked over his glasses, and said, "I notice you ride to work with Michael every day. You live near him out there in Corrales?" This was the first personal question he had ever asked. In fact, it was one of the first times he actually spoke to me. His tone was not friendly, and I suspected that he regarded living in Corrales as prima facie evidence of decadence. My antennae were fully and instantly deployed. Only a few days earlier I overheard him making remarks about the founder and director of the Santa Fe Opera—something to the effect that the "fairy boys" ran the show "up there." It was said with a particular nastiness, the same tone that entered his voice when he sauntered across the city room one day mumbling about "the Reverend Doctor Martin Luther Coon."

"I'm bunking with him while I look for a place," I said. I chose "bunking" as the more manly and western of the options that ranged from "rooming with" to "sleeping there."

His only comment was "Oh?"

It was a day or two later that Bonavita engaged me at the coffee pot and inquired if I was living "at" Michael's. His question was only a preposition away from "living with," and I understood. I wasn't then entirely sure where Bonavita stood on the question of gayness after his earlier question about my marital state, but I was uncomfortable with the idea that he might think I was more than a friend to Michael.

In my seemingly perpetual state of delayed awareness, I had actually debated whether people at the *Tribune* regarded Michael as gay. I now understood that they not only regarded him as gay, they were wondering if I had become his lover. I felt a tremendous urgency to demonstrate that this was not the case, primarily because I feared that Looney would redouble his efforts to get rid of me.

I had two paychecks. With taxes and Social Security deducted, each came to sixty-two dollars. I not only needed a place to live, I also needed transportation. Sixty dollars a week would not soon provide that. In an inspired moment characterized by a mixture of elation and despair, I saw that I might solve my dilemma by resorting to two things I regarded as distinctly distasteful: squatting and borrowing money from a loan agency.

On a country drive the winter before, a friend had pointed out an abandoned house on a country property about fifteen miles north of Albuquerque, near the village of Placitas. He said at the time that the place belonged to a woman who lived in Colorado. She had inherited the property, he said, but had no interest in it. Local gossip held that she had never even visited. Several attempts by a neighbor to locate the woman ended in failure. The empty house had taken on a kind of ghostly existence: abandoned, empty, preserved by the dry mountain air.

The Saturday after Looney's question, I called my friend, Jim Sanborn, and enlisted him for a Sunday scouting mission. We drove to Placitas and located the house, isolated at the end of a seldom-traveled dirt road. Grass and weeds grew tall around the place, but by some miracle it had not been vandalized. The door was unlocked. I pushed it open and went inside, feeling that eerie sensation that always comes when one enters an empty dwelling. Three medium-sized adobe rooms constructed in the traditional New Mexico manner stood in a line with a fireplace on one end and a kitchen on the other. A wood-burning cookstove seemed operable. The house was actually in good condition considering the length of time it had been empty. The roof looked solid. There had been no water damage. The floor was bare stone except for in the kitchen, where a scrap of worn and faded floral-print linoleum still covered most of it. There was an old metal bedstead, a potbellied stove, and in the kitchen some cabinets. Outside, an iron hand pump marked a well. Sanborn pumped vigorously. A hollow echo inside the hole answered his effort. An open cistern nearby undoubtedly contained the remains of various animals and bits of discarded household junk, which meant there was no water supply.

We walked to a barn where a heavy snowstorm in some past winter had snapped the vigas. Favored by sunlight pouring through the open roof, grass flourished in the dirt floor. Lengths of barbed wire and pieces of rusting farm machines littered the area. We found a privy. The air inside was dank. A Sears, Roebuck and Company catalogue from 1951 rested on the two-hole bench. The floor was solid. It was usable.

"I wonder what would happen if she found me living here," I asked Sanborn as we walked back to the house.

"Kick you out," he said, shrugging.

"It's trespassing."

"Yeah," he said. "And it would be embarrassing as hell if the owner shows up, but I don't think she would do anything but make you leave. Or sue you for all you're worth." He shot me a knowing glance and smirked.

"Maybe I could offer to pay rent. I might be able to by the time I found her. I could say I tried to get in touch but couldn't find her."

"You could do that." I sensed that Sanborn didn't approve of my plan. What I didn't know at the time was that his war with his wife, Sally, was heating up again, and he might soon need a roommate. We had shared a house briefly before I left for Mexico, and I think he had me in mind for another sharing arrangement as he contemplated his future without his wife.

On the way back to town, I raised the moral issue of moving into another person's property. "What do you think? You think it's wrong to use the place? It's empty. I'll take care of it while I'm there, and I'm not staying very long."

"It just seems creepy," Sanborn said.

"It is creepy," I agreed.

"Cop to squatter," he said, without looking at me.

"Yeah. Well . . ."

Necessity, wielding a powerful influence on principle, led me to the next step. After work that Monday I stopped in at the Pacific Finance Company and, based mostly on my having seemingly permanent employment, managed to talk them into a $500 loan. The interest rate was exorbitant, but I wasn't the perfect credit risk. I lied about having a lot of furniture, and in a wink-and-nod conspiracy with the young loan officer, I used the imaginary furniture as collateral. I was in the position that most desperate people are in when they borrow money: take it and hope it all works out on the other end.

I bought a very old powder-blue Chevy pickup with part of the money and went to Sears, where to my surprise I was allowed to open a charge account. Having verifiable employment was the key to everything, it seemed. I got a few basics, like a five-gallon water can, a skillet, a small insulated chest, a flashlight, and the other items I would need to survive in my new quarters. Thus equipped, the following weekend I decamped from Michael's palatial adobe in Corrales to the musty rooms of a stranger's house in Placitas, regarding the move as progress.

Michael was gracious about my departure, as he had been about everything in our relationship. He smiled and patted my back and shook my hand and hugged me and invited me back anytime I liked. I felt sad about leaving. I wished that I could reciprocate his affection, or even his lust, but I couldn't. Hugging him good-bye, I felt a kind of love for him, the love one feels for a close relative.

Driving toward the foothills of the Sandia Mountains, where Placitas nestled, I felt lighter and freer than I had in weeks. I had not fully appreciated the pressure I felt in Michael's presence, the pressure to be kind and polite without appearing to invite a physical encounter. My feelings were complicated, but I knew I was happy—very happy—to be headed to quarters that I did not share.

I tied a wet towel over my nose and mouth and set about cleaning the place. This was before we knew much about hantavirus in mouse pee, but my father had taught with great sternness that dust and old medicine bottles in abandoned houses were not to be trusted. It was mostly a broom job, sweeping out accumulated dust, mouse droppings, and cobwebs hanging from the low ceiling. I arranged my gear, unrolled my new sleeping bag across the metal bedsprings, and took an ax to find wood for the stove.

The hills just above the house were covered in cedar and piñon. I was able to knock dead limbs loose and collect pieces that had fallen. In an hour's time I had several days' supply of wood. When the flue on the cookstove proved to be open and working, I knew I could stay, assuming that no one found the owner to report my occupation.

It was only six months earlier that I had left for Mexico, but it seemed years ago that I was a respectable, bourgeois citizen with a job, a badge, a car, and living quarters. Now I had the three essentials back. They were fragile, possibly temporary, and borrowed: the house belonged to a stranger, the pickup would die at any moment, and my boss wanted me gone. My immediate challenge was simple but difficult: to live in this remote house without any modern conveniences—no running water, no electricity, no heat except for the wood-burning stove—and to appear in the city room every morning at seven, clean-shaven, dressed in jacket and tie, ready to work. I was sure I could sneak into my old dormitory at the university for a shower. I could heat water on the stove to wash and shave. I was a competent cook. But even with the skills I acquired over the years while hunting and camping, this situation would require focus and some good fortune if I was to convince Looney that he didn't need to run me off in order to get a real reporter.

With the house clean and my stuff stowed, I made a huge bologna sandwich with extra mayo and pickles and onion and iceberg lettuce. I poured a water glass nearly full of Gallo red and took my lunch outside to sit on the wide stone terrace and let the warm late-autumn sun beat against my back.

CHAPTER EIGHT

As my career in law enforcement wobbled to a close in 1962, I sought out people at the university who were, in most respects, the opposite of law enforcement types, which is to say, people who were more "bohemian," as we called them then. This was in response to my feeling that I was sinking into a kind of cop mentality, and not a very good one. I don't disparage law enforcement people. They generally behave intelligently and responsibly. I respect the profession, and I admire cops who see the worst of human behavior without losing their own humanity. But I was losing the battle for mine. I could feel myself becoming crude and insensitive to other people. I simply lacked the moral stability to resist the pressures that police work brought to bear. Maybe twelve years of strict Catholic education would have helped. Whatever the reason, the police department did not bring out the best in me.

My maître d' for Hotel Bohemia turned out to be Jim O'Connor, a big, garrulous man from Buffalo, New York, who dressed indifferently in dark, loose clothing stained by oil paint and food. Jim was easy to be around, made friends without effort, and permitted a kind of salon in his big living room, where in the evening people hung out to drink cheap beer and talk. I don't remember how I met him, but within a few days of becoming acquainted, I was spending many off hours in his company as he made his way to a master of fine arts thesis, painting copies of work by a dozen or so major contemporary artists: Mark Rothko, Franz Kline, Georgia O'Keeffe, and others. I enjoyed watching the paintings emerge as he worked his way through the pantheon.

In the year before he finished his MFA and departed, I left the police department, and for the short time that I was free of work or school, he managed to teach me quite a lot about art. From time to time he would also enlist me to help build sets for the single legitimate theater then operating in Albuquerque, where he worked as set designer, painter, and carpenter to supplement his meager graduate school income.

Through him I gained my first real exposure to fine art and theater. I had only one class in fine art in my entire twelve years of public school. It was fifth grade, and a nice lady came in two times each week for about a month to show us examples of great paintings and to tell us about them. We constructed little bound notebooks where we mounted poor-quality color reproductions of works by Gainsborough, Turner, Goya, Remington, and others and then wrote a paragraph about the work on the facing page. It was a class designed to teach us to recognize half a dozen icons and to instill a reverence for art that we most likely would never see. I still have the book.

Before O'Connor, my experience with drama was equally thin, confined to the annual senior play in Tucumcari, which was usually something like *Our Town*. There were two movie theaters, both owned by Michael's father, and they were my only window into the world. There was no television in Tucumcari until after I left home for college. Reaching college age without ever watching television clearly placed me in a minority in the developed world, a minority that would soon be gone, and it may help to explain why I did not see the medium as a competitor to printed news and pictures.

My mother did make an effort. When I was fifteen, she hung a large dime-store print of an English landscape on our living room wall. Nearly sixty years later I still recall every detail of the painting: A rustic cottage sits on the edge of a deep wood facing a sloping meadow. In the foreground a gentle stream flows horizontally across the painting. A woman and a boy carrying a walking stick cross a little footbridge on their way to the cottage. I always imagined they were returning home from a trip to their village. A few lazy cows, probably put there to give a splash of ocher to an otherwise very green scene, bask in sunlight in the right foreground. It was a reproduction of one of the thousands of landscapes the English painted in the nineteenth century, all lovely, most looking very much like all the others. Another print, harsh and photographic, depicting a vase of yellow lilies, hung on the opposite wall. It had been my Mother's Day gift to her when I was ten. I wanted to give her something to put on the wall, and it was about the only print I could afford at Woolworth's. Otherwise, visual art was confined to snapshots of family and occasionally, in public buildings, to a print of cartoonish Western art depicting the noble cowboy or the stoic Indian. No Taliban purity squad could have more completely stripped Tucumcari of art and music than had poverty, ignorance, and attenuated southern culture.

It was at O'Connor's house in late October 1962, as we huddled around a radio (he didn't own a television) to hear President Kennedy describe the advent and later the resolution of the Cuban Missile Crisis, that I became aware of the great existential threat in our lives. I remember clearly my sense of disbelief that war would result from the confrontation. "So what if the Russians don't back down?" I said to O'Connor in an offhanded manner. "It's the end of the fucking world, man," he replied with absolute assurance. Then, seemingly for emphasis, he sucked deeply on his Kent cigarette.

A sobering notion. Still, I found it hard to believe that we would actually engage in nuclear war. Many people at the time were not so sanguine. All across the country, people were stockpiling food and supplies and building backyard bomb shelters out of fear that we would be attacked. Years later, as I read the memoirs of our leaders in that period, I understood there was far more pressure in Washington to launch a war on Russia than I ever imagined. The anticommunist rhetoric of the fifties convinced many people that the Russians were just waiting for the right opportunity to begin a worldwide conflagration and that a first strike was not only morally possible, but patriotism required it. The great danger, of course, was that one side would misunderstand the actions of the other, making the Cuban situation very dangerous. When it was over, I was relieved to go on with my probably pointless discussions of aesthetics in O'Connor's living room, but the chilling hours of the crisis, before the other fellow blinked, remained part of the Zeitgeist. The notion that men (they were all men) working thousands of miles away could and might take actions that would instantaneously, irrevocably destroy our lives led to many existential discussions around the pinochle games that seemed to break out in the early evening. Playing cards, drinking Knickerbocker beer at a dollar a six-pack, smoking Marlboros that cost thirty-five cents a pack, we allowed ourselves much talk about our heavy burden of despair, ennui, and futility while we quietly searched for any opportunity to further our ambitions.

It was at O'Connor's that I met Jim Sanborn, who guided me to my quarters in Placitas a year or so later. He was an architecture student who was having trouble finishing a degree. He was good-looking, intense, and involved in a troubled on-again, off-again marriage to Sally, a sophisticated, energetic blonde from California who suffered from insomnia, problems with self-esteem, and what she regarded as the kid culture then emerging in America. By "kid culture," she meant pot and rock and roll. Her father, Jack Stewart (née Sternad), was a literary agent for movie and television writers in Hollywood. He drank too much, drove an old Rolls Royce coupe in the hope that the fancy car would protect him from arrests by the California Highway Patrol, dressed impeccably, and looked down on almost everyone. He, like my father, suffered from a lost, glorious past, except that instead of losing a ranching empire, his family had lost the Austro-Hungarian Empire.

It was never clear to me exactly what position Sally's great-grandfather held in the Austro-Hungarian government before World War I, but her father recalled that they had many servants, a huge established house in Budapest, and eventually enough worthless government bonds to paper a living room in the Brooklyn house where he was raised. According to Sally, who had graduated from UCLA magna cum laude, her father regarded only the ivy league women's colleges as offering acceptable education, except that when it was time to go, he couldn't or wouldn't afford the tuition. Her mother, Kay, a feminist from a stern midwestern Protestant family, put up with Jack and taught high school English in Beverly Hills to provide her own source of income.

In a classical pattern of repetition, Sally disapproved of Sanborn's drinking and was seldom in attendance at the O'Connor salon/saloon. She taught school to earn their living and rightfully, in my view, thought Sanborn should be spending more time on studies and less time drinking beer and arguing the finer points of aesthetics with the likes of me and O'Connor. Sanborn, like her father, was a terrible snob, except that it was Hemingway's code that he embraced rather than Jack Stewart's sense of noblesse oblige.

I didn't see a lot of Sally until she and Sanborn separated the winter I left the police department. After becoming friends at O'Connor's, Sanborn and I rented a house together. From time to time Sally would call and invite me to have coffee so that she could pick my brain about Sanborn's state of mind. These were tricky meetings. Sally was an attractive woman. I didn't want to be disloyal to Sanborn by revealing anything that might hurt his standing or by being so helpful that I became closer to Sally than to Sanborn, but during these brief encounters I began to understand that many of her frustrations and grievances were legitimate. Wisely, I managed to remain neutral. By the time I left for Mexico, Sanborn and I were still good friends.

While I was in Mexico, Sanborn and Sally patched up their marriage, so by the time I was employed at the *Tribune* and staying with Michael in Corrales, they were living together in Old Town, a chic area surrounding the city's oldest church, San Felipe de Neri, built in 1793. Without children, Sally's salary allowed them to occupy a tasteful two-bedroom apartment in a city where tasteful rental property was still scarce. It was there, in their spare bedroom, that I awoke one morning to find a flower on my pillow.

CHAPTER NINE

The first Monday after my move to Placitas, I was able to walk into the city room without apprehension. Filled with confidence, I stopped at Bonavita's desk to tell him, within earshot of Looney, that he should come out and see my new place in Placitas.

"Pla-ci-tas," he repeated loudly. "I assume this is some chic ethnic enclave nearby."

Bonavita rarely spoke in normal vocabulary. He chose archaic phrasing and was either dramatically conspiratorial, archly ironic, or feigning ignorance. He was always performing, except when he was angry. It was a way of avoiding direct communication, and it was alternately amusing and maddening.

"I'm in a traditional adobe abode," I said. "No place for a dyslexic. Small, but very pretty. Really, you have to come out." I felt sure that Looney had taken note that I was no longer "bunking" at Michael's, but to be certain, I went on about the commute being a good half hour and gave Bonavita vague directions. With that bit of business done, I sat down to my pile of press releases.

Just before our first deadline at 11:30, I noticed Looney speaking excitedly on the phone. I watched as he scribbled a few notes on a sheet of copy paper. Except for a few of the senior beat reporters typing furiously to meet deadline, the newsroom was deserted. Looney looked around, then leaped up and came charging to my desk, his soft little body jiggling with each step.

"Some guy on a crane over by Central Avenue just had an accident and smashed the crane into a building," he said. "Take a camera and go over there and see if you can get a story. We'll hold space on page one. You have twenty minutes." He thrust the copy paper at me.

Panic seized me. Thoughts rushed through and over one another. I had to calm down and think how to do this. In the great scheme of things the events in downtown Albuquerque that morning were no more important than a grain of dust blowing against a desert rock, but I regarded it as my big break.

I grabbed pencils and paper and stuffed them into my pockets. I went to the file cabinet where a Rolex camera rested. I had never used it, but I hung it around my neck and headed for the accident scene. Outside, I slowed my pace and heard my thumping heart. I tried to calm myself enough to think clearly. I was only blocks from the accident, and when I turned a corner I saw the crane flipped onto its back like a giant dipper with a handle six stories high resting against an office building. Emergency lights flashed in a confusing show as police, fire, and ambulance vehicles arrived. I pushed through the crowd of gawkers and approached a policeman I recognized from my cop days.

"Hey, Moore, how are you?" he asked, apparently happy to see me. "What ever happened to you?"

"I'm working at the *Trib*."

"No shit. That's great, I guess. You must be here for the big story," he gestured toward the camera hanging from my neck.

"Yeah, what happened?"

"I don't know. I just got here. Go talk to the operator. He's over there, with Wiley and Birch." He pointed to a small, middle-aged man in work khakis speaking with two cops. I hurried over. Wiley and I had been in the police academy together. Sergeant Birch was essentially a stranger because I worked nights and he was a day man. Wiley paved the way. "Hey, I heard you were a reporter," he said when he saw me with the camera. Sergeant Birch looked at me suspiciously. "This is Gerald Moore," Wiley said. "We were in the academy together."

"OK," Birch said without interest. "Let's get this mess cleaned up." He turned to me. "What do you want?"

"Talk to the operator?" I said, indicating the intimidated little man standing beside Wiley.

"Be my guest," he said and turned away to direct other officers handling the traffic that was building.

In limited English, the operator told me how he had attempted to lift a heavy pallet of building materials to a sixth-floor construction site. When the pallet reached the fourth floor, the crane suddenly shifted on its base and began falling forward, pulled down by the load. Reacting instinctively, he released the load. The sudden release of tension caused the crane to recoil violently backward so that it fell off its base and sent the boom crashing into the building across the street from the worksite. No one was injured, and there was minimal damage, despite a huge amount of debris scattered on the street and sidewalk. It appeared that the base of the crane had not been properly prepared. It had shifted and ultimately given way under the load swinging beneath the boom, or he had overloaded the pallet. Had the accident happened anywhere but in the downtown area it would have been insignificant. Had it not happened so near the *Tribune* deadline, it would not have been thought so important. The whole thing struck me as minor, but they were holding front-page space.

I took several pictures and rushed back to the paper, turning in my film and then running to the typewriter to write my first-ever on-deadline story. I used the most violent and active language I could conjure without sounding silly. Before I finished, Looney appeared in front of my typewriter. He took hold of the copy paper and held it loosely as I kept typing, his hand moving with the paper. Then he pulled the copy and went to his desk to begin editing. I rolled in a fresh sheet and finished the story.

The first run of the late edition carried the story on the front page with a large picture of the fallen crane. I read the story carefully, trying to see if Looney had made any substantial changes. He had not. The story was accurate but ultimately not very interesting: "Office Towers Damaged in Construction Accident." I congratulated myself for not failing on my first assignment and went to lunch.

That afternoon, Bonavita stopped by my desk and suggested we go to Al Monte's for a beer in celebration of my little story. I took the invitation as his response to the news of my move, but it could just as well have been because I had arrived, sort of, as a real reporter. As it turned out, he was just lonely and in need of a friend. We settled in over two cold Heinekens that I could not afford and began the process of getting to know each other.

Bonavita served four years in the air force, went to college, and then began working for the *Richmond Times-Dispatch*. It was never clear to me why he came to Albuquerque except that he seemed to find the Virginia social structure stifling. His speech was full of acronyms like FFV (first families of Virginia), references to the "Tidewater aristocracy," and puns, like his name for the Francis Scott Key Bridge over the Potomac River: the "car-strangled spanner." His mind was lively and his contempt for Looney unconcealed. He claimed that the standards of journalism as practiced by the *Tribune* were low, although he never actually offered me any concrete instances. He was interesting and probably trouble where newsroom politics were concerned. He immediately began to pick my brain about "Pla-ci-tas."

I was not about to reveal my status as a squatter. I simply said I found this great place in the country through mutual friends. He seemed interested in the fact that I had a large circle of friends. It turned out he had only one: a television reporter who had moved from Richmond to Albuquerque. I sensed a certain condescension when he spoke to me of journalism, which was as it should be. I knew nothing. By contrast he was responsible for the education beat, which included the University of New Mexico and all the public schools.

It was during the second round of imported beer that I could not afford that Bonavita apparently decided I needed instructions on some customs of the newspaper. Leaning forward in his chair, he adopted a conspiratorial manner and said, "There are a couple of things you might want to know. Have you noticed the large cardboard carton sitting on the table behind Looney's desk?"

"Yes," I said. "I assume it is garbage or something they haven't unpacked."

"Noooo. Those, my friend, are review copies of books sent to us from publishers all over the country. They're up for grabs. If you take one, you write a review, unless it's real junk. A lot of them are. The *Trib* doesn't print many reviews, so just turn in one once in a while."

This news was stunning. He had handed me a winning lottery ticket, a trifecta: free books, an opportunity to say what I thought about them, and a reason to be published in the paper without waiting for Looney to make an assignment. "All the new releases are in there?"

"Yes and no," Bonavita said, pausing to wet his throat. "When the books come in, Looney and Burrows and Baldwin and the other guys up there on the desk take their pick. The ones they don't want go in the box. Then it's first come, first served. Don't expect to find any photo books on New Mexico, or histories of naval warfare or the Civil War, or James Gould Cozzens, or anything like that, but there are often some decent novels."

"I can't wait," I said.

"Keep an eye out," Bonavita said. "Every few days Looney will dump a bunch of books. Some have been in there for months. Nobody wants them."

"That's unbelievable," I said. "You can just pick out a book and review it?"

"Right."

"And does it matter—I mean—does anyone care what you say?"

"Sometimes. I've reviewed a couple of books that the bookstore said they had calls for afterward. And I suppose a few people in town might recognize you as an idiot if you got one really wrong."

"Amazing." My imagination had left the room several minutes before as I began to understand the potential. I wanted to leave Al's and go back to the paper to see what might be in the box.

"And another thing," Bonavita continued. "You can go to the movies on your *Tribune* ID card."

"Free?"

"Yeah. Free. And take a guest. The deal is that if the movie has not been reviewed, you are supposed to review it. If it has already been reviewed, then, 'Be my guest.' You might want to bear in mind that the theater owners give us this privilege and they can get very pissed if you pan a movie they are expecting to do well."

Bonavita would demonstrate this principle just a few weeks later when he panned *Cleopatra* and the theater owner temporarily pulled our free entry.

"Balance is the word, my friend," Bonavita said with as much irony as he could muster. "Balance, if you know what I mean." Then he broke out laughing. "You can say anything you want to about books. Movies are more sensitive."

"I may be in your debt," I said sincerely.

"Thanks are not necessary," he said. "A simple check will do."

We finished our beers. Bonavita straightened his six feet, four inches, pressed a hand against his back, and grimaced. I was admiring his suit when I remembered that all my clothes were in a house I didn't own.

I left Al's feeling optimistic about a real friendship. I liked Bonavita. He struck me as a decent man who, despite his odd manner of speaking and the little roles he sometimes adopted, was essentially open. He clearly was inclined to teach and share what he knew. I could learn from him. The animosity that existed between him and Looney could be a problem if Looney knew we were friends. In a strange twist of fate—God shifting the wind, if you will—the Bonavita-Looney struggle played out in a totally surprising way and was a key in allowing me the chance to go to New York to work as a national journalist.

CHAPTER TEN

The house in Placitas was lonely after the weeks I spent at Michael's. There were no after-work drinks, no conversations about work, and no sexual tension. Being an object of desire can be pleasantly distracting, I discovered, if things don't get out of hand.

The countryside was so still that I became acutely aware of silence. Any noise I made cooking or even turning the page of a book seemed outsize and intrusive. Silence, in my case, begets silence. I began moving more quietly through the house and placing plates and skillets on surfaces with more care to dampen the impact. I lived in a constant state of alertness, always vaguely expectant that the owner would appear and demand an explanation of my presence.

My perception of light changed too. I was concerned that too much light might give me away, even though there were no other houses in sight. In fact, there was not another house within a mile or two, but I was aware that I lived in a pool of bright light in an otherwise dark sea. I remembered all the survival lore learned from older friends who served in the Korean War about the ability of the human eye to see the glow of a cigarette five hundred yards away or how a single flashlight beam shining on a dark night at sea could be seen for miles. I didn't want to be found living in the old house, but more than that, I didn't want anyone to know that I was there alone. I rejected my new Coleman gas lantern as being too bright and settled instead on a kerosene lamp for reading. The soft yellow light reminded me of cozy, secure evenings spent as a little boy in my grandparents' ranch house before they got electricity.

Aside from the fact that I had no right to be there, and there was no place to bathe, I quite liked the old place. It felt secure and substantial in the way that only earthen houses can. I speculated briefly about searching for the owner to see if I could actually rent the place when my financial situation improved, but then I remembered that at seven thousand feet of elevation, the first serious snow of winter would close the road, perhaps until spring. And sooner or later someone was going to ask why I showered in a dorm where I didn't seem to have a room. My tenure was limited. I would have to be out in six weeks or be butt deep in powder. In the meantime, I devised what I hoped would be a sufficient rationale for my presence. If I was confronted by the owner, a sheriff's deputy, or another interested party, I would say that I was on a trip and just intended to sleep over. I had so little gear that the traveling story was marginally plausible.

One thing I would not miss when I moved was the squeaking springs of the old bed. Each time I struggled to turn over in my sleeping bag, they set up a cacophony that brought me fully awake. A mattress, of all things, became a high-priority item, when I could afford one.

Lying in the darkness, hyperaware of my surroundings, I recognized an attraction to country peace and quiet that lingered deep inside me. The early, formative years on the ranch left a mark. Somehow, to be in the country was to feel at home. I didn't give it a lot of thought at the time because I was so completely focused on hanging on at the *Tribune*, but as time passed and the pressures of work and success increased, the appeal of the country would grow strong again.

CHAPTER ELEVEN

The morning after the crane accident, I found a copy of the *Albuquerque Journal*, the city's larger-circulation morning paper, neatly folded and stuck into my typewriter. A headline, circled in a broad copy-pencil line, read,

Hero in Downtown Accident
Quick-Thinking
Crane Operator
Averts Disaster

The story, accompanied by a photograph of the smiling crane operator at the controls of the righted crane, recounted how he maneuvered the machine to avoid hitting the building toward which the crane fell, saving uncounted lives and human damage.

I read the story with a slightly altered sense of reality. The physical facts of the accident were exactly the same in the *Journal* story and in mine. The question of human volition was entirely different. The base under the crane failed. The crane tipped toward a building. The operator dropped the load and the crane recoiled, falling over backward into a different office building. No one was hurt. But the wily *Journal* reporter, playing cleanup on my story, created a hero. The operator, in the split second that his crane was tipping forward, felt a deep concern for the people in the building toward which his crane was falling and, thinking quickly, released the load and spared them injury or death. I could almost hear the *Journal* reporter laughing at me.

"You missed the story," Looney said as he arrived with his arm wrapped around the morning stack of press releases, clearly pleased by my failure.

"That guy was no hero," I asserted. "He just reacted to his crane falling."

Looney looked at me directly, which he seldom did. "How can you go out on a story and not recognize a hero?" He smiled a tired, rebuking smile.

"He was not a hero," I repeated.

"The *Journal* has a good story," he said over his shoulder as he walked away. "Where's ours?"

Looney's thrust left a jagged, bleeding hole in my self-esteem. I did not know the purpose of his nasty critique, but I did not think it was intended to make me a better reporter.

A sense of injustice filled me, but there was no appeal. It would have been fraudulent to call the poor, panicked operator a hero. In fact, I thought as I stewed, the real story was why the base of the crane failed in the first place. Someone had not done a proper job and put people, including the operator, in jeopardy. There had been no time to investigate that, and anyway, no one was interested, except perhaps the insurance company.

I had just bumped into a basic principle of popular journalism: personalize the story. Keep it personal. Keep it local. How many people cared a flip about a badly installed crane base? How many people cared about a damaged office building? Not many even cared about the lowly crane operator. But call him a hero and people would read the story to find out why he was a hero and if they agreed with that judgment.

Once I got over my feeling of being falsely accused and began to think about the story and the events surrounding it, I suddenly recognized a condition that would prove useful. Looney had to assign me to that story because he had no other reporter available. Burrows's frugality kept the staff so small that Looney did not have any choice but to use me. If I wrote decent copy, one way or another, he would be forced to print it. If my work appeared in the paper, Burrows would not consent to my being fired. Of course, if I wrote enough successful copy, then Looney's motive in running me off would be gone, and he would, in effect, have a journeyman reporter at Burrows's price. It was an odd situation. I would defeat Looney's purpose by giving him what he wanted in the first place.

I had managed so far to keep our relationship impersonal. Looney might wish me gone because he wanted a more expensive, more seasoned reporter, but I had taken care not to give him any reason to dislike me personally. The "hero" nonstory was doubly upsetting because it was the kind of thing, I thought, that he could claim as a failure.

With my quota of press releases done, I went to the box of review copies where I found the detritus of the publishing world, the leavings after the staff thoroughly picked over the already leftovers deposited there by Looney and the senior editorial staff. Then, near the bottom of the box, I found a novel that looked interesting: *The Spy Who Came In from the Cold*.

I read the first few pages standing beside the book box. I like mysteries and thrillers, but my pleasure is always diminished by a vague sense that the activity is frivolous, that I ought to be learning facts or reading one of the classics I never cracked. The need for facts came from a sense that ignorance lurked in my mind like a fugitive and could suddenly appear at any moment to shame me.

One of the more humiliating moments of being blindsided by ignorance happened in my second year at the university. While having coffee with friends, we began to swap childhood memories of World War II. One person recalled his feelings when he saw his father in uniform leaving for the war. I talked about evenings in 1943 sitting in front of a battery-powered Zenith radio listening to newscasts about Allied advances or retreats. Sam Levi described the fate of a courageous relative who, "speaking Yiddish as he went," left Poland and crossed Nazi Germany on his way to France in the 1930s. The story did not have a happy ending. His relative made it to France only to be deported back to Poland, where the Nazis murdered him. When Levi finished his story, I asked, "What is Yiddish?"

Levi exploded in shock and anger. "You don't know what Yiddish is?" He was half standing. "You fucking fool. How can you not know what Yiddish is?" He was beside himself and unspeakably rude, but I felt far more upset by my ignorance than by his rudeness. A calmer, wiser friend at the table said simply, "It's a German dialect spoken by Central European Jews." End of story. But I never forgot what Yiddish is, nor did I ever forget my embarrassment.

Oddly enough, Levi was also the source of a second great embarrassment that fall, although thankfully this one was private. The friend who so calmly and clearly explained Yiddish told me later in confidence that he was concerned about Levi.

"Why?" I asked. "He seems OK."

"He has a really hard time keeping a girlfriend," he said. "He gets dumped all the time by women he thinks he likes. I'm worried that he's becoming a misogynist."

Judging from the sound of the word, I concluded that Levi was "massaging" himself. "I guess we are all misogynist some of the time."

"Do you think so?" my friend said. "I honestly don't think I am."

The misunderstanding continued: "You have a wonderful girlfriend. So of course you wouldn't be."

"Right," he agreed. "How could I be a misogynist when I have Megan?"

"Right," I agreed. "I mean if you were, there would definitely be something wrong with you."

We laughed and went on to another topic. Mercifully, I was alone when sometime later I discovered that the words "massage" and "misogynist" may sound alike but stem from entirely different roots, and although being a misogynist might result in a man massaging himself, the word for that is "onanism."

I tucked *Spy* into my knapsack and took it back to Placitas. The cover blurbs made it sound serious, and thriller or not it offered me an opportunity to get into the paper. In fact, the book was not quite like anything I had read before. It was dense and hard to follow. I considered putting it aside, then reminded myself that a review would get my name in the paper. I would have something to show my mother. I slogged on trying to follow the fate of Alec Leamas. The intrigue was complex and cynical, challenging my understanding. The government of *Spy* was not like any US government I could then imagine.

The theme of loyalty and betrayal at the core made it compelling but troubling. It's so human to want to belong completely to a movement, an institution, or a country—to be a true believer. *Spy* showed the cost of letting loyalty blind you to the truth, and that the truth is not always pretty.

I didn't feel enough confidence to write a strong review condemning the book as dense, even though I was never entirely sure exactly what had happened. I settled for a tepid, safe account of the book and reassured myself with the belief that no one would have heard of the book or been especially interested in it. Before Google there was no way to easily research John le Carré. Even a trip to the UNM library would have yielded little. I hadn't heard of him, and I assumed not many others had either. Two weeks passed before I felt safe enough to toss my review into the copy basket, ignoring a suspicious scowl from Looney.

The review appeared with my byline the following Thursday when the *Tribune* printed a weekly Arts Section. I read and reread the review until I had it memorized. I wished I had taken a firmer stand about the book's quality, but I played it safe, except to say that it was not an easy read.

Driving to Placitas after work, I stopped to buy the Sunday edition of the *New York Times*, which in those days reached Albuquerque on Thursday. I feigned laughter at the clerk's weekly joke about needing a week to "read all that" and took the big paper to Al's, where I settled in over a beer. I pulled the book review from the paper and was stunned to see le Carré on the cover of the *New York Times Book Review*. Apprehension rising, I read the review. Graham Greene called it the best spy book ever written. The reviewer agreed, more or less, citing other classic examples of the literature of espionage—Kipling, Dickens—that might possibly be its equal. I was more than ready to defer to the *Times*'s reviewer and hoped that no one at the *Tribune* would see the *Times*. I could imagine Looney's comments about missing the story a second time.

"Hey, ol' buddy." I heard Michael's cheery voice and looked up as he walked to my table and pulled out a chair. "Mind if I join you?"

"Not at all." I quickly hid the review inside the massive paper.

"It seems like months since you moved. I saw your truck outside."

"I know. I keep meaning to suggest we have a beer or something."

"So how's the place in Placitas?

"It's fine. I'm fine."

"You're reading the *Times*."

"Yeah. Great paper, huh?"

"Great paper," he agreed. "Looney and my father both think it's run by a bunch of communists."

"Really?" I said, eager to make conversation. "My father thinks so too."

"Your father reads the *Times*?" Michael asked in surprise.

"No, no. He just thinks that because that's what he's heard."

"Where does he hear that in Tucumcari?"

"Probably from your father."

We laughed. The tension that Michael brought into the room dissipated. He ordered a beer.

"Why didn't you tell me about the books-for-review box?" I asked casually.

"I didn't think you were ready."

"Ready?"

"Ready to start writing reviews. I just thought you should get your feet on the ground first."

I felt patronized by his suggestion that writing a book review was something I wasn't quite ready for. Had he said I wasn't ready to cover a federal-court case, I would certainly have agreed, but writing a book review for the *Tribune* should have been within reach of any good reader. I suspected that he withheld information about the review copies to keep me from becoming too independent. "And the movies. You didn't mention the free movies."

"You know, I never think of that. I never go to movies. I just didn't think to tell you."

"I'm surprised. You write plays, but you don't go to movies."

"They are entirely different," he said defensively.

"Well, maybe." I decided to let it go. I had read only one of his plays, and it was not very good.

"So who told you about the review box?"

"Bonavita." The mention of Bonavita made him uncomfortable.

"Do you see him a lot?"

"No, but he seems very nice."

"I'd be careful if I were you."

"Really?"

"I told you Looney doesn't like him. If he thinks you're friends, he'll make your life even harder."

"He's doing a good job as it is."

"You're doing fine. He has no grounds to do anything. You're fine. Except you missed a day last week?"

"It was bad." I grimaced remembering the morning. "I got up and got ready for work. It was a very cold morning. When I tried to start the pickup, the battery was dead. Completely dead. It groaned for about two seconds and went quiet. I rolled the truck down the hill and nearly got it going, but it didn't kick over. I knew I was fucked."

"You should have called me, but then you don't have a phone," he smiled.

"I was at the bottom of the hill on a dirt road and there was nobody around—nobody. It took me nearly an hour to walk to a pay phone. I walked into Placitas and called Looney from that phone on the road there by the bar. Thank God I had twenty-five cents. I'm calling him an hour after I'm supposed to be at work and giving him this story about how my battery is dead and I had to walk an hour to a phone. I don't know if he believed me or not. I told him it would never happen again."

"Not good," Michael said. I felt my spirits sag with his judgment.

"Maybe you should have stayed at my place a little longer. You're welcome back anytime, you know."

I knew that living so far from work and commuting in an unreliable truck was not the ideal circumstance to maintain my job. I had already decided that I could not afford to miss another day of work and had begun a search for living quarters in Albuquerque. The fact that my tiny salary came weekly was helpful, and I still had some of the $500 I had borrowed from the friendly Pacific Finance Company. Moving back to Michael's place would certainly be the easiest way to guarantee that I could get to work on time every day, but I was determined not to do that.

I pondered the question at length: What do we owe to someone who has helped us in a major way? That is a very different question from the question of how they would like to be repaid. Michael would feel repaid if I moved in with him and became his lover. Or would he? Reflecting on that question in later years, I knew the answer was not so simple. Initially, perhaps, he would have felt that bringing me into his life by helping me to get a job at the *Tribune* rewarded whatever effort and risk was involved. But assuming that I was capable psychologically of having that kind of relationship, there surely would have come a time when we went our separate ways. Would he not then feel even more unhappy that, having brought me on board, nurtured my career, and provided room and board and companionship, we could not finally get along? Would he feel not only unhappy but also betrayed?

It was a moot point because I could not be his lover. There was no moral element in this. I simply was not homosexual. To move back into his house now, knowing what I knew, would truly be exploitative.

"I think I found a place I can afford here in the North Valley," I said. "I'm supposed to see the owner on Saturday."

"Suit yourself," he said.

We finished our beer and made plans to meet for dinner later that week.

Meeting Michael, finding the *Times* review, and the discussion of the missed workday all put me in a somber mood. I took a detour through the North Valley to drive past the place I had found. It was in the oldest area of the city and had adobe walls thirty inches thick with window ledges deep enough for sitting. The kitchen and bathroom were pre–World War II. The neighborhood was dicey, and the yards were bare dirt. The affordable rent of forty-five dollars a month plus utilities reflected all this. I used most of the next Sunday moving, which under the circumstances was not a lot of work. Settled in, I felt I was edging back toward bourgeois respectability: debt, a job, a house, a car.

CHAPTER TWELVE

Looney appeared at my desk Monday morning with the daily ration of press releases. Normally I ignored him, but now he was actually speaking to me. "I liked your book review," he said.

I wasn't sure I heard him right. I looked immediately for the sucker punch. "Thank you," I said cautiously.

"Your timing was great."

"How do you mean?"

"The *New York Times* ran their review last Sunday. Did you see it?"

"Actually, I did. Big review."

"I thought you made more sense."

"Really? Thanks." I was astonished. Without thinking, I pushed my luck. "The *Times* reviewer liked the book a lot better than I did."

"They are full of it," Looney said. "They give good reviews to bad books all the time. They miss good books. Sometimes they catch up."

"Oh?"

Apparently Looney wanted to talk. He held onto the press releases, rocking slightly from toe to heel. He looked into the middle distance somewhere over my shoulder as he spoke. "The critics, all of them, often ignore a book that's good because the author isn't well known. Then the book turns out to be popular and they are embarrassed. Then, to make up for it, when the writer does a second book they give it a rave even if it isn't very good. *The Big Sky* was a great book. They missed it. All the critics ignored it, so they gave a Pulitzer to *The Way West*, which was not a great book."

"I didn't know that." I had not read either book, but I loved the Kirk Douglas and Arthur Hunnicutt movie *The Big Sky*, and I was willing to take Looney's word for the book being superior to *The Way West*.

"I worked with Guthrie at the *Lexington Leader*," he said. "He knew

The Big Sky was the better book, but when you're being offered a Pulitzer you don't whine about the past." Looney made his mirthless chuckling sound.

"Did you know him well?" I was shamelessly impressed by anyone who actually knew a Pulitzer-winning novelist, especially one who wrote about the West.

"Yeah, I knew him. He was an editor, but then he went to Harvard on a Nieman and became famous and started to drink too much." Looney fingered the press releases, thinking. "Then he left his wife. They always do that when they become successful. He'd come back to see us once in a while after he published *The Big Sky*."

The conversation allowed me to relax some for the first time in Looney's presence. "I hope I didn't miss the point in my review," I offered. "I had a lot of trouble following the story, so I was surprised when I read that Graham Greene called it the best spy story he had ever read."

"Do you like Graham Greene?"

"I like *The Power and the Glory*. I liked *The Quiet American*. I thought *Our Man in Havana* was really funny."

"He hates America, you know." Looney gave me a very direct look.

"I didn't know that. I mean, I know *The Quiet American* isn't very flattering, but I didn't know that he hated America generally."

"He hates Americans. He wasn't kidding when he condemned Americans in *The Quiet American*."

"You must know a lot about him."

"I know enough," Looney said. He was finished. I knew everything had changed when, instead of tossing the releases toward me, he laid them gently on my desk and left.

Still in an altered state of mind from the surprise of our encounter, I dug out a copy of my review and reread it, holding the paper behind my desk so that Looney couldn't see what I was doing. I tried to understand what he might have liked about it. My phone rang.

"Congratulations," Bonavita said. "You passed the test."

"I don't believe it."

"He liked your review?"

"That's what he said."

"Go figure."

I never fully understood what transpired. Whether it was my moving away from Michael's house, my diligence in rewriting press releases, or just despair that I would screw up so badly that he could get rid of me, or none of those things, but from that day forward Looney treated me more or less as a fellow human being. For my part I saw him in a somewhat different light when I realized he read literature and thought about things like critics.

The following week I began to get little assignments. The ration of press releases lessened, and in addition there were clippings from the competing paper or clips from the previous day's *Tribune* with little notes like "Follow up" or "Update" or "Check this out." I began to feel less like a fraud when I called someone and said, "This is Gerald Moore at the *Albuquerque Tribune*."

When I started to think more about stories I might develop on my own it quickly became apparent that I knew virtually nothing about Albuquerque politically, socially, or financially. In that regard I was little different from the average citizen who, lacking time or interest, seldom knows how the things around him actually work. Many areas for possible stories were already covered. The courts were assigned to a good reporter. The university was Bonavita's beat. City government, including the police blotter, was assigned to an aggressive reporter. I had to find stories that were not spoken for. The one area I knew anything about, other than the university, was the police department. Then, in the amazing way that things sometimes happen, a friend called to complain about a justice of the peace.

JPs, as they were called, were an anachronism left over from the frontier—citizen judges who operated originally in a region so sparsely settled that to even require a high school education would have meant too few judges. They were elected within a defined district, a precinct, and they held great power, including the power to send a person to jail for up to one year. They functioned as small-claims courts, married people, heard traffic cases, and conducted misdemeanor trials. Owing to the odd political circumstances of their origin, they were almost extrajudicial because they worked under the loose supervision of the local county sheriff rather than a district judge. Bernalillo County in the early 1960s had about forty-five JPs. The job came with a small stipend, but any real money had to be made in court costs levied on persons who appeared before the justices. It was commonly believed that JPs worked hand in hand with the state police officer assigned in any given area of the state so that traffic tickets became a major source of revenue for the judge and there was no hope of ever being found not guilty. Court costs associated with traffic offenses were quite lucrative in rural jurisdictions with major highways.

In Albuquerque, though, most traffic tickets were written by city police and handled by municipal judges—properly qualified lawyers who were also elected but required to hold the credentials normally associated with a judgeship. As a result, JPs had to find other sources of revenue. In a city with a very large population of poor people, many enlisted military personnel, and thousands of college students, fees collected on bounced checks became the key. Debit and credit cards would eventually eliminate checks for small transactions, but in 1963 there were no credit cards. Checks were the only way to buy anything, unless one had cash. Checks written for more than the purchase amount at a grocery or pharmacy or other small business were the major source of cash. Otherwise, a personal trip to the bank was required. We routinely went to the grocery store and bought a quart of milk so that we could cash a twenty-five-dollar check to have money for the weekend.

In fact, it was a twenty-five-dollar check that caused my friend so much trouble and led him to call me, his now-empowered reporter friend. Believing that he had just enough money to cover the check, and having failed to deduct service fees, Tim bounced a check at a local grocery. Without notice from the store, it was handed over to a JP in a routine arrangement between the judge and the store.

"I was working at my desk this morning," Tim said over the phone, "when this big goon with a gun shows up at my door. He has my check and he wants seventy-five dollars. He wants twenty-five dollars to cover the check and fifty dollars for coming to collect."

"He was the JP?" I asked.

"No, no, he was the constable. They work for the JPs. He had an order from the JP charging me fifty dollars in court costs."

"So what happened?"

"I don't have seventy-five dollars. He threatened to arrest me and throw me in jail. He said the court costs would go up to one hundred dollars if I didn't pay right then."

"That's awful. I don't think a check for insufficient funds is a criminal offense. What did you do?"

"I was scared. I didn't know what to do."

"So?"

"So I called Megan"—his fiancée—"and asked to borrow the money.

She didn't have that much either, but she went through the dorm and took up a collection and managed to scrape it together. This guy sat in my living room for over an hour until she came with the cash."

"This may be legal, you know."

"Well, it shouldn't be. I made a tiny error in arithmetic, and it costs me a week's pay, a day's work, and a lot of anxiety. This is a shakedown."

"I'm really sorry," I said. I didn't see how I could help.

"Can't you write a story about this kind of thing? It just isn't right."

"What would I say? You bounced a check and the JP collected it and charged you twice as much for the service?"

"I should have been more careful," Tim admitted, "but damn, they could have called me. I'd have made it good. Fifty bucks. I only make sixty dollars a week."

I commiserated, but I couldn't see the story. Getting jerked around for bouncing a check didn't sound like anything that would start a rebellion or get Looney excited. It had happened to a lot of people I knew. The JPs had a reputation for essentially shaking people down when they were in trouble, usually poor or unsophisticated people. And I knew from my police department days that at least one JP was illiterate. He ruled against any lawyer foolish or ignorant enough to cite a law by handing him the book to read. The situation bothered me enough that I decided to call a cop I trusted, Jim Nunnery, just to talk about it.

Nunnery was a cop I held in high regard for his sense of decency and common wisdom. When I was on the force with him, he once gave me a perspective on my personal life that I would never forget. The divorce had been wrenching for everyone. At one point of extreme depression I was sustained only by my desire to be a continuing part of Cathy's life. I was in terrible pain because Cathy and I were not to live under the same roof, but I had to endure the pain to remain a part of her life, to try to protect her and be her father. Nunnery sat me down one morning after our midnight shift and counseled me on pain.

"You have this wonderful kid in your life," he said. "If she didn't exist, you would not have this pain? Right?"

"Right."

"Would you trade no pain for no kid?"

"No."

"Then suck it up, buddy, and get on with it. You're not the first guy who hurt because he wasn't living with his kids."

As usual, Nunnery's clear view of reality cleared my own vision, and

I accepted the idea that my time with Cathy would be more limited, and that the time we had would be more precious.

Nunnery once told me that in his neighborhood in St. Louis, every young man became either a criminal or a cop. He chose to be a cop, and he was a good one. He was smart, worldly, and so courageous about his principles that the brass disliked him—a lot. He had now been banished to the swing-shift records desk, where he worked as a glorified clerk. Had I had Nunnery's self-assurance, my encounter with Lieutenant Smiley over the drunk driver we released might have gone differently. But then I probably would not have been at the *Tribune*, considering the fact that my job there had been dependent on Smiley's goodwill.

I called Nunnery and asked him what he knew about JPs.

"They're a shady bunch," he said. "Why, did you bounce a check?"

"No, but a friend did."

"And?"

"It was a twenty-five-dollar check. The JP collected fifty dollars in court costs."

"They are allowed to do that."

"So who are these guys, really? I mean, are they part of the political machine? How do they get elected?"

"I don't think anyone pays any attention to who is running. You know, the party does, but the voters don't. They have no qualifications. One guy up there in the North Valley did time for manslaughter or some serious shit like that."

"Really?"

"Yeah, but they have a lot of power. You have to be careful."

"Could you look to see if any others have a record?"

"I could, but I can get into enough trouble by myself. I don't need your help."

"OK, if I got a list of all the JPs in Bernalillo County and got permission from your commander, would you look them up?"

"In my spare time?"

"Whenever."

"Sure."

In 1963 Albuquerque Police Department records were stored on five-by-eight-inch file cards in hundreds of drawers in tall oak cabinets, like the card catalog of a large library. Some were annotated, often in barely legible handwriting. Some went back thirty years in fading ink. All were typed by hand using ribbons of different quality and color. Red type just meant that the black ribbon was worn out and no replacement was immediately available. Searching records was slow. In an age of computers it is hard to remember how inaccessible information was when stored on paper. I knew I was asking a lot of Nunnery, but I also knew that the arrest information he managed belonged to the public. If the police brass didn't see any threat to them in my request, chances were good they would cooperate.

The next day I called the chief, spoke to his secretary, and agreed that I would bring my list and a formal letter of request to the chief the following day. There was no guarantee that he would grant my request, but then he could envision the same headline that I could envision: "Police Chief Refuses Arrest Information on Public Officials." It took two days, but I got a call back that the list was being checked. I was told to expect an answer in two weeks. A lot happened in the world before I got my answer.

CHAPTER THIRTEEN

Bells on the teletype machines rang *bing, bing, bing* without stopping. The UPI bureau chief burst out of his office with two slips of torn copy in hand. I watched through the big office window as he ran past Looney, past the copy desk, and straight into Burrows's office, waving the copy and shoving it into the startled editor's hand in an unimaginable act of familiarity. Burrows looked up frowning, affronted, took the papers, and read them. Normally phlegmatic, he rose quickly and rushed to a little opening in his window, shoved the papers through, and banged hard on the window, gesturing to Looney. It was just after our 11:30 morning deadline, and everyone was distracted. Looney didn't bother to get up from his chair but rolled it backward, kicking the floor to propel himself until he could reach over his shoulder and retrieve the paper in a kind of offhanded, lazy fashion. He scanned first one sheet and then the other. Then he too jumped out of his chair. "The president's been shot!" he shouted. We all stared at him blankly, trying to understand what he meant. The room went quiet. Then, in frustration, he shouted again. "Goddamn it! The president has been shot."

It sunk in. Everyone scrambled, except me. I had no idea what to do. Tony DeCola, the political editor, began immediately typing a story about Kennedy's last visit to Albuquerque. Other reporters hurried to the files. Some began typing. I had no idea what they were writing. I ran into the UPI office and watched the shuddering teletype as it hammered out a line or two, paused, and started again. Looney called to me through the open door. "Take a camera and go out on the street and get reactions from anybody you see. And hurry! And get names!" As I left, I heard him telling the press room to "tear up the front page."

Half a block from our building, I saw a well-dressed woman in her thirties. As she crossed the street, I called out to her, "Excuse me!" Then

94

again, "Excuse me, I'm from the *Tribune*. President Kennedy's been shot."

She looked directly at me and in a firm voice said, "Good!" Then she turned sharply to hurry off. Her reaction so completely surprised me that it penetrated my panic like a slap to the face. She wanted him dead? No time to think about what this might mean. I had to get other reactions. I ran down the street with my news and got far less reaction than I expected. Despite the camera hanging around my neck and the notebook in my hand, many people met the announcement with skepticism. Others thought I was a nut. A woman scolded me, "That is not the least bit funny!" Within a few minutes, people began to tell me they already knew. They heard it on the radio. Ah, the electron carries the news. While I was on the street getting reactions, the radio had carried the story, but we would offer more detail, more analysis, and perhaps more credibility.

By the time I returned to the paper, all the available space was gone. Merriman Smith, the UPI correspondent riding in the Kennedy motorcade, had filed his historic eyewitness account of the shooting, and our first edition was rolling through the presses, delayed by less than an hour. We knew the what, where, and when. Now we would begin on the who, how, and why—the more difficult of the five *w*'s and the *h*.

In the hours that followed, Lee Harvey Oswald was identified as the shooter and captured. Then I watched two days later when Jack Ruby killed Oswald on live television. Then we celebrated Thanksgiving. I felt a great uneasiness as the official drum began softly to beat out the message that Oswald and Ruby acted alone, of their own volition. It seemed unlikely that Oswald, unaided, was able to kill a president. And Jack Ruby, a strip-club operator who as far as I could tell had never done anything in his life out of high principle, suddenly was moved to toss away his freedom to kill Oswald before federal authorities could interview him. But the drumbeat of reassurance had already begun: "All is well, all is known, good people are in charge, the system is working." Presidents are expendable. Faith in government is not.

Albuquerque was clear, sunny, and cold that November—the kind of high desert weather that usually lifts my spirits and makes me happy to be in the Southwest—but the feeling there and in the country at large was raw and frightened. The event weighed on me as I sat in the bedroom at a desk I had fashioned from an old door and eight cinder blocks, reading and rereading the newspaper and magazine accounts of the assassination. I watched the funeral on television and tried to think who had arranged the killing and what "they" might want from the country. I could not believe that Oswald had the passion and the means to commit such an act alone. I was unable to see how Kennedy seriously threatened any established vested interest. He might have been viewed by conservatives as a Yankee liberal, but his policies, even on civil rights, were distinctly moderate. The Russians would not attempt such a high-risk, low-return ploy. The anti-Castro Cubans acting alone seemed to lack the resources. Who did have the resources to kill a president? The CIA? Organized crime syndicates? Castro? What could have happened?

At the time I was unaware of any of the dynamics between the Kennedy family and organized crime, except of course for Robert Kennedy's relentless pursuit of James Hoffa and Carlos Marcello. It did not occur to me until years later that someone might kill a president to neutralize an attorney general and then kill a former attorney general to prevent him from being president. It was unacceptable to me that we might never know for sure what happened.

The quandary would last for decades. It was just too easy to dismiss criticism of sloppy investigation as "conspiracy theory." A few years after President Kennedy's murder, I would find myself in a state of youthful moral outrage once again when I saw that many powerful men in journalism did not agree with me that knowing the answers in these events was of the utmost importance. Two years after Robert Kennedy was killed, I was sent to Los Angeles to look into allegations that the investigation into his death was sloppy, incomplete, and in all likelihood failed to identify everyone involved. I returned with ample evidence that this event was not as it had been officially described. The pistol used to kill Kennedy had been sent to Sacramento and melted down before it could be test fired. Bullets taken from the walls of the kitchen where he was shot were left unprotected, casually tossed into a desk drawer in a plastic bag to be rolled about each time the drawer was opened and closed. There seemed to be too many bullets in the wall for Sirhan to have been the only shooter. Interviews that should have been conducted were not conducted. Credible ballistics experts believed more than one gun was fired in the hotel kitchen.

Back in New York I presented my evidence carefully and as objectively as possible to a large gathering of Time Inc. editors. I had barely finished when I heard Tom Griffith, *LIFE*'s editor, say with finality, "We don't need to reopen this. Stirring this up again won't benefit the country." These were not the words of a journalist. These were the words of a social manager, a politician. What Griffith deemed important in these situations was not so much finding the truth as getting on with business. Robert Kennedy was dead. The past did not matter as much as the future. To know too much might lead into places where the public reaction would be unpredictable. Griffith operated like the good trial attorney who never asks a question without knowing the answer in advance. At lunches like this one, I started to think about the role of journalism in social control, but in November 1963, with three months' experience as a reporter, I still thought we journalists were just the good guys exposing the bad guys, as I was about to do with the justices of the peace.

CHAPTER FOURTEEN

When my list came back from the police department, I saw that Nunnery had done an outstanding job. Every justice on the list was carefully checked, and the entire arrest record appeared with the name. Scanning the list, I saw that of the forty justices then sitting in Bernalillo County, an astonishing number of them had police records. Some of the offenses were serious: assault, receiving and concealing stolen property, drunk driving on more than one occasion. In all, eighteen of them, nearly half, had been arrested and charged. Some were convicted. Clearly I had stumbled into a sensational story, if Looney would let me print it.

There was a slight vibration in my guts as I rolled a sheet of paper into my typewriter and began: "City police records show that 18 of 40 peace justices now holding office in Bernalillo County have arrest records, a *Tribune* check revealed today. Nine of the 18 have been arrested more than once." With the story finished, I took the list and went to Looney, standing quietly in front of his desk until he looked up with his weary gaze.

"What do you want?" he asked.

"I think you should see this." I offered my copy. He looked directly at me as he took the story and placed it firmly in his copy basket with all the other stories awaiting his attention, then went back to reading copy. As I walked away he reached beneath his desk and pulled out the thermos of milk, slowly unscrewing the cap to take a big swig. I felt a thrilling sense of expectation as I sat at my desk making busy work, waiting while the bomb in his copy basket ticked. I didn't have to wait very long.

"Where did you get this!" Looney yelled across the room. He sounded annoyed. Several reporters stopped typing to see what the commotion was about.

"From the police," I yelled back.

"Why did they give it to you?" he hollered.

"I asked for it," I shouted back.

Looney motioned for me to come to his desk. In a quieter, more civilized voice he continued his questions. "Why did you ask for it?"

"I had a hunch."

"A hunch?"

"Yes."

"A hunch?"

"They are known in certain circles to be less than honorable."

"The chief knows about this?"

"He approved the search."

Looney turned and shoved my copy across the big circular desk to where George Baldwin, the managing editor, sat in the slot making up the day's paper. George retrieved the paper, tilted his head back to bring his bifocals into use, and scanned the pages. He looked at Looney and then at me. He rarely talked. He gestured with his chin toward Burrows's office. Looney left me standing and went to Burrows, his pace slow and deliberate, as if he was going to his own hanging. Through the big plate-glass window I could see him conferring with the editor. He came to the door and waved me in.

"You got this from the police?" Burrows asked.

"Yes, sir."

"It came through official channels. You made a formal request for the information?"

"Yes, sir."

"Let me see the list," he said.

I went back to my desk and collected a copy of my original letter of request and the list as I received it from the police. I laid them on Burrows's desk. He read them carefully.

"Fine," he said, looking up, handing my copy back to Looney. "Keep it strictly to the facts. I want every paragraph attributed to 'Police records show.'" He looked carefully at me for just a moment. I sensed he was pleased. "What else do you have up your sleeve?"

"I thought I would check the constables next," I said.

"Sounds good," he said and went back to the work on his desk, completely unperturbed.

I followed Looney back to his desk. On the way he began to chuckle. "I hope you don't get arrested in Bernalillo County anytime soon," he said.

I didn't have to ask what he meant. I was about to make enemies of every justice in the county, and probably of their protectors, the sheriffs. It could be exceedingly unpleasant if I was to end up in front of one of them. I went back to my desk. Fifteen minutes later the paper's photographer appeared. "Looney wants your picture," he said flatly. He took three or four shots with his big Speed Graflex camera and left without a word.

When the pressroom helper made his daily appearance in the city room with copies of the day's first edition, I joined in the crush of reporters to grab a copy. Rushing back to my desk with the intoxicating smell of damp ink in my nose, I scanned the front page. There it was! My picture and byline in the upper left-hand column. Just below the Scripps Howard motto, "Give light and the people will find their own way," a headline announced what I had discovered and what would now be known to anyone who cared to know: a substantial part of our local judiciary did not respect or follow the law. As I prepared to read for typos, I knew this was a turning point. This story would mark a fundamental change in the course of my tenure at the *Tribune*.

I played the story perfectly in the days that followed, revealing new information, asking public officials for their reaction, explaining the political dynamics of the office. When the justices were done I held onto my front-page space by detailing the arrest records of fourteen of the thirty-seven county constables. The series ended with a report of one constable who had served prison time after a murder charge against him was reduced to manslaughter. Here was a case of extreme rehabilitation. A man convicted of manslaughter released from prison, given a gun and a badge, and sent out to enforce a judge's bidding. In time, the revelations would lead to reform, including a new state law that required Bernalillo County judges to be members of the bar.

The experience appealed to every part of my being, to my mind and to my soul. Having my name and picture on the front page of the paper nourished vanity, of course, though I understood the need to conceal any pride in the accomplishment. Feigning modesty would increase the impact of my triumph. In a more positive way, the success of the effort started to heal the raw self-doubt and disappointment that had followed my divorce, my abrupt departure from the police department, the lingering sense that I had disappointed my parents, and the awkward struggle to finish college. Most important was a sense of having found a place in society where I could live and work in harmony with what I felt to be true and good. Showing a little enterprise and a little courage to reveal something corrupt and in need of attention, or something good in need of encouragement, made me happy. Any person who every day looks forward to going to work is blessed, and for several years to come that is the way I felt, for the first time in my life.

CHAPTER FIFTEEN

Ready or not, the apprenticeship ended the week following the justice of the peace series. Looney called me to his desk to say he wanted me to cover Bernalillo County government and every two weeks to check in with neighboring Valencia County. I would have to attend county commission meetings and planning board meetings at night and generally be responsible for whatever happened in county government. He added that there would be no compensatory time off. Beat reporters put in as many hours as the beat required. "The rules are different at some of the union papers," he said. "But we don't have a union here." He laughed his wicked giggle as though the thought pleased him. "And we are not likely to have one either," he added.

Looney got used to seeing me at my desk half an hour early each morning. The new challenge and responsibility filled me with enthusiasm. It had been a long time since I started each day feeling excited, wanting to get up and get going, thinking ahead to what I might discover.

With a minimum of preparation I would leave the city room for the county office building and begin my rounds. Some days produced decent stories. Other days produced very little, but by eleven or so the deadline clock began to tick louder and I would hurry back to my typewriter to write whatever I had.

The most important stories got first attention. Some required follow-up phone calls and further research. Then came the dreary housekeeping: liens filed, tax foreclosures, odd and ends that would be important to the people affected. By one o'clock everything had to be in the copy box. Half an hour later, samples of the paper appeared in the city room for a quick proofread, and then the day wound down.

There is something fulfilling about the short cycle of effort and reward that comes with seeing your work in print at the end of every day. The process of anticipation, excitement, contest, and tension is released when the paper appears. On reflection I suspect that all people who are able to see their work made visible share this reward: masons, gardeners, artists, engineers, designers, farmers, some factory workers, anyone who can stand back at the end of a day or at the end of a week and see some tangible accomplishment. Maybe brokers and bankers can measure the day by how much they made or lost, and maybe sales clerks can tally up the day's receipts, but to actually see work in physical form is a powerful stimulus to do more. With the county beat assignment, my early education in government process began.

Dante Alighieri had Beatrice Portinari, the angelic Florentine beauty, to guide him in the *Divine Comedy*. My guide through the less than divine comedy of county government was no beauty. County Manager John Nunn, a big, rumpled man left badly crippled by childhood polio, knew the *Tribune*'s penchant for attacking public officials on very small issues, so in our first few meetings he adopted a formal manner, answering my questions with vague, technical responses. But after two weeks of talking guardedly and then reading my stories, he began to relax and let a relationship develop. I think he saw that I wanted to treat issues fairly, that I believed people mostly played by the rules and that I still thought politics was conducted according to the principles taught in high school civics. I am sure he found my naïveté amusing. He responded by assuming the role of instructor, and in so doing he became an important source of information, albeit a source of information favorable to him and his administration.

His first lesson began when I appeared in his office about nine o'clock one morning and he announced that he was going to show me a "good" story. He would not tell me what he had in mind. I had to see it. I agreed and then watched patiently as he began his silent, awkward struggle to rise from behind his desk. Years of using steel crutches to compensate for his damaged body left him with large, powerful arms and shoulders that he used to hoist and swing his delicate waist and shriveled, heavily braced legs. He pulled himself up, steadied himself on his crutches, threw back his big head, and took a deep breath. Then, balancing, he grabbed the huge wad of keys lying on his desk and began a rolling, lurching walk. I never watched this process without feeling tension that he might fall, and always with a sense of awe at his courage and grit.

"Come on," he said gruffly, heading for the door.

In the subterranean garage, Nunn struggled again to get behind the wheel of his specially equipped county car. He shoved his crutches into the backseat and started his lecture.

"You knew the state just issued twenty-seven new liquor licenses for Bernalillo and Sandoval Counties?"

"No, actually, I didn't. But I should have," I admitted, wondering why the *Tribune*'s state editor had not reported the event. Liquor licenses were a controversial form of political patronage that always aroused debate.

Nunn looked at me for a moment, trying to decide where to begin. "Do you know who supported Prohibition?" he asked, gunning his official car up the dark parking ramp into the eye-shocking winter sunlight.

"People who thought drinking was bad. Is this a joke?"

"You are half right," Nunn said. "You forgot the bootleggers. The bootleggers and the preachers supported Prohibition." He laughed. "The preachers to force people to be virtuous. The bootleggers because they didn't want legit competition. The cops were in there too somewhere. Prohibition created a lot of opportunities for the cops."

"And the parallel?"

"You don't see it?"

"I hadn't really thought about it. OK—so restricting liquor licenses is like a mini-Prohibition?"

"Shortage creates value. Didn't you study any economics? Wait, you'll see."

He drove west along Route 66 to Rio Grande Boulevard and turned north. Close to Rio Rancho Estates, fifty-five thousand acres of empty desert, Nunn turned west off the main road and followed a dirt track up onto the mesa into an area devoid of anything but jackrabbits, juniper, and scrub cedar. Looking out across the vast, empty expanse, I saw what looked like a Bedouin camp or a squatters' village a mile away shimmering in the clear winter light: two dozen little structures clustered in the desert. The road became fainter, but Nunn pressed on, bouncing the county car with abandon through the bumps and holes in the road. A cloud of fine brown dust rose behind us and hung in the air.

The area had been legally subdivided a number of years earlier. The developers ran small ads in Sunday papers all across the country offering half-acre "ranchettes" in what was essentially high desert. The offers were so misleading that, in response, a friend from Seattle once threatened to sell Puget Sound mud flats to New Mexicans as "beachettes." Few lots had been sold, none had been improved. The whole empty fifty-five-thousand-acre subdivision sat quietly waiting for some future development: a housing boom or a new factory, both of which eventually came to town.

As our car approached the cluster of buildings, I saw they were travel trailers, little boxes on wheels designed to temporarily shelter two people while camping. Lonely, surrounded by nothing but long views of a distant horizon, the scene looked for all the world like a set for a Fellini movie.

"Those are bars," Nunn said.

"Come on."

"I could not be more serious. What you see here are the twenty-seven new bars, liquor licenses issued to real addresses, at least addresses that exist legally on a plat map. In ninety days, they can be moved to another address, one where there are actually houses, and the value will be roughly one hundred times what it is now. All they have to do is be open for ninety days and not get a violation from the Liquor Control Board."

"That would be hard out here."

Nunn drove us to the closest trailer and stopped. Fetching his crutches, he struggled out of the car and found his footing on the sand.

Where the trailers had once been equipped with narrow beds and room to prepare a meal, they now had a large door on the side that could be swung open to offer service. Inside, a table holding a few dusty bottles of liquor and an assortment of glasses completed the equipment. A man in his early thirties, casually but expensively dressed, put down his paperback book and came to the window.

"Are you the owner?" I asked.

"One of them," he said, smiling pleasantly. "What can I get you?"

I was in a Potemkin village. None of the people and none of the structures around me were really what they appeared to be.

"What do you charge for scotch?" I asked.

"Sixty cents. You want ice?"

"You have ice?"

"No."

"I don't actually want anything to drink. I'm with the *Tribune*."

"You're a long way from town."

"So is this a bar?"

"Yes, sir." The man smiled pleasantly.

I was stumped. I couldn't think of anything more to ask.

"So what exactly is the deal?" I asked Nunn.

"If you issue a liquor license to an address where there are people, the bar owners and the Baptists go crazy. They issued these where there are no neighbors." He gestured with his chin toward the surrounding mesa. "And when a certain time has passed, they can be transferred to a location where they actually make sense. The license costs about $100 a year, but resale value is around $50,000, depending, once it is moved."

"So how do we get one?"

"Render some sort of service to the party in power. Or be the cousin of someone who does."

"I'm not sure just what the story is," I said. "I mean this whole thing is strange, but it's more or less legal, right?"

"The scandal is not what is illegal. The scandal is what is legal."

I tried to think of a serious news lead for the story. "Twenty-seven new liquor licenses issued." That would only interest the temperance people. "Biding their time until they find a location in your neighborhood." That was better, but I knew Looney would never approve it. It implied something I couldn't prove, that the licenses were to be moved. I took some pictures and followed Nunn as he struggled through the sand on his way back to the car.

"If you were writing this story, what would you say?" I asked.

"Hey, that's your job," he said, breathing hard from his walk.

"Will any of these guys admit that this is all temporary?"

"Of course not!"

"So how can I write that they will be moved if I don't have a source? Will you 'charge' that they will be moved in ninety days?"

"Nope. But it seems obvious that they won't stay here."

I found myself wondering why Nunn brought me out here, other than for the spectacle of seeing twenty-seven bars in the desert. I asked him, "Why do you care about this?"

He was silent for a moment. "I don't really care. I just hate it when they do stuff like this. It is so blatant."

In the past, as a story began to present itself, I usually understood what the lead should be—the heart of the matter out of which all other parts of the article would flow. Now I was stumped.

Back at the *Tribune*, waiting at my desk for the contact prints to come back from the darkroom, I considered the cultural divide in the state between the conservative, sometimes reactionary Protestant groups who thought alcohol sinful and the people who liked to drink, dance, play cards, and smoke. Sometimes they were the same people, their moral position on alcohol dependent on the day of the week on which they were asked. But in terms of public policy, the wets and the drys were always at war.

Where conflict exists, there is opportunity. Pressure from the anti-alcohol crowd, supported by bar and liquor store owners who feared competition, created an artificial—which is to say not market driven—shortage of liquor outlets. Shortage creates value, as Nunn had pointed out. The political class was more than happy to perpetuate the situation. A governor or state legislator could vote against changing the liquor-licensing laws, benefiting from the support of the religious folks and the established liquor industry. At the same time, the lawgiver could quietly lobby the state liquor commission on behalf of a friend and make himself a silent partner in a new bar or lounge whose license was more valuable than its building and its entire inventory. The kind of explanation my discovery needed was beyond the purview of a straight news story. I decided to consult Looney.

I saw a look of deep tiredness invade his face as I detailed my dilemma. "Just write an expanded caption and give me the contact sheets. It might make a good picture, but it's an old story."

The picture ran three columns on the front page with a caption explaining the situation. I consoled myself with the thought that I had not wasted a day or left Nunn without a story. When I revisited the matter with Nunn the next morning, I made the mistake of casually, thoughtlessly saying something banal like, "I guess this is the way government works."

Anger rose into Nunn's face. He paused for a moment to regain his composure. "It is not the way government works," he said firmly. "It is the way people work. People are always talking about government as if it was separate and apart from them. Who the hell do you think the government is?"

CHAPTER SIXTEEN

After work, on the day Nunn straightened me out on government, I met Bonavita at Al Monte's, where a few of us now gathered several times a week to rehash the day's events, swap gossip, and make plans. Michael often joined us, as did John Hoffman, the television reporter Fred knew from Virginia. The hours we spent there were full of energy and optimism. We were innocently competitive in the way that a bunch of half-grown pups are competitive: trying out our strength on one another without any intention of doing harm, learning from each other—including, in my case, such mundane things as exactly how to dress.

The signs of class expressed in dress were subtle but important to anyone with ambitions beyond the *Tribune*. I adopted Bonavita as my model the first day I saw him. Now my study went forward in great detail. No polyester. Natural fabrics, good tailoring, and no stinting on material—the basics for a well-dressed man. Bonavita kept his wingtip shoes well shined. His dark wool-blend over-the-calf socks coordinated roughly with his shoes and suits. He wore wool in winter, summer-weight wool in summer, and cotton when it was too hot to breathe. His freshly ironed white cotton shirts were of a good weight and never short-sleeved. Ties were tasteful, without words or symbols, wildlife, flowers, or any design intended to attract attention. He did not carry pencils and pens in his shirt pocket. His wallet was flat, and nothing hung from his belt. I did not know from personal knowledge about his underwear, but I would have bet he wore boxers. This was not a complicated uniform. In fact, it had been the general mode of dress for professional men for many years, but synthetic fabrics and easy-care shirts were making inroads. The standard of dress at the *Tribune* was left entirely to the individual, as long as it included a tie of some sort. Urban legend was rife with stories of important job opportunities lost because a man wore the wrong watch (plastic) or the wrong tie (knit, polyester).

Nor was Bonavita just a model for dress. He displayed a wider and more professional curiosity than most of my colleagues. He read magazines and newspapers from other cities. He was current with movie criticism. His cultural awareness extended beyond Dallas to the east and Phoenix to the west. He often brought along the most recent issue of the *Saturday Review of Literature* and read Norman Cousins's weekly column aloud. For someone hungry for words from the outside world, Bonavita was a godsend. In the same way that Michael nurtured my fledgling skills as a reporter, Bonavita was my mentor for moving through a more sophisticated world.

In fairness I have to recognize Looney in this process because he instructed me on important matters: the darker side of things, naked competition, bending the rules, pleasing the readers, appropriate cynicism, and the value of sycophant behavior. As they say now, "It takes a village." One evening as a bull session at Al Monte's was ending, Bonavita and I were left alone nursing a final beer. Something was on his mind, something he wanted to tell me in confidence. I waited as he moved bottles, coasters, and an ashtray around until he had them in perfect position. Finishing what appeared to be a little mental rehearsal, he leaned forward and confided. I could never tell Looney, he said, but he had been named the Time-Life stringer for New Mexico. He delivered this news with an air of great importance. Its impact was lost on me, except for the fact that Looney was not allowed to know. I had no idea what a stringer was. I couldn't help but recall my experience with Levi and my question about Yiddish when I asked cautiously, "What is a stringer?"

Bonavita was surprised, but rather than being insulted, his tendency toward pedagogy emerged. He was delighted by the opportunity to enlighten me. Many national publications employed a local part-time correspondent, he explained, usually a newsman, to cover stories that were breaking too quickly for them to staff or were not important enough to send full-time people from New York or Chicago or Los Angeles, wherever they were headquartered. So the national publication picked a trustworthy local journalist to call on when help was needed and relied on that person to tell the editors at headquarters if something of national interest was brewing. They were paid by the hour at a rate much higher than the local scale. In some rare cases, the position involved a retainer.

Arch Napier, an old Chicago scrivener, had moved to Albuquerque ten or fifteen years earlier for his health and had pretty much dominated the stringer business in Albuquerque ever since. He held the stringerships for *Time, LIFE, Sports Illustrated, Fortune, Architectural Digest,* the *Wall Street Journal,* the *Christian Science Monitor,* and *Oil and Gas News,* among others.

Bonavita said Napier's health was not good and he had decided to lighten his workload. To this end, he shed all the stringerships except for *Sports Illustrated* and *Oil and Gas News.* He kept *Sports Illustrated* because the University of New Mexico was part of the NCAA, and its sports programs required regular, easy reporting. *Oil and Gas News* was lucrative because of intense interest in oil and gas leases in the oil fields in northwestern and southeastern New Mexico and in taxes and regulations affecting the industry. This left the prize publications of *Time* and *LIFE* magazines available.

In the totally interconnected way that things work, *Time* magazine's Denver bureau chief, Barron Beshoar, had arrived in town a few days earlier to find a replacement for Napier. He called the head of the journalism department at UNM to ask for a recommendation. The chairman recommended Bonavita, the reporter who covered the university and would be responsible for writing about the journalism school.

My cynical side said that the head of the department recommended Bonavita in order to curry favor with the reporter who wrote about the university two or three times a week. My more generous side said that the head of the J school recommended Bonavita because he knew and respected his work. My pragmatic side said it was a win-win (although that expression was not around at the time). How could he go wrong? Bonavita would indeed do a good job. He was a consummate professional. How could Bonavita not feel gratitude for having his way paved to a prestigious and lucrative add-on to his job? In any event, I was pleased and impressed. I was pleased that I actually knew someone who on occasion worked for *Time* or *LIFE* magazine. I was impressed that Bonavita, my friend, would be chosen to do the job.

It is difficult to fully appreciate the powerful role *Time* and *LIFE* magazines played in the American mind in 1963. With a combined circulation in excess of eight million paid subscribers, the magazines reached fifty million readers. The magazines' weekly arrival influenced the views of millions of people who were themselves influential members of society. An article in *LIFE* about a new musical on Broadway would absolutely assure its success. Every tourist who blew into town for the next few years wanted tickets for the show they had seen featured in big, attractive color photos in *LIFE*. *Time*'s annual cover story on the "Man of the Year" was highly anticipated and widely discussed. The magazines were often quoted and frequently, in the early days of television news, the source of leads for television coverage. *Time* and *LIFE*, along with the country's great urban newspapers, determined what subjects were worthy of the country's attention. And while any editorial opinion expressed by either magazine was largely ignored by the public, the slant given to news coverage seeped into the national consciousness. Reliably Republican in their editorial stances, the actual news coverage tended, at least in the case of *LIFE*, toward something bordering on liberalism. They spoke with authority and credibility in a time before news and opinion fractured into a kaleidoscope of offerings shaped for every taste and theory. To be associated with either magazine was a matter of enormous prestige. The phrase "I'm with *LIFE* magazine" could get you wherever you needed to go.

Bonavita's announcement that evening did not create a light at the end of the tunnel between Albuquerque and New York City. Rather, it revealed the presence of a previously unknown tunnel—dark and winding, but there. It was possible to be in touch with the people whose names appeared on the magazines' mastheads. They were real. They had telephone numbers. Before Bonavita shared his good news, the distance from the *Tribune* to anything published in New York seemed infinite. Now it only seemed a very long way away. I congratulated Bonavita on his good news and helped him celebrate with an extra beer. My happiness about his success was genuine, but my mind was focused on what his news might mean for me.

CHAPTER SEVENTEEN

I saw the Sanborns frequently that winter. Of Jim's many friends, I was one of the few Sally also liked. I was often asked to come by for a casual dinner. Occasionally, early on, the invitation extended to an overnight stay so that I did not have to drive back to Placitas. I enjoyed their company. I loved Sally's home-cooked meals and found the chance to use a private shower especially thrilling. (One never fully appreciates a private bathroom until there is none.) After one of these sleepovers Sally had left that flower on my pillow. In my perpetual state of arrested awareness and naïveté, I took the flower simply as an expression of friendship. When I thanked Sally, she smiled and lightly dismissed the gesture as something she "just felt like doing." I thought no more about it because Sally and Sanborn were so tightly paired in my mind that I never thought of them as separate people, despite their ongoing marital problems. When I was with one of them, the other was implied. This led to a major crisis early in 1964.

A group of about eight friends decided to attend a sports-car race in Fort Sumner, a small town on the Pecos River three hours from Albuquerque. Fort Sumner is known to western history buffs as the place where Pat Garrett shot and killed Billy the Kid. Excited by the prospect of getting out of town for a couple of days, I arranged to trade a day off with another *Tribune* staffer so that I could make the trip. Bonavita was game. Jim and Sally wanted to go. John Hoffman, our television reporter friend; Ed Lowrance, who ran the local art house / foreign-movie venue; and two other people whose names I have long forgotten made up the group. As the day approached, people began to back out, one by one, until only Sanborn, Sally, and I were going. I called Sally to make the final arrangements.

"Jim has decided he doesn't want to go either," she said. "It's too long a drive."

I was very disappointed. "Well, damn," I said. "It is not something I would do alone, but I was really looking forward to going." I was completely surprised by what she said next.

"I'm very tired of people who only want to sit around town drinking beer. If you want to go, I'll go."

"Without Jim?"

"He makes his own decisions," she said with an air of dismissal. "Do you want to go?"

"Yes, I do."

"Then let's go."

This was a stunning turn of events. Most men would have thought it wasn't a good idea to travel out of town, overnight, in the company of a friend's wife, but the commonsense wisdom of this was lost on me. I thought of myself as a gentleman, a man who could safely escort a married woman—a friend—without risking a loss of dignity in a moment of raging lust. I assumed that Sanborn thought of me in the same way.

"OK, I'm ready," I said. "Can we go in your car? Mine will never make it that far."

We left Albuquerque after work on a Friday. Driving to Fort Sumner, we didn't really talk about Sanborn. I felt it was intrusive to talk about him in his absence, and Sally seemed comfortable with her decision. I assumed that she had told him we were going and that her decision was just another chapter in their ongoing struggle. We arrived in Fort Sumner in time for dinner in a crowded local café where most everyone at the races seems to be eating or waiting to eat. Then we went to our separate beds without anything more than a "See you tomorrow."

Early the next morning we drove to a racetrack laid out on runways at an abandoned military airport. There were nearly as many drivers as spectators, the small numbers creating an informal, collegial atmosphere. We wandered around, listening to the powerful engines straining for acceleration, and watched up close as the racing Porsches, Ferraris, Jaguars, and Corvettes clung to the track at impossible speeds— or, in the case of the Corvettes, almost clung to the track. Cars and drivers were accessible enough that we could look over the shoulder of mechanics making last-minute adjustments or peek into the businesslike cockpits of the racers. The noise, the fumes, the pumped-up drivers, and the powerful, sleek cars in competition all made for a wonderful day. We got back to Albuquerque in the early evening and found Jim in a state of sullen hysteria.

My assumptions had all been wrong. Sally did tell him she was going without him. She neglected to mention that the group attending the races had dwindled to just two people. When he figured this out sometime while we were away, he went crazy.

I tried very hard to convince him that the trip had been innocent, that I had not dishonored his friendship, nor had Sally violated their marriage. He stubbornly clung to his assumptions of the worst behavior. I pointed out to him that if I didn't care how he felt, I wouldn't be sitting there explaining things to him. Had Sally and I decided to engage in a weekend of adultery, why would we bother to talk to him? But in the cynical world where he chose to live, it wasn't possible for a man and a woman to be alone without sneaking into each other's arms. And in keeping with his Hemingway code, there was the very large question of male honor. If anyone thought he had been deceived and that he chose to ignore the insult, his macho standing—that is to say, his value as a human being— would be destroyed. I decided as the evening wore on (and have since come to believe firmly) that he wanted to think the worst because it suited other agendas that were at the time unknown to us. In any case, it was an unpleasant scene, in spite of which the two of them continued to live together for several more days. I kept my distance, feeling abused that Sanborn thought so little of my respect for our friendship.

The tremendous tension generated by all this broke one evening soon after while I was busy at home trying to rehabilitate a pot of three-day-old chile. Sally called and, in a voice filled with tension, said Sanborn was threatening her and could I help. I said I would come immediately and that she should tell him that I was on the way.

Thinking of myself in the role of counselor or mediator rather than savior, I jumped in my car and headed for Old Town just to calm things down. I did not believe that Sanborn would actually harm her, but I knew from my cop days that people do things during domestic quarrels that they would never do in other circumstances. I was just blocks away when I spotted Jim in the black Volkswagen Sally and I had just driven back from the races. As he approached on the other side of the highway divider, I stopped at an intersection, thinking he would also stop and that we would talk. Instead, he drove his car straight into mine, hitting the rear fender and scooting my car over several inches. The violence blasted me out of my counselor frame of mind and sent me speeding off as fast as possible to Sally's apartment, afraid of what I might find. Sanborn, apparently satisfied, drove off in the opposite direction. She was safe, but a deep tension had transformed her.

"Are you all right?" I asked.

"Oh, yes," she said firmly. "He yelled a lot and broke some stuff, but he's gone. I'm OK. Do you have a cigarette?"

"What are you going to do? I mean tonight? I didn't know you smoked."

"I don't. Except once in a while, like now. I'll be OK. He won't come back." She seemed sure of her judgment.

I didn't feel I should offer to take her to my house or that I could stay with her. Either one would make the situation worse. But I felt anxious about her safety. She invited me in, and we settled at the kitchen table, feeling bleak and washed out as the adrenaline burned away. She made a pot of coffee and we talked about what she should do. After all the separations and all the reconciliations, things now seemed to have passed a point of no return.

"He refuses to accept the fact that we went to Fort Sumner as friends and came home as friends," she said. "He now imagines that there was something going on even before. The whole marriage was a huge mess, and now it's worse." She paused, taking a quick drag on the cigarette, blowing the smoke up above our heads. She seemed to ponder a thought. Then, almost as if she were changing the subject, she said, "I'm really sick of him coming home at midnight full of beer, recking of beer, wanting to make love."

This shocked me, not so much because I didn't know he came home at midnight full of beer, but that she would tell me that intimate detail. The image lodged unhappily in my mind. "I should have known better than to think we could go away overnight without causing havoc," I said.

"It is not your problem," she said decisively. "You didn't do anything wrong."

On reflection, maybe I just didn't care that much. I felt deeply tired of the pretense that the two of them would eventually work it out. It just wasn't going to happen that way.

Everywhere I turned there was an elephant in the room, and I was growing tired of pretending the huge beasts weren't there. Sanborn and Sally had a bad marriage and were hanging on because breaking it off was too scary and inconvenient. She was out of her natural element, essentially alone, teaching middle school in Albuquerque. They had come there temporarily from Los Angeles while Sanborn finished an architecture degree, which after three or four years of on-again, off-again effort did not appear to be happening. My own judgment from hours of conversation with him was that he was not deeply interested in architecture. He was interested in drinking beer and making money, which is why he spent more time working as a highly paid construction supervisor for a local home builder than he spent building models at the architecture school. I won't even go into the elephants of living at Michael's or in the city room or in state government, but hypocrisy and/ or a willingness to ignore the truth seemed suddenly to characterize so much of the world around me. I decided that I didn't care any longer what Sanborn might or might not think. I didn't think he would return and harm Sally, but I didn't want to leave worried about her safety. My revolver was in the car.

"I have a gun in the car," I said. "Do you want me to leave it with you?

"Yes, thanks, I do."

I returned with the pistol and offered it. "Do you have any idea how to use this?"

"You point it at someone and pull the trigger, right?" Her mischievous smile felt like a parting of the clouds. "I'm not going to need it, but it'll make me feel better." She weighed the pistol in her hand. "It's really heavy, isn't it?"

"You're sure you want it?"

"I'm sure."

I told her good-night and went home, feeling unhappy about the evening's events. As much as I tried to dismiss the sense of gloom and apprehension left over from the encounter with Sanborn, I could not. I have always hated conflict, even though I have encountered a fair amount of it in the course of my life. My mother's belligerent moods when I was young left me with a deep fear of angry people. My first desire is to flee, but sometimes fear has an opposite effect and I want to destroy the thing I fear. I have seen the violence born of fear at work and it is terrifying, as when someone who is deeply afraid of snakes kills one using far more force and taking far longer than necessary. I am fascinated by the relationship between rage and fear. One of the great rewards of working as a cop was that I never felt afraid, no matter what the situation. Authority, for me, is an absolute defense against fear, but where Sanborn and Sally were concerned, I was without authority. I was just a bystander, and a not altogether innocent one.

Nothing bonds people faster than shared risk—think of cops, soldiers, and illicit lovers. We were not illicit lovers, of course, but we had been treated that way by Sanborn, and the resultant feeling that grew quickly between us was one of being partners in something important. I called Sally the next morning to be sure she was all right and to offer my moral support. We decided to meet after work for a drink, and that turned into dinner and a long conversation about growing up and our parents and all the things people talk about when they are seriously getting to know each other. Without giving much thought to what I was doing, I found myself spending much of my free time with her. She had many attractive qualities. Those I remember best were a pair of sparkling blue eyes and a quick laugh. Her sense of humor was refined and well developed. She had learned the delights of irony, and she was something of a snob—but in an easy, amused way rather than in a nasty, smug way. She appeared to be self-sufficient. She read a great deal, and she enjoyed playing Bach and Mozart on the piano. As we whiled away evening after evening, and as the time away from Sanborn lengthened, I became aware of a powerful physical attraction to her. I suspect the desire had always been there in some nascent form, but suppressed by boundaries of friendship and marriage.

I don't recall exactly how we arrived at this point, but on a given evening not so very long after the races and the blowup with Sanborn, she said that she too wanted to make love, but she would not until her divorce was final. This struck me as an odd and old-fashioned legalism. They had been finally separated by that time and were actively negotiating the terms of a divorce. It was just a matter of time until it would all be reduced to writing and brought to a judge. She and I were clearly building a strong relationship. I didn't understand why a legal divorce was a prerequisite to our intimacy, but she held firmly to this position. Thus it became my goal to expedite the divorce, which I was able to do because, in my new role as county beat reporter, I had come to know most of the county judges. Nothing illegal or extralegal was needed, just an ability to get the judge to move Sally's folder to the top of the pile.

New Mexico law provided that, following a judge's approval, a divorce would become final in ninety days, unless the judge waived that waiting period. Sally and I watched with some excitement as the judge signed the waiver.

"There you are," he said. "It's final." He smiled, pushing the papers back across his desk to where Sally sat nervously rubbing her jaw with her right index finger.

"That's it?" she asked. "I am completely divorced?"

"You are free to do anything a single woman can do. You can get married tonight, if you wish." He smiled then looked at me quizzically, having surmised that I had some personal interest in the proceeding.

Outside, the early spring weather was cool, the light white and harsh. As we walked to the car, I took her hand. She flinched, jerking away, alarmed. Then I watched her expression morph into amusement. She laughed and shook her head in wonder. "I can do that," she said. "I can't believe it. I can do that! We can hold hands!" She held out her hand, and I took it.

While the ink was drying on the divorce document, we drove north, more or less following the Rio Grande, and in just under three hours checked into the Taos Inn, a beautiful old Pueblo-style place on the plaza. Finding our room and making a fire, I suddenly felt awkward. This was new and strange, because until then we had been friends—buddies, more or less—completely comfortable with each other. I opened a bottle of wine, and we sat uncomfortably in two overstuffed hotel chairs, looking at each other while the bed, present in my peripheral vision, seemed to grow larger and larger. Later, as we began making plans for dinner, we agreed that when people make love for the first time, the second time is always better.

Endocrine systems humming, floating on a powerful sense of well-being, filled with the heady mix of hormones that flow from new love newly consummated, we drifted off to dinner at a wonderful Mexican restaurant. There, against astronomical odds, we looked across the dining room and saw John Hoffman staring at us in utter disbelief. He knew nothing of the events of the past several weeks, not to mention the past few hours, but all was revealed in an instant as we sat pressed together in our booth radiating the high glow that follows vigorous successful intercourse. He was shocked and considered acting as if he did not recognize us, but that was no good. We were looking at each other. I waved to him. He came to our table, and without trying to explain anything except to say that we were celebrating Sally's divorce, we bought him a drink and swore him to a secrecy we knew he would not keep. I told Sally on the way back to our room that I would bet a hundred dollars he called Bonavita before he went to bed that night.

On the drive home Sunday afternoon, I felt I wanted to be with Sally all the time. We had been friends. We had been soul mates. Now we were lovers. The fit was complete.

"What do you think?" I asked impulsively. "Should we look for a place together?"

"Oh, God," she moaned in distress. "It is so soon! Yes. Yes, let's do."

I was right, of course, about Hoffman's ability to keep a secret. When I got to work Monday morning, I found Bonavita so excited he could hardly wait to get me alone to find out what was happening.

It took two weeks, but we found a rental in Corrales, about a mile from Michael, and moved in. The house was anonymous, sitting on an unpaved road beside an irrigation ditch. We kept the location confidential. There was no street address. We collected our mail at the post office and had an unlisted phone number. These were probably unnecessary precautions, but I was still not easy about Sanborn's attitude, or my standing with the justices of the peace. Even though Sanborn and Sally were finally and completely divorced and Sanborn was pursuing other interests, I worried he might decide there was still a score to settle. He had alarmed me when he burst into my house one night soon after our evening of bumper cars to give me a "piece of his mind." I was in bed when I heard someone barging roughly through my front door. I sat up, waiting. Beneath my pillow, out of sight, the revolver recently returned by Sally rested in my hand. Sanborn stormed into my bedroom and turned on the light. When I saw it was Sanborn, half drunk, I released the pistol. The situation seemed more likely to require quick hands than lethal force. Neither was needed, as it turned out. He just stood at the foot of my bed and ranted: I was a terrible writer, a faithless friend. I was a lackey to owners of the *Tribune*. I had "sold out." Next, the worst possible insult available to an acolyte of Hemingway: I was also "a phony." Then, with a bit of recently discovered spousal concern that almost made me laugh, he added that if I ever hurt Sally he would kill me. I listened silently. I had no desire to provoke him and no hope that I could make him understand that he was the problem in his relationship with Sally, not me. When his energy was spent, he turned abruptly and left. I never saw him again.

Sally and I were very private and very happy in our new relationship. Our work hours were approximately the same. She dropped me off at work and drove to school. She picked me up after work, and we drove home to Corrales. We shared a bottle of wine with dinner and went to bed early. Michael dropped by occasionally, at times for dinner, and once in a while we visited him.

Bonavita was the other person in our lives, and we saw him fairly often. Then, soon enough, Amy Bunting appeared. I don't know where Bonavita met her, but in a short time they were a couple. Bonavita, a bachelor, used to being pursued by women, now found himself in the reverse situation. Amy liked him, but she wasn't in pursuit of anything other than, perhaps, enlightenment. Independently wealthy, well educated, attractive, interested in her artistic pursuits and in advocating for enlightened social issues like peace, she was happy to have a man in her bed, but she wasn't interested in marriage just then. I guessed that Amy's independence and apparent lack of interest in marriage disarmed all of Bonavita's defenses. It wasn't long after they began seeing each other that he surprised me utterly by starting to talk about marriage.

By early May, Sally and I decided she would go to Los Angeles when school was out and explain everything to her parents. We knew they would be dismayed by her decision to marry again only months after a divorce, but we reassured ourselves that we were, after all, twenty-six years old and able to make these decisions on our own. After Sally had a few days alone with her parents, I would drive out and meet them. Once our business in Los Angeles was finished, we would drive up the Pacific coast to Seattle; take the ferry to Victoria, British Columbia, a suitably romantic town; get married; and drive back to Albuquerque, all in less than two weeks' time. The schedule didn't matter because we were happy whether we were driving or just talking endlessly about whatever came up. In preparation for the trip, we bought a new, bright-red Volkswagen Beetle for $1,760, which we could now afford because we were sharing expenses and paychecks.

Meanwhile, on the eve of my departure, Michael invited me out for coffee. As we were saying good-bye, he handed me an envelope containing a stiff $100 bill. "A little wedding present," he said, smiling.

"Michael, I can't, really." I tried to return the envelope.

"Of course you can," he said. "Buy Sally a fancy dinner in LA and tell her she is wonderful." He looked at me with such warmth in his eyes that a sense of welling affection for his generosity and selflessness made me want to hug him.

CHAPTER EIGHTEEN

Sally gave me good directions. Interstate 40 brought me across western New Mexico, Arizona, and the Mojave Desert. I stopped overnight somewhere in Arizona in a cheap but clean motel and spruced up the next morning for the final leg of my trip.

The little red Volkswagen was a joy. Smelling new, four cylinders pounding away in reassuring rhythm, it inspired utter confidence. As a gesture of insouciance toward bigger cars, I applied a bumper sticker: "You have just been passed by 40 horsepower."

Somewhere in California I picked up I-15, which led eventually to the Hollywood Freeway. I had never before driven in a city the size of Los Angeles. I had never driven in a fast lane. When I strayed into one while it was momentarily empty, my major problem quickly became survival. Suddenly cars were coming up behind me at blistering speeds, swerving around me before I could move over. Drivers in the slower lane on my right sped by faster than the VW would go. I did not close my eyes and steer toward the slowest lane—but something close to that. My new bumper sticker was not cool in California.

More than content to remain in the slow lane after my escape, I marveled at the metropolis spreading out in every direction. It was a bright, sunny day, and the city seemed to glisten white as it stretched off toward the Pacific. I found and successfully made the exit onto Sunset Boulevard. I was in mythic territory long before I turned onto Doheny Drive and headed up into the hills, climbing on switchback streets above Hollywood. Suddenly I felt the same sensation I had known in New York a few years earlier of having entered into an entirely different world, a different reality. The scale and density of Los Angeles were beyond my experience.

Arriving at Sally's house did nothing to alleviate the feeling. The house sat near a narrow street, Flicker Way, and showed the public nothing but a long, blank, white stucco wall, broken near the center by carved wooden double doors set into a shallow porch. Toward the end of the house, the outline of a three-car garage was just visible. I parked in the narrow space between the street and the house and knocked on the front door. Sally answered, offering a bright, welcoming smile.

"We never use this door," she said, fussing with the huge slab of wood. I kissed her discreetly and followed her into a large, beautifully decorated room. On the far edge of the room, I literally drew back in shock. The wall was entirely glass, offering an unobstructed, 180-degree view of the city from the downtown towers to Beverly Hills and Santa Monica. The Pacific Ocean met the sky somewhere in the distance. A generous terrace, complete with large stone planters, ran the length of the house. I felt airborne. I was so stunned by the view that I almost missed the arrival of Sally's mother.

Kay—a tall, slender woman, blonde hair turning to gray, looking schoolmarmish—greeted me politely but coolly. She looked very directly at me with eyes of the purest blue, sizing me up. She seemed beyond the reach of my considerable charm. I surmised she had met and been disappointed by other charming men, and having taught school for nearly twenty years, she was beyond manipulation. After a brief exchange of formal pleasantries, Kay excused herself to return to her studio, where she was painting. "They are terrible," she explained over her shoulder about her paintings as she left the room. "But the activity is pleasant."

Sally, responding to my obvious awe, showed me through the public areas of the house, room after spectacular room, each with the view.

"It must be something at night," I offered.

"It is fantastic. Just wait."

On the cantilevered terrace I looked over the edge and saw that we were probably fifty feet above the ground. "Some amazing engineering," I said, impressed that the house stood so near a precipice.

"They didn't live this way when I was a kid," she said. "They got rich after I left home." She gave me a subversive look and smiled as if she had given away a secret.

We had a glass of wine on the terrace while Sally told stories of how Los Angeles had changed since she was a kid, just twenty years before. "I used to take the streetcar to my violin lessons," she said. "Can you imagine that? Streetcars in LA. They ripped up all the tracks or paved them over."

"Wow. Why did they do that?"

"It was complicated, but a company owned by Firestone, Standard Oil, and General Motors bought them up. I guess they just didn't see the point in mass transit."

I had read some of the history of Los Angeles, mostly about the Chandler family's role in developing real estate while they built the *Los Angeles Times* and fought off unions, but this was a chapter in southern California skullduggery I had never heard. I associated Los Angeles with Hollywood and the movies, but clearly there was a whole lot more than movies going on here.

Sally's father arrived a little after five. A man of polished manners and careful diction, he shook my hand and bowed slightly, as did I. He was attractive, wore a little mustache, and flashed the same ice-blue eyes as Sally's. His dress was expensive, formal California: soft, light wool in muted earth tones.

"Care for a drink?" he asked.

"Whatever you're having," I said. "So long as it's not bourbon."

He soon returned from the bar and handed me a fancy tumbler filled with vodka and a little ice and topped with a splash of tonic water. I tasted the drink. It would only be possible to drink it when the ice had melted. Twenty minutes later, Jack poured himself a second drink and we sat down for dinner.

There was great tension at the table as Kay tried to get Jack to "eat a little something." I noticed both Kay and Sally behaving with exaggerated care in what they said to Jack. There was clearly a proximity fuse here, and the women were determined not to come near it. Jack ignored Kay and held forth with several "cute" stories he had heard that day. They were basically *New Yorker* cartoons set to words, amusing enough and welcome because they seemed to move the evening along without conflict. I wasn't sure whether it was the vodka or a more basic trait of his personality, but I felt a kind of preciousness in the man, an exaggerated concern with his refinement. When he mentioned his office in Beverly Hills, I was reminded of the second most important thing then on my mind and asked if he knew the location of the Time-Life bureau. "Somewhere on Wilshire Boulevard?"

"I'm on Rodeo Drive," he said, assuming that I would recognize the famous street, which I did not. "They are just around the corner. I know the building. It's a bank, I think, on the first floor. Why?"

"A friend of mine was just named the New Mexico stringer," I explained. "I thought I'd introduce myself in case there is an opening someday."

"Sally can give you directions," he said, dismissing the topic. He clearly was not interested in such small potatoes, or maybe not in any potatoes other than his own.

He picked at his food for a few minutes, finished his drink, and went off to bed. It was not yet eight o'clock. Kay tried to get everyone at the table to have another helping. She was clearly distraught by Jack's condition, but I surmised this was a daily routine. Sally and I helped clear the table, then Kay sent us away saying she wanted to clean the kitchen alone.

After Bonavita was hired as the stringer, it occurred to me that he might someday give up the assignment. I had actually mentioned to him that if he ever decided to move on to bigger and better things, I would like to succeed him. He had been noncommittal at the time, but I had voiced my dibs.

Once I knew of the existence of such a position, I decided I should learn more about the organization. Reading a *LIFE* magazine masthead, I saw that *Time* magazine had a one-person bureau in Denver, the bureau to which Bonavita reported. But I also saw that the main western bureau for both *Time* and *LIFE* was in Los Angeles, on Wilshire Boulevard in Beverly Hills, where two dozen correspondents and photographers were listed.

Sally and I walked the family dog after Kay warned us which lawns to avoid because the owners were especially sensitive about finding dog leavings. My head was still buzzing from Jack's drink as we made our way down the hill to an area where more level land allowed for lawns and a place for the Puli to poop.

Back from our walk, Sally and I went out on the terrace, where a trillion lights carpeted the terrain, stretching off in all directions until the dark ocean laid a thin border along the horizon. The late-evening air grew cool and damp. I leaned on the balustrade and thought briefly about the changes in my life in the nine months since I had crossed the border from Mexico, ragged and broke. I liked what was happening. I felt a keen hunger for more of it.

Sally showed me to the guest quarters. Reached by an outside staircase, the suite was comfortable, luxurious by my standards, and very private.

"I'll come back when they're asleep," she whispered, flashing a big smile and leaving me to wait anxiously for her return.

The day began on the terrace with coffee, a croissant, and the *Los Angeles Times*. I don't think I had ever eaten a croissant, except perhaps during my brief stay in Paris, but I tried to act as if the whole scene, breakfast on a beautiful terrace overlooking a vast city, was a daily occurrence. Sally knew better, of course, but it was her parents who concerned me just then. I didn't want them to think Sally was about to marry a hick.

I put aside the strangeness of my surroundings and tried to imagine what it might be like to actually live here. I considered whether it might be possible for me to work at the *Los Angeles Times*, and whether I would want to. It had remained my dream since the day I arrived in New York City to catch the boat for England that I would one day return to New York and work there. It was not something I thought about every day, but it was an unexamined decision that vaguely informed all that I did. Even with all its enticements, I concluded, Los Angeles remained a second choice.

Just after nine, I called the *LIFE* bureau. Lois, a switchboard operator, answered. To my surprise, she was friendly and curious. I explained that I was a reporter visiting from Albuquerque and that I just wanted to drop by and introduce myself.

"I'm sure they would like to meet you," she said sincerely, treating me as if I were someone of standing. "No one gets in until about ten. Why don't you call back a little after ten and talk to Don Moser? He's our bureau chief. I'm sure he'd like to say hello."

Lois's invitation left me feeling slightly high. I expected to be treated with indifference, at best, or told to go away. Apparently, the fact that I was a reporter, even at a small regional paper, placed me in the club and entitled me to talk to the big boys.

I told Sally. She gave a little leap of joy and said she could drive me down when I was ready to go. "It's only ten minutes from here," she said. "Try to go just before noon and I'll get Father to take us to lunch after at the Beverly Wilshire. It's right next door."

I reached Moser at about 10:30. He was cordial, as Lois had promised, and interested in seeing me, but he was leaving for an interview. "Come by and tell my secretary you are here to see Joe Bride. He's a correspondent. I'll tell him to expect you. Leave your numbers and all that stuff with him. When will you be back in town?"

"I'm not sure," I said. "Maybe Christmas."

"Be sure to call the next time you are here. I'm not always so busy."

I was not very disappointed by Moser's absence. Getting to talk to anyone in the bureau was a coup as far as I was concerned, and his invitation for a future meeting was especially encouraging. I put on my best Bonavita-inspired cotton poplin suit, and Sally drove me into Beverly Hills.

Wilshire Boulevard was amazingly clean and orderly. I had the impression that everything was beige. People on the street were all attractive, energetic, well dressed, well coifed, shined, and self-confident. Sally dropped me at a nondescript building on a corner where a branch bank occupied the ground floor, Time Inc. claimed the second floor, and various law firms, psychotherapists, and accountants occupied the remainder of the building.

Lois, wearing a phone operator's headset, greeted me from behind the little switchboard that served the office. An attractive woman in her early forties, she directed me to the bureau secretary, a classy younger woman, who in turn took me down a short hall to the office of Joe Bride, correspondent.

Bride—in his late twenties, smooth, portly, and friendly in a reserved way—invited me to sit down. I was struck immediately by the difference between the *Tribune* city room and the *LIFE* offices. The big open area at the *Tribune* was an active factory floor where things were being hammered and shaped and moved around beneath bright lights, where a sense of great urgency and noise seemed to solidify space. By contrast, the *LIFE* office was sedate and quiet, almost like a law firm, with men and a few women toiling away in separate offices, each office decorated in a style meant to reflect the attitude of the occupant. It felt too quiet, almost lonely, and a little forbidding. Bride understood without my having to say anything why I was there.

"I'm a little confused," I said. "My friend, Fred Bonavita, was hired by Barron Beshoar, who is in Denver, but you *LIFE* people are all here in Los Angeles."

"It's very informal," he said. "Frankly, for us there is not a whole lot going on in New Mexico. There is White Sands Missile Range and Los Alamos, the Indians, and the NCAA at UNM, but those don't produce a lot of stories. We have always left the stringer business up to

Beshoar, but in the end, Moser is the person who decides on the *LIFE* stringers."

We talked for ten or fifteen minutes about our pasts. Bride was from St. Louis and began his career at the *St. Louis Post-Dispatch*, the paper where I understood that Looney began. Then Bride asked about Michael.

"I worked with a guy at the *Post-Dispatch* who left and went to Albuquerque, a guy named Michael Hopkins. Do you ever run into him?"

"My god, he is one of my closest friends," I said. "My fiancée and I have dinner with him often."

"He's an excellent journalist," Bride said. "He was just out of the J school at Missouri when I met him. He was really good, especially on the technical stuff. Tell him hello."

"What a small world! I will tell him."

I left my phone number, name, and address with Bride. I reiterated my desire to be a stringer if Bonavita gave it up, and then I left, stopping on my way out to say good-bye and thanks to Lois.

Sally was waiting on the sidewalk when I came out of the building. She had been successful in snagging Jack for lunch. She directed me half a block down the street to the Beverly Wilshire Hotel, where Jack waited for us in the bar in a big booth upholstered in red leather. He was much more relaxed than he had been the night before. He was jovial and talkative. He ordered a bullshot (vodka and beef bouillon) and actually inquired about my meeting. I was just describing Joe Bride when Joe and two other men appeared at the door. I waved, and Joe came to the table. I introduced him to Jack and Sally. He stayed only long enough to be polite, but the whole thing was great for me. Jack got to see Joe, and Joe got to see Jack and Sally, and we were all eating in the same place.

We were halfway through our salads when Jack paused and said, "You know, you kids don't have to get married."

I wasn't sure how to take it. Did he think Sally was pregnant, or did he mean we had his approval to "live in sin"?

"Oh, we know," Sally said, laughing lightly. "But we want to."

"It isn't necessary," he emphasized.

I stayed silent.

Then the conversation picked up where it left off. Marriage wasn't mentioned again. After lunch, on the drive back to Flicker Way, Sally told me that Jack was always much easier at lunch than at dinner.

"He's good in the morning," she said, wistfully. "He gets up incredibly early and gets a lot of work done. Then he goes over to the Beverly Hills

Hotel and plays an hour of doubles and then he has lunch. Lunch is the first drink, and it all goes bad after that. You don't want to be near him in the evening. But I don't want to talk about him. I hate him."

"You don't actually mean you hate him."

"Yes, I do mean I hate him."

I was shocked. At that time in my life, I had never heard a person claim they actually hated a parent. We rode on in silence.

CHAPTER NINETEEN

The drive to Seattle was spectacular. We stayed as close to the coast as the highways allowed, most of the time within sight of the Pacific. When we arrived, the city was gloriously clear and sunny, as it can be in summertime. We planned to stay there with one of my oldest friends from Albuquerque, Tim Weeks, and his wife, Ramona, who was then managing editor of the University of Washington Press. She and Tim were preoccupied with *Ice Island*, a book they were writing together. The tension in their house was palpable. Ramona, a highly disciplined professional, was beside herself with frustration and fury at Tim's free-spirit attitude. The conflict over the joint project was about to end their marriage. Tim was more than happy to accompany us to Victoria.

The next morning, with Tim as our designated witness, we rode a ferry northwest through the San Juan Islands and put in at Victoria. The little city was as quaint and "Victorian" as we had hoped it would be. We bought a marriage license without trouble and then ambushed a drowsy Presbyterian minister in his study. Vaguely suspicious, uncertain of our worthiness, he was finally persuaded to perform the ceremony. Afterward, we celebrated with overpriced drinks in the elegant great room of the Empress Hotel and then caught the last ferry back to Seattle.

Pressed for time now, we made a beeline from Seattle back to Albuquerque, down through all the arid country between the Pacific Coast Ranges and the Rockies—eastern Oregon, southern Idaho, Utah—scenery now as sere as sights on the trip to Seattle had been damp. It did not matter. We were happy with each other, optimistic, and carefree. Near Durango, Colorado, running out of money, we persuaded a reluctant service-station operator that Michael's $100 bill was genuine and filled the VW for the last time.

With our relationship now public and unambiguous, the distractions of the past few months fell away. We each plunged ahead with our plans. With my encouragement, Sally quit her teaching job and accepted a graduate assistantship at the university, where she began work on a master's in American history.

Just after our return I discovered review tickets for the Santa Fe Opera going unused because no one at the *Tribune* liked opera enough to drive the sixty miles to Santa Fe and back on a work night. When I told Sally, she was almost beside herself with excitement.

"Oh my God, I've wanted to go to the opera every summer I've been here," she said. "We can go, can't we?"

"Sally, I know nothing about opera. How am I going to write reviews?"

She thought for a moment, looking at me with a distracted expression. Then she disappeared into our spare bedroom, where her books were still in boxes. I could hear books hitting the floor as she searched for something. Soon she returned with a copy of *Kobbe's Complete Opera Book*, edited and revised by the Earl of Harewood. Handing me the huge book, more than one thousand pages and weighing three or four pounds, she said, "Here, read this and you'll be fine."

So I did. I took the review tickets, and in late June, July, and August, before each performance, I carefully read what Kobbe/Harewood had to say about the opera, the composer, and past performances. I read the program notes carefully to learn as much as possible about the performers and the production. I did a lot of research before the performance because the review had to be written as soon as I arrived at my desk the next morning. In the end, I felt secure that most readers of the *Albuquerque Tribune* were not going to expect reviews that dwelled on the technicalities of how well a given passage was rendered or on the quality of a singer's voice compared to that of another who had once performed the same role. We were, as a newspaper, taking notice of one of the great cultural offerings of the region. My job, I thought, was primarily to celebrate the opera and encourage attendance, and if I didn't make a fool of myself in the process, that was enough.

There is always a tricky part, of course. Each season, the Santa Fe Opera performed a world premiere, in keeping with the aim of the founder and director, John Crosby, to broaden the repertoire of American opera and to give singers a chance to learn roles they would never get at bigger, more established opera houses. This was not unlike the chance I was enjoying as a reporter at a small regional paper, where a willingness to drive two hours was enough to qualify me as an opera critic. Since there was no history to guide me on world-premiere performances, I tended to treat them as news stories: here is something brand-new to the world, and here is what it looks and sounds like.

The enterprise went well and was greeted with mostly positive notices until I gave in to a moment of chauvinism and defended the opera for sometimes performing in English. A stinging rebuke came in the next mail from a man who was obviously reading my reviews and who knew something about opera. "Mr. Moore," it began, "have you never heard of bel canto?"

Sally and I felt very special mingling with the glamorous opera crowds. There were probably more wealthy, culturally aware people in the audience of the Santa Fe Opera on any given night of the summer than there were in the entire rest of the state. It was wonderful. There were men in Levi's and boots. There were men in evening dress and opera slippers. There were women in Levi's and women in designer dresses and diamonds. It was a completely democratic venue for high art, and I loved it.

The theater was open to the sky in those days, and the star-crusted, high-altitude New Mexico night made a roof of incomparable grandeur. I can attest without reservation that there is no experience in music and few in life quite as moving as sitting in the middle of the desert on a cool summer night as a good soprano and a full orchestra deliver "One Fine Day" (*Un bel di vedremo*) from Puccini's *Madame Butterfly*. I learned to carry a Kleenex or a handkerchief—not for Sally, but for me.

I continued to write movie reviews, both because we enjoyed going to the movies and because I enjoyed reviewing them. I was on much firmer ground when it came to judging and explaining films. I had loved movies since I was old enough to go alone. I paid my ten-cent admission to one or the other of Michael's father's theaters at least once a week until I turned twelve and had to cough up an exorbitant sixty cents. Movies were my window on the world. I saw my first tuxedo in a movie. I learned about the Civil War, mostly from a Rebel perspective, from *Gone with the Wind*. I heard a Brooklyn accent for the first time at the movies, and as Leslie Fiedler pointed out in *Montana; or the End of Jean-Jacques Rousseau*, the movies showed us how to be cowboys. Roy Rogers, Randolph Scott, and Jimmy Stewart with their accents, horses, garb, and stoic attitude defined for us what a real cowboy was. I even judged my grandfather, as authentic a western cowman as any man who ever lived, against the Hollywood standards. "Gee, Papa, your rifle is just like the one in the movies."

Tim, my soon-to-be-divorced friend in Seattle, was head of the University Film Society when I arrived on the Albuquerque campus. As a Korean War veteran he was older and more worldly than most of us. Under circumstances I can no longer remember, I signed on as his assistant, which meant that I got to see many foreign films, learning to read subtitles and not to expect to understand or even to be entertained by every movie I saw.

My stint as a movie reviewer began, luckily, in a great season for American films. A wholly inadequate list for 1964 includes classics such as *The Americanization of Emily, Dr. Strangelove, Fail Safe, The Girl with the Green Eyes, Goldfinger, Love with the Proper Stranger, Marriage Italian Style, My Fair Lady, Night of the Iguana, Woman in the Dunes,* and *Zorba the Greek.* What a feast! There were more movies deserving reviews than the *Tribune* had space for. And now that I knew about the book box, I wrote book reviews regularly, trying to avoid the complications I encountered with *The Spy Who Came In from the Cold.*

All this extra work did not replace my obligation to cover county government. I still headed for the county office building every morning to bother Nunn and cruise the halls, hoping to turn up a good scandal or something of interest to our readers, but I would guess that for every inch of copy I wrote on Bernalillo County government, I wrote an inch on books, movies, and music. This simply would not have been possible at a larger, more fully staffed paper. So in the ironic way that things often unfold, all the inadequacies of the *Tribune* that drove Bonavita crazy were fabulous opportunities for me.

The Bonavita-Bunting relationship continued much as it had been before Sally and I left for Los Angeles, Bonavita wanting to marry and Bunting feeling it an unnecessary step. Then, in early July, the relationship took a dramatic turn. Bonavita called me aside one afternoon as I was getting a last cup of coffee. Motioning for me to follow, he led me behind a row of filing cabinets, where it was possible to talk without Looney watching. He dug into his pocket and produced a blue-velvet ring box.

"Look at this," he said, conspiratorially. He opened the box to reveal a very large Tiffany-mount diamond solitaire.

"What?"

"Amy's going down to spend a week with her parents in Saint Martin. They've got a place down there. I'm going down, unannounced. I'll surprise her and give her this." He held the ring closer to me.

It sounded like a crazy idea. If Amy wouldn't say yes in Albuquerque, why would she say yes in the Caribbean? "Do you really think that will work?" I asked, without trying to hide my skepticism.

"When she sees this she'll know I am serious. She'll say yes." He was confident. "I think she'll be moved by the gesture."

"Well, maybe. You know her better than I do. When are you going?"

"Next week. I have to get some time off."

"Anything I can do to help, and all that."

"Yeah. No, it'll go OK." Bonavita returned the ring to his pocket and walked jauntily back to his desk. Looney looked at us with dark suspicion because we had engaged in private conversation behind the file cabinets.

That night I told Sally what Bonavita was up to. She looked very doubtful. "I don't think that's going to change Amy's mind."

"I don't either, but he seems determined."

An air of anticipation hung around Bonavita during the next few days as he readied himself for the big trip. He drove Amy to the airport and saw her off, without revealing his plan. The next day, I heard him telling Looney that he needed to take a few days off.

"You've had your vacation, Fred," Looney said firmly, without looking up from his work.

"This is very important," Bonavita insisted. "I have to have four days off, without pay of course."

"You've had your vacation, Fred. Go back to work." Looney was unmoved.

"I am taking four days off," Bonavita insisted.

"No, you are not." All the latent animosity between the two men now threatened to erupt into a shouting match. They stared steadily at each other. Reporters in the city room sat dead still, watching the encounter play out.

Bonavita turned quickly and walked straight into Burrows's office. Through the big plate-glass window we watched Bonavita gesturing in the manner of an injured petitioner, palms up, arms waving. Burrows shook his head in the negative. Bonavita walked back to the city desk.

Many people would have said something like, "Take your job and shove it." But Bonavita was too much the gentleman to use that kind of language. What he said instead was, "Ralph, you may consider me resigned from the *Tribune* staff."

Looney was clearly shocked that it had come to this, but he wasn't moving away from his position. "Fine," he shrugged. "Whatever suits your fancy."

I could hardly believe what I was seeing: Bonavita, like a former king of England, giving up his job to be with the woman he loved! He went to his desk and began rummaging through drawers for his personal stuff. Looney kept working, but his eyes were on Bonavita. In a very short time, Bonavita walked purposefully out the door. The whole thing was so sudden, so surprising, so final, and so shocking that I hardly knew what to think. I rushed home to tell Sally and call Bonavita, who I now considered my closest friend at the paper, excepting the special case of Michael.

"What the hell did you just do?" I asked when I got him on the phone.

"I was fed up with that rag anyway," he said. "I can't stand another day with Looney and the Scraps Horrible news chain. Anyway, I've been talking to the guys at the *Journal*. It's a much better paper, and they're interested in me."

I was surprised to learn that he had kept his overtures to the morning paper, the *Albuquerque Journal*, secret from me. I knew he was unhappy at the *Tribune*, but I had not guessed that he was unhappy enough to act. "So when are you leaving?"

"Tomorrow. Tomorrow morning. It's a terrible trip. I have to fly to Kansas City and then to Miami and then to Puerto Rico and then to Saint Martin. It's gonna be a very long day."

"What are you doing about the stringership while you're gone? Do you need someone to fill in for you?"

"I resigned that too."

I felt a little electric charge surge in my tongue. "You quit the stringership?"

"I just got off the phone with Barron Beshoar. I'm clear. . . . No ties to Albuquerque."

I was astonished that he would give up something that just a few months before seemed to make him so proud. It was also unnecessary. His dispute with Looney and the *Tribune* had no bearing on the stringership. "What did you tell Beshoar about a replacement?"

I expected Bonavita to say he had recommended me, or no one. What I heard instead felt like a kick in the gut. "I recommended Bob Lamont."

Utter betrayal! Over the past six months, Bonavita and I had spent many hours together, sharing intimate thoughts and information. We had made weekend trips together and shared a byline on a story about the nation's smallest post office. I regarded him as an ally at the paper, and I was sure he thought of me in the same way. That he would recommend another reporter, not even a friend, smacked of treachery.

"I thought you would recommend me."

"I thought the job needed someone with more experience," he said without hesitation.

I was livid. His attitude was patronizing, condescending. I suspected immediately that he had done this because he was jealous of my relatively quick rise to the rank of journeyman reporter. I held my temper. "So did Beshoar say he was going to hire Bob?"

"Oh, yeah, I'm sure it's a done deal," Bonavita said confidently. He was without concern, as if my desire to have the stringership meant nothing. The fact that he did not appear to think he had betrayed me in any way was beyond comprehension.

Bob Lamont sat at the desk next to mine at the *Tribune*. He was a competent reporter who, like many reporters working then, moved around a lot. He had worked in Albuquerque, left for the Midwest, where he worked on several papers, and then returned to Albuquerque. He smoked a nice, aromatic pipe tobacco, wore run-down shoes, appeared to dress from a Salvation Army store, drove a badly dented noisy older Cadillac by choice, and struck me as a good reporter held back by some kind of personal problem or domestic discord. Under other circumstances I would have been happy for him.

I hung up with Bonavita and told Sally what had just happened.

"What a jerk," she said. "And you went to all the trouble to meet the men in the LA bureau." She smiled. "We'll have to change the meaning of OSC from Old Southern Charm to Old Southern Cad."

I remembered Joe Bride saying that even though they let Barron Beshoar hire the *LIFE* stringer in New Mexico, the final decision rested with the Los Angeles bureau chief. I checked my watch. It was just after five. I knew the Los Angeles bureau was open until six. With the hour time difference between New Mexico and Los Angeles, they would still be in the office. I called. Lois answered. I reminded her of my visit, which she remembered.

"Lois, the stringership here has just opened up, and I need to talk to Joe Bride about it."

"Joe and all the correspondents are in San Francisco," she said pleasantly. "At the Republican National Convention. I don't think you can reach them."

"There must be a way."

"Well, I can give you a number up there. Maybe someone will be willing to track him down for you."

I took the number and called. A woman answered. There was a great deal of noise in the background, but I thought I recognized the voice of the bureau secretary whom I met in May. I explained who I was. "I need to speak to Joe Bride," I told her. "It is urgent and very important."

"Joe is out on the convention floor somewhere," she said.

"Can you send someone to find him?"

There was a long pause as she considered the magnitude of my request. "Do you have any idea how hard it is to find someone on the convention floor?"

"I do," I lied. "I know it must be almost impossible, but this is really quite urgent."

My certainty seemed to sway her. "Well, I guess I could," she said. "Are you sure this is important?"

"Yes, yes, it involves something that just happened here in New Mexico. I really must speak to him."

"Well, OK," she agreed reluctantly. "Give me a number and I'll try to get it to him."

In half an hour Joe called back. I apologized for calling him off the convention floor and then I explained what had just happened. "When we spoke in Los Angeles this spring," I said, "I felt I might have the job if Bonavita ever left. Now he has resigned, and I understand that Barron Beshoar is going to hire someone else."

The urgency and utter unimportance of my request in the middle of the Republican National Convention amused Bride. I could hear a certain playfulness in his voice. "Don't worry," he said simply. "You are the New Mexico stringer."

"I am?"

"Yes, consider yourself the *LIFE* magazine stringer as of this moment. I'm naming you the *LIFE* stringer for New Mexico."

"Will you send me something that says I'm the stringer? Is there a protocol?"

Trying to reassure me and get off the phone, Bride said again, "You are the New Mexico stringer, OK? I can assure you of that. Right now, I'm pretty busy here. They are about to nominate Goldwater and things are getting nasty, but next week, when this is all over, call me and I'll tell you all about it, OK?"

"Thank you, Joe. This means a lot to me."

"I'm sure. Good luck."

I put down the phone and sat still for several moments, finding what had happened in the past few hours hard to believe—the shock of Bonavita's resignation, the despair of hearing that he had recommended someone else to fill his position as stringer, and now the astonishing news that I had the dream job.

"So tell me! Tell me!" Sally said.

"I am the new *LIFE* magazine stringer in New Mexico."

"I don't believe it!" She jumped into my lap and kissed me.

CHAPTER TWENTY

I wasn't able to forgive Bonavita right away. When he returned the next week I called him to gloat because I had the stringership in spite of him. I was also very curious about what happened in the Caribbean. A sadder but wiser Bonavita, still in possession of his ring, answered the phone.

Amy was indeed surprised to see him, he said, but not in a happy way. His unannounced appearance in Saint Martin meant she had to explain him to her father, with whom she already had a complex relationship. Her father was inclined to send Bonavita away to find a local hotel on his own, but through Amy's intervention he was allowed to stay in the guesthouse as an unwelcome visitor. The elder Bunting quickly made it clear that an ink-stained reporter was not what he had in mind for his daughter.

"Her father holds reporters in contempt," Bonavita said. "He thinks of us, like, just workers, like clerks."

"Really?"

"He has no respect for the profession—none. And he does not approve of Amy's peacenik, artsy ways either. He approves even less of her sister out there raising horses with her cowboy husband. And he's a big Goldwater supporter."

"Sounds like you took a beating," I said, without feeling a lot of sympathy. "I mean socially."

"Yeah," he said unhappily. "I hope I can return the ring."

"What are you going to do for a job?"

He brightened slightly. "I'm starting at the *Journal* in a week."

"Oh, good. Looney was shocked when you walked out."

"It wasn't as rash as it looked. I'd been talking to the *Journal* for several weeks."

I was actually happy that Bonavita would be around, even if he would be at the morning paper, the *Albuquerque Journal*. In spite of his behavior, I enjoyed his company, but that didn't make my revenge any less sweet. I delivered my news casually, as if it were hardly important.

"While you were gone, I got the *LIFE* stringership."

"What do you mean?"

"I mean the guys in the LA bureau named me the new *LIFE* stringer."

"I think Barron Beshoar is in charge of that. That comes out of Denver."

"*Time* magazine, yes. Not *LIFE* magazine."

"Are you sure?"

"Yes, I just talked to them."

"So Bob will be the *Time* stringer, and you are the *LIFE* stringer. They are willing to split it?"

"Apparently."

He wasn't happy about my news. "Well, I hope you are up to it."

"Me too, but it won't be on you if I'm not, will it?"

"No."

"They sent me a letter and a pile of supplies—you know, shipping labels and expense account forms and those big red envelopes."

I knew the mention of "big red envelopes" would add credibility to my news.

Because raw film was the lifeblood of *LIFE*, there was no greater responsibility than assuring that a roll of film made it as swiftly as possible from the photographer's camera to the processing laboratory in the Time-Life Building on Sixth Avenue in New York City. To accomplish this, *LIFE* maintained an elaborate and efficient system for moving film. A principal element, and the one that impressed me most in the beginning, was the big red *LIFE* envelope. Approximately sixteen by twenty inches and dyed bright red, the envelope carried a shipping label addressed to the Avenue of the Americas building. Another label instructed, "Film— Do Not X-Ray." And finally, another large label sternly commanded, "DO NOT OFFLOAD!—HOLD FOR MANCUSI." The urgency of delivering film and the clout of Time Inc. working together resulted in a system in which V. T. Mancusi, a customs broker and freight expeditor, was allowed to send agents aboard arriving airliners to dive into the baggage hold, personally search out the big red envelopes, and rush them into Manhattan. The envelopes were so deliberately garish that a British postal official once turned away a film shipment under a regulation that allowed him to refuse "embarrassing parcels."

Nothing about stringership impressed me as much as the envelopes. They spoke of power, urgency, importance. I took the half-dozen that Bride sent me and carefully stacked them on my desk at home, ready for the urgent movement of film.

Until my appointment as stringer, I looked at every event, every new piece of information as a possible *Tribune* story. As a stringer I looked at every event as a national news story, but only if it could be photographed. Bride made it clear that without pictures there was no hope of getting into the magazine.

This way of thinking was entirely new to me. I now had to revise my judgment of television reporters, who, like Bonavita's friend John Hoffman, I always regarded as lesser journalists because their stories depended on pictures, on "good film": no film, no story. Without understanding what was happening, I was joining the ranks of an entirely new and soon-to-be-dominant approach to journalism in which the image was more important than the word. In many respects I am conservative or at least conventional, or perhaps just traditional, and I held the written word superior.

In a moment of hauteur months before the stringership became a possibility, I had pronounced *LIFE* magazine "a magazine for illiterates" because one could "read" it just by looking at the pictures. It was a line I regretted after I read the July 24, 1964, issue of *LIFE*, the issue reporting on the Republican National Convention I had "interrupted" to get Joe Bride to the phone. In a brilliant column, Loudon Wainwright Jr. wrote, "Inside the San Francisco Cow Palace the sounds were boisterous, but the look was sleek. Tanned, leggy women with ash-blonde hair paraded in shocking pinks and greens through a crowd which purred in self-appreciation. It was a gathering of the utterly comfortable, come together to protest that they should be having it better." Wainwright's words reassured me that this was an organization where I might one day work without serious ethical compromise—that among all the stunning photographs there was still room for stunning words.

Goldwater's nomination set off an immediate attack by President Johnson, portraying the Arizona senator as a warmonger who would attack Russia or China and turn us all, prematurely, to ashes. I was not inclined to support Goldwater, but Johnson was not behaving well on the war front either. By August that year, he had ramped up the war in Vietnam, using the constructed provocation of the Gulf of Tonkin incident to justify bombing in the north.

Conducting war without national debate or congressional approval was worrisome, but there were other ugly things going on in the country that summer. Before August was over, Johnson's high-handed actions on foreign policy had been pushed aside by the murderous response to African American demands for civil rights in the South. A wire service story from Mississippi announced the discovery of three bodies: civil rights workers who had disappeared in Philadelphia, Mississippi, in June. It was a disturbing time, a frustrating time when many people felt powerless to confront bad things that were happening, so when a local story involving injustice came my way, I welcomed the chance to champion an underdog.

A small farmer living in Valencia County, south of Albuquerque, called the *Tribune* to say he would like to speak to a reporter. He didn't say why. He just asked if a reporter could come by his small farm to see him. It was common to get this kind of request. People often believed they were in possession of information that would "blow the lid off this town" once it appeared in the paper. Most often they proved to be cranks or people with mental-health issues, but speaking to Mr. Padilla, I sensed that he was sane and serious and might have something to tell me. I made a date to drive to his farm near the town of Belen the following afternoon.

Padilla, a Spanish American farmer, spoke sincerely and without passion in heavily accented English as he described how the New Mexico State Highway Department had condemned forty acres of his farm to construct a new interstate highway, I-25, crossing the country from northern Wyoming to southern New Mexico. The land was more than a commodity to him. The farm had been in his family since the eighteenth century, and forty acres represented a sizable portion of his holdings. He said he understood that his land would be condemned, taken by eminent domain, so he agreed to sell the land to the state, but he did so with the understanding that if the land was not used to build the highway, he would be able to buy it back.

Less than a year later and without any public notice, Padilla's parcel, along with about seven hundred acres taken from other small farmers in the area, was leased to a Belen rancher and businessman for $200 an acre, under a contract to buy the land outright for $50 an acre after he tidied up taxes and assessments against the acreage.

Padilla didn't raise any issues of legality. He just felt the action was unfair. He would gladly have paid $250 to $400 per acre for the land

141

had he been given the chance. Research confirmed Padilla's story. I wrote an article explaining what had happened. When I dropped the copy in Looney's basket, I felt certain I had disturbed a rock. Something ugly would soon crawl out.

Two days later I received a delegation from the New Mexico State Highway Department bearing sundry maps and technical expertise to explain why selling Padilla's land, and 109 other small tracts, to a local businessman made perfect sense for the taxpayers of the state. These were all small parcels, the highway department people said, and to find all the owners and return the land to them, once the state realized it did not need the land, would have been a burden.

My opinion that morning was that if the actions of the state were not illegal, they should be. If they were legal, then it was a case of very high-handed behavior by the government favoring the rich and influential over citizens of modest means. It was, in fact, unfair. The chief engineer of the highway department told me quite sincerely, "We sometimes sell land to the abutting property owner, or the former owner, or at auction, but it is up to us to decide the best way to sell the land." Public notice was not required nor generally given. "Once we take the land, we own it."

"So," I said, "you can take private land that you think you might need in a project. Then less than a year later you can decide you don't need it and sell it quietly, without notice, to whomever you like at whatever price you name?"

"That's pretty much the case," he said, smiling confidently.

"God," I said. "I love New Mexico."

I think the engineer and his party were offended by my attitude. We were talking here about small parcels of land owned by poor and generally hard-working Spanish American farmers, or, more crudely, "Mexicans." The man who received the land was an Anglo rancher and successful businessman with friends in Santa Fe, including the state highway commissioner. That I failed to understand why this was fair made me an apostate.

I reported the visit from the highway department and the official explanation of what had happened. The next morning, Padilla's state senator called to say he intended to write to the state highway commissioner, calling the action "gross abuse and violation." The senator, later a lieutenant governor, said he would pass legislation in the next session to make actions such as this illegal.

Padilla did not get his land back. Several other landowners in other parts of the state who had similar experiences sued and lost. The highway department had acted within its authority. So what was accomplished? The articles revealed an abuse of power that had not been questioned before, and eventually legislation was passed to rein in the highway department. Several years of effort were required, but the highway commissioner was eventually forced out by a reform-minded governor, and I was energized once again because I could tell my fellow citizens what was going on in their government.

While I was still annoying the state highway department, one of the most bizarre stories I would cover as a *LIFE* stringer began to unfold at the Isleta Pueblo south of Albuquerque. A priest, German-born Monsignor Fredrick Stadtmueller, assigned to St. Augustine Church, built in 1716 on the Isleta Pueblo grounds, did not look favorably on the fact that the people of Isleta retained some of their traditional pre-Christian, preconquest beliefs. He decided to revivify the centuries-old struggle between Roman Catholicism and the spiritual practices of the conquered/converted people. The instrument of his attack was a load of ready-mix cement.

Traditional Isleta Pueblo people believed that it was necessary to dance barefoot on bare sacred ground each year to help nature along and assure a good harvest. The word "dance" is probably misleading, unless one is willing to call a procession of bishops a "dance." It was a religious observance, like saying the stations of the cross. In any event, the practice was as harmless to Christianity as dragging a fresh-cut tree into the living room at Christmas. Over the years, the people of Isleta had conducted their dance in the courtyard in front of the church. Priests in the past had simply looked the other way and welcomed everyone to Mass when it was Christianity's turn. But Monsignor Stadtmueller apparently felt he must put an end to pagan practices. A few days before the annual dance, he ordered in a ready-mix concrete truck to pour a slab into the courtyard so that no bare feet would touch bare earth there again. One might ask why the dance wasn't just moved to another venue, and the answer would be that generally churches were built in the New World, as they had been in Europe, on grounds traditionally considered sacred—that is, grounds that were considered sacred before the birth of Jesus Christ. Dancing just anywhere would not work.

In the confrontation that followed, the Pueblo governor decided he was fed up with this annoying priest. Showing more mercy than Henry II in a similar circumstance, the governor ordered Stadtmueller's arrest and expulsion from the Pueblo. In full view of a good photographer who had heard rumors of the pending confrontation, Pueblo deputies handcuffed the struggling priest, while members of his household staff tried to intervene. The stout deputies frog-marched the cleric to the edge of the Pueblo territory with instructions to go and never return. The whole dramatic event—angry and snarling priest, lamenting women, aggressive and burly deputies wielding shiny handcuffs—looked for all the world like an illustration for *Foxe's Book of Martyrs*.

There were, of course, all sorts of repercussions—threats of mass excommunication and much public discussion. The archbishop came down from Santa Fe to perform Mass and snub the governor. Some of the more Catholic members of the tribe tried to oust the governor, but throughout the dispute it remained a matter between the church and the pueblo. Within the pueblo, on their sovereign property, the pueblo authorities had the final say. I called Joe Bride. When he finally understood what had happened—that some Indians had legally arrested a priest and thrown him off their reservation and that I had access to good photos of the events—he wanted them shipped to New York ASAP. I was now, so to speak, on the map as a stringer.

I knew this for certain when the next assignment came to me. Moser called to say, "The FAA, NASA, and DoD have built a small town out there in your desert somewhere near White Sands. They're going to fly some planes over at supersonic speed to prove, I suppose, that the sonic boom is harmless. They've scheduled a press demonstration and briefing for next Wednesday. I'm sending a photographer out to cover it. I don't think it will make a story, but just to be on the safe side, I think we ought to go. "

God, how I loved the word "we" in that sentence!

"We won't write much," Moser said. "The whole debate is too complex, but it might produce some pictures."

Moser told me to meet *LIFE* photographer J. R. Eyerman and go along for support, captions, and whatever else was needed. In the fashion of *LIFE* editors, Moser praised Eyerman profusely so that I would be sufficiently impressed to do a good job of supporting him. I suspect that he had also praised me to Eyerman to make him comfortable that his assistant was equal to his great status as the man who had developed a special electric eye years before to allow historic photographs of the atomic bomb explosions at Yucca Flats, Nevada. "He's at the top of his game on this technical stuff," Moser said. "Just help him, however you can."

Happily, my floating day off that week coincided with Eyerman's arrival. Afflicted with a slight intestinal tremor in anticipation of my first assignment, I drove to the airport and waited to meet a real *LIFE* photographer.

Eyerman arrived in a scene that I would witness a thousand times in the years to come. Accompanied by what looked like dozens of boxes and shiny-aluminum hard-shelled cases covered in stickers from traveling the world, his baggage contained all manner of camera equipment, lighting apparatus, ladders, electrical cords, and God knows what else. No duchess ever traveled with more luggage than a *LIFE* photographer. Hoping for the best, I introduced myself to the heavyset, middle-aged man and quickly found he was not at all interested in the New Mexico stringer. We worked silently, loading his equipment into the big rental car I had arranged for the shoot.

Eyerman seemed distracted and a little cranky as he thought about the assignment. We were still loading the car when he spotted two network-television crews collecting their massive piles of luggage, all marked with big imposing network logos. He turned almost glum then spoke the first full sentence of the morning. "That's our competition," he said. "Those are the guys we have to beat." He was right, of course. He had already understood that television, not *Look*, was *LIFE*'s deadly competitor.

On the five-hour drive to White Sands, through mostly scrub-dotted desert, I tried again for conversation, but talk was not Eyerman's strength. After an hour of driving in silence I began to think about the terrible landscape through which we drove. South of Socorro, the country takes on a kind of empty, foreboding beauty. At sunrise and sunset it is awesome—what the Romantic poets would call sublime: thrilling and chilling in its vast, frightening beauty, reflecting some deep, distant mystery. At midday it approached hell on earth: hot, dry, and empty.

A broad, gently sinking depression in the earth's surface called the Tularosa basin spreads out between the Black Range and the Sacramento Mountains. Within the basin is a one-hundred-mile stretch of waterless sand and gravel known as the Jornada del Muerto, the journey of the dead man. When I was a kid, I thought the name referred to the struggles of the sixteenth-century Spanish colonial soldiers walking and riding from Mexico City to the pueblos along the Rio Grande as they looked for water for themselves and their horses where there was none. Eventually I learned that the journeying dead man was not Spanish at all but a Protestant German merchant—called Aleman for want of a proper name—who died there of thirst in the 1670s as he fled the Spanish Inquisition. Who would have thought that an arm of that savage, deadly ecclesiastical inquiry would have reached so far from its source? There were even indications that it reached into the mountains of northern New Mexico, like a virus spread by its victims, into an area where little government of any kind long survives.

Three and a half hours out, near Alamogordo, we passed an innocuous roadside historical marker commemorating the Trinity site, where the United States detonated the world's first atomic weapon. I recalled that my father was one of the few people to witness that first atomic explosion, although from a considerable distance. He was outside at 5:30 a.m., milking our cow, doing the morning chores at the barn on our ranch near Vaughn, when he was stopped by the sight of an immense fireball that suddenly appeared on the southwestern horizon. Hair on his neck stood as he watched the fire spread, climbing the sky, turning from purple to green to white—strange unearthly colors. He would later describe the sight as similar to the blinding light produced by a welding torch, but the size was unimaginable.

He ran back to the house and told Mother to turn on our radio. It was, as I recall, nearly an hour later when a report finally came that an ammunition dump had exploded near Alamogordo. Dad scoffed. "That was no ammunition dump," he said. "That was whatever the hell they've been working on up at Los Alamos."

People in New Mexico knew something was going on in Los Alamos, just as everyone seemed to know that the night bartender at the La Fonda Hotel in Santa Fe was an FBI agent. They knew that very important scientists were working at Los Alamos on what they assumed to be a powerful secret weapon. Los Alamos was a mystery, but it was not a secret.

I remember the discussion continuing at breakfast. I had turned seven two weeks earlier. I don't remember anything about that birthday, but my memories of the morning of July 16, 1945, are clear and still unsettling. I understood perfectly when I read years later the Robert Oppenheimer anecdote that, upon witnessing the fireball, he recalled Krishna's words from the Bhagavad Gita: "Now I am become Death, the destroyer of worlds."

Nearer to the White Sands site, Eyerman seemed to perk up a bit. His earlier churlishness may just have been jet lag. Then I learned that he knew almost nothing about the controversy that produced the tests we were on our way to witness.

I tried to explain, without seeming presumptuous, that in the 1950s, when it became technically possible to build a supersonic passenger plane, questions arose immediately about the effect of a sonic boom. Would the impact of the boom produced by planes traveling faster than Mach 1 prove highly annoying or even destructive? The boom became a football in a complex game involving environmentalists, aircraft manufacturers, foreign interests, and the US regulatory agencies. The tests Eyerman and I were driving to witness, while not conclusive, would have a major impact on the future of the supersonic transport (SST) program in the United States.

We arrived at the aptly named Oscuro testing area of the White Sands Missile Range at about lunchtime. The government had prepared a small town in the desert, empty of residents but perfectly representative of a thousand American towns. There was a main street with businesses of various types. Big plate-glass windows that might be found in an auto showroom glistened in the bright New Mexico sun. Houses of every style from two- and three-story Victorians to ranch-style bungalows lined streets equipped with utility poles and wires. On one side of a warehouse were three representative glass storefronts with nine panes of glass, including two eight-by-ten-foot glass show windows. A greenhouse was constructed on site.

I was reminded of the photographs of towns built in the desert and destroyed in tests of the atomic bomb. The place was a little spooky but soon came alive as the network television crews arrived and began their noisy preparation to film. Print reporters started wandering through, speculating on what might happen.

I had no idea how to illustrate a sonic boom hitting a small city, so I followed Eyerman around as he pondered the same problem. According to a briefing by Gordon Bains, director of the federal SST program, the plan was simply to fly military jets over the village at supersonic speeds and to let the press witness the impact, which he predicted would be minimal. It was an OK plan for the print reporters, but it was going to be hell for the picture people.

Eyerman eventually settled on an idea. He set up a number of cameras with motor-driven shutters aimed along the horizontal plane of big plate-glass windows. His hope was that the vibrations of the boom would cause the windows to shake, and by using a slow shutter speed he would capture the big glass moving in and out. It was not a powerful image, he complained, but what else was there?

Through the afternoon, the F-104 flew high over the village and delivered weak booms that did shake windows but caused little else of interest. The CBS camera crew was the first to pack up and leave in frustration, persuaded there was nothing to see. By midafternoon, a press corps, whose members had driven five hours into the desert and who would have to drive five more to get out—some of whom had flown in from Los Angeles or New York, all of whom had to write about what did not happen—were showing signs of being dispirited.

"This is bullshit," Eyerman said. "I'm packing up."

As soon as he spoke, word came over the public address system that in response to requests by television cameramen, the F-104 would make a final low, subsonic pass over the village so that pictures could be made with the plane and the village in the same frame.

Eyerman wearily tended his cameras in preparation for the shot. Inside the briefing room, Bains began explaining to the gathered print media that in his view, people who claimed damage from sonic booms were imagining things. As he spoke, the F-104 pilot flying at five hundred feet, having misunderstood his instructions, streaked across the village at Mach 1.

A heavy ruby-glass ashtray flew off Bains's desk and sprayed shards over the briefing room floor while reporters ducked under desks. Outside, both panes of the mocked-up storefront blew in a great shower of glass out into the street, a glass window in a trailer caved in, and sixteen out of ninety panes in the small greenhouse blew out. There was absolute silence for thirty seconds and then pandemonium as everyone outside began shaking glass from their hair and everyone inside ran out to see what had happened.

Eyerman's cameras, whizzing and snapping as the motors ran film past the shutters, caught it all: great sparking shards of glass exploding into the air as an F-104 looms huge and menacing against a blue, blue sky.

"Holy shit!"

"What the hell happened?"

"He broke the sound barrier!"

"Holy shit."

"Did you get it?"

"I think so. I think so. Did the TV guys get it?"

"No, no. They had their cameras on the plane."

"Here, here. Help me with this stuff. We've got to get this film to New York."

CHAPTER TWENTY-ONE

Hanging out for a day with members of the national press corps, seeing their confusion, anxiety, and uncertainty, helped me understand that there was not a great deal of difference between them and me as we wandered around in the desert trying to figure out exactly what the story was. They were more experienced and more aggressive than I, but we were clearly made of the same stuff. With very little more experience, I could do what they were doing. I felt a new sense of confidence.

In the first days after Burrows hired me, I was keenly aware that I knew nothing about journalism, despite his kind observation that cops and reporters do much the same thing. I knew how to write and I knew how to ask questions, but it quickly became apparent to me that being a reporter was a great deal more than asking questions and writing down the answers. Among other things, in any story involving controversy there is a kind of elaborate game, a fugue that goes on between reporter and subject as the reporter tries to keep the story alive. Part of a story's impact is its duration: how many days it appears in the paper. A skillful reporter can actually moderate a public debate that goes on for days. A charge is made by someone on day one of a story ("The state took my land and sold it to an insider"). On day two the charge is answered ("We had to do it to build a highway and protect taxpayers"). On day three the answer is answered (a local senator says, "The state is wrong"), and in each iteration of the story, the major points are reiterated, driving them through the cluttered attention field that makes up a reader's consciousness. Nothing in police work that I know of mimics this or the many other techniques available to a good reporter as he tries to convince the public, as opposed to a prosecutor, of his point of view. And I soon discovered, even though I tried to be fair, I always had a point of view. I dutifully reported both sides of the story, but only in the rarest cases did I believe that truth and right rested equally on both sides.

Michael and Fred and, in an odd way, Looney were all wonderful teachers, and I was an eager and willing student, but in spite of their efforts (or in Looney's case, because of his efforts) I had to learn some lessons the hard way. The humiliation of missing the hero in a crane operator's panicked response to an accident was an early indication that in journalism, as in life, things are not always what they seem. I understood after that day that I had to pretend to be a reporter until I became one. In the fourteen months after I first said to a source, "This is Gerald Moore with the *Albuquerque Tribune*," I lived in a steady state of anxiety, worrying that I was missing the point, missing the hero, stating the obvious, being deceived, or was about to write something that others would find monumentally stupid. After my trip to the desert with Eyerman, the fear began to subside.

The peak of my anxiety probably came the day I shut my eyes and dove into the cold water of opera reviews, mostly to acquire the tickets that Sally so coveted. I relied heavily on the established authority I found in *Kobbe's Complete Opera Book*. I was careful not to go where I lacked experience. I stuck to descriptions of the opera's history, the sets, and the weather (a real factor in the open-air theater in Santa Fe). I tried to keep my reviews simple, descriptive, and supportive of the young company and its young staff. Even though the reviews appeared to be well received, I still felt a nagging sense of fraudulence. What standing did I have to critique an opera? In the end, my standing was that no one else would do it. Was a scared, half-informed, but conscientious reviewer better than none at all? I decided the answer was yes. It sounds like the worst of clichés, but I decided I had to live with the fear if I wanted to keep writing for a newspaper.

Barbara Taylor, the *Tribune*'s Women's Page editor, must have sensed this new confidence, because late one afternoon, not long after the sonic-boom event, she walked to my desk and said, "Why don't you write a weekly column for me? We could call it something like 'Moore on the Arts.'"

An intelligent and stylish woman who favored pencil skirts and silk blouses, Taylor's responsibilities included a weekly section of about six pages that covered most of the cultural news offered by the *Tribune*. The practice of grouping book, movie, and music reviews with recipes and syndicated columns on good manners or advice on raising happy children and then calling the whole thing the "Women's Page" said a lot about social attitudes toward both women and culture.

A column would give me space on a weekly basis to make known my views as they related to the arts. It would make me responsible for writing something intelligent and reasonably interesting once a week in a space bearing my name and photograph. It meant adding another 1,500 well-chosen words to my weekly workload. It also meant dealing with ideas rather than events, a much tougher task.

"I have already spoken to Ralph," she said. "He's OK with the idea. As far as I am concerned, you can write about anything you like, so long as it relates to art. Once you start, you can't miss a week. I want it to appear every Thursday, and I need copy COB Tuesday, OK?"

"OK," I agreed, plunging ahead, smiling, nodding assent.

What actually qualified a person to be a "columnist"? I asked myself. A Nobel Prize in the subject being considered might be a good start, but in the real world, being interesting and making sense to readers, especially the better-informed readers, was probably enough. Then a thought, both comforting and deflating, came to mind: the future of culture would hardly be affected by my little column in a regional paper. It was only my fledgling reputation that was on the line. Some doubt was probably a healthy thing, an antidote to the raging certainty that can befall a person paid to regularly write opinions.

A more mundane side of this was not lost on me. By offering the column, Barbara now had a guaranteed twenty-odd inches of copy each week to help fill the space for which she was responsible, and Looney didn't really care one way or another because the column would not replace any of my other duties.

I was still a long way from stardom. The column did not come with any more money. The $2.50 raise I got at the end of my first year pushed my total compensation to $75.00 a week. There was no profit sharing, no medical insurance or sick leave. We got ten days of paid vacation and a $5.00 bonus at Christmas. Writing a column would change none of this. It did not really matter. I rolled out of bed at 5:00 a.m. every morning, excited to see what the day held. There was no place on earth I would rather be than in the newsroom at seven each morning. That was incentive enough.

I began the column while continuing to write about government in Valencia and Bernalillo Counties. There were articles about crowded jail conditions, delinquent taxes, and proposed commercial developments.

When washday suds began to foam up in the Rio Grande, I wrote about the pollutants now present in a river used for drinking and irrigating food crops along its winding route all the way down to Brownsville, Texas, a thousand miles away. An editor drew a line through my zeal when I wondered in print how many sets of kidneys Rio Grande water passed through before it reached the Gulf of Mexico.

When I finished writing about the real struggles and failures of the little world around me, I turned my attention to the finer things in life: the struggles of art and literature and music to achieve some indefinable goal that could be experienced but not ultimately defined. In the column, I held forth on pop art, current writers, and the National Endowment for the Arts. Without anyone to rein me in, I said some pretty rash things—some of which I would later regret—but the freedom was heady and thrilling.

In late November, Sally's mother sent us plane tickets and an invitation to come to California for Christmas. Los Angeles was beautiful that December. Just days before we arrived, a weather pattern brought unusually clear and cool air into town, blowing away the smog and sprucing up the city. The San Gabriel Mountains put in a rare appearance, looking like a Disney movie illustration painted overnight on the eastern sky.

Our first morning in town, I took myself out on the Stewarts' terrace to write the column I would phone in the next day. As I looked out over the sprawling city, it occurred to me that I might actually be qualified now to work in a place like this, if I could convince a national publication or a major newspaper, like the *Los Angeles Times* or the *New York Times*, to take me on. It was a strange moment and one that would stay with me, because I had never before seriously thought that I could work professionally outside of New Mexico. I could deliver pizza anywhere, of course, or work nonunion construction, but writing news stories for a major metropolitan daily would require a worldliness and sophistication that until recently I felt sure I lacked. I was still daydreaming about the big time when Sally came out to sit with me. Happy and well rested, she wore a fresh white blouse and perfectly fitted shorts. A light breeze ruffled her blonde hair. She smiled, took my cigarette, and after a long pull returned it to my fingers. Her look and easy, confident manner was so thoroughly California that I found myself wondering how we ever got together: the golden girl and the desert rat.

"You ought to think about writing some scripts," she said, settling in next to me on a double chaise. "There's nothing to them. You should see some of the crap Father sells."

"And because they are crap, you think I could write them," I said, teasing.

"No, no, I mean you are *so capable*, it should be easy for you."

"Crap is not easy," I argued. "In fact, for a quality guy like me, crap is hard. If crap were easy, there would be thousands of Harold Robbins. Anyway, do you think your dad would help me learn?"

"Oh no, no. He's way too jealous." She was serious. "If you wrote something good it would upset him terribly. He basically has two modes: worshipful and sneering. He is not a collaborator. And if you wrote something bad, he would be unbearably contemptuous."

A harsh and frightening thought.

"Really! He won't help. But I can get you a stack of scripts, and you can look at them. You'll see. They're not all that complex, at least not for a series."

"Like what series?"

"*Naked City. Bonanza.* Let me get you a pile of scripts." She gave me a knowing, seductive smile. "Pays better than the *Tribune*."

"OK. I'm willing to be a trekker in the vast wasteland, but in the meantime, I'm due at the *LIFE* bureau to remind them I'm alive."

Again my snobbery came into play as I thought about writing for television as opposed to writing for a national magazine or a big newspaper. I just could not take television seriously.

My reception later that morning at the Time-Life offices was surprisingly cordial. Lois looked up from her switchboard and smiled and gave me a big hello. Moser came out of his office, greeted me happily, and called over Hal Wingo, destined to become a stalwart at *People* magazine a decade later but currently his number two, to introduce us. Joe Bride wandered up from his office when he heard the commotion. He said hello and then smiled contentedly as Moser told me Joe was leaving soon to take a lucrative job with Budweiser back in his native St. Louis.

"Have you eaten?" Moser asked. "Let's have lunch."

A block or two away and across Wilshire Boulevard, Moser ushered us into a cool, dimly lit Italian place with deep-red tablecloths. Even though it was lunchtime, big candles flickered on each table. When a waiter appeared to take a drink order, Wingo asked for a Coke, explaining to me that as the son of a Baptist minister from Texas, he preferred not to drink alcohol. That he needed to explain this should have told me something about the culture of magazine journalism in the 1960s, but I thought little of it. I knew a lot of Southern Baptists who didn't drink. What I found unusual was that Bride and Moser asked for martinis. Drinking at lunch was a practice I knew to be detrimental to the workday, but ignoring my experience, wanting to be like the big guys, I threw caution to the wind and went for the gin.

Moser truly was one of the big guys. Only a few years older than me, he was already an accomplished journalist who, as a graduate student in Wallace Stegner's writing program at Stanford, had been passed on by Stegner to Interior Secretary Stewart Udall to help write *The Quiet Crisis*, a book that, together with Rachel Carson's *Silent Spring*, laid the intellectual foundation for the modern environmental movement. This fact alone gave him such standing in my eyes that I was amazed to be sitting at the same table with him, and even more amazed that he was actually asking questions about me. He was unassuming, supremely confident, intelligent, and sensitive to irony, especially where he was personally concerned.

After some small talk, he asked, "Do you ever think about working at a place like this?"

My heart may not have actually leaped, but it sure felt that way. "I have thought about it, and I would very much like to," I replied as nonchalantly possible.

"But you seem to be a fairly big deal at the *Tribune*. Are you sure you would want to give that up?"

I couldn't understand how he would think this. I never imagined myself as anything more than a scared reporter trying to hide my ignorance and keep up with the pack. "I'm flattered," I said, still off balance and not recovering my footing very quickly. "I actually never thought about it that way. Yes, I'm very happy at the *Tribune*, but I would love an opportunity to do more national stuff."

"I liked what you wrote about the Rio Grande," he said. "And now you have a column, right?"

"Thanks, yes, that's right." I laughed and said, "'Moore on the Arts.'"

"Well, you know, some people are very happy where they are, and they're not interested in going to New York or LA or Saigon. You must have a lot of family in New Mexico."

"I do. I have a daughter there, but I think her mother is going to take her to Seattle this fall, so that becomes moot. My wife is actually from here." I gestured in the general direction of the Hollywood Hills. "I think she would be delighted to come home. And," I added quickly, "I'm sure she would also love living in New York."

Wingo allowed that he thought New York was "a really crazy place, but lots of fun."

"How did you know about the column?" I asked.

"We get the *Tribune*," Moser said. "We take a lot of the regional papers. I looked through some back issues before you came in. I noticed your paper didn't cover the sonic-boom tests."

"No, they used wire copy."

"Even though you were there?"

"You know, I don't think I told them I was going."

"Really?"

"Our editor is quite conservative. He's uneasy about having reporters travel. He won't let anyone fly on assignment. Our travel is very restricted, two counties. We don't even go to Santa Fe. Insurance, I guess."

"Yeah, well, it's an afternoon paper. I suppose the *Journal* covers most of the national and international news."

I was surprised again that Moser knew as much as he did about Albuquerque and our two papers. The *Albuquerque Journal*—the morning paper, the paper of record—circulated statewide, maintained a Santa Fe bureau, and was generally thought to be the more responsible paper. This was part of the reason Bonavita was so happy to make the switch. The *Tribune*—smaller, feistier, a Scripps Howard outpost—was in fact a better place for me, considering my experience.

The conversation drifted off to other topics: Vietnam, President Johnson's civil rights initiatives, Hollywood gossip. We drank another martini and then, after a light lunch, made our way back to the office. After two hours in the near darkness of the café, the bright California sun was blinding. My head buzzed and snapped from the gin, but I held on as though nothing unusual had happened, pretending to be sober until I was.

Back in the office, Lois distributed a stack of pink phone messages. Moser motioned for me to follow him into a big corner office, where he flopped into a huge office chair, quickly looked at his messages, and turned his attention back to me.

"Sometime soon they are going to be looking for new people," he said. "If you want to put together a book of clips and anything else you think matters, I'll be glad to take your stuff to New York. There's no rush. This won't happen until late spring, maybe summer. No promises, but they'll get a chance to see your work. You just need to be sure that is the direction you want to take. You obviously like to write. Maybe you should be thinking about *Time* magazine?"

"No, no. I love *LIFE*. I truly like working with photographs."

This was only half true. I did like working with photographs, though not necessarily with photographers. I liked taking photographs. In fact, I had recently bought a professional-grade Nikon camera with two lenses in the hope of illustrating some yet-to-be-determined freelance work. Photographs pleased me, and I found good ones to be art, but one important reason to choose *LIFE* was pragmatic: my best chances of successfully making the transition from local to national journalism lay with Moser and *LIFE*. Why, having been offered a ski trip to Vail, would I say I preferred Aspen?

I could not divulge the most powerful reason that I preferred *LIFE* over *Time* without seeming grossly ambitious: *LIFE* printed bylines on important stories, and at that time *Time* did not. The possibility of seeing my name on an article in a national magazine was a pleasure so great that I didn't even like to imagine it. The enormous ego boost that came from seeing my name on a good piece of writing in a regional newspaper was worth at least as much as my weekly check, which had now risen another $7.50 a week, all the way up to $82.50.

I thanked Moser as sincerely as I could without sounding like a grateful serf who had been granted his freedom and told him I would put together something for him to show the people in New York. Outside, I stood on the sidewalk and watched traffic on Wilshire Boulevard for a moment, trying to regain my sense of equilibrium. I could hardly believe what had just happened.

Back at the Stewarts', Sally hugged me and rushed off to tell her parents. Jack and Kay were too sophisticated to get excited over a new son-in-law being a potential candidate for a reporter's job at *LIFE* magazine. They were polite, but they were far more interested in the fact that we all were going to the film premier of *My Fair Lady*, opening the next day in Hollywood.

Two days later, Sally and I flew back to Albuquerque, excited and apprehensive about the future. I had half a dozen television scripts weighing down my luggage and a suggestion from Mr. Stewart that a script about Maria Callas could be very commercial, as if Greece and the Metropolitan Opera and Onassis's yacht were just down the road from Albuquerque. It didn't matter. My mind was on New York and national journalism.

CHAPTER TWENTY-TWO

The divorce decree I signed with Hellyn in 1962 stipulated that neither she nor I could take Catherine out of the state without the other parent's permission. I remember being surprised by the clause when I read through the agreement prepared by Hellyn's lawyer. I was still on the police force and trying to get through school. I could not imagine a time when either of us would move away, but it was really too much to hope that Hellyn, Cathy, and I could continue to live near one another. While I worked at the *Tribune*, Hellyn pursued a degree in fine arts at the university, and until I moved to Corrales with Sally, we lived only blocks apart. Hellyn's success as an art student led to the phone call that changed all this.

"I've been offered an assistantship at the University of Washington, in Seattle," she said. "I'm going for an MFA. I need permission to take Cathy."

I had never imagined when Hellyn and I divorced that Cathy might live a thousand miles away. Now, if I got what I wanted, she would be 2,800 miles away.

"There are a hell of a lot more direct flights from New York to Seattle than there are from Albuquerque to Seattle," Sally said, when I pointed out that my daughter might be on one coast and I on another. "And," she added, "you'll come a lot closer to affording airfare on a *LIFE* salary than with a *Tribune* check."

I gave my permission.

Now we began to talk seriously about living in New York City. Sally and her sister had been frequent visitors there all the years of their childhood. Jack Stewart loved New York in the way that only a New Yorker living in California can love the city. He dragged his often-bored daughters through dozens of trendy restaurants, fancy hotels, museums, and galleries as they were growing up. He fully captured their attention on the one occasion that he took them to see the house in Brooklyn where he was raised—a painful trip for him because he was completely, though mysteriously, alienated from his siblings. His parents were dead. I often speculated about why he had cut himself off. He alone changed his surname from Sternad to Stewart. Perhaps that decision played a role, but it seemed so self-destructive. His brother, Rudy, was Stanley Kramer's art director, right-hand man, and sometimes producer. Another brother was a successful architect. There were four brothers who had all done well in the world, yet he acted like an only child.

Sally's concern about New York was simply that such a huge change in our lives might disrupt our relationship. We were, in many ways, living a perfect American life, though on a modest scale. I had developed into a respected local reporter. The column had given me a certain social cachet in circles that read the local paper and had an interest in the arts. Sally had performed brilliantly in her graduate work, so much so that she was being urged to continue for a doctorate in American history. We lived in a comfortable, if rented, three-bedroom house in Corrales surrounded by accomplished people, creative people, small farmers, and horse breeders. We went to the opera in season and to as many movies as we cared to see. I brought home review copies of as many good books as we could read. We were able to have Cathy with us on weekends and some evenings. Bonavita and Amy Bunting and Michael Hopkins and John Hoffman were good and frequent companions at dinner. Sally had started to think about having children, or at least a child, encouraged by her sister's happy motherhood. It was this aspect of our lives to which Moser referred when he asked if I really wanted to give up Albuquerque. When I examined the question, I had only one doubt: I would fail and have to return with the knowledge that this was the best I could do.

I reminded myself that Moser's offer to carry my clips to New York was hardly a guarantee of anything. I half expected that I would never hear another word about the matter, except perhaps if he was kind enough to make some excuse as to why no one called.

Sally agreed that I should pursue Moser's offer. We could decide what to do, if anything, as events unfolded. I put together a book of clippings of my strongest stories and what I regarded as my best columns and reviews and shipped them off to Los Angeles. Moser reiterated his promise to take the work to New York and once again counseled patience. I pressed on with my work at the *Tribune*.

CHAPTER TWENTY-THREE

The call came into the city room in the way most requests for coverage arrived: directed from the switchboard to the city editor and, after a brief screening, transferred to a reporter—in this case, me. The caller identified himself as a local doctor, "part of a group of doctors who own planes," he said. "We fly into very remote parts of the world to bring medical services to people who have none. We usually stay for a week or ten days, and we try to arrange some follow-up, but that isn't always possible."

Dr. Thomas thought the *Tribune* should be interested in the group's next undertaking. Seven doctors from Albuquerque and nineteen from other states would fly planes loaded with donated medical supplies into the very remote Sierra Madre Occidental, the rugged and remote range of high mountains and deep canyons lying south of Arizona in western Mexico. Using a tiny, isolated Spanish colonial mission where a rudimentary airstrip was periodically maintained, they would treat members of a group of indigenous people, the Tarahumara, the same people who inspired my epiphany about literacy as I traveled through Juárez on my Mexican trip two years earlier. The Tarahumara maintained a Stone Age culture, had a life expectancy of about forty, suffered an infant mortality rate of about 75 percent, and perhaps more important, suffered greatly from diseases and conditions that yield readily and completely to modern medicine. They were also, improbably, the best distance runners in the world, able to cover seventy or eighty miles without rest at a pace that still confounds all observers.

Clearly a good story: local doctors, flying their own planes, join with colleagues from around America to treat people living in Stone Age conditions only a thousand miles away who have no Western medicine available to them. I did a fairly extensive interview with Thomas. I called some of the other doctors he mentioned to confirm they were going and wrote a feature story that appeared the following day.

The doctor called the next morning. "Why don't you come down to Mexico with us? We would be happy to pay you something and return your expenses. We need coverage of this effort. I promise you there are many good stories that will come out of this."

At first glance the idea seemed like an impossibility. The *Tribune* would never send me. I doubted they would even give me time off to go on my own, but I decided to approach Looney, who had changed recently from an antagonist into a supporter, based, I assumed, on my more professional work.

He listened carefully to my pitch. Then he shrugged. "Mr. Burrows will not let anyone fly on assignment."

"Would you consider letting me go on my own time? I'll do some articles when I get back."

"Maybe. Let me check."

Looney went off to Burrows's office, where, through Burrows's picture window, I could see them conferring. Looney returned to his desk and motioned for me to approach. "He's willing to give you time off without pay. He wants it to be clear that you are not on assignment for the *Tribune*, but if you return safe and sound"—Looney laughed his bitter laugh—"he will be happy to run your stories."

I laughed too, from pure amusement. "Good. I'll do it."

I had no idea how I would make enough money to replace the four or five days of lost wages. Even with Sally's small stipend from the university, our finances remained very tight. The doctors' offer of pay was no help, because I could not report the story while being paid by them and still think of myself as a journalist. It was an important technicality. If I took money, I would in effect be a public relations person for their organization. I felt sure they were doing good work, and I doubted I would be tempted to write anything critical. But what if I discovered that this was just an elaborate ruse to get a vacation to Mexico and deduct part of the cost of their airplanes as charity? Financial independence was critical to my integrity.

Another plan came to mind. Since my recent Los Angeles trip and Sally's suggestion that I try writing scripts, the notion of freelance work had been much on my mind as a way to extend the scope of my work and income beyond the bounds of the *Tribune*. The Mexico venture seemed like a perfect place to begin. I would not be on the *Tribune*'s payroll. The story would belong to me, and I could sell it wherever I liked, once I wrote something for the *Tribune*. Surely there were magazines or newspapers that would be interested in the story.

As so often happened in those days, the immediate solution to my money problem came in a most unexpected way. Somehow word spread in the newsroom that I was going to make the trip. Two days before we were to leave, the Associated Press bureau chief came to my desk.

"I understand you are going to Mexico with the DOCARE guys."

"Right. How did you know?"

"I heard."

"Oh."

"I'll put you on per diem and pay your salary if you can find a way to file a story for AP every day."

I had never thought of AP as a customer for my work. They had the rights to everything that appeared in the *Tribune* and they had picked up any number of my stories, but this was different. I was not a *Tribune* reporter for this outing. I could offer my work directly to them.

"That's great." I was delighted. "Absolutely. The only thing is, I understand that where we are going there is no electricity and no phone. Certainly no telegraph. The place is a hundred miles southwest of Chihuahua in the Sierra. You can imagine that filing daily might be a problem."

"If you make every effort humanly possible to get copy to me as often as you can, I'll deal with that."

I called Dr. Thomas and told him the good news. I don't think he fully appreciated the difference between a story in the *Tribune* and a story moving on the AP wire, but in time he would see what "nationwide" meant. When I explained my need to get copy to the AP every day, he easily solved my problem. "We'll have lots of planes down there. Someone will be flying out to Chihuahua every day. They'll take your stories out."

AP, working through its vast international network, quickly made arrangements for my copy to be wired from Chihuahua to the Albuquerque bureau on a prepaid basis. All I had to do was see that copy was handed into the Chihuahua telegraph office. I did not have to fly out.

The day before my departure, Looney came to my desk wearing a big smile. "Mr. Burrows feels it would be embarrassing to run stories written by our reporter over an AP dateline. He wants to print your stories under your byline, as a *Tribune* staffer, so he proposed that, when you return"—he laughed—"if you do, we will just forget you were gone."

Plausible deniability. "Fabulous," I said. My now restored salary of $2.06 per hour (before taxes), for five days, would pay the rent. My AP check was, as they say, all gravy.

It was once famously remarked that "all politics is local." The same can be said about most daily journalism. Looney and George Baldwin, the *Tribune*'s taciturn managing editor, constantly reminded me of this. "What's the local angle?" was the question asked of any story where the local tie was not obvious. If two men went into space, we would have to find that one of them had a cousin in Albuquerque and interview him. When President Kennedy was killed, we wrote about his visit to Albuquerque. The lesson was not lost on me as I planned coverage for my Mexican trip. Local doctors would be grist for the *Tribune* mill. Doctors from Ohio and Indiana and California and elsewhere would satisfy the AP's needs to service the local angle from a great distance. "Here," the AP could in effect say to subscribing papers all over the country, "is a firsthand account of your local doctor doing good things in Mexico."

On Saturday, equipped with my new Nikon, three dozen rolls of Kodachrome film with ASA ratings of 200 and 400 for bright sunlight and dim interiors, a portable Smith Corona typewriter, a change of clothes, and a few personal items, I met my doctors at the private aviation area of the Albuquerque Sunport, where just a few years earlier I had worked gassing planes.

The assembled aircraft were mostly modest single-engine machines, four-place Cessnas and Beechcrafts. A few doctors flew bigger twin-engine planes, but this was still about people who just loved to fly. The days of ostentatious private aircraft as a display of wealth and power were yet to come. Packed with medical supplies, big boxes of bandages, bottles and jars of things I didn't recognize, drugs of various kinds, and equipment, the planes had just enough room for pilot, copilot, and, in one instance, me. I felt a certain sense of relief as I watched and listened to the men and concluded that they were careful, serious pilots truly in love with flying.

The trip to El Paso, Texas, took about two hours. We landed to top off the fuel tanks before hopping just across the border to Juárez to clear Mexican customs. This was accomplished with a minimum of bribery.

The Mexican officials seemed to recognize that the doctors were on a mission of mercy and that their medical supplies should not be held for a ransom too high, even though the importation of medical drugs into Mexico was highly restricted—in spite of a more or less open market within Mexico in medical drugs. Benzedrine and other pills were available at any pharmacy without prescription. Some cash was involved and a lot of personal diplomacy, but the whole affair was relatively hassle free. In another three hours, we landed in the city of Chihuahua, where we spent the night.

The doctors proved to be a pretty typical group of American men on an out-of-town trip. After dinner, some retreated to their rooms to pursue whatever private activities interested them. Others hit the bar for more talk and a few more rounds before bedtime. A few found female company for the evening. I watched the scene for half an hour and then went to my room to write an account of the day. I would have to deliver it to the wire office early, before we left for the tiny mission in the mountains that would serve as the base for the doctors' work.

Early the next morning, we flew out of Chihuahua, rising above the low-lying cloud of beige dust that seems to hover above every Mexican city. Dr. Thomas explained that takeoff or landing in Sisoguichi was better accomplished very early or very late in the day. The landing strip was at the bottom of a deep canyon with high peaks on three sides. Elevation had to be quickly gained or lost, depending on whether we were landing or taking off. By hugging the sunny side of the canyon, a pilot could take advantage of the warm air rising in the sun to help lift him out of the canyon. Conversely, a landing approach on the shady side would take advantage of falling cooler air and bring the plane down in time to hit the end of a makeshift runway, a dirt strip approximately 30 feet wide and 2,800 feet long that featured, halfway along its course, a rickety wooden bridge over a shallow ravine. A broad pasture feeding a variety of livestock surrounded the strip. Without radio communication, pilots on final approach had to watch for sheep, goats, little boys, dogs, and other creatures on the runway. The first pilot to land each day typically had to pull up and go around before the runway was cleared.

The doctor's description of the landing field did not fully prepare me for the reality. After flying over the vast Chihuahuan desert for half an hour, we could see the terrain begin to rise, and a canyon on the scale of the Grand Canyon appeared. We flew down where we saw more canyons, and more canyons, like a Chinese box, until at last I saw the landing strip, a narrow line in the bottom of a box canyon. On three sides the mountains appeared sheer and unforgiving. The fourth side was open, but winds being what they are, our approach was not to be over the open end but over the high end of the box. "We'll come in very low over the mountain," Thomas reassured me. "Then where the canyon opens, we'll hug the shady side and drop right in."

I don't know how many feet of altitude we lost between the bluff and the runway. My innards were pressing hard against my lungs when Thomas made a perfect touchdown. Then the tail wobbled and he quickly accelerated to gain control as he lined us up to cross the narrow bridge. I heard the hollow *pock, pock* of tires hitting wood as we passed over the ravine and into the safety of the second half of the runway.

"I'm glad we don't have to do that every day," Thomas said as he taxied to the edge of the field.

"Have you done it often?"

"Only once. Last year," he said smiling. "It's exciting, isn't it?"

As more planes landed and taxied into parking position, the mission grounds soon resembled the resupply of a forward military base. Packages and cartons were offloaded, and people arrived to help move them to the clinic. Doctors converged on the mission where the small staff gathered to greet new arrivals. Lots of hustle and bustle ensued as the doctors set up a simple operating room and turned other rooms into clinics.

Several days earlier, word of the doctors' impending arrival had gone out into the mountains. Lines had begun to form outside the clinic even before we arrived. Sick people, young and old, many of whom had walked for days to be there, waited patiently for the doctors to call them. Women nursed infants while small children clustered quietly nearby. More people arrived every few minutes until the lines were very long. Most of the Tarahumara seemed to prefer standing to sitting, and they stood for hours. This would go on and on as word of the doctors' presence penetrated deeper into the mountains and bestirred the sick and suffering to begin the long walk for help.

I now faced an entirely new kind of reporting, something I had not done before. Covering county government, I reported on things that had already happened: money spent, decisions taken, land bought or sold. Even scandals were past events that had to be uncovered and reconstructed. What I witnessed now was more like covering a war or a political campaign. The story was large and dynamic; it sprawled. I had to find a way to grasp some manageable part of a narrative that would allow me to sketch the larger picture.

I was elated. Here was my own treasure in the Sierra Madre: twenty-six doctors, each with his own story, his own motivation for being in Mexico. There were airplanes and the problematic 2,800-foot dirt landing strip. There was Father José Liaguno, head of the mission, devoted to mankind, fluent in Tarahumara (a dialect of the Uto-Aztecan language family), ready to explain in depth the life and condition of the people he served. There was the exotic locale and the indigenous people. I had an Associated Press bureau chief in Albuquerque waiting on my dispatches. My only competition was a film crew from National Educational Television whose report would be weeks, if not months, away. I felt like a spring bee in a clover field.

I wrote about the doctors mostly, hewing to the idea that local people in the United States would be more interested in their local physicians than in a group of isolated and primitive people. But describing activities of the doctors gave me many opportunities to write about the Tarahumara and the life they lived, and the problems their lives presented to modern medicine. How do you explain that a pill should be taken every four hours when no one has a clock or can tell time? How do you make mothers understand that sugar-coated pills are not candy to be eaten all at once? When a doctor gave a woman birth control pills to stop erratic menstrual bleeding, he resorted successfully to the phases of the moon to explain when she should stop the medication. Discovering that the Tarahumara lacked any concept of a microbial world, doctors sought ways to explain the need for basic sanitation in terms that could be understood. At the end of one long day, a tired doctor turned to me and mused, "It's not a very Christian attitude, I know, but sometimes I wonder if we are trying to perpetuate a people that nature is trying to stamp out." He would have been surprised to learn that, in the belief system of the Tarahumara, they were the superior beings. The rest of us had yet to catch up.

There were some striking differences in the physical conditions the doctors saw. Excessive weight that afflicted so many people in their practice at home was nowhere in evidence here. And there were striking similarities, such as ulcers caused by heavy drinking.

Awash in wonderful material, I filed long dispatches, sending copy out to Chihuahua every morning with the pilot/doctor going out that day. On our third day I volunteered to go along when an expedition was mounted as a kind of medical outreach to take a jeep caravan into even more remote country. We rode for an hour on powder-dry roads with fine white dust boiling into the jeep. I tied a T-shirt around my face and mouth with little effect. When we finally stopped in a tiny village, I looked at my companions and saw a group of Kabuki players; everyone was so completely covered in white dust that only their eyes moved. I felt I would suffocate. I walked a few yards and found a clear mountain stream. Washing my face, I drew water into my nose to clear the dust. Then, feeling better, I accompanied the doctors as they climbed up the mountain to a few caves where Tarahumara families lived. The only metal I saw was a few steel axes and a rare aluminum cooking pot. The caves were shallow, clean, and virtually empty except for a little firewood stacked near the entrance. Our interpreter announced that the doctors were available to treat anyone who was sick or injured, but no one volunteered.

"I don't think they understand what you want to do," the interpreter said finally. "They don't understand why you are here." Imagine, I thought, if one day a group of witch doctors from some remote jungle showed up in Cleveland and went door to door, calling on people to bring out their sick for treatment. In time, the doctors gave up, and we drove the tortuous road back to the mission. I washed again and went to bed exhausted.

What I did not know at the time was that my stories, moving on the AP wires, were being picked up by papers all over the country. Papers in the East and Midwest ran stories that involved local doctors. Some papers found the whole effort worthy of notice. Still others, apparently fascinated by the news of a very primitive people living so close to the United States, ran stories that focused primarily on the Tarahumara. And the *Tribune* ran my stories every day. I was their very own foreign correspondent.

Some stories never lose their draw, and this was a classic example: a nineteenth-century story of good doctors taking medicine to primitive people. It would be too much to say that I held the nation in rapt attention, but the clipping service hired by the doctors did produce bundles of news clippings from papers all across the country. The doctors were thrilled. I was astonished by the reach of a national wire service.

On the trip home, we flew through terrible turbulence. In Truth or Consequences, a spa town between El Paso and Albuquerque, we landed for two hours to wait out a dust storm. I attributed my illness to the rough air, but the next day back at the *Tribune* I stood up to go to the bathroom and almost blacked out. I gripped the corner of my desk until I could focus again and knew I had to see a doctor. Within a couple of hours, I was connected to a strange, noisy machine that pumped chemicals through my sinuses.

"I don't think I have ever seen anything quite like this," my nose and throat specialist said. "But I think we can kill it."

The clear mountain stream I had used to wash the awful white dust from my nose contained a parasite that now seemed determined to eat my head from the inside out. I was relieved that my doctor seemed so certain he could cure me and baffled by how I forgot about the world of microbes in the middle of a story that often featured their work.

The AP bureau chief came around to say what a good job I had done and hinted that, if I ever wanted a wire-service job, he would be interested in talking to me. Looney treated me like a returning hero because, among other things, my trip ended Burrows's edict against flying to cover a story. Then Dr. Johnson came in with an envelope containing three $100 bills. I considered the situation and decided that the stories were done and done honestly. I saw no harm in taking the money.

At home, I became known affectionately as "IFC"—intrepid foreign correspondent.

CHAPTER TWENTY-FOUR

The rapid click of high heels on terrazzo caught my attention. I turned to see Phyllis, the county manager's secretary, waving frantically as she hurried toward me. "Mr. Moore! Mr. Moore!" she called. "You have a phone call from New York City!"

"New York City?" How would anyone in New York City know I was in the Bernalillo County Courthouse? I didn't know anyone in New York City. I hurried along behind Phyllis, trying to think who might be calling as she led me back to her office, where the phone receiver lay on her desk.

"Hello? This is Gerald Moore."

A deep baritone voice came over the phone. "Mr. Moore, before you make the mistake that most people make, my name is Miss MacPhail, Marion MacPhail. I'm calling from *LIFE* magazine."

Her voice was as deep as any man's, and despite the warning, I had trouble picturing a woman on the other end of the line. "Yes, OK. Hello."

"Don Moser brought your clips by the other week," she continued without further formalities. "We liked what we saw. We thought maybe you'd like to come to New York so we can look you over and you can look us over. What do you think?"

"I'd like to do that. Very much."

"When do you think you could come?"

My heart said, "This afternoon," but I quickly thought better. I'd have to make reservations and arrange time off from the paper. This was Tuesday. A week would be an eternity, but I probably needed that much time. "I could come next Monday or Tuesday."

"Oh, that soon?" She sounded surprised.

"Is that all right?"

"Yes, of course. That's good, actually. We are going to start running into vacations soon. I just thought it might take you a little longer to arrange your schedule."

"I'm sure I can come on Monday, but it will take most of the day to get there."

"We'll reimburse your travel, and we'll get you a hotel room. Let me give you my number and a number for my secretary. We'll talk again when your plans are firmed up."

We hung up, and I sat for a moment at Phyllis's desk, utterly stunned. When I came to, I saw Phyllis staring at me, clearly expecting me to share the news from New York City. "Just some business in New York. I'll have to go there next week," I said. I tried to dismiss the call as unimportant.

"You have business in New York City?" Phyllis looked at me as if I were a movie star.

"Nothing important," I lied. I knew that if I told Phyllis what was going on, she would tell Nunn, and he would tell someone else, and in a day or two word would be back to Looney that I was trying to get another job. That would be all right if I got the job. It would not be all right if I didn't and had to go on working for a paper that knew I tried to leave. An interview was a long way from a job. But if *LIFE* magazine thought I was worth an air ticket to New York and a hotel room, which I found astonishing, then the job was probably mine to lose.

Since the day Bonavita told me about the *LIFE* stringership, I had pushed and schemed for this to happen. Now I was shocked. The difference between what I wanted and was willing to work to get and what I actually expected to achieve was a large and more or less permanent dichotomy in my life. I found it hard to imagine that people like me actually wrote and edited magazines like *LIFE*. I always imagined, without close examination of the thought, that there were adults, genuine grown-ups, running things in New York and Washington. People like me were a sort of faux grown-up. Had Bonavita not demonstrated that people like him, people like me, could work at the level of national journalism—had I not recognized our common qualities when I met the network television crews at White Sands—I would never have imagined it possible. When the opportunity for the stringership opened, I went for it with all I had without ever really believing I would get it. I kept asking for things and being surprised when I got them. There was a sense in which it was alarming to know that people with my level of ability were running important enterprises.

I tried to call Sally at the university, but she was away from her desk. I had to contain my news until four o'clock, when I picked her up in front of the library. She had barely settled into the car when I said, "*LIFE* magazine called this afternoon. They want me to come to New York for an interview."

"They what?"

"They want me to come to New York for an interview. Next week."

"As in, they want to offer you a job?"

"That's what it means."

I could see that the news came as a shock, perhaps as great a shock as it had to me. My success at White Sands and in Mexico had been fun but changed nothing fundamental. The thought of moving to New York and going to work for a national magazine changed everything. Sally looked excited and frightened.

"I can't quite make myself understand this is real," she said. Then, without lingering over the metaphysics, she moved on to the more important question. "What will you wear?"

Once again, thanks to Bonavita's fine example of how a young man should dress to succeed circa 1965, I had all the clothes I needed, but for some reason that I have never unraveled, I decided I would also need an umbrella. Why I thought I would need an umbrella in New York in July remains mysterious, but it was probably a good thing, because our two-hour search through every department and specialty store in town burned off lots of nervous energy. It was nearly time for dinner when we concluded what should have been obvious: with an average annual rainfall of 9.4 inches, most of which fell on three afternoons in July or August, no one needed an umbrella in Albuquerque.

We treated ourselves to a big Mexican meal at one of the tourist traps in Old Town where the decor was great and the food passable. Anxiety more than anything else characterized our conversation that night. Could we afford to live in New York? Where in the city would we live? What if I got the job but couldn't do it? What then?

We were very comfortable in Albuquerque. I was doing well at the paper. Sally would be invited to pursue a doctorate in history. We loved Corrales and our rambling house. I sensed that Sally would want to begin a family soon, which would be much easier to afford in Albuquerque than in New York. And though Cathy would soon be in Seattle, I would be closer to her in New Mexico than in New York. There were many good reasons to stay, but I felt a powerful desire to go. The siren call of the big time came before I had time to order myself lashed to the mast.

I spent the week trying to imagine what the interviews might be like and what I might be asked. Eventually, I conjured up a scenario that involved a formal interview before a panel of editors, something like the oral exams for an advanced degree. The scenario I imagined was, of course, completely wrong.

TWA, the only airline then serving Albuquerque, had once been a part of a plane-train system for making the two-day crossing from New York to Los Angeles. Planes did not fly at night, so they landed in Albuquerque late in the day and passengers were put on the *Santa Fe Chief* to travel to California through the night. Service had improved by 1965, but not as much as one might hope. To reach New York, my plane made two stops, one in Kansas City and a second in Saint Louis. On Monday morning, Sally drove me to the airport. Filled with uncertainty, I boarded my flight.

The strongest memory I have of that journey is the greasy, yellowish cloud of pollution that spread in the early evening light above New York and New Jersey. It looked for all the world like an oil slick on water, the particulate matter so dense that it refracted light into the spectrum of colors. Rather than being repelled by the sight, I took it as a sign of passage into the fast-moving, tough, urban East. As we plunged through the miasma, I felt my spirits expand almost to bursting. I was in the Arena, and that was where I wanted to be. Miss MacPhail had booked me into the New York Hilton, just two blocks up Sixth Avenue from the Time-Life Building. I was due at her office at 10:30 the following morning.

Wearing my best dark-blue summer-weight wool suit, a white cotton shirt, a simple red tie, and well-shined oxblood wingtips, I found my way to the twenty-ninth floor and Miss MacPhail's office, where I introduced myself to an attractive young woman whom I took to be MacPhail's secretary. Realizing that I had arrived, Miss MacPhail herself ordered me, in a very commanding voice, to come in and sit down. I settled myself before a big, efficient woman wearing heavy horned-rim glasses. She could have been a school principal or chairwoman of the League of Women Voters: formidable, informal, almost overwhelming in her self-assurance. As chief of research, she commanded a very large and well-appointed office with a view toward the Empire State Building and Lower Manhattan. I think I appeared calm, but she must have sensed my tension, because she made easy conversation as she inquired gently about my interests and background, my opinions and my ambitions.

"During the course of the day," she said, "I'll introduce you to three of our assistant managing editors. They're the people who make the hiring decisions. They're nice guys. Don't be intimidated by them."

Later on I would come to understand that she was a person who never, ever revealed the full range of her power. Without her approval, the editors she spoke of would not hire me. Over the years she had been involved in hiring so many members of the editorial staff then working at *LIFE* that she had become a kind of tough but loving den mother to the whole crowd of researchers, reporters, and editors. Had she been male, I would say she was avuncular. Somehow the female counterpart just doesn't convey the same combination of authority and warmth.

I honestly do not remember the morning interviews. I am sure they were with Roy Rowan and Ralph Graves, both then assistant managing editors. What I remember best is being back at MacPhail's office as lunchtime approached.

"I suppose you have dozens of friends in New York who you are meeting for lunch," she said.

"Actually," I admitted, "I don't. Is there a decent place to eat nearby?"

"You don't have a lunch date?"

"No."

"Well, then," she said decisively, "come with me. There's a little hamburger joint around the corner that I like. We can go there."

She adjusted her lipstick, went to the bathroom, found her purse, and in short order we arrived at Toots Shor's, the fabled bar where the likes of Joe DiMaggio, Frank Sinatra, and Jackie Gleason mingled with the city's sportswriters, gamblers, politicians, and other "crumb bums." Toots himself greeted us in cheery good humor. "Hello, Miss MacPhail, come in!" Then, looking at me, he went on. "And this must be Mr. MacPhail." He ushered us to a table for two.

I didn't know what to think. Luckily, I said nothing. I followed MacPhail's lead and ordered a martini, though I suspected this was a bad idea since I still had an interview to complete.

"So, Gerald, what does your father do?" she asked.

"He's an electrical engineer," I replied, feeling justified in the misrepresentation because his job running Tucumcari's electrical-generation facility qualified him through experience and responsibility for the title. After all, there were many graduate engineers who were doing far less technical and demanding work. And when not so many years later he was placed in charge of all electrical-power generation for the Military Assistance Command in Saigon, I would regard my answer as having been prescient.

I was intensely curious about MacPhail's history, and in spite of thinking it cheeky, I asked her the same question.

"Oh," she said, with utmost casualness, "my father owned a bunch of little midwestern banks."

She could have said, perhaps more accurately, that he also owned baseball teams, like the Brooklyn Dodgers and later the New York Yankees, but we were each enjoying a little leeway in describing our father's occupation.

What she left me to discover on my own was that her grandfather had founded twenty-odd banks in Michigan and left an enormous fortune to his son, Larry MacPhail, who became the owner, general manager, and president of the Brooklyn Dodgers and later the New York Yankees. Her brother Lee was, among other things, president of the American League. He, along with his father, would be inducted into the Baseball Hall of Fame, the only father-son duo to be so honored. Her brother Bill, president of CBS Sports, had introduced the instant replay to televised sports just two years earlier. But what did I know?

Oh yes, her husband, Dr. Walsh McDermott, was a venerated figure in medical research related to infectious diseases and a professor at Cornell University Medical College. She told me none of this. She never even hinted that she lived at the nexus of the American establishment. She was just "Miss MacPhail," whom Toots Shor enjoyed kidding.

"Ready for another martini?" she asked, as we worked on our enormous hamburgers.

"Um, sure," I said, thinking that I better keep up. I was already feeling a heavy buzz from the first round, but I assumed that whatever Marion was doing was how it was done, and I had better follow suit. Our waiter was a man who had waited on Miss MacPhail before. Two fresh drinks arrived almost as quickly as I nodded assent.

We wandered casually over various topics. She asked me what I thought of John Lindsay, then a candidate for mayor of New York. I answered safely, I thought, by saying he seemed like an attractive man, a man who could win. We talked about current affairs and about theater. My regular reading of the Sunday *New York Times* put me in decent shape in this regard. I at least knew what was playing on Broadway.

I couldn't finish my second drink. When she noticed it lingering, MacPhail said, "Had enough?"

"Yeah, I still have another interview."

She reached across the table and dumped my leftover gin into her glass. I was never sure if the drinking was a kind of test to discover if I drank and if I could hold my liquor or if that was just a typical *LIFE* magazine lunch. When she relieved me of the rest of my drink, things seemed to change very subtly between us. She took me seriously under her wing.

"When you interview with Phil Kunhardt this afternoon," she said, "no matter what happens, just keep talking."

Being coached, I felt sure, was a very positive sign. If MacPhail was willing to give me advice, even the slightest help, that must mean she was on my side.

We made our way back down Sixth Avenue and up to Kunhardt's office, where a tall, athletic man about ten years my senior looked up from the work on his desk as though our arrival was completely unexpected. It took him a few seconds to recover from his concentration. Then he stood. His greeting was minimal. I did not know at the time that he was a very serious amateur historian and Lincoln scholar. I knew he had played football at Princeton because I had looked up all the assistant managing editors in *Who's Who in America* before leaving Albuquerque. (Somehow, I had missed the MacPhail dynasty in my research.) I sat down and waited. He remained silent for a full minute, apparently waiting for me to speak. Remembering MacPhail's advice, I started talking. It was like being in a boxing ring with a fighter I had never seen before. I made little conversational jabs and feints, hoping to draw him out or to get him to commit. My efforts worked, but very gradually. After fifteen minutes, we were talking about photographs and using photographs and words together. Ansel Adams came up, and Kunhardt asked me a few questions about the Indians in New Mexico. In half an hour, by which time I was exhausted but completely recovered from my lunchtime drink, Kunhardt ended the interview and sent me back to MacPhail.

"How did that go?" she asked.

"I don't know."

"Did you talk?"

"Yes, we talked about photography and Indians."

"Oh, well, then," she said seriously, "you'll be fine."

We had been at lunch from one to three o'clock, and I began my interview with Kunhardt at three thirty. It was now well after four, and I felt real fatigue creeping in.

"So," I said, resuming my seat in front of MacPhail's desk, "where do we go from here?"

"Give us a day or two," she said with alarming casualness. "I'll talk to the guys, and we'll get back to you. We might want you to come back for another round."

I had walked on eggshells since the moment I got off the plane. Now I dropped all caution. "Is there any chance you could tell me today? I've come a long way, and I have to tell you that waiting will be agony."

MacPhail studied me for a moment, pondering my request. "Wait out there," she said, indicating the area outside her office. I got up and went out. The door closed behind me. I sat down and looked at the pretty secretary who gave me a wonderful smile.

"Hi," she said. "My name is Brooke."

Though it seemed longer, I believe the door opened again in about fifteen minutes. MacPhail waved me in and indicated a chair. She returned to her desk and sat down very deliberately. My throat felt as if it might explode. She clasped her hands together on her desk and said, "May I offer you a job at *LIFE* magazine?"

I didn't say, "Oh, my God," because people didn't say that. I took a deep breath and exhaled slowly. I nodded my head slowly, affirming the news, and said, "You have no idea how happy this makes me."

"Welcome aboard." MacPhail stood up, offering her hand. "I'm glad you're going to be part of the circus."

I didn't want to seem so grateful that I lost my dignity, but my grin was very wide and I may have squeezed her hand a little too tightly.

"We can take care of the details later," she said. "You've got all the numbers. I'd guess you have some calls to make." She walked me to the elevators and said good-bye, waving as the elevator doors slid shut.

I returned to my room at the Hilton in a state of disbelief. It simply did not seem possible that a person who had no prospects—a divorced college dropout without a place to live—could, in two years' time, have acquired a wonderful wife, some self-respect, and a job at one of America's finest magazines.

I called Sally. The prospect of leaving Albuquerque and moving to New York overwhelmed our imaginations. There were just too many things to think about and to decide and to discuss. After an hour on the phone, we hung up, and I called my parents. They were pleased, but not nearly as pleased I had hoped they would be. My father had never regarded New York as a good place to live. I think he imagined it too ethnic, too European, not really American as he understood the word. He congratulated me quietly and put Mother on the phone. She was thrilled that one of her children would get such a prestigious job, but I think she was also thinking that we would be a long way away. In any case, she began immediately to give me advice about how to conduct myself to assure that I kept the job and succeeded. Her pointers ran to things like, "I just hope you'll make sure you get to work on time every day." When I hung up with them, I went down to the hotel dining room for dinner.

That may have been the loneliest evening I ever spent. I looked around the room and saw happy couples at every table, laughing, staring into each other's eyes, lifting wine glasses. I was alone, bursting with good news. Even when camping solo in the New Mexico desert, the big stars had offered more company than the faces around me. Now that I knew what sophisticated people drank, I ordered a martini. The gin was harsh and burned my throat. I finished it anyway. This was, I decided, a taste I should acquire.

After dinner I walked to the theater district and found a movie, *The Great Race* with Tony Curtis, Jack Lemmon, and Natalie Wood. It cheered me up. On the way back to the hotel, a heavy rain suddenly swept the streets, turning them a shiny black. I ran the last few blocks to the Hilton, arriving in my room wet and soon enough cold, as well as extremely annoyed that I had failed to find an umbrella in Albuquerque. There was no control to modify the air conditioning in my sealed room—no thermostat and no opening windows. Instead of complaining to the management as I should have, I spent half an hour in a warm shower before finding I was too excited to sleep.

CHAPTER TWENTY-FIVE

On the trip back to New Mexico I warned myself repeatedly against arrogance and the unpleasant smugness I had seen in friends who suddenly enjoyed a great professional leap forward. I walked down the ramp from airplane to tarmac and saw Sally waving energetically from the crowd. Despite all my earlier admonition, the laurel wreath appeared above my head and a sense of triumph overcame me. I gave a big arm-swinging wave to Sally and felt really fine.

Walking through the Sunport, arms around each other, we acknowledged a special bond, a secret we shared. We might be walking around Albuquerque looking like normal denizens involved in a daily routine, but we were not. At any moment, we might step into a phone booth and emerge as Big City People, Manhattan bound with great things ahead.

Driving in from the airport, I sensed that I no longer lived in the state where I was born. Something fundamental had changed twenty-four hours earlier in MacPhail's office, when I agreed to leave all this and cast my lot with the Eastern Establishment and the world it had created. Albuquerque looked the same, but I felt an entirely different relationship to it now. When Tucumcari was my reference, Albuquerque was vast and urban. With New York in my future, Albuquerque seemed small. In a spiritual sense I was homeless. I didn't belong to Albuquerque, and New York remained an enigma to be explored. My roots in New Mexico were deep but not fully nourishing. My roots in New York were entirely aspirational.

We elected to have dinner at home, where much of the conversation concerned parental reaction to our news. When I called my father from New York, a subtle disapproval in his restrained reaction troubled me. I was not entirely certain, but I guessed my decision to move east carried an element of implied disloyalty to southwestern culture—his culture. At our house, easterners were often a subject for mild ridicule when they were discussed at all: "Living back there, doing each other's laundry." The same disdain did not extend to people from California or southerners or people from the Midwest. It was just "easterners" who were thought to be arrogant or ethnic and odd.

The more I thought about it, the more regional prejudice I remembered. When we took our lambs to market, I inquired who ate lamb. We knew no one who ate lamb. With the slightly superior air of a beef eater, Dad said, accurately enough, "They eat it back east. The Jews and the Italians like it."

When I was ten or eleven, after reading a book about the Mafia, I tried to enlist my father in my sense of impending crisis. "Oh," he said, dismissing my concerns. "That's an eastern problem. It's just a bunch of Sicilians killing one another."

There were other instances, all innocuous enough, of his prejudice. He thought men in shorts ridiculous. He disliked people who talked too fast or wore hats with narrow brims or who seemed to be putting on airs. But mostly, I think, he felt intimidated by the East. He knew that the money and the power were there. He probably feared that my move east would result in my having less respect for him.

I never saw my father treat any person of any color or religion or national origin with anything less than complete respect. He genuinely admired his successful Italian, Spanish, and Jewish neighbors. His prejudices did not concern a person but a region, its culture, and a way of life. In time I would discover that he was not alone in this. In fact, my education in this regard began that night at dinner.

"Father would never, ever come to visit me in Albuquerque," Sally said, laughing. "He'll be in New York to see us thirty seconds after we arrive."

"He never came to see you?"

"Never! This is Hicksville. Who would appreciate his accent, his manners, the quality of his clothes? Who would tell him if the melon is good today? He as much said he regards Albuquerque as beneath his standards as a place to visit."

"Yeah, but what about you? You're here."

"It is not about me. It's about him."

"Right. I forgot."

A mutual feeling of vindication emerged slowly from our conversation.

Securing the job in New York settled many old scores. The doubters, the critics, those who had lost faith—like our fathers—were silenced, at least in our minds. Whatever they had thought or said was now nullified. Getting the job in New York was like getting baptized; we arose sputtering from the water with all our past sins washed away.

Sally did not understand her father, but she was able to predict his behavior with uncanny accuracy, a skill common to children of alcoholics. Jack didn't show up in New York thirty seconds after we arrived, but he and Sally's mother landed the second day we were in town. It turned out to be a very good thing.

Though he had chosen long ago to live in Los Angeles, New York was Jack's city. In the same way that my father felt we had abandoned his culture, Jack was thrilled that we had adopted his. He led us with unusual enthusiasm on a wonderful four-day tour of Manhattan. He walked us around the campus at NYU and pointed out the Washington Mews, where he believed faculty still lived. We walked Fifth Avenue from Washington Square to Rockefeller Center. That evening, we ate at Lüchow's, the famous German restaurant then on Fourteenth Street. I don't know that I had ever eaten anything strictly called "German food," but the fare, while delicious, did not seem especially foreign except for the amount of vinegar involved. What most impressed me was the sudden arrival of the whole Fonda family: Henry, Jane, and Peter. Henry looked just as he did in the movies. Jane, only seven months older than me, was stunningly beautiful, more beautiful in person than on screen, and Peter looked as cool as he would look in *Easy Rider* a few years down the road. They were quickly whisked into a back room, and we did not see them again. Astounding. I was eating in the same restaurant as the Fondas.

The next day, Jack took us to meet an old friend, Robert Russell, and his wife, Rinaldina, on West Fifty-fourth Street, across from the Museum of Modern Art. Russell had been nominated for two Academy Awards in the 1940s and 1950s, but his screenwriting career was now in a slump, and he had turned, unsuccessfully it seemed, to writing plays. He was coauthor of the book for *Flora the Red Menace*, which had just closed its Broadway run after only eighty-seven performances, losing most of the money its backers ponied up and Bob's hope for making some serious money on a long-running Broadway show. He was so obsessed by his anger at Liza Minnelli that he could hardly be sociable.

Awestruck to be in the presence of anyone who had written anything that appeared on Broadway, even for only eighty-seven days, I wanted to talk to him about writing. He wanted to talk about Liza, the "childish, spoiled, self-indulgent, arrogant, amateur" star who caused his play to fail. The fact that she had just won a Tony Award for her performance as Flora made his complaints less than credible, so I turned my attention to the apartment. Modest as it was, it looked down into the sculpture garden at the Museum of Modern Art. The experience created one of those odd associations that haunt memory; every time I visit MoMA and happen into the sculpture garden, I look up at the yellow brick building across the street and think of Bob Russell and Liza Minnelli.

We left Bob stewing and had a drink at the Top of the Sixes. We rode the Staten Island Ferry and went to One Fifth Avenue to meet another friend of Jack's, a Mad Man who led the Phillip Morris account for his ad agency and who was a member of the New York Yacht Club. This visit segued into a trip to the yacht club itself, where we were able to stand next to and stare at the actual America's Cup, now housed in a glass case. The case, we were told, was occasioned by an incident involving a well-oiled guest who grabbed the cup off its pedestal, bending the elegant, soft sterling-silver handle in the process; this was potentially a terrible scandal for a club that had taken custody of the now-iconic traveling trophy in 1851.

During the days of our orientation, we basically walked Manhattan from the Metropolitan Museum of Art on Eighty-Second Street to the Customs House and the Battery, from the Hudson to the East River, listening to endless bits and pieces of history in the process. "Look," Jack exclaimed, "there's Federal Hall, where George Washington took the oath of office as the first president. Look, there's Cooper Union, where Lincoln gave the speech that made him president. Look, there is the Bowery, where Steven Foster lived. . . . Greenwich Village, where Dylan Thomas drank . . . and Chelsea, where . . . ." The city came alive, vested with history and meaning and myth—Teddy Roosevelt's birthplace, Washington Irving's home, the mighty Rockefellers' Baptist church, Grant's tomb. By the end of our tours, I knew I had reached the nexus of something deeply American and important. Any doubts I had about coming to New York were gone. My task now was to stay.

Jack and Kay helped with that too. They knew a couple, Bob Russell's sister and her husband, who were part owners of an East Side apartment building where they occupied the penthouse. It was not the kind of building I would have chosen, left to my own devices, but we had a connection. The building, one of those absolutely characterless white-brick apartment buildings that are ubiquitous on the East Side, housed mostly airline stewardesses and other nomadic types who signed three-year leases and stayed six months. We agreed to take a one-bedroom on the fourth floor, becoming the fourth tenant on what remained of a three-year lease. The paperwork-passing responsibility from one tenant to the next was by then many dozens of pages long and required an hour to read. My new salary at *LIFE* was twice what I earned in Albuquerque. When I signed the lease on East Fifty-Third Street, I increased our rent by a factor of six. Even before our furniture arrived, Sally went looking for a teaching job.

CHAPTER TWENTY-SIX

Our lives now became surreal. We awoke each morning in an empty apartment. Our furniture, inexplicably delayed—lost, I suspected, somewhere between Albuquerque and New York—did not appear in spite of repeated, frantic phone calls to the moving company. We slept on cheap air mattresses found in a Modell's sporting-goods store, cooked in three cheap aluminum pots, and used the Manhattan phone directory and its companion, the Yellow Pages, as pillows to get our butts off the floor. We had clothing and little else.

Complicating our situation, Sally was snapped up by the New York City Board of Education the moment she appeared and was sent to teach American history at Mabel Dean Beacon, a vocational high school for girls on East Twenty-Second Street. Despite our circumstances, Sally managed somehow to look completely professional each morning as she left the apartment to catch the Lexington Avenue bus to her classroom.

Without furniture, life at home was very restricted. We lounged on our air mattresses to read. We spent the few hours we were home sitting on our phone books, eating, talking, and on one occasion sliding a bottle of port wine across the floor between us, congratulating ourselves on having made it to—not yet in—Manhattan. Big changes were only weeks away.

In my short time at the *Tribune*, I developed a surprisingly strong identity as a news reporter. The combination of telling people what was happening and outing bad guys appealed to all my tattletale instincts. I liked being a cop with a pen. The stories most satisfying to me were always about official misbehavior: unqualified justices of the peace, bribery, cronyism, misuse of public funds, district judges who failed to file income-tax returns. I liked hero stories too, when the heroes were real, like my doctors flying into Mexico to treat a forgotten people.

A tendency to be didactic is essential in a reporter, and I had it in abundance. Blah, blah, blah.

During my interviews with *LIFE*, I just assumed I would be assigned to report on news, public affairs, and national events, but I had missed a couple of clues along the way. I felt very left out when I first arrived at the Time-Life Building and found that the three other young reporters hired that same summer were assigned to the bullpen in Newsfronts, where they would fact check and report on hard news, while I was sent to the entertainment department.

"Moore on the Arts" had been a kind of spare-time project for me— enjoyable but not something I took to be essential to the serious business of a newspaper. Writing opinions about movies, music, and books was a challenge and very fulfilling, but at the time I never thought it was what I did best or that it was my most important function. As things turned out, it was the column that smoothed my path to *LIFE* and determined my assignment. George Hunt, our managing editor, believed that entertainment stories were critically important to the success of *LIFE* magazine and assigned some of his most able people (not necessarily me) to work in the entertainment department. While I imagined that my prospective employers were looking at my ability to expose wrongdoing, they were actually looking at my columns on the arts and imagining a creative entertainment reporter.

I soon learned I was wrong to be disappointed. I was made to feel welcome in the entertainment department and encouraged to eat freely from the huge cultural buffet that is New York City. I was offered tickets to every play opening in New York that fall and sometimes sent to see the pre-Broadway tryouts in Boston. Movie screenings were a must. Concerts, classical and otherwise, were often required listening. There was so much entertainment in New York that running full-time, sixteen hours a day, one could not experience it all. Still living out of suitcases, using our phone books for stools, Sally and I became regulars on Broadway, at the old Metropolitan Opera House, and at Carnegie and Philharmonic Halls. We saw two or three plays a week: *Man of La Mancha, On a Clear Day You Can See Forever, Marat/Sade or The Persecution and Assassination of Jean-Paul Marat as Performed by the Inmates of the Asylum of Charenton under the Direction of the Marquis de Sade, Royal Hunt of the Sun, The Country Wife, The Devils, The Odd Couple*. We were hungry for culture in Albuquerque. New York offered a surfeit. We hardly had time to change clothes between performances.

Sally was in heaven. Her students were streetwise, mostly ambitious girls from minority families. They responded well to her sharp sense of humor and her equally worldly point of view. They actually energized her for the potentially exhausting whirl of culture in which we now found ourselves. Sally loved classical music, opera, and theater. Now there was more than she ever imagined she would experience. It wasn't long before she could annoy her father (a favorite pastime) by exclaiming, "Oh, you must see such and such *when it gets to LA.*"

I wasn't expected to actually report on any of the performances. Unlike the newspaper, where no reporter ever did anything without the expectation of a story, the magazine could support reporters as they developed expertise, and in any case there was far too little space in the magazine to publish even 1 percent of the potential reportage from the staff. Even though the department was staffed by experts in every area of entertainment—people who knew drama, movies, music, and dance at a depth I would never achieve, all hungry to get their favorite story published—I was still free to attend any performance.

I quickly discovered that my colleagues in the department were all worthy of their own profile in any popular magazine. *LIFE*'s theater critic, Tom Prideaux, a Yale man (as was Henry Luce), was Jason Robards's first cousin and knew everybody in the theater world. Walking with him anywhere near Broadway was like accompanying Cary Grant on a walk down Sunset Boulevard. Everyone looked, spoke, and smiled. Prideaux had covered Broadway for *LIFE* magazine as long as I had lived, literally writing his first review for the magazine the year I was born.

Prideaux, as everyone on Broadway knew, was the guy who decided which musicals got the coverage. He was an absolute gentleman with a natural, easy ability to sense and acknowledge the needs of others. His manners were as natural to him as his bushy gray eyebrows and glittering blue eyes. Unlike me, he was utterly comfortable in any setting. Eating at a fancy buffet, he routinely dropped his silverware into the handkerchief pocket of his jacket to free both hands. He wadded his money into one big ball and stuffed it into his pants pocket. Provoked, he would whip off his jacket, throw it on the floor, and perform a perfect pantomime of an awkward angry man to the complete amusement of everyone in the department. He eased me through what would become one of my most embarrassing moments when he simply smiled a confused smile (and refrained from patting me on the head) when I asked him, as we returned from lunch one day, if he ever thought about writing something serious. By that, I think I meant a novel. He had been editor of the Yale literary magazine and 1930 class poet, written a respected book on theater history, and was at work on a book about the Romantic French painter Eugene Delacroix. The impertinence of callow youth seems the kindest way to explain such a stupid blunder.

Mary Leatherbee—Tom's dear friend and frequent companion, and for many years the de facto number two in the department—was a woman of enormous energy, taste, and concern. Blonde and tending toward the manic side of normal, she had already lived an astonishing life by the time I met her. I heard rumors first and then had it confirmed that this "crazy blonde woman," still very attractive in 1965, had interrupted a promising acting career in World War II to fly newly built bombers to Britain. I could picture Mary, the freshly minted WASP pilot, at the controls of a B-24 taking off from some airport in Michigan to deliver a bomber still smelling of welding flux and grease to some haggard American bomber crew in England. She would undoubtedly have worn exactly the right costume, probably something involving a long white scarf, as she gave the thumbs-up sign and cranked the 1,000-horsepower Pratt and Whitney engines that would take her to England.

Mary was one of a small, very elite, and largely unacknowledged group of women who ferried bombers to England through most of World War II, freeing male pilots to fly them into combat. Not that she would have avoided combat had she been allowed to fly bombing runs. Instead, being a woman in 1944, she towed targets to provide gunnery practice, and when the war ended, she went back to study acting at the Royal Academy of Dramatic Art in London. Through her older brother, Josh Logan, the ubiquitous producer, writer, and director of such productions as *South Pacific*, *Picnic*, and *Bus Stop*, she was directly connected to Broadway and Hollywood royalty. There was hardly a fact or an insight concerning the dramatic arts, no matter how clever or obscure, that had escaped the combined attention of Prideaux and Leatherbee.

Tommy Thompson, the entertainment editor and my direct boss, was an aggressive, high-energy, six-foot-six-inch storm of a man who was completely stagestruck, desperate to write a respected novel, in love with Natalie Wood, and one of the better reporters in American journalism. He became semifamous on the day John Kennedy was assassinated when he rushed to Dallas, where he had been, at age twenty-three, city editor of the *Dallas Morning News*. He quickly located Marina Oswald and convinced her to hide from the press under a false name in a hotel room he provided. Keeping her whereabouts secret, he negotiated exclusive rights for *LIFE* magazine to the story of her life with the killer. In any other environment, Tommy's awe-inspiring energy would have used up all the oxygen in the room, but in *LIFE*'s entertainment department in 1965, he was merely a commanding presence. Laura Bell and Ann Guerin covered dance and opera and brought a sense of ladylike restraint and sober reflection to the otherwise manic crowd inhabiting the southeast corner of the thirtieth floor of the Time-Life Building.

Then, on September 29, the Metropolitan Opera's National Company opened its first season, at Clowes Memorial Hall at Butler University in Indianapolis. Made up of younger artists, the company would tour America, bringing opera to audiences that would otherwise go without. It was an effort to encourage an interest in opera and to give younger performers a chance to sing major roles, not unlike the goals of the Santa Fe Opera. *Susannah*, an American opera by Carlisle Floyd about which I knew nothing, was to be the offering. I was assigned to cover the event.

With rented tuxedo, air tickets bought with my new Air Travel Card (which charged airfare directly to the magazine), and many butterflies swarming in my stomach, I made my way to Indianapolis, where Henry Groskinsky, "my" photographer, and I found the young singers of the National Company. Within an hour of our arrival, we were hanging out with beautiful young sopranos, rubbing shoulders with important opera people, and watching Rudolph Bing, a man whose behavior defined impresario. We mingled happily in the excitement of a national cultural event in a provincial setting. We set up photo shoots with various cast members and tried to cover the general social hustle and bustle that such an event entails. When the evening was done, we retired with the cast and various donors and supporters to a mansion in the suburbs, where the owner had tents erected on the manicured grounds of his estate. Soon more than two hundred guests were enjoying champagne and carefully prepared food in what was the most opulent setting I had ever seen. I was in a philosophical frame of mind, comparing my life that evening with what it had been just weeks before, when I suddenly found myself in conversation with our host, a very polished gentleman in his midfifties.

"You're the *LIFE* magazine reporter?"

"Yes. Yes, I am. What a nice party. Thank you for having us here."

"It is my pleasure entirely."

"Did you enjoy the performance?"

"It was wonderful. I really hope this National Company thing works out. It would be so great to have opera like this in Indianapolis."

"There seemed to be an audience for it. At least tonight," I said.

"Oh, I think there is an audience," he said. Then moving to a tone of confidentiality, he went on. "I know you people from New York think we are pretty provincial out here in Indiana, but we love the arts too."

With the dust of Albuquerque hardly off my shoes, I was being called a "New Yorker." It took a moment to think it through. If he was willing to think of me as a New Yorker, I would play the role, or try to. Honesty would have disappointed him. Part of his current pleasure was awing a reporter from *LIFE* magazine, showing his social skills and the depth of his resources. Impressing a reporter from New Mexico would have been no fun at all.

"No, no," I reassured him, assuming my new role. "We don't think people in Indianapolis are provincial at all. The Met knew there was a large and knowledgeable audience here when they decided to open in Indianapolis."

"Yes, well, I hope that's true," he said. "My wife and I have season tickets to the Met, you know, but opera is not an easy sell, even in New York."

We went on with our conversation about the financial vagaries of opera as I tried very hard not to be outed as a rube by a man of vastly superior knowledge of opera and probably the world. I was rescued when his beautiful, smiling daughter and perfect son-in-law arrived from a mansion down the way—the house he had built for them, he said, to keep them close. He excused himself and left me to enjoy my champagne and to wonder about being thought a New Yorker.

CHAPTER TWENTY-SEVEN

It was just after 2:00 a.m. when the buzzer rang. A tired southern voice announced that he had our furniture. I looked out the window to see an enormous green and yellow Mayflower van four stories below, blocking Fifty-Third Street.

"It's two in the morning," I said, incredulous.

"I know, I just got here. I got to get you unloaded and get out of here."

From the panic in his voice, I guessed he had never driven in New York. "You have someone to help?"

"No, just my wife. You're gonna have to help me."

Sally was awake, listening to my conversation. "Can't he come back tomorrow?"

"Can't you come back tomorrow?" I said.

"No, no. I'm leaving town tonight."

"I'll come down."

I pulled on some clothes and went down to the street where I found a lanky, haggard man of my own age standing beside the idling truck. A sleepy, disheveled blonde woman studied us from the truck cab.

"I'll help unload," I offered, "but I don't think that was part of the deal."

"I hate this damned place," he said, ignoring my thrust.

"Yeah, well, I've been waiting for my furniture for a month. Where have you been?"

"You had this little bitty load. We put it up front 'cause you was first on and I kept gettin' sent to other places. I been all over the country since I loaded you."

"I had to wait all this time because my stuff was in the front of the van?"

"More or less," he said, pulling on his gloves. "You don't have a lot of things. It shouldn't take too long, except for that mattress."

I had forgotten our king-sized mattress and single-unit box springs, an ungainly package even in the spacious quarters of New Mexico. It could be a problem. A cab driver was already impatiently eyeing the space between the truck and the line of parked cars. Horns would start at any moment. I asked the driver to move the truck enough that a car could squeeze past. Even at two in the morning, East Fifty-Third Street, the Midtown exit off the southbound FDR Drive, was busy.

We hauled the heavy cardboard boxes awkwardly through the double doors of the building and into the elevator and up to our door. The work went fairly quickly until we discovered that the box springs would not fit into the elevator.

"Ain't there a big freight elevator or somethin'?" the driver asked.

"Nope. This is it."

We decided without discussing it that we would simply force the box springs to fit. And we did. I heard a lot of cracking and crunching as we bent the last corner of the springs through the elevator door. The struggle repeated itself when we arrived upstairs. Sweating and panting, I announced to Sally that when we left this apartment, the springs would stay behind.

We worked in silence for another two hours without any sign of the bond that mutual effort is supposed to engender. When we were done, he offered an invoice for me to sign. I signed and returned the paper.

"You move here?" he asked as he ripped off my copy.

"Yeah."

"From out west?"

"Yeah."

He shook his head in dismay. "I don't know why anybody would do that," he said. "I'd rather go to prison than live here."

One man's paradise is another man's hell. How to account for that?

It was nearly four when I went back to bed, still hoping to salvage part of a night's sleep. Sally greeted me holding shards of a mosaic lamp her sister had made for us, the first evidence of what would turn out to be major damage to all of our things as a result of a month in a truck and thousands of miles of bumps and turns. The next morning, we began a long and ultimately unsuccessful struggle with the moving company to recover some of our losses. We soon discovered that moving companies had lobbied the Interstate Commerce Commission, in the absence of any consumer representation, to achieve an almost liability-free relationship between shipper and customer. Our insurance would cover about 20 percent of the loss. We ate the rest. We simply threw out the broken plates and glasses—and one beautiful Pueblo pot—and wrote off the cost to experience.

At the *Tribune*, I would have written about this experience and felt better for it. Now I was in the big time, where there was no space and no audience for such discussions. I was a junior staffer at one of the great communication organizations in the world, and my personal ability to communicate was severely curtailed. In time, that gap between the things I cared about and the things my editors, often correctly, believed our audience wanted to read would prove to be a serious problem for me. It was a problem that would grow slowly and eventually turn deadly as the shine wore off my new toy. Part of my problem rested in an immature understanding of human nature. The famous H. L. Mencken quote "Nobody ever went broke underestimating the taste of the American public" would come to seem profound. But more important, I would eventually discover that I was not always happy to tell people what they wanted to know rather than what I thought they ought to know.

With the little furniture we owned in place, the apartment was much more comfortable and much, much smaller. Our big mattress filled the bedroom, leaving only a narrow, shin-skinning path around its perimeter. A small dining table and two chairs, a couch, and two Mexican-made wicker chairs took up most of the living room. Phyllis, Jack Stewart's penthouse-dwelling friend from upstairs, soon showed up with four really ugly op-art paintings made by an artist whose career she was supporting. We suppressed our distaste and hung the things just to civilize the bare walls. With furniture and some "art," we were finally at home in New York.

CHAPTER TWENTY-EIGHT

In September Pope Paul VI announced plans to visit New York, the first pope ever to set foot on North American soil. In a typically elaborate, if not actually grandiose, move, *LIFE* magazine planned to cover the pontiff from the time he got out of bed at the Vatican the morning of October 4 to board his plane in Rome until he landed there again at the end of a marathon one-day visit: fourteen hours in New York City. He would meet with President Lyndon Johnson at the Waldorf-Astoria Hotel, visit St. Patrick's Cathedral, visit Cardinal Francis Spellman, address the UN General Assembly, visit the World's Fair, say Mass at Yankee Stadium, wave to one million people gathered along the way, appear on television before one hundred million more, and never be out of view of a *LIFE* camera. The effort would require all of the *LIFE* staff. I was drafted for a pool of reporters who would team up with *LIFE* photographers and establish positions at every strategic point in the pontiff's itinerary. I was assigned to support photographers at two locations: St. Patrick's and Yankee Stadium.

On a perfect autumn day in New York City, I awaited the pope's arrival perched in an open office window in Rockefeller Center across Fifth Avenue from St. Patrick's. Days of work had gone into preparation for this moment. I got credentials from the NYPD and permission from the building manager. I scouted the various floors of the building to choose a window that could be opened at the right elevation with an unobstructed view of the cathedral entrance. I got Art Rickerby, my photographer, to agree that I had chosen the right spot. The day before the pope's arrival, we brought several large cases of photographic equipment up to the office and set up. As I made my rounds seeking permission to do unusual things, like take over an office in Rockefeller

Center and use an open window thirty yards away from the pope, I was struck by how much goodwill the public held for *LIFE* magazine. It was a phenomenon I would see over and over: a request made for *LIFE* was nearly always granted, usually with delight. People loved us.

I watched as Rickerby anxiously prepared for the forty- or fifty-second opportunity he would have between the time the pope left his limousine at the curb and disappeared through the high Gothic arch at the front of the cathedral. If we hoped to get a photo published in the eight- or ten-page essay the magazine planned, we would have to produce something to compete with the twenty-eight other *LIFE* photographers working that day, including the one riding with the pontiff.

It may have been the scent of camera oil or the sound of metal parts moving against one another that triggered in me a comparison of photography to hunting. There is equipment to be selected and tested beforehand, oiled and readied for the job. There is the selection and preparation of a position, the blind, where the photographer would lie in wait to shoot his subject. There is great anxiety that everything will work correctly at the appointed moment. (Often enough, it does not.) There is the uncertainty as to exactly how the subject will behave. Will it move fast or slow? Then there is the wait and ultimately the adrenaline-filled seconds when the subject appears and the motorized shutters whir and snap until the subject disappears. Had we been hunting big game, we would have seen the quarry go down or run away. Hunting with a camera just prolonged the tension. We would know if we were successful only when the film was developed and we could see the images. As I watched Rickerby, I wondered if he would agree with my comparison, that the verb "to shoot" when applied to photography was not accidental. There was no time for such idle speculation. When he was ready, we settled in quietly to wait.

A seemingly endless parade of New York City police officers preceded His Holiness, but in time the limo arrived and the man in white robes stepped to the sidewalk and began his measured trip to the door. Rickerby, who had photographed the Japanese surrender on the battleship *Missouri* and recorded the first-ever no-hitter in a world series game— and who would prove to be one of the best sports photographers ever to work—moved with polished precision between his various cameras until, at the final moment, just before he disappeared into the cathedral, the pope, seeming to sense our presence, turned and stood facing

Rickerby's cameras. The west facade of St. Patrick's rose in the background. The pope raised his hand and blessed us as Rickerby's cameras pumped 35-mm Kodachrome past the lenses.

"That absolutely has to be a cover," I said, feeling my heart pounding.

"What?" Art asked, still in his professional trance.

"The pope in front of Saint Pat's."

"I think I got it."

"I'm sure you did."

He began the process of retrieving film from half a dozen cameras, and within a few minutes I was on the way to the Time-Life Building, just blocks away, with the precious cargo.

I was wrong about the cover. A pope in front of a cathedral, even an American one, did not tell the story of a papal visit to America. A pope saying Mass in the middle of Yankee Stadium said, "Pope in America." I would not realize that, of course, until several days later, when the magazine was published.

The Rickerby film delivered, I headed to Yankee Stadium, where I met Bill Eppridge, one of *LIFE*'s youngest photographers. Eppridge was destined for a date with history three years down the road, when he would follow Robert Kennedy into the kitchen of the Ambassador Hotel in Los Angeles and snap the iconic photo of the mortally wounded senator lying on the floor beneath the ministrations of a distraught busboy.

Almost exactly my age but light-years ahead of me in experience and worldliness, Eppridge was utterly relaxed, confident, and self-sufficient. He exhibited none of the neurotic, worried concern I had come to expect in *LIFE* photographers. By contrast, he was sardonic, nonchalant, happy, and busy. A slender, focused man wearing aviator glasses, he had everything under control by the time I arrived. The idea of "supporting" his efforts quickly became ridiculous. I tried to make myself useful by getting us coffee.

The closest I had ever been to Yankee Stadium was listening to radio broadcasts of Yankee games when I was a kid. The structure alone, with all its history, was enough to create a sense of awe. Here I was, in Yankee Stadium. It was another moment in the amazing journey that my life had become.

I hesitate to estimate the number of nuns crowded into the stadium, but it seemed literally to be filled with women in habits, each bearing a cheap flash camera. So here was this great cathedral of sports, now filled with nuns as excited as a crowd of teenage girls gathered outside the Warwick Hotel when the Beatles were there. Surveying the scene, I felt grateful for the opportunity to be present and grateful that I did not have to write anything about it. How would one make sense of it all? Yes, it was a historic visit by the pope, and the pope was the head of an enormous congregation of faithful and not-so-faithful Christians. He was going to say Mass, evoking the name of Jesus and his solemn sacrifice, but the event had all the emotional trappings of a really big rock concert. When Paul VI appeared at the improvised altar, now occupying a place normally used for second base, the stadium exploded in a near storm of flashes from tiny cameras. None of the light would carry far enough to improve a photo, but collectively the flash cameras disrupted the ambient light so much that I heard Eppridge cursing behind me.

"Son of a bitch," he exclaimed as he peered through a viewfinder. Looking up at the constant twinkling of flashes, he asked, "What the fuck is going on?"

"Everyone has a flash camera."

Eppridge retrieved his light meter and tried to make sense of the phenomenon. "This is not good," he said. "The light's not steady."

"What can you do?"

"I'll have to bracket everything and hope for the best."

I don't know if he changed shutter speed or aperture settings or both, but he got very busy firing shots and readjusting his Nikons. We had a lot of time. The Mass took its allotted hour. Eventually, the spectators began running low on flashbulbs, and everything settled down so that Eppridge worked with more confidence.

At the half-hour mark, we handed his exposed film to a motorcycle messenger swathed in black leather and gleaming studs who ran it to the lab in Midtown. When the event ended, we packed Eppridge's gear and made our way to his Aston Martin DB5, which he had managed to park in a restricted area next to the stadium. What followed was one of wildest rides of my life. There was an urgency to get the film delivered and processed to assure that his photos were among those considered for the essay, but Eppridge drove as though we had a badly bleeding man stuffed in the trunk. I was concerned as he sped through the Bronx, but when we hit Central Park and the bending streets leading to Fifty-Seventh Street, I was in a panic—not just because I thought he might kill us but because I really thought his driving was so over the limit that he would be jailed if we were stopped. The Aston Martin's tires shrieked on the shiny black pavement as I watched shrubbery flashing past. Luckily, it was late enough and cold enough that the park was almost abandoned. Somehow we emerged onto Fifth Avenue without a cop in sight. I acted as cool as I could, as if I had driven through Central Park at eighty miles an hour many times. I didn't discuss the ride until later in the week, when I remarked to an older reporter that Eppridge was an impressive driver.

"Oh," he said. "I could tell you some stories."

The pope flew home that night after what everyone agreed was a triumphant visit. *LIFE*'s new and very expensive high-speed color presses enabled the magazine to hit the newsstands on Friday, five days after the event, with page after page of stunning, intimate photographs. Before the following week was over, another five and a half million copies would land in mailboxes around the country. The enormous effort seemed wholly justified.

That the entire visit had been covered live and in color on three television networks drained away some of the excited curiosity that always greeted *LIFE*'s appearance before the arrival of television, but page after page of gorgeous still photographs, produced by twenty-eight of the finest photographers in the world, allowed readers to savor the event at their leisure, to examine detail and revisit special images. It was on this unique experience that the strategists at Time-Life were counting to keep the magazine viable with readers and advertisers.

CHAPTER TWENTY-NINE

The fluorescent lights in my office flickered nervously and then steadied. They flickered again and dimmed and then came back. I knew from power outages in Albuquerque that we were experiencing a drop in voltage and that in all likelihood the lights would go out in the next few minutes. I went to my door.

"Looks like we're going to lose the lights," I announced casually.

It was just over a half hour before the end of our workday, and my colleagues were busy finishing up various projects in anticipation of a six o'clock departure. Ann Guerin looked up from her work, smiled indulgently, and went back to work.

I left my cubicle and walked out into the public area of the office suite. "I think we're going to lose the lights," I repeated, a little louder.

Laura Bell looked at me as if I were losing it. "The lights don't go out in New York, Gerald," she said firmly, stopping just short of calling me a hick.

I was trying to decide whether to argue my case when suddenly we were in the dark. Everything stopped. Tom Prideaux came out of his office and looked around to see if the outage was general. Mary Leatherbee rushed out into the hall and returned to announce that the light were off on the *entire* thirtieth floor. Everyone went to the windows and saw Manhattan without illumination. The sun had already disappeared over the Hudson River, and we were rapidly losing the little twilight that remained. The realization arrived slowly that the metropolis might be without electricity.

"I see some buildings way downtown that seem to have light," someone said.

"They have generators," came the reply.

I was used to losing electricity, but I had never thought of the consequences of losing power while on the thirtieth floor of a Manhattan skyscraper.

"I guess we'll just have to have a drink and wait for the power to come back," Prideaux said.

I would discover that this was essentially the default mode at Time Inc. When we were confused, delayed, or otherwise bumped temporarily off course, we had a drink. The office of every department head was provided with a well-stocked liquor cabinet. By "well-stocked," I don't mean Dubonnet and brandy. I mean lots of scotch, bourbon, and vodka. Only serious drinkers were accommodated. Within a few minutes, someone had found his way in the dark to the ice machine and we were happily drinking and speculating on how long it would be before power was restored. It was exciting. It was different. It was fun, in the beginning.

We began to get reports from other offices where battery-powered radios were available. Most of the larger radio stations—WCBS, WABC, and others—had emergency generators that kicked in almost immediately. Their problem was not power, it was information, but slowly a picture emerged of an Eastern Seaboard without power. The blackout reached all the way into Canada.

We sat in the dark, drinking and talking by the light of little birthday candles that someone had saved from an office cake. Even burning them one at a time, they lasted less than an hour. The idea of spending the night in my office was not appealing, but that option was being seriously discussed. We were all feeling helpless, as if we simply could not do anything without power. In the back of my mind I knew that I was not really trapped. I could walk down the thirty flights of stairs in the dark if I simply took my time and felt my way. About seven o'clock, I decided I should not drink anymore because the stair walk was looking more and more like the only alternative to sleeping on the thin, not terribly clean carpet in my office.

Then word came that a large group of people was organizing to walk out of the building. We collected all the grease pencils we could find and went to the stairwell. Grease pencils burn with a dim smoky flame, produce toxic fumes, and drip hot red wax on clothes and fingers, but they will produce enough light to reveal stairs, once one's eyes have adjusted to the dark.

I was reminded of a scene from an old Tom Sawyer movie where the townspeople carried torches as they searched a cave for Tom and Becky. Ahead of me, a long line of writers, editors, researchers, secretaries, and photographers stretched down the stairs, moving slowly and carefully from stair to stair, a grease pencil flickering in the hand of every tenth person or so. Step by step, landing by landing, we made our way to the lobby. The trip was longer and harder than I had imagined, but soon enough we were free.

Outside, a full moon cast a dim light over a general air of carnival. Ordinary people stood in the middle of intersections directing traffic. Bars were crowded. Hotel lobbies were full of people who could not get to their rooms because the elevators were dead. They didn't seem to mind. People were drinking, excited, and having fun. All by candlelight. Where, I wondered, did all the candles come from?

I was fortunate to live only blocks away. Some of my colleagues were walking home across the Brooklyn Bridge. Others had a long hike to the nether regions of Queens. People living in the suburbs mostly elected to spend the night on their office floor, hungry and uncomfortable, unable to get supplies because no one was admitted back into an office building after leaving. When I arrived at our apartment house, I found the front doors propped open to defeat the electric locks that normally operated them. Making my way up the stairs, I heard a commotion on the third floor. In the elevator lobby, three people were prying on the elevator doors and speaking to a person trapped inside.

"Want some help?" I asked.

"Yeah."

"You trying to get somebody out?"

"No, no. We just need to get these damned doors open enough to give him a drink."

A woman standing in the shadows held a martini. With my added heft, we opened the doors wide enough to permit the cocktail to pass through. Sounds of great delight issued forth from behind the thick doors.

"Will he be all right?"

"Yeah, yeah. We'll stay here and talk to him, give him another drink. The power should be back on before long."

I hurried on up the stairs where beside our door I found a candle burning in a saucer on the floor. A note taped to the wall read, "Come to PH. Jack and Phyllis serving drinks. They have candles."

Everyone expected that power would be restored at any moment, so the first several hours of excited social interchange by candlelight were pleasant enough, but as the night dragged on, a sense of boredom set in. As midnight approached, we said good-bye to Jack and Phyllis and several of our neighbors and went down to bed.

When we awoke at seven the next morning, we calculated from our electric clock that power had been restored to us at about 4:30 a.m. We had been without power for about eleven hours. With the disruption of everything familiar, it seemed like days.

Walking to work that morning, I felt a new sense of community. We had all been in it together, and we had turned it into a great party. I was almost sorry the power was back. There were people who had suffered, of course. The *Times* (printed in New Jersey) carried accounts of people in hospitals without power and of other emergency situations, but those individual hardships did not diminish the fact that New Yorkers had behaved decently when the normal social controls were gone.

Later that morning, I found myself pondering the blackout. Even though I was born in Albuquerque and lived there as a student, as an adult, as a police officer, and as a reporter; attended the birth of my daughter there; and passed other important milestones of life there, I never felt as close to that community as I felt to New York City the morning after the blackout, and I was still virtually a stranger here. What was that about? I would learn in time that I was not alone in experiencing this rather mysterious phenomenon. Many people find they have a sudden feeling of deep connection to a city where they have hardly any history.

Cathy's mother called just a few days later to say that being a single mother and a graduate student was getting her down. She wanted us to take Cathy. I jumped at the chance, and a week later we took a cab to JFK to meet a nonstop flight from Seattle. Cathy, just turned five, never looked smaller or more vulnerable as she walked hand in hand with a nice stewardess to where we waited. The sight of her in a beautifully cut, royal-blue wool coat, her long, dark hair shining—so small, so full of courage—brought me to tears. She had just flown six hours, essentially alone, and she pronounced the whole trip just fine. "They had me sit up front," she said. "They were very nice to me."

In front of our apartment, the tension caught up with her as we were getting out of the cab. She threw up. Not very much, but it was enough to signal the strain. Our cabbie, grizzled, in his sixties, seemed to sense the tenderness of the situation. When I asked him to wait so I could get a towel to wipe up the cab, he said decisively, "You go on. Take care of the little girl. I'll take care of the cab."

"Are you sure?"

"I'm sure. Go on!"

I did tip him generously, but he could have made an awful fuss about his cab and he didn't.

Cathy's arrival bumped up the pace of our lives by a notch or two. We were each new at our jobs, living in a new and challenging city, and now we had a five-year-old to shepherd. Cathy kept pace with a demanding schedule. It helped that only two months earlier she had been spending weekends with us. Sally, with uncanny skill, quickly found a suitable school, and we settled into a domestic routine. Luckily, our schedules accommodated Cathy's school day. I did not have to be at work until ten, long after Sally left for her eight o'clock class. Then Sally was free midafternoon to pick up Cathy from school while I worked until six.

The prospect of acquainting Cathy with New York excited me, and I found myself playing Jack Stewart's role, constantly pointing out things that probably made little impression on a five-year-old. There was one exception, however.

It was a clear, cold day when I put Cathy on my shoulders and plunged into the crowd along Sixth Avenue to give her a better view of the giant balloons floating above us. Like a lot of experiences in life, the Macy's Thanksgiving Day Parade was made worthwhile by the presence of a child. I'm not entirely sure what Cathy saw or felt, but as we watched the inflated characters floating down the street, tethered between rows of high buildings, I felt a lot of excitement on her behalf. She hung in until the end, and then, cheeks shining pink from the frosty weather, she said, "I'm cold, Daddy. Let's go home."

This was all too good to be true, of course. Hellyn, scolded by her mother for being a negligent parent, called before December was over and demanded Cathy's return. I considered the possibility of simply ignoring her request. Sally and I discussed the idea, and in the end we decided it was not in Cathy's best interest to go to war with her mother. With a lot of guilty explaining and reassuring talks, we arranged for Cathy to retrace her path and return to Seattle for Christmas. It was the saddest day I could remember since Hellyn and I had broken up.

CHAPTER THIRTY

I spent an afternoon in early December interviewing Leopold Stokowski in his sumptuous apartment overlooking Central Park. The maestro, now in his eighties, seemed no less full of himself than I understood he had been years earlier when he conducted great symphony orchestras, collaborated with Walt Disney on *Fantasia*, and squired Gloria Vanderbilt around Hollywood. With white hair; a round, pink face; and a refined demeanor, he tolerated the inevitably trite questions of an inexperienced young man from New Mexico, and he did this simply because my name was followed by the magic phrase, "from *LIFE* magazine."

I knew in advance that the meeting would never produce a story. When my editor, Tommy Thompson, sent me out to do the interview, I sensed that his motives were more managerial than journalistic. He knew Stokowski would be flattered that *LIFE* was still interested in him and his American Youth Orchestra, and Thompson knew that the assignment would keep me busy and perhaps relieve some of the boredom that had set in since the pope left town. For my part I was happy with the assignment because I was curious about this icon of classical music, and I was sure the interview would give me a chance to demonstrate that I could write a *LIFE* story.

Over the course of a long career, Stokowski had answered every question that could possibly relate to his life and work at least ten dozen times. I can't imagine how many hundreds of reporters had preceded me to the well, trying to offer an interesting query, trying to reveal some part of his life or personality that would interest readers or at least intrigue an editor. His repertoire of answers was as vast as his repertoire of music and as well rehearsed. I asked the questions. He recited the answers. I looked out his windows and admired the view of Central

Park. He indulged my amazement. I looked on as a student appeared for a lesson, no doubt a very advanced lesson. What I would recall about the place later when I sat down to write was how much white and gold I had seen. How very Hollywood 1938.

I worked hard writing the piece. It was difficult to bring anything current or topical to an eighty-year-old icon whose many accomplishments were mostly behind him and all well documented. Nor was *LIFE* magazine the right venue for a reinterpretation of his contribution to music, even if I had been capable of such an effort. Eventually I had done all that I could with the material and turned it in to Thompson.

Aware of Thompson's truly breathtaking ambition and his tendency to occupy all available space relating to entertainment matters, I made carbons of my text and circulated them to Prideaux and Kunhardt, our assistant managing editor, just to be certain that my first effort at writing for *LIFE* didn't disappear into Thompson's in-box to die a quiet death.

My strategy was sound. Thompson read the text, aware that other copies were in circulation, and made the pronouncement I most wanted to hear: "OK, you can write!" Then came the pronouncement I fully expected: "But this is not the right time for a story on Stokowski."

This was all fine. I had been given the opportunity to demonstrate that I could write. I had met a man of great talent and accomplishment. I had enjoyed a view of Central Park normally reserved for billionaires and their servants. I had established my right to circulate my work beyond my immediate boss. The tension and excitement of the assignment reminded me how much I missed actually being a reporter.

As the end of the year came hurtling toward us, I began to worry that I was not making any visible contribution to the magazine. There had been no pressure from anyone to produce anything, but I felt sure that hidden beneath *LIFE*'s collegial, laissez-faire management style was an organization in which initiative was prized and where, eventually, a group of senior people would sit down and tally up the contributions of the newly hired. Offering clever insights at editorial lunches, providing astute criticism of a new issue of the magazine, dressing for success, and the other secondary modes of participation were all well and good, but what was needed to relieve my growing anxiety was to write something, or conceive and execute with a photographer a photo essay that actually appeared in the magazine. I didn't see the opportunity for that in an entertainment department staffed by people who all outranked me in every way—in experience, contacts, and the skill of crafting a story idea and proposing it to the right editors. I was also bothered by what might loosely be termed my work ethic. I was only truly comfortable when I was in the process of producing something real. Sucking up culture on a *LIFE* expense account made me nervous. I decided the apprenticeship had gone on long enough. I had to take action. Kunhardt was the only person who could help me.

A man of legendary talent as an editor of photo essays, a man blessed with intuitive good taste the way some people are blessed with perfect pitch, a Lincoln scholar, a Princeton man, a college athlete, and a really nice guy, Kunhardt was also thought to be the most sympathetic of the assistant managing editors when personal matters were at issue. This reputation had the unfortunate result that many people chose Kunhardt's shoulder when they needed one to cry on. He heard complaints about how the magazine was run, how it was edited, how stories were selected, why we were or were not relevant in the "complex modern world." He was also, among other things, responsible ultimately for the entertainment department and therefore my top boss. One evening in mid-December, scotch in hand, I made my way to Kunhardt's office and planted myself in a chair in front of his desk. He paid no attention. After a few moments he looked up from the work that engaged him and gave me the "Kunhardt stare," a level, absolutely expressionless look that betrayed nothing but the notion that whatever you had to say should be worthy of the interruption.

"Phil, I was a reporter when you hired me. I like being a reporter. But I don't feel that I have been able to function in that way since I arrived here in September."

He waited, saying nothing.

"I love going to plays and screenings and concerts. I've learned a tremendous amount in a very short time. I work with wonderful people. In many ways, I have a dream job, but I really need some work."

The Kunhardt stare continued. My greatest fear at that moment was that he might say, "Well, then, go apply to the *Daily News*."

"I honestly don't know what to suggest," I said, hoping I had not gone too far. "But I need to do some honest reporting."

Without any change of expression, he straightened in his chair and lit a Marlboro. "You have to keep this to yourself," he said quietly. "You can't tell anyone." He waited for my reaction.

I nodded my assent to secrecy.

"We're shipping you out to the Los Angeles bureau in January."

I was speechless. There was no ambiguity about being promoted from reporter/researcher to regional correspondent. I would be assigned stories and expected to report on them. I would hold the same position that Joe Bride held when I called him off the GOP convention floor two years earlier to ask for the stringership. It was unimaginable that I was now to occupy the same position as the person I then held to be years ahead of me in his career as a journalist. I reminded myself that it would not be good to reveal how amazed I was by this news. I understood that to some degree I needed to convey a sense that I expected all this to happen, felt comfortable with it, and was, in general, just a bit blasé about the whole correspondent business. I didn't want anyone second-guessing a decision because I seemed surprised that they would think I could do the job. This may have been the first time that I consciously recognized a split in my psychological posture—a split that would grow wider and deeper as time went on—between how I felt inside and how I knew, or thought I knew, I had to appear on the outside. Had I acted solely on the emotions rolling around inside me, I would have come off as a kind of foot-scraping, forelock-tugging, "Aw, shucks, you shouldn't-a done it" kind of guy. Nor did I want to seem ungrateful. They were offering me a vote of confidence and a wonderful opportunity. Acknowledging the news, I tried very hard for just the right mix of gratitude, pleasure, and nonchalance—in other words, poise.

Kunhardt refreshed his drink from the bottle sitting on a copy table behind him. "I had a wonderful time in Los Angeles," he said. "You are going to have so much fun out there."

I kept hearing people talk about "having fun." I found the concept foreign. I was terrified most of the time—watching every move I made; constantly examining my thoughts and motives; assessing and reassessing my work, my dress, my tone of voice; watching for signs that other people liked, admired, and trusted me; or, God forbid, the opposite. Excitement? Yes. Challenge? Yes. Fun? That must be something you want to do again and again. I could think of almost nothing I had done professionally that I would want to do again. The important stuff was high tension and the unimportant stuff was drudgery. Going wilderness camping in early fall with a woman you love and a bottle of gin is fun. Staying in a first-class hotel in a capital city with a woman you love is fun. Manipulating the truth, or some version of it, out of a recalcitrant public official; stroking the swollen ego of a celebrity to collect the sweet golden residue they sometimes excrete; pretending friendship and solidarity with a subject, knowing à la Janet Malcolm (the journalist who blew the whistle on journalists), that the resulting article will in some measure betray their trust—these are acts of major emotional investment for anyone with any degree of moral development. I had heard many stories about escapades in California involving Kunhardt and Wainwright and large quantities of alcohol. These stories were the stuff of legend, but I was hesitant to think of them as "fun."

As much as I was heartened by news of the move to Los Angeles, the thought of leaving New York this soon distressed me. I wanted to work. I wanted to report stories, but I would have preferred to stay in New York. I had to face the reality that most of what we wrote about in *LIFE* did not happen in New York. California and Hollywood would offer dozens of stories.

Making my way back to the thirtieth floor, head filled with a hundred thoughts and tips of thoughts tumbling over one another, I remembered Sally. She would have perfect justification to feel put upon. Only months after moving to New York, settling into an apartment, and getting a job she liked, my career now required us to pick up and move again. But at that point in our marriage, she was still along for the ride. I had a hunch she would look at the news as an opportunity to go home in triumph. I was right, as it turned out. She left Los Angeles as the schoolteacher wife of a frustrated architecture student. She would return bearing a master's degree, with time spent engrossed in New York's cultural scene, as the wife of a "junior editor for *Time-LIFE-Fortune*," as her father liked to describe me. For the second time in less than six months, our lives were now filled with the energy generated by a happy anticipation—but our joy was not pure. We had fallen deeply in love with New York, and now, like newlyweds about to be separated, we had to say good-bye while our passions still ran hot.

The sense of loss at leaving New York grew more poignant just before Christmas when we wandered unexpectedly into an evening that infused our hearts and minds—infected us, really—and made us determined to return to the city as soon as circumstances would allow.

We left our apartment on East Fifty-Third Street a little after 7:00 p.m. that evening and walked uptown in the early darkness of late December to have dinner with John and Linda Kurland at their splendid apartment in the East Sixties. It was cold, threatening to snow, but not bitter. The glow of the city reflected off a smooth layer of low-lying clouds. We walked quickly, arm in arm, until we arrived cold and invigorated at the Kurlands', ready to drink a scotch and linger near their blazing fireplace. John's efforts to make a fire spoke of a special evening.

The Kurlands were stylish California transplants now very much at home in the New York entertainment world. Linda, a Hollywood princess, beautiful but chronically unhappy, came cursed with all the neurotic baggage often associated with that strange background. Her father spent most of his professional life as the number-two man at Twentieth Century Fox, a surrogate for Darryl Zanuck. She desperately wanted to live up to his achievements but had no idea how. John's past was harder to determine, except that he had enjoyed early success in the record business, came from an affluent family, and had evolved into a publicist, producer, and general dealmaker for a circle of musicians that included many of the Brill Building crowd, such as Barry Mann and Cynthia Weil, who had just written (with Phil Spector) "You've Lost That Lovin' Feelin'."

I met John soon after my arrival at *LIFE*, when he called to introduce himself to the new entertainment reporter and to tout his clients. We had lunch a few times and soon became friends, independently of our mutual interests in placing a story in *LIFE*. Sally and I were pleased and touched when the invitation came for a pre-Christmas dinner.

The other guests were Millie Perkins—the actress best known at the time for her portrayal of Anne Frank—and Millie's husband, Robert Thom, a screenwriter, director, and ex-husband of the actress Janice Rule. Linda's mother was there, aloof and imperious. Jake Ross, an editor at Doubleday, articulate and opinionated, and his wife, Shirley Kaplan, an artist, playwright, and illustrator of Broadway show bills, made a fourth couple. Pauline Kael, already well known in New York for her film reviews but not yet at the *New Yorker*, came alone as well.

Witty conversation, show-business stories, good food, and the best wine I had ever drunk—it all delighted me. Sally seemed to feel perfectly at home. She had grown up around entertainment chatter and accomplished people, but for me this was like being admitted into a coveted fraternity. These were the people who actually wrote, produced, and acted in movies, the only dramatic medium I had experienced in any depth before Sally and I began regular attendance at the Santa Fe Opera. These were the people, in John's case, who brought us the music we heard on the radio. I was, for an evening at least, engaged with the people who made popular culture. It was a short arc from writing about these things in Albuquerque, where the process of their creation remained mostly mysterious, to John and Linda's dinner table, where I could listen to the attitudes and strategies of their creators. This was what I had come to New York hoping to experience, and now had to leave. After dinner, we gathered near the fire for more alcohol and conversation.

It was near midnight when we said good-bye and left. During the evening, a foot of snow had fallen. The city was pristine, covered in a fresh layer of white fluff that hid every flaw. All the corners and hard edges were now softly turned or hidden. It was as if we had walked into a sanctuary, preternaturally quiet and peaceful. The cold air revived us from the torpor of rich food and wine, creating a kind of euphoria.

We made our way slowly down to Sutton Place, where we found a balustrade overlooking the East River. We stood there watching the snow fall, the big white flakes disappearing into the dark water of the river.

CHAPTER THIRTY-ONE

Without formal training in journalism, it took me a while to understand that when a large number of people start to do something they have not previously done, it is called a "trend"—or less politely, a "fad"—and that these phenomena are news. Trends do not normally begin in places like Albuquerque, Des Moines, or Chillicothe, and so reporting for a local paper I had not been instructed to watch for this sort of group behavior. In Albuquerque, our task was binary. Either we should find things of which we approved: hero firemen, lower taxes, beauty queens, real-estate development, tough sheriffs, and all things American. Or we should seek things of which we disapproved: higher taxes, wasteful government, most crime, foreign style, and anything that smacked of socialism. National journalism, by contrast, thrives on reporting trends and fads, and so it was that, arriving in Los Angeles, I was immediately assigned to accompany a photographer, Lawrence Schiller, to document the fact that large numbers of people were suddenly dosing themselves with a newish and highly psychoactive drug called LSD.

Larry, an aggressive photojournalist who understood his market the way Bill Gates understood the market for software, had arranged to cover an LSD party where half a dozen twenty-somethings had agreed to be photographed while tripping. The drug would not be outlawed until later that year, so being photographed while using it was not thought to be particularly risky. This cooperation was also smoothed, I learned later, by free acid, cold cuts, and a safe place to trip. Larry made the arrangements, but if he hoped to sell the photos to *LIFE*, he needed a reporter along to provide some supporting words and verification that the event was authentic. Moser, my rabbi, was still the Los Angeles bureau chief, though he would shortly depart for Hong Kong, Saigon, and the Vietnam War, where nearly a quarter of a million US troops were fighting. Moser briefed me quickly and, without much fanfare, sent me off with Schiller on what turned out to be my first truly national story.

I had heard of LSD, of course. Articles from *LIFE*'s comprehensive clipping service included accounts of the dismissal from Harvard University of Dr. Timothy Leary and Richard Alpert (later Ram Dass) for providing LSD to people who were not officially involved in any research project, some of them underage. There were also reports of serious research projects that sought to find psychiatric uses for the drug. Though details were still secret, the navy and the CIA were experimenting with LSD, hoping it would prove to be a truth serum. Rumor also had it that Aldous Huxley had used the drug as an extension of his interest in the mystic and religious aspects of drugs first discussed in his book *The Doors of Perception*. What I did not know was that Henry Luce, the founder of Time Inc., and his wife, Clare Booth Luce—former ambassador to Italy, paramour of Joseph Kennedy Sr., friend and adviser to Richard Nixon, hard-right Republican, and probably the person who first conceived of the picture magazine *LIFE*—had also taken LSD.

I don't know when they first became interested in the drug, but when they decided to try it, they did what powerful people often do: they called a leading expert and told him what they wanted. Dr. Sidney Cohen, associate professor of psychology at UCLA and LSD expert, flew out to their Arizona retirement home and delivered the drug and some guidance about its use. Clare was later quoted as saying it "saved" her marriage. Henry would reveal his experience in a surprisingly nonchalant manner two years later before the entire *LIFE* staff assembled for a celebratory dinner at the Plaza Hotel in New York City. Personally, I had been completely unaware of the drug, although I had once experimented with peyote and smoked pot half a dozen times while in Mexico. I had a healthy respect for and fear of drugs, except for alcohol, and only considered for the briefest moment taking the drug to better report the story.

A few days after meeting Schiller, now armed with my newspaper clippings (the only contemporary research source then available), I climbed into Schiller's black Mercedes diesel sedan and fell down the rabbit hole into Wonderland.

We drove to a nondescript one-bedroom apartment in a complex somewhere in Hollywood, where we met six very nice young men and women who had assembled for the "trip." Soon enough, they downed the little white pills that were passed around and conversation stopped. Had Schiller and I gone to an apartment to observe and photograph half a dozen people getting drunk or high on pot, the possibility of serious boredom would have concerned us, but somehow we imagined that watching people trip would be different.

It was different. It was worse.

If we had been observing drinking or smoking pot, there would have been some social interaction: conversation, debate, a display of sexual desire, fights, great laughter—something. Watching six people tripping on acid was more like being in a room with six people sleeping—people who, on occasion, cried out from a nightmare or laughed out loud before settling back into peaceful staring.

The drug seemed to pull each person deep into an inner space where communication was neither desired nor possible. Our subjects sat on couches, chairs, or on the floor, and simply stared. Occasionally, there was a noisy outburst or moaning and crying. I could see Schiller desperately looking for something to photograph. When one young woman cried out and bit her hands, Schiller leaped into action, shooting a roll or two of film. Otherwise, the photographs were distinguished more by the ingenuity of their angles and lighting than by any real information.

Sometime after midnight, the lonely cold cuts began to dry out. The bread grew hard, and my head started to ache. I made a few notes, but since no one wanted to talk about what was happening, I was left to describe the physical scene and to record my own imagination. Schiller, growing insufferably bored, taped a camera so that the setting could not be changed, handed it to me, and said, "If anything happens, shoot a few frames." Then he left for home.

Around three or four in the morning, with the acid wearing off, people returned slowly to the world I inhabited. Mostly, they were exhausted and not interested in giving details of their experience. Descriptions tended to be single words or exclamations: "amazing," "scary, but wonderful," "terrible," and "I can't think right now."

As people fell asleep or drifted away to their daily lives, I bummed a ride with our host, who had not tripped, and arrived at my new Brentwood apartment a little after four. Sally woke up when I let myself in.

She watched me undress and then asked, "What happened?"

"Nothing," I said.

Day by day over the next two weeks, Schiller and I became more plugged into the world of LSD. Connected to the grapevine, we heard news of upcoming events, and names like Owsley and Kesey and the Merry Pranksters. It became apparent to me that either the network of people using and interested in using LSD was vast and unknown or that experimenting with the drug was a phenomenon moving rapidly and exponentially into California's population of young people. In either case, I knew I was onto a big story. The problem for me was how to tell it. The "trippers" didn't make great pictures, and so far I had not encountered anyone who was especially articulate about the experience. I had read *The Doors of Perception*, Huxley's book about his experience with mescaline, but I was not sure that it was right to extrapolate from one drug experience to another. Huxley was dead, and as far as I knew then he had not written specifically about LSD. Academic reports were vague and filled with jargon.

With Schiller's encouragement, I decided to just follow the story wherever it led. This, of course, required me to shed the parsimonious attitudes I had developed working at the *Tribune* where every penny spent on a story was weighed against a few lines of copy. The *LIFE* magazine style with which I was still uncomfortable was to spare no expense in getting the story. If we needed weeks, that was fine. If we needed air tickets to other parts of the country, that was fine. If we needed to charter a plane, even that was fine. As it turned out, we did all of these things and more, but first we had to attend—not pass, but attend—an "acid test." We were told to show up at an abandoned garage in Compton, near Watts, where scars of the 1965 riot were still very apparent and racial tension still threatened to break out into violence. There we could observe an acid test.

"What the hell is an acid test?" I asked, reflecting my ignorance.

Our guide explained that a group of people who called themselves the Merry Pranksters, led by Ken Kesey, author of *One Flew over the Cuckoo's Nest*, would come to Los Angeles from Northern California in a school bus painted in the bright colors that were coming to be known as "psychedelic." For a modest entrance fee of something like two dollars, they would make LSD available to all who attended their event. They would be accompanied by a rock group called the Grateful Dead. Their major sound tech and archivist, bearing the unlikely name of Augustus Owsley Stanley, an acid cook nonpareil, would supply LSD.

The whole effort, I was told, was to introduce LSD into the culture at large. It was a holy mission, because the changes in values and point of view that resulted from an acid trip would help to end the strife, the competition, and the hatred that characterized so much of modern society. Rousseau's dream realized through drugs, I thought. Evil could be cleansed from society by giving people a peek deep into their heads. Apparently the Pranksters thought that LSD actually had the power to change human nature. Or maybe they just liked tripping and wanted everyone else to enjoy it too, the way a committed drinker wants everyone to join him for a cocktail.

Nineteen months earlier, Kesey and the Pranksters had gone on the road on an acid-fueled journey to Washington, DC, New York, and Texas in the wildly painted school bus that would soon enough become famous. I had heard of none of this. In fact, in June 1964, when the Pranksters were New York bound, Sally and I were en route to Los Angeles to tell her parents we were planning to marry. While Kesey, Owsley, and the others were plotting to change the world, I was plotting to get a better job.

"We have to go to this," Schiller said. "There'll be good shots there."

I agreed and decided that in the meantime I should find out more about the Merry Pranksters. I found their school bus, painted to look like what I guessed a person saw during an acid trip: wild, fully saturated colors butting into one another. It was parked outside a large rundown Victorian house in an equally rundown neighborhood in South Central Los Angeles. The Pranksters had just arrived, and some were still on board. I climbed into the bus and had my conventional sensibilities instantly assaulted by the sight and smell of several diaper-less babies and the messes they can make. Picking my way down the aisle, between tie-dyed dresses and scarves, between sandals and baby poop, I soon learned that no one was interested in talking. Or more accurately, they were not interested in talking to me. They were especially not interested in talking to Time-Life, the establishment press. And in reality, they just weren't very interested in talking at all.

I wandered around in the house, where people seemed to be settling in. I had never heard of the Grateful Dead, so I was not very interested in people who appeared to be musicians. If Jerry Garcia had offered me a cigarette I would not have known him from any other twenty-something hippie. No one seemed to know where I could find Kesey or Owsley. I needed someone to begin at square one to explain to a square reporter just what the hell was going on. Unsuccessful after an hour, I left and went back to our offices in Beverly Hills. On the return drive, I found myself struggling with several apparently conflicting notions. These people were, at least in their view, leading an effort to make the world a better place. If their motives were pure, I should respect them. Somehow, that was made difficult by their personal hygiene and the presence of small children who appeared to be poorly tended. I believed that the way people treat children is an absolute index of their character. I didn't want to leap to conclusions, but the dirty kids disturbed me. Had I visited a group of people devoted to heroin I would have expected to be appalled, but these people were said by some to be the vanguard of a new and better world. Maybe LSD was just another drug, and all the social improvement and personal enlightenment rhetoric was just cant. I needed to answer that question before I could properly report the story.

That night Schiller and I drove to a dank building in a dicey neighborhood. The place looked like an abandoned garage: dusty, greasy, forlorn. A few people milled around outside. Half a dozen more loitered near the door. We paid the admission of two dollars and walked in. I was surprised and relieved that no one seemed especially interested in the fact that Schiller, in a suit that made him look like a loan shark, carried three cameras around his neck.

The concrete floors, soaked in old grease, complemented the dark yellow, heavily stained walls. The room was bare of any furniture except for two large plastic garbage cans standing near the door. They were filled with Kool-Aid of some dark-colored flavor, grape perhaps. One garbage can sat quietly beside a stack of Dixie cups. Heavy vapor rose from the other as dry ice, bubbling in the liquid, released CO_2 as it disintegrated. "The one not smoking is for the kids," someone behind me whispered.

"The smoking one is acid," Schiller said, leaning in to my ear. "Stay away from that one."

The Grateful Dead looked like they were preparing to play, but after a fumbling effort to tune up, members began to walk away and something recorded and amplified came through the big speakers. A strobe light flashed in the dark room, threatening to create motion sickness in anyone watching too closely. A man danced, whirling in tight circles before the strobe. Schiller shot a few dozen frames using a very slow shutter so that the flashing light created multiple images of the dancer, like Duchamp's *Nude Descending a Staircase*. Again, not much happened. People talked quietly. Some sat on the floor and stared. The level of the smoking Kool-Aid began to drop. I kept waiting for the event to begin, not suspecting that the event was in full swing. It was just out of sight, inside the head of every person in the room who enjoyed the smoking Kool-Aid.

Near midnight, my feet hurting from standing for hours, I walked to the LSD, took a cup, and dipped it into the acid-laced liquid. It would be easy enough to say that I didn't know the drink was spiked with acid. I was debating my decision when I saw cigarette butts floating in the soup. Suddenly, I imagined what else might be there and decided against a drink. I dumped my cup and told Schiller that it was time to go.

Sally roused herself when I got home at 2:00 a.m. She propped herself on an elbow. "So what happened?"

"Nothing," I said once again.

"Nothing? How can you do a story about nothing?"

"I don't know yet."

CHAPTER THIRTY-TWO

On the same December evening that Sally and I strolled along Sutton Place enthralled by our first Christmas snowfall in New York, Tim Leary and his daughter Susan were undressing before US Customs agents in Laredo, Texas. Earlier that day, the Learys and three other people in their party had attempted to enter Mexico to begin a Christmas-week vacation. Exactly why the Mexican authorities refused them entry is unclear, but they were summarily turned around and sent back across the Rio Grande bridge into the United States. Even though the group had entered Mexico in only the most superficial way, hardly crossing the international bridge, US Customs officials conducted a careful search of their car, discovering a few marijuana seeds on the floorboard. As a result, a personal search was ordered, and the little group was marched off to undress before the customs agents. When a small silver snuffbox containing three roaches—remnants of marijuana cigarettes—was found in Susan's underwear, she and Leary were charged with serious federal crimes. His charges carried a penalty of thirty years in federal prison. Susan, eighteen at the time, could be detained in a juvenile facility until she reached age twenty-one. The charges seemed to reflect the official attitude toward Leary and his proselytizing for LSD more than the seriousness of the crime. The government, spending taxpayers' money—the only money it spends—was prepared to support Leary in a prison cell for thirty years, ostensibly for transporting three New York joints, all half smoked, hidden in a teenager's underwear, back and forth across an international bridge.

Schiller, who practiced a kind of scorched-earth journalism where nothing was left unexamined—no source left without an interview, no possible lead not followed, no question not asked—insisted that we must go to Laredo for the trial, which was then in progress. I agreed that Leary was an important part of our story, but I was shy about climbing on a plane to fly 1,400 miles in pursuit of an interview. I was still stuck in the transition from regional daily newspaper to big-time national journalism, but Schiller made sense when he insisted that it was important to maintain control of the story and that meant covering all of it, personally. He would prove to be something of a mentor in this regard. In time, I would come to admire his drive, his obsession with every detail of a story, and his willingness to requisition any resource needed from any source, even though I sometimes found his assertiveness embarrassing.

I once watched in amazement as Schiller confronted a total stranger in a New York City elevator and told the man that the two rolls of film Schiller was then wrapping in note paper must be delivered to the *LIFE* magazine film lab immediately. He gave the bewildered man the film with a slip of paper bearing the address of the Time-Life Building and the film-lab manager's name. Then he sent his startled messenger off on an errand of dubious urgency. I don't know whether I was more bemused by Schiller's gall or the willingness of his designated messenger to accept the assignment. Schiller's self-confidence was such that the man actually seemed to feel honored that he had been chosen. Not only would I never have summoned the nerve to try such a thing, it would never even have occurred to me. Somewhat more notoriously, Schiller had once convinced a Marine Corps commander at Camp Pendleton that he should supply a landing barge and a platoon of Marines to storm the beach at Santa Monica so that Schiller could shoot a fashion assignment involving armed Marines charging past models in bathing suits.

I was no match for Schiller's powers of persuasion and soon enough arrived at the Los Angeles airport feeling vaguely guilty about spending *LIFE*'s money on what might be a marginal part of our story, but I was convinced that it must be done. In San Antonio, when we confirmed there really was no scheduled air service to Laredo, Schiller insisted we charter a small plane, raising my level of anxiety to even greater heights. He was right to insist on the charter. We would have used up two days driving to the border and back, and I suspect that our savings on his "day rate" more than covered the charter.

Laredo, its streets mythic largely because of an old song about a dying young cowboy who knew he'd done wrong, probably harbored more intrigue per square mile than any other small town in North America, certainly more than any town I had ever been in. A torrent of American goods, televisions, appliances, luxury items, and European imports were smuggled nightly into Mexico by legitimate businesses operating on the US side of the border, where the merchants maintained small showrooms and catalogs of thousands of items available. Wealthy Mexicans flew into Laredo as they returned from skiing in Aspen, gambling in Las Vegas, or visiting New York. They dropped off shopping lists for goods that soon enough would be delivered to their homes in Mexico. Moving the other direction were, of course, mostly drugs. It was a classic trade pattern: manufactured goods exchanged for agricultural raw materials. Once it had been cotton and tobacco traded for steel tools and finished cloth. Now it was television sets exchanged for cocaine and pot.

A local reporter I met at Leary's trial enlightened me in this regard when, one evening, he took me down to a bank of the Rio Grande, where we could see the supports beneath the international bridge. Large boxes lined the footing of every pillar, waiting to move until the right customs inspector came on duty. Long lines of loaded trucks idled on both sides of the river awaiting the signal that they could safely cross.

"That's all contraband, stuff to be smuggled?" I asked, shocked by the openness of it all.

"It goes on twenty-four hours a day at every bridge, in both directions," he said. "Want to get a beer and watch for a while?"

We stopped into a dingy Veterans of Foreign Wars club nearby, picked up two Lone Star longnecks, and settled in for an hour to watch what could only laughingly be called a "border." Leary's predicament, smuggling three roaches, seemed more absurd every hour I was in town.

Over the next few days, I interviewed Leary while Schiller took some nice pictures of him sitting on the floor talking, his adoring daughter snuggled against him. We hung out with his crowd and secured an invitation to visit his headquarters in Millbrook, New York. Walking to and from the courthouse, we endured the hostile stares of the federal police, who took our presence as support for a man they believed to be dangerous and disgusting. After Leary and Susan were sentenced and filed a notice of appeal, they were released on bail, and Schiller and I headed back to Los Angeles.

Dick Alpert, soon to be Ram Dass—heir to a railroad fortune and Leary's partner in LSD research at Harvard—had come down for the trial. He was articulate, open, and friendly. When he said he was returning to Los Angeles as soon as the trial ended, we agreed to take the same flight back to continue our conversation. Alpert, keeping our date, showed up in San Antonio to board our flight. As the reporter on the story, I was able to claim Alpert's attention, sitting next to him in the big first-class seats we had, alas, been forced to book, because all the cheap seats were gone. He regaled me with wonderful stories of his adventures with Leary in the early days of the LSD saga, like the day a quart Listerine bottle, filled with a nearly pure solution of LSD, broke in his suitcase while it was being off-loaded at Kennedy Airport. "Most of it soaked into a gray Brooks Brothers suit," he said. "It was actually my favorite suit. We took it home, carefully hung it up to dry, and then cut it up into little squares. I think we tripped on that suit for at least a year."

Little of what he told me would be directly useful in a *LIFE* story, but it was extremely important in the history of the phenomenon we were reporting. Somewhere over Arizona, I could see Schiller, sitting across the aisle from me, growing agitated at being excluded from the conversation. Before we landed I understood that photography, though he was very good at it, was not Schiller's primary interest. At heart he was a producer. He insisted on switching seats with me before we landed, and soon enough he secured Alpert's tentative agreement to collaborate on a book when the *LIFE* story was done. He then set about trying to hire me to ghostwrite it.

Beginning with the little party in the West Hollywood apartment, our LSD story grew larger and more important as we pursued it. It was the small rock protruding from the bottom of a hole that, probed and poked with a shovel, is revealed to be a boulder. Nothing I had done at the *Tribune* began to compare in size and complexity with the story now revealed to me day by day as I continued to interview people and attend events. I alternated between elation that I had hit the lottery and abject fear that this one was so big I would miss something essential and look like a fool.

The Merry Pranksters and Owsley had managed to "turn on" thousands of people in and around San Francisco without much public notice. Venice and Santa Monica were awash in LSD, but a person had to be there to know that. Kesey and the Merry Pranksters, using their wildly painted bus to advertise the psychedelic experience and the Grateful Dead to provide accompanying music, were on the road energetically spreading the message and the drug. Even the Hell's Angels were in on the act, although it would be another year before Hunter Thompson made that widely known. A whole subculture, complete with art, music, fashion, metaphysics, and a vision of human destiny, was quickly evolving, and the general public didn't have a clue, making it a perfect *LIFE* story. Six million subscribers would be told about an important trend happening all around them that they had yet to notice.

My weekly reports on the progress of our research and the film piling up in New York attracted enough attention that the walls normally separating editorial departments began to collapse, revealing that several people knew about LSD and had dibs on the story, my story. Barry Farrell, a columnist for the magazine—hip and closely associated with the avant-garde scene in art and music—had suggested writing a text piece on LSD months earlier. His record as a writer and his prior claim to the role of explaining the phenomenon trumped any claim I could lay. I was both disappointed and relieved. My ambition drove me to seek a byline on a major story. My common sense told me that it was a high-wire act and I should be careful.

I should have been more confident. I was in the field doing primary research. I had interviewed Tim Leary and Dick Alpert, pioneers in the social movement toward using LSD as a learning tool. I had observed the Merry Pranksters and seen their bus. I had interviewed Dr. Sidney Cohen at UCLA and read his articles. He was as expert as anyone on the subject of LSD, and his views about acid were far more cautious than the crowd who was convinced it would save the world. "We'll know in twenty years what the long-term effects are," he told me. "People are doing to themselves what no researcher would ever be allowed to do."

I had attended acid tests and sat for hours in apartments all over West Los Angeles watching people trip while they stared at oozing blobs of color projected on home movie screens. I had made arrangements to visit Leary again, at the Millbrook, New York, mansion provided to him by William Mellon Hitchcock, an heir to part of the Mellon family millions and the Gulf Oil fortune. I continued to hear rumors of the Luces' encounter with LSD, though I still had trouble believing them. I interviewed Aldous Huxley's widow, Laura, and learned that he had experimented with the drug and that she had given Huxley LSD as he lay dying. I was beginning to feel confident that I had a grip on the story, but I couldn't be sure.

I gave a lot of thought to the possible social consequences of widespread acid use. I couldn't predict the future, of course, but against the backdrop of the Vietnam War, growing more savage, more intractable, and more dispiriting each day, the prospect of a substance that would make people less aggressive and more self aware did not seem a bad thing. After all, if Henry and Clare were dropping acid, who was I to say it was a bad idea?

Another very powerful but subtle force was now at work on my thinking. The war in Vietnam was simply eroding my respect for traditional authority. Growing up as I had in the 1950s, in a middle-class family that went to church on Sunday, obeyed the law, paid its taxes, and respected older people, I held parents, governments, and the traditional centers of authority in great respect. The conduct of the war and the insistence with which the government pursued it, in the face of what I regarded as clear evidence that the war itself was extralegal if not illegal, had started to raise doubts in my mind about the government's moral worthiness. When a son discovers a father's adultery, it is hard to take moral instruction from the man ever again. When a man discovers his president is lying and that his policies are killing people day by day, wasting the national treasury, and that the purpose of the war is more about political survival than national interest, it grows harder and harder to grant the government one's obedience. The whole edifice of authority—universities, corporations, civic organizations—seemed unable to even question, let alone challenge or thwart, the misbehavior of "Daddy." The old ropes that held us all together in some orderly social contract frayed and broke. I grew up with "Father knows best," and now it appeared that Father was a crook. "Drugs are bad, therefore LSD is bad" was a proposition far more acceptable in 1962 than in 1966. I wasn't there yet, but I was drifting toward the corrosive but perhaps inevitable opinion that the government and traditional organizations of authority were not to be trusted—an opinion that would increasingly include my own corporate hierarchy.

Of course, the philosophical and psychological trappings that accompanied the emergence of LSD—the association with Harvard faculty and old-line American millionaires—made it hard to think of it as just another drug. This led me to miss the commercial aspects. Here was a new drug and a unique commercial opportunity. LSD was not yet owned by the traditional networks of producers and distributors—rogue governments, large criminal organizations such as the Mafia, certain intelligence agencies, and revolutionary/terrorist groups—in the way that cocaine, heroin, and cannabis were. It presented an opportunity for people to get into the drug business without getting killed. This was not lost on the Hell's Angels or on some of Leary's associates or on Owsley. At the time, it was totally lost on me.

CHAPTER THIRTY-THREE

Accompanied by Irene Neves, a reporter in *LIFE*'s human-affairs department, I left Manhattan in a rental car, driving north on the Taconic State Parkway, a road once described as a "misanthropic little road divided in the center by a low mean rail." Other people, like Lewis Mumford, disagreed, calling it a masterpiece of engineering and aesthetics. For me, it just seemed long and winding. I still held a westerner's smug notion that the East was small and the West was big, but after an hour of avoiding the dinged-up center rail without really leaving suburban New York, I began to revise that belief. I would have been shocked to learn that we could drive another five hours and still be in New York state.

Irene was good company, although she was reserved, regarding me as square while she was Greenwich Village hip. It was rumored that she had once been married to a jazz musician who used heroin, placing her in a special category of haute hip. She was along because she was yet another staffer who had laid claim to the LSD story and because she knew Leary's current partner, Rosemary Woodruff, soon to be his wife. "Ro" had agreed to see us when we arrived.

Just north of the Poughkeepsie exit, we left the Taconic and headed northeast toward Millbrook, an old-money section of Dutchess County where thoroughbred horses and packs of beagles are among the toys kept for weekend amusement. It was midafternoon when we rolled past the Bavarian-style gatehouse and into the grounds of a 2,500-acre private preserve created by the man who founded Union Carbide. Ironically, Leary and his crowd now occupied a place that had originally been conceived as a kind of ideal Bavarian ministate. Where American capitalism and German romanticism had once held sway, Leary and his group now conducted their form of research and enjoyed a kind of casual communal life. It was a sort of decaying paradise where they were temporarily undisturbed by the larger world. It was too good to last, of course. The serpent that would eventually undo them already lurked in Poughkeepsie, where G. Gordon Liddy, a Dutchess County assistant district attorney, former FBI agent, and soon-to-be felon as a result of the Watergate imbroglio, watched and plotted.

We were welcomed by a group of people whose role in the commune was never clear to me. Rosemary, Leary's mistress, was a remarkably beautiful woman—animated and open in her attitude. I was attracted to her and intimidated by her at the same time. It did not especially surprise me some years later when I learned that she had arranged for the Weathermen to break Leary out of a federal prison and whisk him off to Algeria. She was clearly a force within the commune, guarding Leary's privacy and in control of more than was apparent. She was having a great time, which always makes a person more attractive. We spent the afternoon talking. I did some interviews with various people, and then Irene borrowed the rental car and left to tour the grounds with Rosemary and three friends.

They wanted to get high, and being unsure of just where I stood on that question, they left me to my own devices. I wandered through the old palace, checking out the bowling alley, the meditation pavilion, and the other artifacts of nineteenth-century excess. The place created a deep sense of melancholy in me. It was too big, too grand, and too run-down to offer any excitement or comfort. While it was not literally a ruin in the sense that the Coliseum or the Parthenon is a ruin, it was a cultural ruin. The attitudes and fantasies that underlay its construction were gone—off to the Hamptons and Palm Beach.

Afternoon turned into evening, and sometime after dark I began to feel profoundly lonely and very annoyed that Irene had not returned. About nine I saw the car roll into the driveway, slathered in mud with the side caved in. They had, they said, slid off a muddy road into a ditch and had to call a wrecker from Millbrook to pull them out.

Back in New York I returned the car and filled out insurance papers to cover the damage. Within days I received an angry rejection. The local insurance agent had interviewed the tow-truck driver, who reported that the group with the car was all "high on drugs" and that the Hitchcock estate was a known "drug den." I was shocked by the hostile language of the rejection. I refused to be refused, and eventually the problem went away, but I had a taste now of the contempt many people felt for this drug and the people who used it. Possession of LSD was not illegal in March 1966, but the locals clearly believed that whatever was going on at the Millbrook estate was not to be tolerated.

The Monday after our return from Millbrook, we began the process of "closing" the LSD story, something I had never done before. Schiller flew in from Los Angeles to represent his interests, mainly seeing that he got ample space in the magazine and credit for his work. Barry Farrell wrote a long text piece that he wanted run without cuts, and I worked to assure that the subject was treated fairly, which is to say that LSD was not portrayed as just another street drug, and the people taking it not simply as junkies of a different stripe. Of course, I was flying blind, as is so often the case with journalism. There was no way to look into the future and know the ultimate outcome of the big experiment now launched in America. I just didn't want to be part of an effort to make experimenting with the drug a felony.

In the end, we got ten pages and a cover, which is about as good as it got at *LIFE*. I didn't get a byline, but Schiller and I shared an editor's note lauding our efforts, and I came as close as I would ever come to being on the cover of *LIFE* magazine. Schiller shot a picture of my hand holding an LSD capsule. Art Director Bernie Quint laid six transparent squares of color over the photograph. It would run as the March 25, 1966, *LIFE* cover.

I was at ease with what we had written, except for the cover slug: "The Exploding Threat of the Mind Drug that Got Out of Control: LSD." The slug was meant to appease the more conservative minds on the editorial staff, to boost newsstand sales, and to give the magazine some protection from the law-and-order crowd sure to be upset by the more balanced treatment inside the magazine. Nowhere did we actually document either a threat or an epidemic of drug use, but *LIFE* was often a little schizophrenic, reflecting the enormous range of opinion on the editorial staff and the complex pressures that fall on a popular national publication. LSD was a mild debate compared with what would eventually develop out of the war in Vietnam.

CHAPTER THIRTY-FOUR

I was ready to leave New York for Los Angeles when a call came in for Schiller. Unable to find him, a secretary directed the call to me. A pleasant male voice reminded me that he had given the "party" we photographed (and given me a ride home that morning). I remembered him acting as a kind of casual host. I was upset when he said he supplied the acid and the cold cuts, arranged the party, and invited the people we photographed because Schiller asked him to and that he expected to be paid. I knew the photos had not been literally staged because I was present when they were made, but if the party was something Schiller arranged and paid for, then the photos were not quite what we claimed they were—an event that we recorded without interference. I found Schiller and confronted him with the news. He was evasive. I decided to seek guidance from a higher authority, who in this case was Dick Pollard, *LIFE*'s director of photography. Pollard was a polished, attractive man about my father's age. He worked at the magazine practically from its inception and was associated with directing many iconic photographs, like the 1941 cover photograph of Rita Hayworth kneeling on silk sheets on her bed wearing a silk nightgown, a picture that practically defined "sexy" for forty years. As I laid out my concerns, Pollard was sympathetic and listened carefully, but I saw he really did not want to know what I purposed to tell him. The story was in print. The deed was done. We had ten pages and a cover, so what the hell was the problem? I decided the best course was to forget it and move on. I knew I had bumped into a troublesome ethical problem for photojournalism, one I had never encountered at the newspaper, but one I suspected I would bump into again.

Reporting, as I understood it, was meant to convey events as accurately as possible. Reporting was history written in real time. The idea, à la Heisenberg, that the observation of any event changes the event was clearly true. No person facing a camera behaves exactly as he would without the camera present. But the goal, I believed, was to come as close to unaltered reality as possible, unless of course it was clear that the subject and the photographer were engaged in a mutual effort, like photographs of a dancer or Rita Hayworth.

The idea that truth can sometimes be more powerfully portrayed by well-structured fiction than by reported fact is a concept requiring rather high and refined intellectual sensibilities. At *LIFE* and at the *Tribune* we were never even near that arena. Our readers believed (and were entitled to believe) that what we wrote was as nearly the truth of a matter as we could ascertain it. We were reporters, not producers. It was significant, I would come to believe, that the head of a television news team was known as the "producer" and the person reporting was known as the "talent."

In my view, working with photographs as a primary reporting tool created a new burden for journalism. The average reader brings a certain healthy skepticism to a written story. Sophisticated readers are at least vaguely aware of the bias of the publication they read, and those to whom such things matter glance at the byline on a story to get an even better fix on the cant that might have crept in. Pictures are another matter. To a very large degree, the adage is true: seeing is believing. Because *LIFE* magazine reported through pictures, it bore a special responsibility not to fake photos. The issue, as it turned out, was not as simple as it first seemed. My next assignment, to report on the conditions in Watts a year after the riot there to determine if anything had changed, brought the matter up in a way that Schiller's actions had not.

The civil disturbance in August 1965 shook the nation by its size, intensity, and duration. I was still at the *Tribune* that summer, and I remember the feeling of anxiety and dread I felt even at a great distance as parts of Los Angeles burned and crowds stormed through the streets stealing, fighting, drinking, and just watching the scene. Over the course of six days, thirty-four people died and $40 million in property damage was inflicted on the city. Most of the mischief was opportunistic, fueled by alcohol, deep frustration, and a sense of injustice going back three hundred years. Now I was assigned the task of going back to Watts a year later to see if the conditions that produced the riot had changed.

The answer to our question "Had things changed?" seemed obvious to me from the outset. Nothing had changed. What would have changed?

Human nature? The economic conditions, both cultural and structural, complex and years in the making? The posture of white America toward what amounted to a black ghetto? Adults who have never held a steady job are unlikely to suddenly find and keep one in an area where unemployment is triple or quadruple the national rate. I decided to adapt the ironic view: the question was rhetorical.

My editors were not obtuse. They knew nothing had changed, but pondering the question offered an opportunity for the magazine to revisit the causes of the riot with a year's worth of hindsight in a cooler, more contemplative atmosphere. LIFE's coverage of the riot itself had tended to focus on the action, the violence, the fire, and the faces distorted by the excitement of rebellion. There were many fire-truck photos, heavily armed cop photos, and graffiti exhorting "Burn Baby Burn." The word "seething" seemed a favorite to cover the temper of the area.

Bill Ray, a veteran LIFE photographer and one of the most cynical men I would ever meet, was assigned to the story with me. We hardly knew where to begin. Neither of us had ever been to Watts. We were well informed in a general way about conditions in the inner cities, but we possessed no special knowledge to help us shape a story. As so often happened, we had to begin our assignment by educating ourselves on the topic we hoped eventually to explain to our readers. We decided to seek out some of the community leaders in Watts and go from there.

We quickly saw that interviewing community leaders might be a perfectly good way to begin a story that could eventually sprawl for a few thousand words, but it was a decidedly unpromising way to begin a photo essay meant to reveal social conditions that might produce a riot. As in any American city, poverty and despair and barely repressed anger are manifested in mostly subtle ways. There are no naked children with bellies distended by malnutrition. No one in Watts was begging. Even the poorest in urban American in 1966 could afford to dress well enough to look like everybody else on the street, wearing clothes that spoke more of style than economics. Crowded living conditions, lack of public transportation, poor education, high unemployment, dysfunctional families, and drug and alcohol abuse are not easily photographed, at least not in ways that might excite or move a mostly middle-class white readership. A kitchen uncleaned in the month since a pan of oatmeal boiled over and ran down the stove might show a decided lack of domestic skill and motivation on the part of a young mother living there with three small children, but a dirty stove was hardly a *LIFE* photograph. Groups of young men hanging out in the middle of the day who in other communities would be working or in school might illustrate unemployment, low skills, and poor educational opportunities, but it was hardly an exciting photograph. Sociology makes interesting journalism only in the hands of the most skilled observer and often must rely on graphs, not photos, to illustrate its findings.

So we drove to Watts every day to interview people. We trudged through the streets hoping to be inspired. We tried to understand the difference between the Black Muslims and other black radical groups and in the process came across a number of ambitious young men hoping to start an organization of angry men who might successfully, in the words of Tom Wolfe, mau-mau the flak catchers. In the end, we produced what amounted to a series of portraits of individuals who represented the different forces at work in the community. We had the congressman, the social organizers, the dropout, the angry, the radical, the resigned. We ignored the baffled, the confused, and the somnolent. We found street scenes reflecting what had happened a year earlier. Ray produced beautiful photographs, perfectly composed and balanced for color and light, but as a more seasoned *LIFE* staffer than I was (everyone was more seasoned than I was), he knew we needed something more compelling than faces and graffiti.

One afternoon, sitting with a group of five young men we had followed for a week, Ray astonished me into silence by saying, "You guys ever make Molotov cocktails?" Our subjects looked at one another suspiciously and then gave an evasive answer. Ray pressed on. Maybe they would like to make some cocktails and demonstrate their use for his cameras. We could go to a vacant lot somewhere at night, he said, and they could toss the bombs.

I don't think Molotov cocktails—bottles filled with gasoline and ignited by a rag stuffed in the neck—were really a big factor in the Watts riots, but they occupied a lot of ink and haunted the fears of people outside the ghetto who were worried that the Los Angeles violence might spread, as it indeed did in the next two years. The little weapons of Russian resistance to German aggression took on a special symbolic quality, so much so that the Los Angeles City Council passed a law against selling gasoline in portable containers in certain parts of town— like Watts. On the way home that night, Ray and I stopped for a drink in a Westwood bar near Ray's home.

"We can't do that," I said with the firmest conviction. "First of all, it is illegal to make or help people make firebombs. We could get into serious trouble. Second, it is really pushing the story in a way that is not true."

Ray noticed part of a scotch label floating in his drink. He signaled a young waitress who came quickly to our table, flashing a perky smile. "Yes, sir?"

"Will you please bring me a long spoon," he said evenly, "so that I can remove this label from my drink?" He held his glass so that the dissolving paper tab was visible to us all.

Embarrassed, the waitress took the offending drink away and brought another, but without an offer to make it on the house. Ray's sole compensation for a polluted drink was humiliating the waitress.

Satisfied with his new drink, he turned to my question. "You think these monkeys didn't make Molotov cocktails and throw them during the riot?"

"Possibly, I don't know, but that's not the point."

"You think if there is another riot that they or guys like them won't make bombs and toss them around?" He broke into a dry, cynical laugh. "I'm not proposing that we say they are throwing these things. I'm saying they know how to make them and they demonstrate for us how it is done."

"It's provocative, and even instructional. They would not do this without our encouragement."

"It will make a hell of a picture. One of those faces lighted by the flame of a gas-soaked rag. A Seagram's bottle full of gas in his hand."

I started to feel like a Sunday-school kid, a goody two-shoes. Ray was clearly a tough, seasoned journalist. He was arguing that arranging a demonstration of firebombing would bring the sense of drama and threat to our story that it presently lacked. If we clearly stated that the photos were a demonstration, we were not technically being dishonest, but the whole business bothered me.

The next day, Ray stopped in a gas station in an area of town where it was assumed that gas sold in plastic containers would go into the lawn mower. He bought a gallon to go. I didn't intervene. That night, in a vacant lot littered with broken concrete slabs, taking care not to spill gas on their nice clothes, our subjects made Molotov cocktails and threw them, the flames arcing in wide parabolas against the night sky until they burst in an eruption of yellow fire against the concrete. The motors on Ray's Nikons whizzed and popped as he shot roll after roll of film. I expected the police to arrive at any moment and haul us all off to jail.

I wasn't happy with what we had done, but it was done. My greatest fear now was that the film would become separated from my captions as it moved through the editing process in New York. I could imagine a headline over the photos declaring rioters getting ready for the fire next time.

We finished the story in late May, and as had been the case with the LSD story, I was relieved to learn that it would not be up to me to explain Watts and what had happened there in the past year. *LIFE* bought excerpts from a book by two *Los Angeles Times* reporters who were part of the *Times'* Pulitzer Prize–winning team covering the riot. They would offer their view of what Ray and I had looked at and discussed and finally, I believed, understood after three months on the streets of Watts.

We shipped everything off to New York. The story was scheduled to run in July, a few weeks before the August 11 anniversary of the riot. Assuming the article was done, I turned my attention to other matters. Ray continued discussions with our editors and Pollard about the photo coverage.

The week the article appeared, Sally and I were driving Cathy back to Seattle. She had spent much of the summer with us in Los Angeles, and Hellyn was anxious for her return. We decided to drive her home to lengthen our visit and to add a camping trip into Canada after we dropped her off. Along the way, we stopped in a little town in Oregon and I ducked into a drugstore looking for the current issue of *LIFE*. I was stunned when I saw the cover: four handsome little black boys about ten years old, dressed in bright yellow sweatshirts with a lion stenciled on the front. In another generation it could have been an ad for *The Lion King,* except for the context and the militant wannabe in a green dashiki marching behind them, as if they were recruits in a new army. "The young lions," the caption proclaimed, "'Simba'—for lion—young militants are drilled in Watts."

The whole picture and all it implied was utter and complete fantasy, but there it was. I called Ray. "So where did you find the cover picture?"

He explained that after I left the story he had fortuitously gotten in touch with a new group of militants, a group we had somehow failed to identify in two months of research. They were recruiting children to their cause. Of course, they were too laid back and disorganized to actually get uniforms for the new army, so he arranged for the sweatshirts to be dyed, printed, and distributed, and he paid for the cost. The cover photograph was, I gathered, entirely his inspiration.

The Molotov cocktail photos also ran. "Rehearsing with firebombs," the caption said. Not, "Acting out a scenario created by a *LIFE* magazine team." It had just the quality Ray had suggested it would have the night we discussed it in the Westwood bar: a menacing black face holding a handful of fire.

"That cover will scare the shit out of the folks in Dubuque," Ray said, delivering his dry, mirthless laugh.

Well, maybe it will, I thought, but was that our purpose? I was still operating under the innocent assumption that we were journalists trying to discover the truth and report it. Maybe Ray and I simply had a different idea of the truth about Watts.

The article was huge by any standards: twenty-six pages of photographs and reportage. As had been the case with the LSD story, I had no argument with the text. My reporting contributed significantly to what was said about the present situation, namely that not much had changed in the year since the riot. The photos did what they needed to do. None were memorable, except for the cover. That would become an iconic image of the sixties' racial strife.

CHAPTER THIRTY-FIVE

In Seattle we left Cathy with her mother and headed north for the camping trip in British Columbia. I had come to expect that the sadness and guilt I felt after saying good-bye to Cathy would linger, casting a gray tint over my emotions for a day or two, but that was not to be the case this time. As we crossed the border into Canada, a Canadian customs officer broke the mood.

Fully equipped for a week in the woods, our Oldsmobile convertible was laden with camping gear, an inflatable boat, and all the nonperishable goods we anticipated needing for the trip. A very correct customs officer inspected our load and then focused on the cache of assorted liquor we were hauling. He did a little calculation and concluded that we had more than Canada would allow us to bring into the country.

"How much too much?"

"Three bottles of beer too much." He smiled pleasantly.

"What can I do?"

"Well, you can go over there," he indicated a little grassy area on the US side, "and drink it. Or you can donate it to the queen."

I chose the queen.

I followed the officer into his guardhouse, where he took the three bottles of warm Olympia beer and placed them in a locked container as if they were evidence in a criminal trial. Then he prepared a very formal receipt in which the queen, beneath the royal coat of arms, gratefully acknowledged my donation to the Crown of "three pints of lager." By the time I got back in the car and showed the receipt to Sally, my funk over leaving Cathy had dissipated. We spent a night in Vancouver and then headed into the Canadian Rockies.

My memories of going into the country with Sally are among the best I have. She was a city girl who loved fine music and fancy shops, but there was an atavistic streak in her too. She made me teach her how to shoot a gun and how to fish. She loved being in a tent at night with a fire outside. She didn't complain when we spent hours in misting rain perilously huddled in our inflatable boat or rowing across a cold lake beneath gray Canadian skies. The beautiful trout we brought home for dinner, and breakfast, and the joy of being in the country were enough reward.

After three days of fishing in the rain, we gratefully accepted an invitation to shower at the cabin of a Canadian couple we met at Lake Kamloops. Warm and dry after what seemed like a month in damp clothes, we headed south to visit Yellowstone Park on our way back to Los Angeles.

We slept in the park in our little tent. Sometime before dinner I looked around the pristine US Park Service campground and realized that we were the only people not sleeping in a metal box of some sort. There were campers and RVs the size of school busses and pickups with caps over their beds, but we were the only people who were sheltered by a simple piece of canvas. I didn't think a lot about it until later.

Just as we were finishing dinner, a black bear, coat glistening with health and wearing a stiff orange tag like a jaunty feather on one ear, ambled up to the table and ate everything in sight. I banged on a pan and shouted, which annoyed it only mildly. Sally watched in alternating terror and amusement as I danced around the picnic table shouting and banging while trying to stay a safe distance from the animal. Presently the bear, satisfied for the moment, ambled off to the next camp. I listened as the beast moved from one camp to another, setting up a ruckus of pan beating and yelling in each one as it made its way around the large circle. The bear returned to us about 10:00 p.m. We had been in our sleeping bags inside our tent for half an hour.

Before we retired I packed all our food into a sturdy Coleman ice chest and tied it beneath the picnic table with a length of half-inch nylon rope. The rope wound around the ice chest, around steel table legs set in concrete, and around the chest again. I felt sure our food was safe and that failure to get food would discourage the bear from any return trips.

I was just drifting off to sleep when I heard the steel chest scraping on the concrete pad beneath the picnic table. I scrambled out of bed, grabbed a flashlight, and got outside in time to see the bear rip the top off the chest as if it were a plastic refrigerator container. Resigned,

I settled in to watch as the bear devoured three nice Canadian trout (without removing the foil), a pound of sharp cheddar, a pound of butter, bacon, most of a dozen eggs, and some cold cuts, while ignoring all the healthy vegetables. Then, for dessert, our bear batted a can of fruit cocktail around as if it were a hockey puck before stabbing through the steel with two-inch-long claws. Lapping up the syrup pouring from the can in noisy ecstasy, our bear finished its meal and ambled off into the night.

"Well," I said to Sally, who was peeking from the tent. "I guess we can get some sleep. The food's all gone."

Just before 4:00 a.m., I awoke to the sound of ripping canvas. I first thought the bear was tearing into our tent. Then I realized it was the convertible top being assaulted. Outside, in my underwear, I found the bear perched on the trunk of my car, ripping at the canvas top. I lost all sense of caution. Yelling at the bear and throwing the largest rocks I could find, I bounced one the size of a softball, hurled with all my adrenaline-powered strength, off the bear's back. It jumped down and walked off. The rear Plexiglas window of the little Olds hung limply along a rear fender.

"It's time to break camp," I said to Sally. "We'll get an early start." We had been spared any personal injury, and I had no intention of risking another encounter.

I taped up the window as best I could. We loaded everything back into the car, except the destroyed ice chest, which I decided to donate to the US Park Service garbage haulers, and we headed out of Yellowstone at first light.

In the odd way that such things happen, the bear delivered a great gift to us, even though it was impossible to see it at the time. Because we were on the road just at the break of day, we drove through a phantasmagoria of nature. We saw herds of elk and deer grazing in the little meadows where mist rose out of the grass. A badger scampered along the road, his stiff coat undulating as he ran. There were birds and rabbits and more animals than I could imagine in one place. We drove, eventually in silent awe, for half an hour, watching a world we would have never seen if we had not been up at dawn. It all looked remarkably like a Disney nature film.

Back in Los Angeles I took a chance and wrote about the bear and sent it to Davie Sherman, *LIFE*'s editor of a feature called "The Scene." Then I called my insurance agent and began the process of convincing him that a bear had torn the window out of my car. When we found a muddy bear footprint still showing on the white paint of my trunk, the previously skeptical agent shook his head and smiled. "I'm going to have a lot of fun with this back at the office," he said, offering his hand.

A few weeks later, my first byline in a national magazine appeared in *LIFE* on a little story Sherman titled "Bruin: The Forest's Prime Evil."

CHAPTER THIRTY-SIX

After the intensity of the LSD story and two months in a semihostile Watts, I welcomed an opportunity to work mostly on entertainment stories. I never considered writing about entertainers to be as important as covering news and social trends, but the circumstances of reporting were vastly preferable. Instead of walking through strange neighborhoods where no one was sure of his safety, or hanging out with radical druggies and enduring the suspicious, sometimes hostile attention of police, I now spent time in Beverly Hills restaurants, on movie sets, and in the homes of important people in the movie business. The greatest danger in these stories was humiliation at the hands of a tough studio public-relations person, or failing to be hip enough to fit in with a very sophisticated crowd.

Nor was there the same sort of pressure that attended a news story, where it was important to discover new facts and circumstances, or to try to understand an often-complex situation. By the time *LIFE* assigned an article on an entertainer, the reason was manifest: they had just done a terrific new movie, they were up for an Academy Award, they had recently met and charmed a senior editor, or they had gone more or less unnoticed by *LIFE* as they accumulated a long string of accomplished performances. That was the case with Walter Matthau when I was sent to do a profile of him after I returned from my camping vacation.

Matthau was one of those actors who it seemed had always been around. He had played in movies, on Broadway, and on television. He was so good in his roles, blended in so well, that one thought only of the character he played, not the actor who created the role. When he played the Bernalillo County sheriff in *Lonely Are the Brave*, I was still in Albuquerque reviewing movies for the *Tribune*. I marveled at how well he captured the style and attitude of a southwestern sheriff, but his performance didn't set me to thinking about all his other roles and his body of work as an actor. It was only later in his career that he emerged as a star, an actor with an individual personality apart from his roles.

Working again with Bill Ray, I linked up with Matthau while he was making *A Guide for the Married Man*, with Inger Stevens and Robert Morse, directed by Gene Kelly. The production had a dozen cameo performances, so we met enough stars to light a Texas night: Lucille Ball, Jack Benny, Terry-Thomas, Jayne Mansfield, Sid Caesar, Carl Reiner, Joey Bishop, Art Carney, and Wally Cox, among others. All were on the set at one time or another. I was both starstruck and amused at my own reaction. I was determined not to be unduly impressed, but the effort required to do this was a good measure of just how impressed I was. I was never sure if their blasé attitude upon meeting me was because they were not impressed by *LIFE* or if they were just jealous of the attention we lavished on Matthau. There did seem to be a show-business ethic that required actors to stay out of the way when the press was fawning over someone else. In any case, everyone was polite, but reserved.

This reservation was new to me. I was used to people treating me with exaggerated respect once they learned I worked for *LIFE* magazine. People in Watts had been more guarded, but even their hard-bitten attitude was softened by the presence of a national picture magazine. "Take my picture! Take my picture!" was the chant of every group of inner-city kids we met.

Halfway through our story, we were invited to come for drinks before a dinner at the home of the film's producer, Frank McCarthy. Matthau and his wife, Carol, joined Henry Fonda, Jack Lemmon, Jane Wyman, and their spouses at a home McCarthy said was Japanese inspired. It was certainly one of the most tasteful and beautiful houses I would ever see. Talking to McCarthy, holding a glass of good scotch, I again marveled at the idea that I was sharing life with people I had so recently seen only on the screen and who had heretofore been slightly unreal to me. Shaking hands with Henry Fonda, who looked exactly like Henry Fonda in the movies, I refrained from mentioning that a year earlier I had watched him whisked past our table at Lüchow's with Jane and Peter in tow.

Until that night my attitude toward actors was singularly uninformed and parochial. I'm not sure why. It may have had something to do with the snobbish views I developed as a college student, where I decided that the study of philosophy, math, physics, and such were serious, while art and drama were not. I thought of actors as glamorous, lucky people with a peculiar talent for learning lines, but essentially shallow. I did not respect them in the way that I might respect a concert violinist or a good doctor. I think it was at McCarthy's dinner that night that I began to understand that being an actor was a lot more than just having a lucky break one afternoon in Schwab's Pharmacy. The training and dedication of good actors, their understanding of literature and poetry, their substance as educated people began to seep in. It began, in fact, when Lemmon sat down at the piano and began to play beautifully.

"I didn't know he could play like that," I said to McCarthy.

"He taught himself," McCarthy said, "while he was at Harvard. He also plays guitar and double bass."

Later I learned that Lemmon had been president of the Hasty Pudding Club at Harvard and had otherwise distinguished himself there before serving in the navy.

McCarthy, as it turned out, was well into a third career, as a producer. He had been chief of staff to General George C. Marshall during World War II—chief of staff to the chief of staff—while still in his twenties. He left the army with the rank of brigadier general to become the youngest-ever undersecretary of state at age thirty-three. I learned some of this history when I asked him if there was a movie he had always dreamed of producing.

"I want to make a movie about General Patton," he said, without hesitation.

"Why Patton?"

"I worked with him during the war. He was the most unusual man I have ever met. General Marshall was a great man, but Patton was unique."

McCarthy worked on behalf of General Marshall to keep Patton pointed in the right direction, and he described that assignment as one of the most trying he ever faced. Only a few years after our conversation, I watched on television as McCarthy accepted a Best Picture Oscar for producing *Patton*, starring George C. Scott.

Matthau's sense of just what we needed to make a story was actually keener than mine. He fed me great stories about his early life as a poverty-stricken kid on the Lower East Side of Manhattan, but when I brought up the fact that he served as a radioman/gunner on B-24s making incredibly dangerous bombing runs over Europe, he dismissed the whole discussion. "Jimmy Stewart did the same thing," he said.

We were short of interesting pictures when Matthau crawled out of the studio limousine and performed an elaborate buck and wing on the sidewalk. It was 6:30 a.m., and he was on his way to a 7:00 a.m. call. He spoke openly about the gambling addiction that had once landed him in serious trouble with the Mob, but he claimed that was all in the past. Now, he said, he was satisfied to speculate in the stock market. I had so much fun hanging out with Matthau that I delayed writing the piece as long as possible.

The story appeared just about the time that John Kurland, the friend from New York with whom Sally and I had spent our romantic New York Christmas, made a dramatic reentry into my life. He and Linda began to spend more time in Los Angeles, and after we put them up for a few nights during the Academy Awards, they invited us to spend a few days with them at their beach house on the Connecticut shore.

Early that August we arrived at a rambling Victorian house on the Long Island Sound near West Haven. That evening after dinner, John took me out to the big screened porch and dropped a record on the turntable. He was then representing, among others, a folk-rock group called the Mamas and the Papas. I listened to "California Dreamin'" and loved it. He showed me photos of the quartet, and I suspected we could do business. The four were attractive enough and just odd enough to make an interesting story for *LIFE*. Also, I could understand and appreciate their music. I assigned a photographer in Los Angeles to take pictures of the group and arranged to see them perform in Chicago.

Kurland and I stayed in the same hotel with the group. It quickly became apparent that the quartet lived complex personal lives. Kurland tried to bring me up to date on just who had had affairs with whom and what the current tensions were within the quartet, but as with any group of talented people who drink a lot of alcohol, use drugs, and suddenly find themselves rich and famous, the dynamics were too swift and complex to track for very long. What I did observe was that the enormously fat Cass Elliot often ordered table after table of food into her room, where, joined by an equally obese friend, she locked the door and ate for hours. Denny Doherty, slender and shy, was never without a bottle of Seagram's Crown Royal in his hand, always kept in the signature blue velvet bag. He was a native of Nova Scotia, so I took his choice of Canadian whisky as a sign of his patriotism, and what a patriot he was, judging from the intake. John Phillips, clearly a brilliant composer, hid his vices better than the other two. Drugs would eventually destroy his life, but that was years away and not then so obvious. Michelle, John's erstwhile wife, a soprano and a blonde beauty, had only one vice that I could observe, and that was overweening ambition. She was clearheaded, vain, and calculating. I soon gave up on my character study and decided to concentrate on their music, which was fabulous.

I have other powerful memories of that trip having nothing to do with music. One was understanding for the first time how terrified entertainers can be just before they face an audience of thousands with very high expectations; another was understanding for the first time how a crowd can literally tear performers apart out of hysteria and trophy hunting, and why security is so necessary for a concert performed in a popular venue. And finally, I remember, somewhat vaguely, how weird it can be to watch an air show by the Blue Angels roaring in their jets over Lake Michigan while way too high on very strong cannabis supplied by a story subject. I suppose that last item was against the rules of good journalism, but then having a drink with a subject was a standard practice when doing a profile. Having a joint together was just a more sixties' version of the same thing.

I enjoyed writing the piece. I had listened carefully to their music, watched them sing, and talked to them about how they did it. I was able to explain in simple terms how they made it sound so good. I was surprised to hear after the story appeared that John Phillips expected a hatchet job and was pleasantly surprised when I praised his work. He did not understand that *LIFE* rarely if ever spent time writing about entertainment the editors did not like. That was part of the success of the magazine—its happy enthusiasm about the music, movie, or play it chose to present to readers.

As fertile as Los Angeles proved to be, I never stopped wishing to be in New York. And while it was true that most of the stories *LIFE* published did not originate in New York, I still felt that the city was the center of everything interesting.

In some respects my longing was irrational. Even in 1966 or 1967 New York was an expensive place to live, and my salary at *LIFE* was not sufficient to keep us in any sort of middle-class comfort in Manhattan. Living in Los Angeles was easy. We had the sleek little Oldsmobile convertible and a nice two-bedroom apartment with a fireplace and a pool in Brentwood, a reasonably fashionable neighborhood between UCLA and Santa Monica. The beach was fifteen minutes away, and the magnificent countryside of the Monterey Peninsula an easy weekend drive. Sally, a native, knew everything anyone might need to know about California. I had good access to the film community and could have started peddling scripts. Somewhere, somehow I had decided that until I was in New York City I was not in the real arena, so instead of enjoying myself and looking at the opportunities all around me, I pined for cold, dirty New York City.

Any thoughts about returning to New York in the near future were erased in November when I got my first big break as a writer. I was asked to compose a major text piece—that is to say, a magazine article of somewhere between three thousand and four thousand words—to assess whether college students had suddenly changed. Were they still the dull, quiet, careerist people I had gone to school with—the so-called Silent Generation—or had they changed into politically committed, risk-taking young men and women who would reshape the world, hopefully for the better?

Responding to a query from my editors in New York, I doubted if there was much change in the souls of the new generation. Rather, there were two obvious differences between my own undergraduate years and the period on which I would be asked to report: the Vietnam draft and the baby boom. There were a hell of a lot more of them, and they were all, all the males at least, under a constant threat of being hauled off to Vietnam and killed or maimed in a war that could only be justified by something called the domino theory.

This phrase served to obscure any careful analysis of why we needed to defend an unpopular, undemocratic regime in South Vietnam. George Kennan once observed that the American public can only be united behind a foreign policy goal on the "primitive level of slogans and jingoistic ideological inspiration." Lyndon Johnson understood this and cannily offered the idea that if South Vietnam fell to the Communists, Japan would be next, followed maybe by Hawaii, like a line of dominoes standing on end, one falling on the next until all are down. The peculiar notion that the fate of nations is like dominoes was largely accepted by the public, at least until the last American fled Saigon and not much happened in the rest of the world except for decades of US shame and recrimination. Oddly enough, my father was in Vietnam just before it fell, but that is a story to be related elsewhere.

Knowing that my editors, at least most of those at the very top of the Time Inc. pyramid, were generally committed to the domino theory, or at least to the military-industrial complex from which it sprang, I did not spend a lot of time analyzing the advisability of the war in my response to their query. I simply offered the Selective Service System—the draft—as a prod that was making students more politically aware and active. I did not propose any change in human nature.

My editors liked what I told them enough that in late November I found myself living in an undergraduate dorm at Indiana University, studying my subjects firsthand. We deliberately chose a mainstream state university where I hoped to find representative American students.

For the most part, undergraduates were even duller than I remembered them. They watched television to avoid worrying about not studying. They drank a lot of beer. They spent a lot of time thinking about the opposite sex. The men worried about the draft. They felt under constant pressure to perform but often lacked a good understanding of exactly how to do that. There were the bright, energetic, politically motivated exceptions, of course, but that wasn't new. There were always a few of those. Some students had been radicalized by the war, but they were few and they tended to be on certain campuses: Berkeley, Columbia, Wisconsin, Michigan, and a few smaller elite schools. If there were any dangerous radicals at Indiana in the winter of 1966–1967, I couldn't locate them. What I did locate was the terrible, dark hypocrisy of the war.

One of the students I chose as a subject for the article was the affable son of an Indianapolis dentist. When my subject's father heard that his son might be in a *LIFE* story about students at Indiana, he drove to Bloomington to tell us that he thought it was a bad idea. At dinner I asked him how he felt about the war.

"I completely support the war effort," he said. "I just don't want my son there. If he spends time with you and fails to make his grades, he might be drafted."

"Is it acceptable for other men's sons to be drafted and sent to Vietnam?" I asked.

"Yes," he said without any doubt. "But not mine. There are other people who can do that."

So there I had it. We needed to fight the war, but not with anyone who mattered. Here, in 1967, was the seed of the so-called all-volunteer army.

We went ahead with the story, of course, and the young man in question made his grades and was spared the ordeal of defending his country from the falling dominoes. Thousands of others didn't make their grades, or didn't have any grades to make, and a lot of them died. I always believed that the obsessive attention Americans paid to the MIA question and the act of erecting black flags of defeat showing the silhouette of a bowed American soldier on half the flagpoles in America represented a symbolic Jungian response to what we really left behind in Vietnam: a general faith that when we asked people to die for their country, the risk of life was actually necessary to save the country—not to support a dubious theory, protect the oil business, or prevent internecine slaughter.

The article "Who Says Students Have Changed?" appeared that spring. I was very happy to have finally scored with a major article, and I was beset with doubts as to whether I had been brilliant or completely off the mark. I wasn't prepared to consider the possibility that the article was neither, that it was just another magazine article expressing the reporting and opinions of a writer and his editors.

After nearly two months of Indiana winter, I was ready to go home to Los Angeles, but that was not to be. Roy Rowan, the assistant managing editor in charge of news and to some extent the news bureaus, called me and told me that the Chicago bureau chief had suffered a health crisis. "I want you to go to Chicago and run the bureau until he gets better," he said. "Do it quietly, but go right away."

In twenty months I had gone from an inexperienced reporter wondering how to get home from Yankee Stadium to the surrogate midwestern bureau chief, responsible for nineteen states and innumerable major cities, such as Cleveland, Chicago, Detroit, Des Moines, and Denver. Events did not wait for me to settle in. I was still living in a residential hotel in Chicago when Detroit went up in flames.

CHAPTER THIRTY-SEVEN

Except for a brief respite at Christmas, my two-month residency in an Indiana University dorm kept me away from home and Sally most of the winter. Now absence became semipermanent. Because Rowan wanted to be discreet about the illness that sidelined my colleague, I had to live in Chicago as though I was just filling in. It was an awkward situation. I couldn't establish a home or move Sally to Chicago, something many men would have demanded. I was so ambitious that I was prepared to accept almost any hardship.

Alone in a strange city, responsible for three correspondents, a stable of contract photographers, and events in nearly half the geography of the United States, I felt deeply afraid of failure. I also felt for the first time that I was in control of something important, something that potentially could change the way people think. There is a frustrated teacher lurking in me, and a moralist, too, although I hated to acknowledge that part of my personality. I had a strong sense of what I thought to be right and wrong, not that I always lived up to those standards. With the help of amply applied Scotch whisky, I could rationalize deviance from many of my personal standards so that I could join whatever party was in progress at the moment. But public and professional ethics always remained clear in my mind. Cops should be brave and strive to know the truth, politicians should speak the truth as they see it and act for the greater good, journalists should report the truth, and everyone should strive for the general improvement of America. I was a patriot and in many respects a prig. The world was a serious place, and only serious people were worthy of my respect. It would be years before I fully appreciated the notion, so perfectly expressed by the critic Kathryn Schulz writing in *New York* magazine about why she hates *The Great Gatsby*: "When you apply a strict moral code to the saturnalian society to which you are attracted—you inevitably wind up a hypocrite."

Because I felt from an early age that I had failed to live up to the expectations of my parents, especially my father, I always called home immediately to tell them any positive news, like a sixth grader running home with a perfect report card. What I always took to be disapproval on the part of my father was actually just disinterest. He was concerned for my general welfare—that I had enough to eat, no untended cavities— but he was never a good audience, not for me or anyone, though I never stopped trying. In my senior year of high school I persuaded him to attend one football game, on Father's Night, in which I played an outstanding defensive game as a middle linebacker. After the game I asked what he thought of my performance. "I didn't actually see you much," he said. "I usually just watch the quarterback."

I was hardly off the phone with Rowan when I called my father. "They asked me to run the Chicago bureau," I said, trying to sound nonchalant. "It comes with a very nice raise."

"That's wonderful news," my father said. "Congratulations. And I have some news for you."

"What's that?" I was surprised because there was rarely anything like real news from my parents. "News" was that they had bought a new car, or my aunts and uncles had visited. None of those things were even remotely in the same category as their son's appointment to a high post in national journalism.

"I'm leaving for San Francisco in the morning. Then I'm going to Saigon."

He had me. His news definitely topped mine. "You are what?" I knew what I heard. My question was just to buy time until I could sort it out.

"I'm going to Saigon. I took a job with Pacific Architects and Engineers. I'm going to run all the electrical utilities for the Military Assistance Command in Vietnam."

"What's that?"

"They call it MACV, the 'Pentagon East.' They've built a hell of a big power plant over there to supply the military headquarters and all the support staff. It's a first-class facility, completely new, the best of everything. They support enough air conditioning to cool Dallas, and they want me to run it."

The whole proposition was so beyond anything I had ever imagined for him that I didn't know how to respond. There had been many occasions when national corporations had attempted to recruit him. Companies like Westinghouse and Nordberg and Pratt and Whitney offered him jobs after their representatives worked with him on projects at the local power plant where he was then chief engineer. He always demurred, saying that Buffalo was too cold or Milwaukee was too German or that he didn't know anything about Pennsylvania. The truth was that he was comfortable and didn't want to leave the life he had.

"Well, that's great news," I said finally, wanting to be positive. "But if you are leaving tomorrow, why didn't you tell me sooner?"

"I know how you feel about the war. I just didn't want to get into a discussion. I figured I'd tell you once I was there."

"Will you be safe?"

"Oh, I think so. The plant is near the big Tan Son Nhut Air Base. It's well protected."

"What about Mother and Lisa?"

"I can't take them. They'll stay in Tucumcari for now."

Lisa, my niece, had been adopted by my parents after my sister sent her to live with them during a difficult period in her personal life. Lisa's arrival excited two powerful emotions in my mother: loyalty to an apparently unwanted child and resentment toward my sister for not taking better care of Lisa, no matter what her situation was. My mother reacted with outsized emotion. She insisted on adopting Lisa, though that was never necessary; this was understandable to anyone who knew Mother's history. She had been cast off, as it were, when she was two. My grandmother remarried after a brief World War I marriage and divorce and sent Mother to live with her in-laws while she got her new marriage under way. Those years with harsh step-grandparents who found her very existence a reminder that their only son had married a compromised woman scarred Mother for life. She never felt completely sure that anyone, other than my father, regarded her as valuable. She was determined that Lisa not repeat her experience, but she was ill equipped to prevent emotional damage in others.

What an astonishing turn of events! My parents had never been apart for more than a few days at a time, and now Dad would be half a world away, and Lisa would be alone with Mother. Trying to fathom what might have motivated such a radical departure from routine, I called a friend from high school who still lived in Tucumcari.

"We sort of figured something like that would happen," Charlie said. "You probably didn't hear about the city-council business, did you?"

I hadn't heard. I knew that as the head of the power plant my father reported to the city manager, and that in turn the manager reported to an elected city council. I knew that the city council was made up of very ordinary people, the kind of people who might be interested for one reason or another in trying to oversee local government in a town of seven thousand people. I knew that the power plant was a reasonably complex operation where large diesel engines—12,000 horsepower, more or less— were used to generate electricity for the city. Simply operating the plant was not an especially complex task, but maintaining it and making the changes required to keep it running—to keep the lights on—required not only a detailed understanding of the complexities of large diesel engines but of the mysterious nature of electricity as well.

Members of the city council—merchants, farmers, and railroad workers—were not especially well acquainted with the skills that went into maintaining the infrastructure of a city. The lights burned, the garbage was collected, the water flowed, and the council assumed this was all very simple stuff. It was too dependable and too common to require much skill on the part of those who made it happen. Also, in small towns at that time, only doctors, lawyers, and bankers were regarded as having any important specialized knowledge. Everyone else was thought to know about what everyone else knew. Even so, the council refrained for many years from meddling with operations, being content to provide financial oversight and policy direction.

During the period after World War II, Tucumcari grew—not very much, but a little—and its need for electricity increased. Then, in the prosperity of the 1950s and 1960s, as people began to buy more appliances, bigger air conditioners, and television sets, demand grew rapidly. Soon, the electrical capacity of the Municipal Light and Power Plant had to be increased. The city would have to buy a new engine at a cost of about $200,000—probably the largest single purchase the city had ever made.

A notice of intent to purchase went out. Within weeks, representatives—salesmen—from five or six major engine manufacturers arrived in town and began to court members of the city council, taking them and their wives to dinner and offering perks, like a weekend in Albuquerque. It was heady stuff for a group of men who normally worked in obscurity.

The salesmen were good at what they did. They managed to create the illusion that each city-council member, regardless of his training or experience, was qualified to judge which engine would best serve the city. Men who had spent their lives selling cattle feed or cotton shirts, or switching railroad cars, were made to believe that they were suddenly qualified to choose between the five or six competing engine designs.

No one from the council consulted my father or the city engineer. Either they did not trust their own experts or they just felt no need for their opinion. My father grew increasingly concerned. There was no single "best" engine, but there were a couple that he considered outstanding and a couple that were "real dogs." He would have to oversee installation, maintenance, and operation and would ultimately be held responsible for the performance. He began to feel desperate, boxed in, as council members started to firm up their opinions based largely on which salesman they liked best. He was experiencing one of the weaknesses inherent in a local democracy.

Detailed specifications had to be written before bids could be submitted, and at this point my father devised a plan of action. He suspected the city engineer, whose job it would be to write the specifications, had no idea how to go about the task, not a simple one and not one for which a general engineering background would have prepared him.

My father went to his files and found blueprints and specifications for an engine he liked. He stopped by the office of the city engineer and offered the documents. "I know you have to write specs," he said. "I had these lying around, and I thought they might be useful." The city engineer was grateful. He dreaded the task and now my father offered him a template.

Specifications were duly prepared describing in minute details the engine the city would and could buy: bore, stroke, fuel consumption, brake horsepower at a specified RPM, on and on with measurements in tons and in thousands of an inch. They were duly presented to the city manager and passed on to the city council for approval. Approved casually and unanimously, the specifications were packaged into a call for bids and offered to engine manufacturers. Then the trouble began.

Only one manufacturer could meet the specifications written by the city. It happened to be the company that made the engine my father wanted, the engine described in the specifications he offered the city engineer, the engine whose specifications appeared to have been simply transferred from one document (the manufacturer's) to another document, the specifications in a call for bids.

My father got the engine he wanted, but only after threats of lawsuits by losing manufacturers and counterthreats from the successful bidder. The city council wasn't exactly sure what had happened. The city manager had his suspicions, while the city engineer vigorously defended his specs as describing the best engine the city could buy. Most of the members of the city council soon forgot the whole matter. Having enjoyed their moment in the sun, they went about their business. But one member suspected that my father had somehow controlled the outcome and resented his interference with a "council matter." He began to scheme, and that is where the "city-council business" began.

A union member and supporter of the quasi-egalitarian traditions of unions, this council member soon called for a review of the salaries of all city department heads. This was accomplished without much resistance, and it revealed, not surprisingly, that the department heads were generally paid in accordance with the skill level of their jobs. My father was the highest paid. The head of the sanitation department was paid the least. This constituted an inequity, according to the union councilman, and he proposed to solve the problem, not by increasing the lowest pay to be equal to the highest, which would have been a traditional union solution, but by reducing the highest salary to conform to the lowest. Heedless of any consequences and seeing an opportunity to save money, the council voted in favor of the measure.

Blandishments of higher salaries, better opportunities for advancement, better schools for his children, a chance to experience more of the world—none of these ever moved my father or even tempted him to leave Tucumcari. But an assault on his pride was a very different matter. When he got the news of his salary reduction, he left work and came home to tell my mother.

"They think that getting half a dozen garbage trucks out of the barn every morning is worth the same money as running that power plant," he fumed. "I am supervised by hicks and idiots." This was true, but he had managed to overlook the problem until now. It took a week or two, but he soon found that he was eligible for early retirement, which he took.

Pacific Architects and Engineers, a big international construction and operating firm now staffing up for huge contracts in Vietnam, was scouring the United States for capable men. When my father told them he was available, they offered him a very attractive package. He would be paid at the rate of a lieutenant colonel and have an equivalent rank in the civilian pecking order. His wounded pride made the offer irresistible.

Mother, seeing him finally ready to better use his abilities, rashly encouraged him to go, imagining that she would be all right home alone with Lisa for a year or two while he piled up money they needed for retirement. The city council refused to be distressed over losing him. They simply promoted his assistant to fill his job and went on with their somnolent deliberations.

As Charlie filled me in on the city council's effort to bring equality to their department heads, I understood immediately what had happened. I was still stunned that he would be in Vietnam, but I understood his decision.

Just over a year later, the people running the plant piped high-voltage current the wrong way through a huge conduit and destroyed the plant, burning out tens of thousands of dollars worth of equipment, setting the plant on fire, and ending the era of cheap, municipally owned electric generation in Tucumcari. The whole operation was sold to a large commercial utility. Electric rates nearly doubled. Some on the council said my father was to blame. They were not sure exactly how he had caused the explosion, having been in Vietnam for over a year when it happened, but they were sure it was his fault.

CHAPTER THIRTY-EIGHT

After a long absence from home, I was asleep beside Sally in Los Angeles on July 23, 1967, when the Detroit police raided an after-hours joint, a "blind pig," at about 3:00 a.m. Two hundred people, celebrating the safe return from Vietnam of several local soldiers, were in no mood to go home quietly. The raid was a bad move.

Initially it didn't seem as if the trouble would develop into the worst civil disturbance in America since the draft riots during the Civil War, but in less than a week the rioting would claim 43 lives, do $50 million in property damage, injure 1,000, send 7,200 through arrest procedures, and destroy 2,500 stores. I woke up that Sunday morning planning a leisurely day with Sally by the pool. When I heard news of the trouble, I reacted in a most un-*LIFE*-like way: I hoped it would blow over rather than blow up and I could stay in Los Angeles a couple of days longer.

Instead of going to the airport as I would have on any other day, I called Chicago and asked Richard Woodbury and Bob Bradford, the bureau correspondents, to take a photographer and go to Detroit. If the trouble ended in a day, or even two, there would be no story for us (there had already been riots in four major cities that summer), but I could not risk ignoring the possibility of widespread violence. My main fear was that Detroit would explode and I would be caught in Los Angeles when Rowan called to ask how our coverage was going.

Sally and I enjoyed a quiet, much-needed Sunday together, even though my instincts kept nudging me to head back to Chicago. By evening, it was clear that I had to go. I packed and caught what I later discovered was one of the last planes allowed to land in Detroit. Flights into the city were cancelled as the violence grew. Before leaving, I recruited two more reporters from New York and laid on two more photographers to help with our coverage.

While I was in the air, Governor George Romney called out the Michigan National Guard and began discussions with President Johnson about getting regular army troops. They quickly reached an impasse. Romney was the presumptive Republican candidate for president in the coming 1968 election, and Johnson wanted to avoid anything that would strengthen his chances. He wanted Romney to declare the situation beyond his control—in effect, admit defeat—before Johnson would send federal help. Romney balked, but only for a few hours. There were too many fires burning and too many people being shot and killed.

I arrived to find the entire *LIFE* crew watching television in a room at the Harland House Motel. There were empty pizza boxes but no photographs and only a few notes taken from the television coverage. No one had ventured into the streets, conducted an interview, or sought any original information. Television news, it appeared, had become the primary source of information, even for reporters.

I had been exposed to violence as a police officer. Even in this very chaotic moment I felt clearheaded about what needed to be done. I organized everyone into teams, assigned each team an area of the city, helped them plaster *LIFE* shipping stickers on their cars, and then sent them off, hoping they would actually go out and report, not just circle back to the motel or hang out in a Howard Johnson's until things cooled down. No one was really prepared for this kind of assignment. Most had been enjoying expense-account lunches only hours before, and now we had to drive into a burning city where it was assumed our color (or lack of it) would make us targets. My colleagues had not signed up for combat reporting. The idea would take getting used to. Personally, I was ahead of the game. I felt a need to be cautious, but truth be told, I did not feel afraid.

About midnight I drove slowly down a nearly deserted street heading into the area of the most intense violence. Lee Balterman, a veteran photographer, and Julie Greenwald, our Detroit stringer, accompanied me. Only blocks from our motel, a young National Guardsman stationed in the middle of the street signaled for us to stop. He was in what then passed for combat gear, a steel helmet and wrinkled fatigues. He held an M1 rifle recently loaded with live ammunition. He looked tired and tense and hardly old enough to be in uniform.

"You can't be out here," he said angrily.

"We're press."

"I don't care."

"The governor said very clearly today that the press would have full access to the city."

"You can't go down this street. I'm tellin' you."

"Soldier, we have the right to go down this street, and we have the governor's permission."

The M1 muzzle trembled slightly as he moved it toward my face. Balterman, sitting behind me, moved to the other side of the car.

"You ain't goin' down this street."

I saw a sergeant standing under a streetlight half a block away.

"I'll tell you what, soldier," I said. "I'm going to drive up to where that sergeant is and ask his permission."

"You don't understand," he said, weighing the M-1 in his hands. "I'd just as soon kill you as to kill a nigger."

I was relieved by his lack of prejudice. The sergeant was watching us now. I waved to him. When the guardsman turned slightly to see who I waved at, I eased off the brake and let the car begin to roll. The guardsman withdrew his rifle, and I drove very, very slowly to the sergeant, who, luckily, was aware of the governor's orders. He waved to the guardsman who had stopped us and then waved us on into the dark and apparently deserted streets. When I turned to look at my passengers to share my sense of triumph, I saw masks of fear.

We could see that the city was now full of young men, mostly white, woefully untrained, fearful, and without much information. What they did have were weapons, some of them heavy machine guns, and live ammunition. Before it was over, rumors of a sniper in an apartment building would cause a National Guard tank crew to rake the building with .50-caliber machine-gun fire, the heavy bullets tearing through brick, turning shards into secondary projectiles and killing a four-year-old girl clinging to her floor for safety. Other than her family, no one paid much attention to the event. She was just another victim of the violence.

As we prowled the streets looking for our story, a woman staying at our motel walked to a lighted second-story window above the reception area. As she stood peering into the darkness, a sniper killed her with a single well-aimed shot. Whether she was shot by a guardsman, a rioter, or a panicked police officer was never determined. Just another victim of the violence.

For the next three days, we worked virtually around the clock. The people who couldn't deal with physical danger left (with my blessings) and returned to New York. The cooler heads, the people who could work under dangerous conditions, got better and better as their confidence grew. They became battle hardened.

Fires and confrontations between citizens and police made great pictures. Our major obstacle was lighting. Much of the violence took place at night, in deep darkness except where fires burned brightly. It is safe to say that no photographer welcomes a situation where the range of light is extreme, and fire at night offers the greatest of extremes.

High-contrast light had been a problem in Watts. It was a problem in Detroit, and it was a problem not too many months later when I watched this technical dilemma played out in wonderful human detail.

I was sent to cover Gordon Parks, the African American artistic polymath, as he directed his first feature film, an adaptation of his autobiography, *The Learning Tree*. Gordon, a suave, savvy man who made his way from a Kansas farm to the photographic staff of *LIFE* magazine and beyond, long before affirmative action, now had the opportunity to make a movie, perhaps many. He was nervous, though he need not have been. Consort of Gloria Vanderbilt, poet, composer, photographer, and writer, Gordon was about to master movies. His son, Gordon Jr., assigned by the studio as the unit photographer for the film, became, with me, the *LIFE* magazine team responsible for producing a story on Hollywood's first black director. Gordon Sr., in keeping with his Kansas heritage, wore a big gray cowboy hat that hid his face from the blazing Kansas sun. Gordon Jr. shot many rolls of film as the movie unfolded, and I shipped them to New York. At the end of the first week, Dick Pollard, the director of photography, called.

"You have to talk to Gordon Jr.," he said. "The film is unusable. Gordon just disappears."

I gently broke the news to Gordon Jr. He was astonished. "Look," he said, flipping open his light meter. He took a reading on his father from a few yards away. He showed me the meter and then showed me the setting on his cameras. They corresponded.

"OK," I said. "Now go take a reading on your father's face, under the hat."

Gordon Jr. walked to his father, sitting on a director's chair. He held the meter to his face and watched the needle drop to near zero. Gordon Jr. studied his meter for a moment, then looked at his father and said, "You people of the dark-skinned race make it hard on us photographers."

Gordon Sr. didn't miss a beat. "We're goin' to miss you around here, boy."

We worked it out. Gordon Sr. agreed to push the hat back on his head a bit, and Gordon Jr. used a (horrors!) flash fill. We didn't have the luxury of consulting with our subjects in Detroit, so each photographer found his own way of dealing with the difficult night shots. None were perfect. Everyone felt relieved each morning when the sun appeared.

Daylight revealed downtown Detroit as a field of rubble and trash. Looting is messy. Burning homes and buildings are messy. Where nighttime brought tension and excitement, daylight brought a sense of sadness and loss, not unlike a wild drunken evening followed by a sick, gray hangover.

Then, rather suddenly, with the arrival of regular army troops under General John Throckmorton, the tide turned. Where the Michigan National Guard was poorly trained, loosely disciplined, armed with live ammunition, and inclined to create even more violence than it encountered, the regulars were highly trained and tightly disciplined. Even their pressed uniforms gave them an air of authority that set them apart from the clownish wrinkled uniforms of the Guard.

When a sniper was reported in a building (reports that were often unfounded), Guardsmen fired on the building. Sometimes innocent people died. Sniping was never verified, and the sense of indiscriminate violence grew. By contrast, reports of a sniper caused the regular army troops to form small teams and storm the building, covering one another, going door to door, floor by floor, until the building was cleared or the sniper was caught (none ever were). No shots were fired. Watching the process gave one enormous respect for discipline and training.

When it was finally over, it was clear that the black citizens of Detroit had suffered nearly all the damage. Mostly, it was they who died, who lost their homes and businesses and jobs. It could hardly be called a race riot. It also became clear that much of the violence was personal. What better time to settle a score than under cover of an alleged riot? Burn the house of an annoying neighbor. Kill an enemy. Redeem your clothes from the cleaners, free. Stock up on liquor while you can. The Detroit police settled some scores too, having more to do with their attitudes about race than anything else. Politics, racism, and frustration may have led to the outburst, but the specifics were mostly personal. Eventually, official commissions and investigations would sort out what had happened and why, but by then public attention had moved on, and first impressions, as so often happens, held.

CHAPTER THIRTY-NINE

Franklin Roosevelt was president the year I was born. As a child I knew little about him except that he was respected and admired by my parents and that he led us to victory in World War II. The conflation of a highly respected man with the highest office in America set the tone for my emotional—and to some degree, my intellectual—posture toward the presidency, toward authority, and in an odd way toward being an American. Harry Truman, a man of the people, was similarly admired by my parents (except for a brief falling out when he fired General Douglas MacArthur, one of my father's heroes). General Eisenhower was never criticized at our dinner table for being dull or playing golf. He was held in high esteem as a wise, steady leader who put the interest of the country ahead of all else. Our esteem for him only grew when he delivered his farewell address and warned, "In the councils of government, we must guard against the acquisition of unwarranted influence, whether sought or unsought, by the military-industrial complex. The potential for the disastrous rise of misplaced power exists and will persist." Then there was John F. Kennedy, and who could not love him? We didn't know all there was to know, of course, nor had we known all there was to know about the others, but the presidency remained an office with nearly mystical properties for probity, wisdom, and compassion, for Americans and for the world. This was, for me, a deeply rooted and completely unexamined pillar of my system of belief. It was part of the framework that informed my life.

I had seen Lyndon Johnson up close once when he came to Albuquerque as vice president. I was completely unable to square the big, brash, ugly man with anyone who might ever occupy the highest office in America, the office of Roosevelt, Truman, Eisenhower, and Kennedy. When he asked an aide to find him a "little nigger kid" to sit on his lap for a picture, I witnessed firsthand the contradictions of the man, but as a freshman reporter I didn't understand then what I saw and heard. Without knowing why, I didn't like him. There was something about him that scared me and set off a feeling of wariness. He was not the first big, ambitious, grasping Texan I had come across in my life as a citizen of humble New Mexico, once described as "so far from heaven and so close to Texas."

When Johnson succeeded Kennedy after the assassination, I didn't pay a lot of attention to him because I remained caught up in what Kennedy might have done and in what it meant to our country that elected leadership could be changed by a bullet. The Democrats got my attention when they branded Barry Goldwater as an extremist who might resort to nuclear weapons to settle an ideological dispute. The Republican National Convention in San Francisco, the convention I had interrupted to ask Joe Bride for the New Mexico stringership, had not helped. It was a nasty affair. Partisans cut the wires of television broadcasters because they hated the "liberal media." John Chancellor, the suave NBC correspondent, was arrested on the convention floor for failing to relinquish his space to the "Goldwater Girls," famously signing off, "This is John Chancellor, somewhere in custody." The tone of the gathering, as Loudon Wainwright so perfectly caught it, was the whine of very well-off people come together to complain they didn't have it better. Johnson became more appealing each day.

Now, with nearly half a million Americans in mortal jeopardy in Vietnam, with 11,150 Americans killed in action, Johnson hardly seemed like the levelheaded man of peace we had chosen over the "warmonger" Goldwater. (The number of Americans killed would rise to nearly 60,000 before the war ended.) The fact that he had appointed Thurgood Marshall to be the first black justice of the Supreme Court did not, for me, counterbalance the wholly illegal war he was conducting in Asia. The Voting Rights Act of 1965 was an amazing accomplishment, yet the summer of 1967 saw the worst riots ever in black neighborhoods. Gradually, America's greatest moral battle, the battle for civil rights, was being eclipsed by the awful war in Asia.

The fact that I now began to get an occasional letter from my father praising the commitment, moral fiber, and dedication of the young officers he had met and obviously admired in the villa he shared with ten or twelve other men somewhere in Saigon only added to my frustration. He didn't understand, as many of my fellow citizens did

257

not understand, that opposition to the war was not about the quality and integrity of the US military. That was never seriously in question. It was about the moral and legal foundations of the action our president continued to pursue—in effect, an elective war now killing thousands each year.

By October that year, about the time one hundred thousand people gathered in Washington to protest the war, Rowan agreed that I would be the permanent Chicago bureau chief and Sally could move from Los Angeles. It was wonderful to have an established home once again, but new dark currents appeared, coursing through my mind as I watched the country morph into something I had never seen.

Who could respect a president who took the law into his own hands to pursue a widely despised war with goals and outcome not defined—a president who seemed to double down with each defeat? Respectable people were taking to the streets to protest and be arrested. Young men were using every possible ruse to avoid the draft; thousands enrolled in graduate school with no purpose other than to avoid the war, some went to Canada, others declared themselves to be gay or addicted. Those with family connections managed to get into the National Guard, a reserve force that more and more appeared to be a safe haven for sons of the rich and powerful, many of whom supported the war but not for their sons. Others with clout found their way into exempt government jobs with organizations like the US Public Health Service or USAID. The war was turning ordinary people into frauds, liars, hypocrites, and even criminals—and those who went and fought, either out of duty and valor or because they lacked the resources to avoid it, would find a shocking general lack of appreciation for their sacrifice. It wasn't shaping up anything like World War II.

The old standards were dissolving. Thousands of young people were rejecting the social values of their elders, opting for free love, dope, and rock and roll. They actively embraced highly abstract values like "unconditional love of all mankind." The Summer of Love in San Francisco in 1967 and other similar enclaves around the country brought together many thousands, celebrating a new rejection of America's middle-class values: consumerism, sexual restraint, work, and deference to authority.

It was the beginning of the ascendency of popular culture over traditional culture. When John Lennon said, "The Beatles are more popular than Jesus now," he was denounced, but he understood in

258

his gut what was happening. When Tim Leary said that summer that people should "tune in, turn on, and drop out," he was taken seriously as a lifestyle coach.

I had never thought of myself as a conservative, but the line of demarcation between liberal and conservative was moving fast to the left. Not being ready to go into the streets, wear tie-dyed clothes, or give myself to rock and roll didn't make me a conservative, but it did make me suspicious that I was getting stodgy. I let my hair grow a little longer and bought a pair of bell-bottom trousers to wear on weekends. I honestly felt more at home in the Brooks Brothers suits I wore all week, but if bell bottoms were the wave of the future, I didn't want to be left entirely behind.

The notion of a carefree existence, a kind of return to the Garden of Eden, was appealing, but I was old enough to know better. Those naked babies with dirty bottoms crawling around on the Merry Pranksters' bus in Los Angeles were the morning after of the hippie dream. As appealing as the total rejection of responsibility seemed at times, I knew it would come to a sorry end.

It was a time that fostered resentment and self-indulgence. I resented the national leadership's cowardice and pigheaded refusal to admit a mistake. I understood the feelings that led some people to commit crimes of civil disobedience in pursuit of peace. I understood the rage and frustration of some of the peace marchers. Given the political climate and the tsunami of social change sweeping the country, self-indulgence was easy to justify. If the hippies were taking tons of dope and sleeping with everyone, then how bad was a double scotch and a discreet one-night stand? Resentment and self-indulgence are a toxic mix. Feeling angry at authority together with feeling that official moral failures justify personal excesses is more than just a slippery slope. It is a formula for self-destruction.

The late 1960s was a time to be wise, morally cautious, and sober. Professionally, I handled it well enough, delivering the goods for my editors week after week. Personally, I could have done better.

CHAPTER FORTY

The upheavals of 1967 were just the opening act. Events in 1968 pushed beyond anything we could have imagined. The year began happily enough for me. On New Year's Eve, Sally and I went to a black-tie dinner given by one of the *Time* magazine correspondents who shared office space with me in the Prudential Building in downtown Chicago.

Leaving our new apartment on the Near North Side, I got my first feel of a Chicago winter. It was a clear night and ten below zero. Tires on the cab that came to pick us up squeaked as they rolled along the frozen street. My wool overcoat barely turned the cold, and Sally began talking about the need for a good fur coat. I felt my breath freezing in my nose. Soon enough we arrived at a beautiful apartment where we shed our coats and gathered briefly before a big, hot fire. Looking around the room, I saw that the men in their tuxedos were all handsome and the women in their New Year's gowns were all beautiful. We were young. We were professionals. Either by age or by service, we were beyond the draft. I felt glamorous and free of care, mingling, drinking champagne, and eating caviar. The civil strife tearing at the country and the killing in Asia were temporarily banished.

That sense of being aloof from the troubles and confusions of the world, of being in a special place where things were in order and where permanence was possible, did not last much beyond New Year's Day. Before the month was out, I was off to Colorado to do a story on the controversial new state law that permitted abortions in the case of rape or incest or in cases where the pregnancy compromised the health of the mother.

Until Colorado acted, I assumed that legal abortion was beyond the bounds of what American society would ever permit. I wasn't alone in this belief. There had not been much organized opposition to passage of the Colorado law, because no one thought abortion *needed* to be opposed. Researching the story I discovered that this was another of those fault lines in American society where, just beneath the surface, great forces were grinding with increasing weight against one another. I would soon discover an enormous, though largely unvoiced, belief among many men and women that, in certain circumstances, abortion was the right and perhaps the only choice. At a deeper level, women were beginning to think and feel that decisions about their bodies belonged to them. This thinking would come as a shock to the large but shrinking number of men and women who believed that everyone agreed that abortion was essentially murder.

The assignment recalled whispered stories from my college years of men driving girlfriends to Juárez for abortions. The stories were repeated as scandal, meant to be shocking, and they were. Abortion was not discussed in polite conversation. In 1950s New Mexico, even desperate circumstances threatening the life of a mother or the possible birth of a horribly deformed child were not held, on a public level, to be cause for an abortion. It was understood that women of means who had an ongoing relationship with their doctor could arrange a quiet procedure to deal with an unwanted pregnancy, if it was done early enough. Poor women and young women without family support suffered the shame and dangers of illegally performed abortions. They were, of course, largely without voice or power, so their suffering remained hidden.

Then, in 1962, Sherri Finkbine, a married mother of four children living in Arizona, discovered that she was carrying a fetus without legs and with only one arm, horribly deformed by the drug thalidomide. Sold in Europe and England to calm morning sickness but never approved by the FDA, thalidomide would eventually cause seven thousand babies to be born deformed, more than half of whom would die. Mrs. Finkbine discovered this after taking the drug, obtained in England, and now she needed an abortion. Hers would have been another case of a quiet procedure known only to her and her doctor, but in an effort to warn other women of the dangers of thalidomide, she spoke to a reporter. Her identity and her intentions were soon revealed.

Her plight set off a great debate in Arizona when she was ultimately denied access to the procedure. She flew to Sweden, where the fetus, said by her doctors not to be viable, was removed. Back home, she suffered great abuse, including the loss of her job. Her plight aroused the sympathy of women across the country and began a serious debate as to just exactly who should decide the question of how a pregnancy is managed.

I remember my mother's outrage at Finkbine's plight. "The very idea that a bunch of men can tell this poor woman that she has to give birth to a monster," Mother said, almost in tears of rage. "That they would put her through that! It just burns me up!"

By "a bunch of men" she referred accurately to the all-male legislature and the largely male medical and judicial establishment. That was probably the first time I had discussed the topic with my mother, and it may have been the last, but in those few moments I understood the depth and intensity of the solidarity among women on the issue. It was not primarily abortion that drove my mother's anger; it was a woman's right to her own body. It was about a line between the state and the individual woman, an issue on which my mother had strong libertarian tendencies.

Sally was as interested in the abortion issue as my mother was, and since we had not had a lot of time together after I got the Chicago assignment, we arranged for her to go with me to Denver. She had taught school in Los Angeles, as she had in New York and in Albuquerque before that, but with my slightly higher salary as bureau chief, we felt we could afford for her to quit. She didn't love teaching, but the main motivation for her leaving the profession was chronic insomnia. She spent many, many nights lying awake, knowing that she would be exhausted in the morning as she faced a long day in the classroom. Relief from that dread was a tremendous liberation. She blossomed in her new leisure, returning to the piano with gusto, making friends, and enjoying her life. Part of that enjoyment was being able to accompany me occasionally.

In Denver I looked up Richard Lamm, the young member of the Colorado House of Representatives who had written the abortion law and shepherded it though the legislature. It was not a single-handed effort, but he was the most important single actor. Bright, energetic, and iconoclastic, he would soon become a three-term governor. I made a mental note that I would be back in Colorado to write more about him.

It was not a complicated story. The disagreement on who should make decisions about abortion was well documented. The news was simply that Colorado had made it legal in certain circumstances. I did a few other necessary interviews, wrote my report about how the law came to be passed, filed my copy, shipped our film, and then Sally and I left for New Mexico, where I wanted to spend a few days.

It had been two and a half years since I left Albuquerque for New York and *LIFE* magazine, but the pace of events had been so fast that it seemed more like months. In Denver, enjoying the clear, high-altitude light and the sere western scenery, I realized how much I missed my home state. We decided to go to Santa Fe for a couple of days to eat the incendiary native green chile, smell a piñon fire, walk in the bright January sun, enjoy the soft lines and warm colors of the adobe buildings, and recharge that part of ourselves that New Mexico fed.

We splurged on a room with a fireplace at La Fonda on the plaza. After a long walk through town, we came back to our room as the sun started down. We opened a bottle of wine and made a fire. When I turned on the evening news, Walter Cronkite appeared and announced a large-scale offensive by Communist forces under way all across Vietnam. Cronkite was calm and even, but a sense of urgency in him communicated something big and dangerous going on, with heavy fighting even in Saigon itself. When I heard that Tan Son Nhut Air Base was under fire, I thought of my father. I called Mother to see if she had any news.

"No," she said. "I haven't heard a word, but it just happened. I'm sure your dad will call soon. I'm sure he's all right. You may not realize it, but he's wily."

We talked for the first time about my father's safety and his decision to go to a war zone. I understood that she fully supported the undertaking, but she sounded lonely. I sensed that things were not well with her. We speculated about what had happened, about why, only two months before, General William Westmoreland had told the National Press Club that as of the end of 1967, the Communists were "unable to mount a major offensive." I didn't understand how he could be so wrong. What Cronkite now reported sounded major. Even the embassy in Saigon was under fire. Mother was less concerned, but she promised to call the minute she heard from my father.

As was often the case when I spoke to my mother on the phone, I hung up feeling dissatisfied, as though there was unfinished business that could never be finished. Ours was a relationship that Sisyphus would have understood.

The Tet Offensive did not ruin our little vacation in Santa Fe, but it certainly cast a shadow over the rest of our stay. Before we left for Chicago, Mother called to say that my father was fine. He had witnessed some of the action and said the Vietcong never had a chance.

After Tet, my sense of the war as a personal burden grew daily. My opposition was not just intellectual. I felt the war. In complete disregard of the idea that one should only deal with what is real and present, I could not still the empathy, abstract as it was, that I felt for the people who fought, who were wounded, and who died. Each evening the news reminded us of the continuing carnage, fire, and destruction. There was so much blood, sweat, and mud. I felt none of the team spirit that caused me to exult in 1943 when the radio reported a crushing victory over Axis forces. The day Italy surrendered, I was carrying water from the well into my grandmother's kitchen when I heard the news. I sang, "One down and two to go," over and over as I finished my chores. When I watched newsreels reporting Allied advances before a Saturday movie began, I was able to feel real pride, real solidarity with the troops. Photographs of exhausted or wounded US soldiers gave me a sense of belonging to a tough and enduring people, not a sense of shame that they were being needlessly hurt on my behalf. America had become a bully, and our soldiers were being squandered to save face for the big, ugly Texan in the White House. When I walked through the waiting room of Washington National Airport that winter and saw dozens of young men fresh out of Walter Reed Hospital, all missing arms or legs or eyes, waiting to fly home, I wanted to cry. They were kids. I wanted to apologize to them for not having done more to stop what hurt them.

They did not need or want my sympathy, of course. Perhaps they felt good about what they sacrificed, the way my father felt good about what he was doing. That didn't change what I felt. Day by day, the sense that the country was on a disastrously wrong course grew and inhabited my mind. Now, Jeremiah stalked my consciousness. Even Cronkite, the "most trusted man in America," said the war should end. But who would step forward to make it happen?

CHAPTER FORTY-ONE

Late in November 1967, I paid little attention when an obscure senator from Minnesota announced his intention to run for president, challenging Lyndon Johnson in his own party. Two days after his announcement in Washington, Senator Eugene McCarthy came to Chicago, where he delivered what I thought was a decent speech but one that was harshly criticized by the left-leaning Democrats in the audience of the Convention of Concerned Democrats. They wanted to hear a fire-and-brimstone speech denouncing the war and a direct attack on Johnson. McCarthy, as I would soon learn, was a man of moderation, a man of carefully measured words. He wasn't Their Guy, but he turned out to be The Guy.

After the Chicago speech, and after much urging by supporters, McCarthy entered the New Hampshire primary and campaigned throughout January and February, essentially without any political organization or much money. He tended to rise above the necessary political activities of fundraising, flattery, and networking—believing, he said, that he represented a cause, not just himself, and if people believed in the cause they would come and help. Even people of good faith who wanted to help found him difficult and distant, a reluctant champion, but the only one around. The better-known liberal warhorses, such as Hubert Humphrey and Robert Kennedy and George McGovern, had been co-opted. They refused to challenge Johnson on the war and were actually supporting him for reelection.

In the beginning McCarthy appeared so inept and distant that the *New York Times* was said to have issued orders to its reporters to ignore him. Then an odd thing happened. Young people, mostly college students, who were desperate for leadership on the issue of the war began to show up uninvited to help with the campaign. Knowing that the people of New Hampshire were socially conservative and not likely to be persuaded by a bearded bigmouth, the students shaved, put on conventional clothes, got "clean for Gene," and began canvassing the state, house to house in the cold and dark. As word of their efforts spread, thousands more began the trip to New Hampshire—until they threatened to overwhelm the state. Word was sent out at higher and higher volume that no more should come. Their efforts were rewarded when, on the second Tuesday in March, McCarthy won 42 percent of the votes in the Democratic primary, a clear demonstration that Johnson was vulnerable.

As new as McCarthy was at running for president, I was even newer at covering people running for president, so it was with no experience in covering national politics that I showed up one cold March morning at Chicago's O'Hare Airport to join the ragtag group of reporters now assigned to McCarthy's campaign as he began his effort to win the Wisconsin primary.

I self-consciously tried to blend in with the press corps. It was a small group, perhaps fifteen of us, and it included some very experienced and able reporters. Ned Kenworthy of the *New York Times* was the most senior and able among us. He was articulate, thoughtful, and filled with kinetic energy that made younger reporters seem slothful. (After the New Hampshire primary, the *Times* changed its mind about McCarthy, as did much of the professional political establishment.) Kenworthy was a constant thorn in the side of Seymour Hersh, McCarthy's press secretary, on leave from UPI in Washington, DC. Kenworthy's major gripe was McCarthy's nonchalant disregard for deadlines. He often made important announcements too late to make the evening news, and he delivered speeches at times that were inconvenient for press or television reporters. I felt sorry for Hersh, caught as he was between a demanding press corps and a laid-back candidate who would fly the whole bunch of us (at our expense) to a distant state so that he could deliver a speech for a fee in order to pay his daughter's tuition, all in the middle of a presidential campaign. In a way I felt superior to Hersh. He represented to me the fall of a man who leaves journalism for politics. The Pulitzer Prize he won two years later and the ten books he would publish over a prize-showered career would demonstrate how quickly one can recover from a fall.

Most of the really big papers were on board: the *Los Angeles Times*, the *Chicago Tribune*, and the *Boston Globe*. The wire services were there:

Associated Press, United Press International, and Reuters. Periodically we would be joined by network television crews and famous reporters from other magazines, such as Michael J. Arlen of the *New Yorker*. William Styron, a month away from a Pulitzer Prize for *The Confessions of Nat Turner* and accompanied by his beautiful wife, the poet Rose Burgunder, briefly joined the campaign. Though they were not members of the press corps, they hung out with us, and when they held court at the bar in the Pfister Hotel, reporters were three deep around them. The sense of hope created by McCarthy's showing in New Hampshire was like a pheromone lure to those hungry for peace. Hundreds, then thousands—some of them very rich and famous—made the trip to Milwaukee in the next few weeks to offer their help.

The casual structure of the campaign allowed me far more access than a reporter normally has. I was able to spend time in the senator's suite and hang around his senior staff. John Dominis, an accomplished *LIFE* staff photographer, already semifamous for his work during the Korean War, joined me, and we traveled with McCarthy to New York and back to Washington, DC. In a limited sense we behaved with the senator as friends might when sharing a meal and drinks. Even in those hours of relative intimacy, I understood that if McCarthy's campaign ever really took off, I would be elbowed away from the table by serious heavyweights, but it was still too early for that. The New Hampshire primary brought McCarthy to national attention, but Johnson was still a tremendously powerful president in full control of the party machinery. Robert Kennedy was—almost literally—lurking in the wings, and McCarthy gave no sign that he was prepared to give up the huge chunks of himself that a serious national campaign would require. He was not yet considered a real player. Hanging out with him, if one could ever be said to hang out with Gene McCarthy, I began to see a very complex man. He was skeptical in the way that intelligent people are. His doubts could easily be read as cynicism. He once said, "Being in politics is like being a football coach. You have to be smart enough to understand the game, and dumb enough to think it's important."

He was deeply read in history, and he loved and wrote poetry. His formal Catholic education instilled a rigorous Thomist method in his thinking. Without illusions about the fallibility of man, he was optimistic about the ability of people to form and maintain civilized societies and communities, and he seemed to think they had a duty to do so. What some people took to be a lazy attitude toward the rituals of politics, I saw as a refusal to be consumed by it. I believe he feared and disliked social chaos and that part of his motivation for running against the war was the hope that moral, moderate voices might keep the peace movement from being hijacked and run off the rails by the far left.

One of the most important tasks of good political reporting is the reporter's ability to look into the character of his subject and understand the kind of person who seeks to lead us—and, of course, to assess whether that person has the energy, desire, and charm to make a successful run. My job was made especially difficult by my lack of experience in this rather refined task and by the simple fact that McCarthy was fifty-one and I was twenty-nine. He was elected to the US House of Representatives when I was nine years old. He was a US senator. I was a relatively green reporter. He was far better educated than I, experienced in the ways of Washington and seeking to become, as they say, the leader of the free world. I was seeking to write three thousand words that would make it into the magazine and not embarrass me later.

CHAPTER FORTY-TWO

McCarthy had written four books by 1968. The most salient of them for my purposes was *The Limits of Power*: *America's Role in the World*. I read this carefully, along with a number of his poems—which I found to be generally obscured by allusions to material with which I was not familiar—and then I retreated to Chicago to write my essay.

My instincts about McCarthy were clear: He was an intelligent, moral man. He was literate, learned, charming when he chose to be, and aloof by default. He was impatient with foolishness and with much of the silly theater that accompanies politics. He was vain and arrogant by nature, but his religious training had given him some insight into these flaws and the tools to deal with them, when he saw fit to use those tools. He was competitive, but he wrote the rules for the competition. That he was an intellectual who had been the highest scorer on his college hockey team in Minnesota said something about his character.

I didn't write a love letter, but the first ten pages of my piece pointed out the man's virtues. The second ten pages discussed his shortcomings and the difficulty he would have ever actually being elected president. He wanted the war in Vietnam to end in a manner that did not disgrace America, but I was pretty sure he did not really want to be president. A burning desire to hold the office has historically been a basic requirement.

I sent the piece ahead and then flew to New York for the editing. I waited nervously in an empty office I had claimed on the twenty-ninth floor of the Time-Life Building, wishing the phone would ring and dreading the call. Several of my editors were busy reading the piece, the most important of them being Roy Rowan, the assistant managing editor who had sent me to Chicago and the man who came as close to being a mentor as I would ever have. At about 7:30 that evening, Roy called.

"I read your piece," he said. "Good piece."

"Oh, thank you." I was about to give in to exultation when he went on. "I think it begins on page eleven."

"Really? Why?"

"Well, you make him out to be a great man, but do you really want this guy's finger on the trigger?"

"I guess I hadn't thought about that," I said lamely. "I may prefer it to Johnson's."

Roy's reading of my piece was that I wanted to elect McCarthy president. What I really wanted was for McCarthy's candidacy to end the war. In order for him to have a chance to do that, his candidacy had to be credible. A story in *LIFE* magazine essentially endorsing the man might scare the moral laggards in Washington into some sort of self-examination. I was trying to make a three-bank shot. Rowan just wanted to sink the eight ball.

I argued briefly, but it was pointless. I could either cut the piece, rewrite the last half to make it whole and move on, or I could raise a huge stink and take my name off the piece and watch them run something even less flattering than what I might eventually get through the process. Dominis's photographs were good, and we got a lot of space between my three thousand words of running text and his pictures. The headline, something over which I had no control, read, "Everybody Loves Gene, until He Takes the Stump."

We ultimately accommodated the good-guy part of the man and essentially played into the hands of the hard Left by repeating their claim that McCarthy lacked the cojones to take down Johnson. Rowan was not entirely wrong. In fact, as a journalist, he was probably closer to the mark than I was. I had let my disgust with the war turn me into an advocate, and without really thinking about it I was promoting my candidate. There was nothing wrong or unusual about that. I was just too junior to get away with it.

I was in Chicago when the piece came out. I didn't hear anything from McCarthy's people, although I was sure they read it and felt sure they would be disappointed. They had pegged me as a fan, but Rowan had backed the piece down several notches from fandom. In the odd dynamic that happens between journalist and subject, especially between journalists and politicians, I found myself wondering if the McCarthy people would think me disloyal. They had allowed me virtually unlimited access to the candidate, and I had failed, at least in print, to be completely charmed. I understood that my loyalty was due first to my employer, my principles, and my readers, but I did not have to meet any of them face to face. I would have to show up at the McCarthy camp and rejoin the press corps, probably without the special access I had enjoyed. Also, the political professionals understood that I was a one-shot. *LIFE* would not publish a second story about McCarthy written by me. My useful life, as far as the campaign was concerned, was over.

"Ah, the rats return to the ship," McCarthy's senior aide teased when I showed up to rejoin the campaign.

"Did he hate it?" I asked.

"You accused him of a serious sin."

"I what?"

"You said that he 'adores Sir Thomas More.'"

"Yeah?"

"Well, obviously you're not Catholic."

"No, I'm not."

"In Catholic theology it is a sin to adore anything but God. You have accused him of breaking the First Commandment."

"Are you serious?"

"Not entirely, but it does make you look foolish—doesn't it?—that you didn't know."

That was part of the payback. The mistake bothered me. Who knew that "adore" held such a special meaning among serious Catholics? And, I wondered, why didn't one of *LIFE*'s crack researchers catch my error? I slogged on, a spent cartridge now following the campaign just in case something truly spectacular happened, like an assassination attempt.

As March progressed, we were not on the plane so much. McCarthy began serious local campaigning to win the Wisconsin primary, which meant a killer schedule of appointments, speeches, personal appearances, news conferences, interviews, and long bus rides. We were loaded onto buses each morning at 5:30 to begin the daily schedule, which often included an appearance at 6:30 or a breakfast speech at 7:00. The day ground on and on until he made a speech at dinner somewhere in the state, and we returned to the hotel at 9:00 or 10:00 p.m. Sixteen-hour days were not an empty brag. They were the stuff of a serious campaign.

My habit was to hit the hotel bar after the last event to discuss the day with other reporters over two or three drinks. I couldn't sustain it.

After a week, I was so tired at my 4:30 a.m. wakeup call that I could hardly get out of bed. I recalled some advice I'd received at the *Tribune* six years earlier when President Kennedy came to Albuquerque. I went to the airport to cover the president's arrival. *Air Force One* sat on the tarmac, proud and impressive. Behind it was another aircraft of the same size and type carrying the national press corps. After I handed the president off to the reporter who rode in the motorcade, I climbed onto the press plane just to see how the big time looked. The seats were a tangle of briefcases, coats, newspapers, and half-eaten food. A few reporters who had skipped the president's in-town visit remained on board, typing, sleeping, or reading papers. A very friendly and very attractive stewardess who surmised from my dress and notepad that I was a local reporter engaged me in conversation.

"How about a bloody mary or a martini?"

It was 9:00 a.m., but I saw that the bar on the plane was in full operating mode. "Are people drinking already?" I asked. "This early?"

"Oh, sure," she said. "Let me get you something."

"No, no thanks." A drink would wipe out the rest of the day.

When I returned to the paper, our managing editor, George Baldwin, asked me about the national press corps. Slightly scandalized by what I'd seen, I said, "They were drinking already."

"Some of them," George replied. "That's all changing. They used to drink all day, but you can't do that anymore. Can't compete. The young guys, the ambitious ones, they don't drink." He went back to his layouts.

I began to notice on the McCarthy press bus that many of the reporters I saw working busily all day as we rode from appearance to appearance were not to be seen in the bar crowd at night. They were mostly the younger men. I began to feel negligent. I chided myself for not paying closer attention to my work.

I was right to observe that I was staying up too late drinking. I needed to feel fresh at 4:30 a.m., and I couldn't do that if I stayed up until eleven nursing a scotch. But I was mistaken to think that I wasn't working hard enough. That year I had reported and written an article about an Arkansas prison farm where, for years, inmates had been tortured, beaten, and killed—their bodies buried in unmarked graves, recently opened as part of an investigation initiated by Governor Winthrop Rockefeller. "Buried Secrets of a Prison Farm" was followed by a major text piece, "The Ghetto Block," which appeared in the March 8 issue. It had required six weeks of hard work interviewing gang members in one of the most dangerous areas of Chicago's West Side ghetto. That article, combined with articles by Gordon Parks and Jack Newfield, won the National Magazine Award for *LIFE* in 1968. The McCarthy piece made three bylined pieces in three months, a record as good as anyone at the magazine—except for columnists, such as Hugh Sidey, Shana Alexander, and Loudon Wainwright, who appeared weekly or biweekly, whether or not they were ready.

In early March, the monotony of the campaign routine was broken early one evening when McCarthy got a call from Senator Robert Kennedy. He wanted to send Senator Ted Kennedy for a meeting with McCarthy, presumably to persuade McCarthy to support Robert when he announced that he was entering the race. McCarthy agreed to the meeting, but privately he wanted the world to know that the Kennedys had reached out to him wanting him to withdraw. A McCarthy aide quickly leaked Ted Kennedy's plans to the ABC network team covering the campaign. At about nine o'clock that evening, I followed along behind the television crew as they got into position in the hall of the Pfister Hotel. When the elevator doors opened on McCarthy's floor, the big television lights went on, catching Ted Kennedy and two aides standing in the elevator, looking literally like deer in the headlights. They blinked for an instant, and then someone leaned over and coolly pressed the button to close the door before they could be asked any questions. This was McCarthy's answer to Robert Kennedy's request.

We did not see them again. The next day, March 16, Robert Kennedy announced that he would enter the race for the presidency.

The McCarthy people were upset by the announcement. They felt McCarthy had shown enormous courage in challenging President Johnson. Only now that McCarthy had shown Johnson to be vulnerable was Robert Kennedy, who perhaps should have led the charge, willing to enter the race. They also understood that Kennedy enjoyed broad support and would be very hard to beat. Everyone was still stewing two weeks later when we turned on the television on Sunday night, March 31, to listen to an address by President Johnson. After some preliminary discussion about the war in Vietnam and his next move against the Communists, Johnson announced that he would not run for president again. I was alone in my room watching the broadcast. I ran for the elevator and went to the lobby, where a crowd of journalists and campaign aides were in pandemonium. Every phone in the place was in use. People looked stunned. There would be celebrations, but not until much later. The news was too shocking and too unexpected to be processed in a short time. Now everything had changed.

The next morning as I hurried through the hotel on my way back to Chicago, I passed a large meeting room where perhaps fifty people were gathered. I was curious, so I ducked in to see what was happening. Richard Nixon stood at the front of the room. Tall, dark, dressed in a perfect navy-blue suit, he looked like an elegant undertaker. I was shocked to see him. My thoughts at the moment would come back to shame me. He's a has-been, I remember thinking. Doesn't he know it's all over for him? He had been defeated in a run for governor of California six years earlier and seemed to be leaving politics when he declared to the press, "You won't have Dick Nixon to kick around anymore." How could he hope to be president if he couldn't get elected governor? If there was ever a year in which making predictions was a fool's game, it was 1968.

On April 2, McCarthy won the Wisconsin primary with 56 percent of the vote. Next came Indiana, where he would face Robert Kennedy head to head.

CHAPTER FORTY-THREE

As I flew to Indianapolis to cover the primary, I reflected on the relationships between reporters and candidates. Most newspapers and newsmagazines, unlike *LIFE*, assigned a reporter to cover each credible campaign. If the candidate dropped out or was forced out of the race, that reporter was reassigned. If the candidate went all the way, the reporter who covered him during the campaign often became the White House correspondent. The fortunes of the candidate and those of the reporter thus became deeply entwined. Reporters walked a narrow path between being too fawning or reporting too critically and alienating their subject. A campaign staff could easily keep a reporter at a distance. In the competitive world of political reporting, getting information even minutes late can put one out of the running. Generally, reporters become fans in spite of themselves. It's like hanging out in the Yankee dugout day after day. Eventually, you want them to win.

Time magazine writer Robert Ajemian once told me how, early in John F. Kennedy's campaign, he filed a story that was not critical but was not wholly supportive. After *Time* published the story, he was sitting in a press car in a Kennedy motorcade when the door flew open and Ethel Kennedy, Robert's wife, slid into the car beside him, hip to hip, literally in his face. "When are you going to get on the bandwagon, Bob?" she demanded. "Politicians are really thin-skinned," Ajemian went on. "They all want to be universally, unconditionally loved."

I concluded that it was too late for McCarthy and me. I had revealed my hand, or at least the hand of the *LIFE* editors, and it was not unconditional love. Still, Indiana was part of the geography for which I was responsible, and I had invested a lot of hours with McCarthy. Indiana could prove to be a landmark if McCarthy was to beat Kennedy. I decided to show up and see if McCarthy and his staff would take me back.

Soon after I arrived in McCarthy's suite, someone said that one of my colleagues was on the way up. I was trying to think who that would be when *LIFE* columnist Shana Alexander came through the door looking like a fifties movie star. She brought a fine pedigree, an absolutely winning smile, a silver pocket flask of Irish whiskey, and, beneath her arm, a thick volume: *1000 Years of Irish Poetry.* I knew my days covering McCarthy were over.

Shana would have the freedom to write some of the same ideas I had written in those first ten pages that were cut, and she would probably go much further in her praise than I had. She was part of a group of McCarthy supporters that had formed at the magazine, and together they had enough influence to support the man openly. I was happy for Shana to replace me, but I felt diminished that she had.

Shana's next column, written just a few days later for the April 12 issue, confirmed what I had predicted. Its title was "A Poet's Voice Stirs the Land." It was the first of many columns lauding McCarthy and the beginning of a close friendship between the two of them. I packed up and returned to Chicago just in time to hear that Martin Luther King had been murdered in Memphis.

I was sitting at my desk at home trying to think what I should be doing to respond to the event when the phone rang. Sally, playing a Chopin nocturne, stopped when I picked up the phone. It was a woman we knew well, a very wealthy woman living in one of the posh northern Chicago suburbs. We met when *LIFE* covered a charity she ran. Sally and I occasionally had dinner with her and her husband.

"Did you hear about Martin Luther King?" she asked.

"Yes, of course."

"I was glad. It's a good thing."

I was astonished. "Is that why you called?"

"I just wanted to be sure you had heard."

"How can you be glad?"

"He was always stirring up trouble. Maybe things will settle down now that he's gone."

"I can't stay on the phone. We'll have to talk another time." I hung up.

Almost simultaneous with my conversation, Robert Kennedy was in Indianapolis before a large crowd of grieving and angry African Americans. Some of the crowd were calling for violence. Kennedy reminded them that his brother had been killed by a white man, just as it was thought King had been killed. Then, in one of his greatest speeches, he said, "What we need in the United States is not division; what we need in the United States is not hatred; what we need in the United States is not violence or lawlessness, but love and wisdom, and compassion toward one another, and a feeling of justice towards those who still suffer within our country, whether they be white or whether they be black." The crowd was calmed by his words, and in contrast to many other American cities, there was no violence in Indianapolis that night.

Events around the King killing moved too fast for me to get to Memphis. I called New York to see how I could help. They already had a dozen people working on a story, but even with such a major effort, this was the kind of story where television would be absolutely dominant. We had closed the next issue of the magazine the night before King was killed. Now it would be seven days before another came out and almost eleven days before it reached most of our subscribers. There would be very little left unsaid. We could rely on iconic photographs that people could hold and study, unlike the fast-moving images on television, but the urgency would be gone.

In a rather pathetic attempt to be current, the editors managed to switch covers late in the current press run. They pulled a photo of President Johnson announcing that he would not run again and replaced it with a black-bordered image of Dr. King, showing the dates of his life. A week later, the cover was a photo of enduring impact, showing Coretta Scott King in mourning. A full story inside brought the magazine current with events.

This problem of speed and mass audience was central to *LIFE*'s survival. Before television there was only one place, *LIFE* magazine, as the 1930 prospectus stated, "to see life; to see the world; to eyewitness great events; to watch the faces of the poor and the gestures of the proud; to see strange things—machines, armies, multitudes, shadows in the jungle and on the moon; to see our work—our paintings, towers and discoveries; to see things thousands of miles away, things hidden behind walls and within rooms, things dangerous to come to: the women that men love and many children." There was *Look* magazine, of course, but that competition had long ago fallen into an equilibrium that threatened neither magazine. It was television that was slowly eating into the revenue stream at *LIFE* and *Look*.

In the early days of television, when images on the screen were still small and grainy, the big, perfectly executed, and beautifully presented photographs in *LIFE* were in a different league. Then, as television improved, *LIFE* responded by printing color. Then came color television. *LIFE* responded by working with R. R. Donnelley, the Chicago printer that produced the magazine, to develop high-speed color presses. The operation was so financially risky that Time Inc. had to hold the mortgage on the presses. No one else would.

By 1968 the back of the book, the pages of the magazine that could be completed and closed well in advance of publication, were still the home of beautiful color photographs printed with the old "slow-color" technology that required color separations and sequential printing from the various color plates. The front of the book, where news and current events were reported, was printed in black-and-white or high-speed color of a lesser quality. Film shot on Monday, Tuesday, or even Wednesday, if it was really important, could be included in the next issue. That issue would close on Wednesday night and appear on some newsstands by the weekend. But the majority of the magazines would be delivered to eight and a half million mailboxes over the course of the following week.

Through the 1950s and early 1960s, *LIFE* held its own, but television news grew better and better at covering important news and getting film on the air within hours of an event. Sadly, *LIFE* and television were competing for the same audience—people who bought mass-market consumer goods: cars, toothpaste, cigarettes, shampoo, booze. *LIFE* had to print, address, stamp, and mail 96 percent of its circulation. Television simply broadcast. To deliver eight and a half million items to individual subscribers each week involved enormous logistics, not to mention millions in postal fees. I was often struck by the amazing difference in the business model that *LIFE* followed and the one that was now making *Playboy* an absolute gold mine. When Henry Luce started *LIFE* magazine in 1937, he practically gave the magazine away to subscribers and relied on advertisers to pay the bills. Now, faced with television offering huge audiences for very little money, *LIFE* could not easily raise ad rates. Subscriptions were priced so low that to make them pay for the magazine would involve huge increases. Circulation could not be maintained at the prices necessary. By contrast, *Playboy*, because of its risqué content, had been unable to sell much advertising in the beginning. General Motors did not want to be seen next to a nearly naked starlet, so Hefner charged a cover price that paid the bills and relied mostly on newsstand sales for circulation. Then, mores changed. Now General Motors didn't mind being in the same magazine as nude women if their ads were being seen by men age eighteen to thirty-five, who bought a lot of cars. By 1968 advertisers were flooding into *Playboy*, and all that revenue was profit, because the cover price paid the bills. Poor *LIFE* magazine was saddled with eight and a half million subscribers who would not pay much more for the magazine and advertisers that wouldn't either.

Playboy's prosperity would eventually be cut back too as the availability of pornography diminished the lure of the centerfold. And TV, which had taken the power of the immediate image from *LIFE*, would soon enough struggle to adapt to change, to the digital era's 24/7 cable and internet output, which not only "scooped" newspapers but did so at minimal cost. For now, though, in 1968, it was *LIFE*'s existence that was on the line.

I didn't hear a lot of talk about the economics of the magazine, but periodically there would be a meeting of the top editorial people and the top business people, and news of our worsening condition would leak out. I didn't pay much attention to the leaks and rumors until June, when George Hunt, our managing editor, invited all the bureau chiefs to join a group of selected editors for a big editorial dinner in the corporate dining room on the forty-fourth floor of the Time-Life Building.

There had been talk that Hunt might retire following the elections that fall. Time Inc. followed a federal calendar, with big staff changes coming after a national election. Managing editors and Washington bureau chiefs were replaced when the White House got a new occupant. This was both a conceit that imagined the magazines to be almost a branch of government, and a wise practice that prevented a new bureau chief or managing editors from having to get on their feet in the middle of an established administration. If Hunt had run his course and tired of the problems of falling revenues and increasing postal costs, then perhaps it was time for a different editor. A lot of anticipation surrounded what might be hinted at or announced during the dinner.

Hunt was a man of contrasts. He stood well over six feet tall. A Marine Corps officer decorated for his performance in combat in World War II, he also held a fine-arts degree from Amherst College and thought of himself as a painter. He was soft spoken, almost shy, except that he exuded an air of enormous authority. He was a man of large gestures. In anticipation of Winston Churchill's funeral in 1965, he ordered a Boeing 707 to be fitted out with a complete color-film lab, darkroom, and editorial office so that the magazine could be edited and closed in the air as the plane flew from England directly to Chicago. Photographers were stationed at strategic points around England, along roads, in cathedrals, and at public buildings where every aspect of the high pomp of Churchill's funeral was captured on Ektachrome. The film was rushed by motorcycle couriers to the waiting plane. When the last roll of film came on board, the plane left for Chicago. Over the Atlantic, film was developed, pictures selected, pages laid out, text written and edited. When the plane landed in Chicago, the magazine was ready to go to the printers. *LIFE* didn't beat television to the story, but a gloriously illustrated account of one of the great funerals of the century was on the newsstand only hours after the story was on the tube. The act was not sustainable, of course, but it was great fun, and it gave advertising salesmen something very dramatic to talk about when they spoke of *LIFE*'s commitment to excellence and timeliness.

The forty-fourth-floor dining room where we would meet with Hunt was a restrained corporate space that spoke of understated but substantial power. Twenty-foot ceilings capped a room framed by floor-to-ceiling windows offering splendid views of Manhattan. A long mahogany table ran nearly the length of the room. Wide and heavy, it could seat twenty-five people in comfort. A large portrait of Henry Luce looked down on the room from one wall. The carefully designed minimalist decor was altogether tasteful. The room was quiet and dignified, staffed by waiters as carefully dressed and perfectly poised as those in any restaurant in the city. Entering the room, one left all frivolity behind. The feeling was not unlike entering an important church or temple or any place where great power is thought to reside. Reverence and even a little awe were in order for what might happen there. It was a serious place for serious discussions—discussions about how the country was run or should be run, conducted by people who, more often than not, had a hand in running it. Over the course of several years I would share that table with Georgia governor Jimmy Carter, Nixon treasury secretary John Connolly, Jane Fonda, Sophia Loren, CEOs of major corporations, and others whose thoughts and opinions Time Inc. editors might wish to hear.

We gathered for Hunt's dinner at about 6:30. The most immediate topic on everyone's mind was who would win the California Democratic primary. After Gene McCarthy's substantial win in Oregon in May, common opinion held that Kennedy had to win California. Early polling reports indicated that he was indeed on his way.

Jordan Bonfante, the Los Angeles bureau chief for whom I worked before going to Chicago, was getting a drink as I came in. He was the first person I knew who predicted, improbably I thought, that Ronald Reagan would become governor of California. I respected his political instincts and wanted to know his guess about a Kennedy victory. We spoke for a minute about the election and agreed to meet after dinner to go watch the California results.

After two rounds of drinks and a bowl of soup, Hunt opened the discussion by asking what we thought *LIFE* magazine should be in the future. The question seemed to imply that the magazine needed to change and Hunt and others were searching for the right direction. Several opinions were offered, most of them predictable, given the interests of the person speaking. There were the usual clichés that always accompany discussions of news: "hard hitting," "penetrating," "surprising," "insightful." As the discussion progressed, over a main course and dessert, it became clear to me that we were searching for a strategy that would allow the magazine to be current and timely without having to compete directly with television. Then Hunt surprised me by asking to what extent we thought the magazine's role involved entertaining people.

The very word "entertainment" offended me. We were serious journalists. Our role was to inform and teach, to expose wrongdoing and stupidity. We weren't actors or clowns or musicians. I was filled with moral zeal that night, but I had the good sense to keep my mouth shut. Hunt was much more on track as to where the future of magazines lay than I was. In four years, *LIFE* magazine as we knew it would be dead, and two years after that, *People* magazine would be Time Inc.'s leading money-maker.

After dinner, Jordan and I left to find a bar with a television set. I was depressed by what I had heard. The part of my job that I liked most and that gave me the greatest satisfaction was reporting on issues, social movements, and politics, especially abuses of power, like the behavior of a whole series of prison superintendents at the Arkansas prison farm. I enjoyed the show-business stories I had done, but were they really entertainment? I was unsure just what Hunt had in mind when he said "entertain," but I surely didn't support making the magazine any more frivolous than it already was.

Jordan and I sat down at a nice bar somewhere off Sixth Avenue. The television set above the bar was tuned to a news report delivering final results of the California primary. We ordered drinks and watched Robert Kennedy give a victory speech. We both felt that he had a very strong chance of becoming president now that he had won in California. Only minutes after the victory speech ended, the program was interrupted abruptly. A confused announcer said that Senator Kennedy had been shot in the kitchen of the Ambassador Hotel as he was leaving. We were dumbstruck. We thought there must be some mistake. We listened as the television news people got themselves together, and soon enough they said that it appeared that Senator Kennedy had been killed.

It was simply too much to comprehend. What was going on in America? We had turned into a country of political killers. No one was safe. The drinks and wine I had consumed over the past three hours exaggerated my sense of despair. Jordan and I rushed back to the Time-Life Building to see if we were needed. People were crying and cursing. The frustration and anger rolled along the halls. We desperately wanted to find an appropriate response to the enormity of the events, but there was none. After a few hours I returned to my room at the Warwick Hotel, feeling empty and profoundly lonely, and went to bed.

CHAPTER FORTY-FOUR

"I helped you out. Now you got to help me," Peter said over the phone. "They got my momma and my sister. You got to help me."

This was not a voice I wanted to hear. Months earlier, Peter, a gang leader on Chicago's West Side, had provided protection and guidance while a photographer and I virtually lived in a ghetto neighborhood, profiling life along one city block in a dysfunctional area of the city where violence was high and employment low. The result was an award-winning article called, simply, "The Ghetto Block."

Even though I had been generous with meals and other incidentals as we worked on the story, no one had been paid to participate. When the story appeared in March, many of the people whose photos had been used thought they were due compensation. It seemed reasonable enough to them that the magazine was making money using their image and they ought to share in it. I stuck to my position that I was reporting news. They were photographed in public places. They were aware that we were taking pictures for *LIFE*, and they were not due any money. But Peter's request was different. He wasn't asking to be paid. He was asking me to return the help he had given me.

"What do you want me to do?"

"You got to bring some money and come to night court. You got to talk to the judge."

"OK, but what am I trying to do?"

"They're going to set bail. You got to get the judge to set it low so we can get them out."

"What are they charged with?"

"A whole bunch of shit. Receiving and concealing stolen property. Heavy shit."

"OK," I said. "I'll come."

I got directions to the court from Peter. I drew $300 out of petty cash, without any idea of how I might justify the expense, and headed downtown. I found my way into a big municipal courtroom fitted with the standard oak benches and echoing acoustics. The room was sparsely occupied and not well lit. Peter and his sidekick J. J. and several other members of the gang were there when I arrived. I sat down with them.

"So what happened?"

"Somebody hijacked a Sears delivery truck," he said. "They parked it in the alley behind my house, and they dragged all that shit into my basement. When the cops came, they busted my momma and my sister."

In time I would learn that a loaded Sears delivery truck had indeed been stolen and driven into the alley behind Peter's mother's house. The thieves unloaded refrigerators, washing machines, television sets, and other large items and dragged them into the basement. Then, inexplicably, they left the truck in the alley, back door open, tracks in the dirt leading to the house, and all went off to do something else.

When the police arrived, there was no one around but Peter's mother—a woman in her late forties, polite and dignified—and Peter's sister, who was living at home while her husband fought in Vietnam. The police clearly did not believe that these two petite women had dragged several heavy appliances down stairs and into the basement, but they calculated that if they arrested the women, the pressure on the culprits to come forward would be unbearable.

"You got to talk to the judge," Peter repeated with great urgency.

I didn't know what he meant by "talk." What would I say? I was trying to understand what was required of me when a bailiff appeared.

"Excuse me, sir, are you an attorney?"

"No."

"Then what is your business here?"

I was shocked by his question. I didn't have to state my business, but I kept my cool. "I'm a friend of the family," I said. "I'm here to try to help them."

The bailiff looked surprised. He straightened up and looked around the room, thinking. I followed his gaze and realized that the bailiff and the judge and I were the only white people in the room. "Why do you want to help?" he asked, looking back in my direction.

"Peter, this fellow here, and his friends helped me get a story. I work for *LIFE* magazine. I want to return their help in some way." I was still absolutely baffled by what I should do.

"Come with me," the bailiff said.

I looked at Peter. He was nodding vigorously, indicating that I should go. I followed the bailiff into a small office at the back of the courtroom, where he offered me a chair and then sat down himself.

"You have some ID? A press card or something?"

I produced my *LIFE* correspondent's ID card. He looked at my picture and returned the card.

"So tell me again why you want to help."

"These boys—well, young men, I guess—they sort of paved the way for me to do a big story on the West Side ghetto. It's dangerous over there, as you probably know. You may have seen the story if you read *LIFE*." He shook his head in the negative. "One of them called this afternoon and told me his mother had been arrested and that I should come down."

"Did you bring money?"

I thought he might be referring to money for bail. "Yes," I said. I pulled a $100 bill out of my pocket. The bailiff opened the book in his hands and held it out. I placed the bill in the pages and he closed the book. "Wait here," he said. He got up and left. In a few minutes, he returned and sat down, without the book.

"You understand that we are helping you," he said. "You are not helping us, OK?"

"Yes, I understand. I just want to help Peter's mother."

"We are clear about that, right? That we are helping you."

"Yes, clear."

"OK," he said. "The judge wants to meet you."

I assumed that the judge wanted to get a good look at me in case there was trouble later. Peter and company watched carefully as I followed the bailiff through the courtroom and into the judge's chambers. The judge sat behind a desk piled with papers. A reading light hung over the mess. He stood when I entered and offered his hand.

"So," he said, "you work for *LIFE* magazine?"

"Actually, I'm the bureau chief here," I said, shaking his hand.

"Please, sit down."

I sat.

"That must be really interesting work."

The man wanted to chat. I was astonished. I was in the middle of the most officially transgressive transaction of my life, loaded with adrenaline, and he wanted to chat. "It is great work," I said. "Tense at times, but always interesting."

"How about the Bobby thing, huh? That was a shock. Were you out there when that happened?"

"No, no. We had a team traveling with him. They were right there when it happened."

"He would have been president, you know," he said, somewhat wistfully.

"Absolutely."

"Well," he said, offering his hand again. "Good luck."

I returned to the courtroom and sat down beside Peter.

"You talked to him, right?" Peter asked.

"Right."

We waited in silence while the judge mounted the bench and disposed of half a dozen cases. Then Peter's mother and sister were brought out to stand before the bench. The judge shuffled his papers for a moment. Then he addressed the room.

"In my review of this case, I see that neither of you have any criminal record," he began. "And that your husband is serving in Vietnam." He motioned to Peter's sister. She nodded. "I see no indication that either of you is likely to leave the city. Therefore, I set bail at $1,000 each."

Peter jumped up. Then sat down. "You got the $200," he said. I handed him the rest of my cash.

When the time came, Peter posted the bond, 10 percent of the bail, and the women were released. We all retired to the street. Peter's mother, a woman raised in a small town in Arkansas, was polite but wary. I had met her before and she had been cordial, but her brush with the law was an embarrassment. She was cooler than usual. I said good-night to everyone and left.

A few weeks later, the charges against the women were dismissed. The $200 bail money was refunded. Peter kept it.

CHAPTER FORTY-FIVE

It is a truism, but nevertheless amazing, that a single brief moment of insight, or even imagined insight, can alter the future in profound and permanent ways. I don't mean Newton's understanding of gravity after being conked by an apple. I mean that instant when we see a gesture, a look, an unguarded moment that reveals the nature of another person to us in a way that we had never before understood it. Watching Sally with Cathy and my niece Lisa in the summer of 1968 I experienced one of those moments.

That summer, after all the trauma and tension of the primary season and the assassinations of King and Kennedy, I needed to get my personal and spiritual balance back. I had run at full throttle for over a year since taking over the bureau. It had been a productive time, but it had taken its toll.

I was enthusiastically upholding the *LIFE* magazine tradition of two drinks at lunch and more after work. What began as scotch and water became a dry martini straight up, not a formula for steady peace of mind. The fact that I was drinking more than was healthy was not especially apparent, because most of the people I socialized with drank about as much as I did. Sally might have seen booze as a problem, except that compared to her father I was practically abstinent, and she enjoyed drinking too.

The satisfaction and excitement attached to my early success at the magazine was now dimmed by the dawning realization that its days might be numbered, that I might be racing toward a goal that would disappear as I neared the finish line.

I was troubled by the state of the nation—meaning the war in Vietnam that grew deadlier every month—and by the unstringing of the social fabric. It was a small but telling moment when, sometime that June, two journalists I knew from California arrived in town to do a story for a new magazine called *Rolling Stone*, a publication devoted entirely to rock and roll. When I asked them about their assignment, they said they were in town to photograph and interview the Plaster Casters. And who were the Plaster Casters? They were two young women whose shtick was making plaster casts of the erect male members of well-known rock-and-roll musicians. There was a boxed set of four for the Beatles. Jimi Hendrix held the title for size. Would I like to go along, they asked, implying that I too might enter this pantheon of immortals? I demurred, shocked that anyone thought this legitimate material for a magazine, even one devoted to rock and roll.

Hair opened on Broadway that April. I found it transgressive and completely to my liking. Here was a Broadway show that included songs with titles like "Colored Spade" and "Sodomy." The lyrics clearly defended rebellion against the generation in charge, and the show featured a full-frontal nude scene at the end of the first act.

The more convention failed to adequately address the world I saw around me, the more rebellion seemed in order. I found myself feeling increasingly out of step with all the assumptions I brought to adulthood— assumptions about the dignity and probity of the presidency, about respect for authority, hierarchy, and our institutions. I felt like a rock climber, reaching anxiously for the next hand- or toehold as I edged my way forward.

Sally was not faring much better. She alternately enjoyed our high-speed life and found herself beset by unhappiness. There were times when she was full of energy and optimism, laughing and funny. Then she would fall into a period of deep self-doubt and restlessness. I first assumed that the cause was the pressure of teaching, combined with chronic insomnia. I mistakenly thought that when she quit teaching, her unhappiness would disappear. I had always thought of her as the most competent person I knew, but that confidence started to waver, and she began having a harder time making simple decisions. She wanted a piano. We got her a baby grand, and for a time the return to playing seriously seemed to quiet her discontent. Still, moments of deep unhappiness seemed to come and go without any apparent cause.

Our domestic situation was not the easiest. I was gone a lot, working late many days and often distracted by the story that currently engaged me. Sally wanted me to be happy, but as time went on I found that harder and harder to do. I felt disoriented and dissatisfied. In time I came to believe that if I could go back to New York as an editor, I would be happy. Chicago was too far from what I regarded as the center of things.

In an effort to address what seemed to be a gathering crisis for each of us, I decided in June that I would take advantage of *LIFE*'s generous policy of a month of vacation each year. I took off the entire month of July. I was about to turn thirty, which at the time seemed significant. It was a good time to pause and take stock. I invited my mother and Lisa to come stay with us, and of course Cathy would be there. We planned two weeks in the city to show the girls the sights of Chicago and two weeks on Washington Island in Lake Michigan off the coast of Door County, Wisconsin.

We carried American flags and marched in the Oakdale Neighborhood Association annual Fourth of July parade. We celebrated my thirtieth birthday, and while looking at a photograph taken that day from a second-floor balcony, I saw that I was rapidly losing my hair. We went to the Art Institute and the Science Museum and saw the city. Mother left Lisa and returned home. Then the four of us headed north for the island.

It was a lovely time. We walked the beaches. We swam. We watched fishermen return to port followed by clouds of gulls screaming for the fish scraps being thrown overboard. We read. We cooked out and took long walks. It was a healing time. I began to wonder if I had made the right decision when I decided to pursue a career at *LIFE*. The idea that a quieter, more rural life might be more fulfilling, or at least less upsetting, appeared in my mind and took me completely by surprise. That night when the girls were asleep, I raised the subject with Sally.

"What would you think about a different life?" I asked.

"Like what?"

"Well, what if I found a job as a reporter or an editor at some small paper in a rural place, like here, and you taught school?"

Her face registered utter disbelief. "I think if you rest for another week or two you'll feel better," she said.

I decided not to pursue the idea. My feelings were clear. I would be less troubled in a simpler environment, but writing about sewer-bond issues could get awfully dull too.

That spring, Sally had broached the subject of having a baby. I was wary after the trauma of separation from Cathy. I did not want to bring another child into an unstable marriage, and I was not sure just then how stable ours was. Still, I didn't feel it was right to just say no and leave Sally with the prospect of living without her own children. Reluctantly, I had agreed. Then, in the last week that Cathy and Lisa were with us, I saw the attention required by two normal little girls begin to wear on Sally. One afternoon, as they were preparing for an outing, I looked into the bedroom where the girls were dressing under Sally's supervision and saw a look of absolute despair on Sally's face. She was overwhelmed. What seemed to me a routine task that every parent must repeat ten thousand times was suddenly more than she could bear. I felt as if I was looking into the future, a future where the normal stress of being a parent had utterly defeated her. I felt more strongly than ever the fear of having another child. I didn't know what to do, as I had already said, "Yes, let's try." I resolved my problem by doing nothing. I decided to put myself in the hands of fate. If Sally got pregnant, we would do our best.

When the girls were gone, I asked Sally if she was still sure she wanted a kid. She said she was. When I tried to raise the question of her energy to deal with a child, she misunderstood. She thought I was worried about my own ability to parent.

"Don't worry," she said. "The nanny will bring them to you all bathed and in their nighties. You won't have to do anything but kiss them good-night."

Nannies were not a part of a future I was beginning to imagine.

The whole question was soon buried by the impending 1968 Democratic National Convention. I began to prepare for our coverage almost the day Cathy and Lisa left. In just over three weeks, all the forces that had been building in the country and in the Democratic Party over the past year would be brought together in the crucible of the convention. McCarthy, Johnson, Humphrey, the Yippies, Mayor Daley, the Chicago cops, the antiwar and the prowar factions, the radicals, the anarchists, the union men, the southern conservatives, and the liberals would all be in town at the same time, many of them in the same room.

That there would be some sort of trouble was clear days in advance of the convention. The Yippies arrived in town with a 145-pound hog, Pigasus—their candidate for president. They staged various media events meant to antagonize the cops and city officials. They understood the essentially fascistic nature of the Chicago political structure and counted on their taunts to produce a wild overreaction. They believed that if the "establishment"—that is, the Chicago cops—acted out violently, it would prove what they said about American society and they would win wide support among Americans whom they mistakenly supposed to be deeply antifascist.

In the meantime Mayor Daley had gone to work to assure complete control over events in the city during that last week of August. The phones in my office and in the *Time* magazine office were tapped. I assume the phones in other media offices were too. Time Inc. was not that special. My home phone was probably tapped, though I never confirmed that. The route from the downtown hotels to the convention site, the International Amphitheater, was completely refurbished. The fronts of dilapidated houses along the route were freshly painted, courtesy of the Chicago city government. Homeowners were not given a choice in the matter. The front of the house got painted. If the owners wanted the rest painted, that was up to them, and if difficult owners did not want the house painted, they could go to court after the convention to protest the city's gift. Vacant lots were not cleaned up, but a solid eight-foot-high board fence was erected along the street and painted white. It was a corridor of uniformly fresh paint that existed nowhere else in the world at that moment. Telephone-company workers and taxi drivers were sent out on strike by their union leaders, controlled by the mayor. Richard J. Daley now had absolute control over all communication and transportation in the city. All delegates would be loaded on buses supplied by the Democratic Party and driven along the approved route to the amphitheater. Even rental cars were mysteriously booked. No one would see the parts of Chicago the mayor wanted hidden. Cell phones were huge and rare. People attending the convention would have phones only if the mayor wanted them to have phones. Humphrey's contingent got as many phones in their rooms and offices as they requested. Gene McCarthy's forces fought bitterly to get nine or ten.

The week before the convention opened, I did a story on the Chicago Police Department's preparations for the convention. We published a cover showing two police commanders standing behind a chain link fence looking very serious. It was a balanced story, mostly recounting preparations for traffic and crowd control, but during the editing process on the phone with my editors in New York I made fun of the cops. An hour later I called the ex-newsman who was spokesman for the police department to ask for one more interview. We had worked together cordially all week as I prepared the story. Now, suddenly, he was furious. "I don't see why I should help you with anything, not now or ever," he shouted, and hung up the phone.

I was baffled. What could have happened? Then I remembered my conversation with our New York office an hour earlier. Someone had listened in. That was the only plausible explanation. It would be months before the tap was outed, and then the phone company would simply pretend to fire a low-level employee who, they would say, had been listening in on our calls on his own initiative.

This was why I was suspicious when a man called my home that week and said that we had met at a bar the week before. By his voice I guessed he was African American. He mentioned a reporter whom I knew and recounted a brief conversation that I didn't recall. The bar in question was one I frequented after work. It wasn't impossible that I had met him. When he said he had marijuana for sale, very good marijuana and a very good price, my defenses came up in full battle dress. If I'd like to meet him at a Lincoln Park transit station in a couple of hours, I could pick up an ounce. I declined. He pushed, more than a pusher should, I thought. I hung up knowing that I would never know.

Remembering our experience during the Detroit riots the year before, and wanting some way to identify our reporters out on the street, I ordered half a dozen crash helmets and had the *LIFE* logo pasted on the front and back. I put them aside. I reserved three of the last rental cars available at O'Hare Airport, brought them into the city, and left them unmarked.

A few days before the convention began, George Baldwin, my old managing editor from the *Tribune*, showed up to interview me. Having worked at the *Trib*, I would provide the local angle he thought essential to any story. His story would not be about the convention but about how someone who once lived in Albuquerque saw the convention. When he asked if the cops could handle the situation, I assured him they could.

Even a day before the convention began, it was unthinkable to me that a major metropolitan police force in America's most important midwestern city would viciously attack and indiscriminately beat its citizens, most of them peacefully assembled in the streets. Even people who came out on their porches to see what was happening would be clubbed. Identity as a member of the press just increased the likelihood of a beating. As the day of the convention neared, the editorial offices in New York City opened wide and disgorged every shape and size of journalist imaginable, all wanting to buzz near the candle of power. They were all there—my colleagues from *LIFE* and *Time* and every other publication and channel and network: Teddy White and Mike

Wallace, Dan Rather, Walter Cronkite, William Buckley and Gore Vidal, everyone.

I reflected that it had been just four years since I called Joe Bride off the floor of the Republican National Convention in San Francisco, where Barry Goldwater was nominated, to ask for the New Mexico stringership. Events in both the country and my own life had accelerated so quickly, and so many things had changed in those four intervening years, that now I hardly recognized either the country or myself.

CHAPTER FORTY-SIX

I split my time between the convention hall and the streets, because in 1968 we had two stories playing out simultaneously. The senior *LIFE* people arriving from New York pursued various angles for articles on the convention itself while I assigned four reporter/photographer teams to follow the street action. Then I rushed between the two venues. I had no intention of letting the confrontation between protesters and cops cause me to miss the first national political convention I would have a chance to attend.

The first violent clash came even before the convention opened, on Sunday night, August 25, when police ejected protestors from Lincoln Park. The Yippies had sought a permit to sleep in the park, and the city denied the request. When the park closed, several thousand protesters remained. Police entered the park and began clearing it, not by arresting people who were in violation of the city ordinance but by clubbing and gassing them until they ran. This was not going to be a case where the tactics of nonviolence worked well. The protestors might choose nonviolence, but the police soon demonstrated they were more than willing—in fact, were anxious—to practice violence. Seventeen newsmen covering the action were beaten, including a *Washington Post* photographer whose skull was badly fractured. On Monday he was in critical condition in a local hospital.

One of our reporters returned from the street early and took me aside and told me that he wanted to return to New York the following day. He did not apologize for his fear. "I saw a woman come out on her porch to see what was happening," he said. "Three cops just ran up on the porch and hit her with nightsticks. They just beat the shit out of her. She had nothing to do with the Yippies. It is not safe out there—for anyone."

When our other teams returned from the melee late that evening, their clothes were so saturated with tear gas that people working in the office began coughing and wheezing. We instituted a rule that anyone returning from the street had to shed all outer garments in the hallway before they entered the office. The helmets I prepared were initially met with humor and skepticism. Now all of them were taken.

By Monday morning there were 10,000 protesters in the city. This seemed like a big number until one considered that there were also 11,900 Chicago police, 7,500 Illinois National Guardsmen, 7,500 regular army troops, and 1,000 Secret Service agents. All in all, the city was now crowded because in addition to the 40,000-odd troops, cops, and protestors, there were all the delegates and newsmen and hangers-on for a national political convention.

Violence continued to break out sporadically in different areas around the city as the protesters taunted the cops, engaged in acts of provocation like raising a bloody shirt on a flagpole, and looked for different routes to allow them to march to the convention hall. And again, the press was not afforded the immunity we expected, possibly because the police widely believed that the press was on the wrong side.

On Tuesday, at the request of virtually all media outlets, a meeting with Police Chief James Conlisk Jr. was arranged to discuss police attacks on newsmen. The meeting brought about fifteen journalists, mostly editors, to a room with Conlisk and several aides. Ben Bradlee, managing editor of the *Washington Post*, as the most visible member of the group, became our spokesman. I thought Conlisk might claim the incidents had been accidental or say that he would issue an order for the police to be more careful, but he did neither of these things. He refused to talk. He sat silently without expression and listened as we recounted tales of outrageous police behavior against newsmen doing their jobs. Bradlee saw quickly that the meeting was useless and left. I pressed on, actually making an argument about First Amendment rights. I soon realized that Bradlee had it right. Nothing was going to change. I gave up and left too. Outside, embarrassed by the innocence of my performance, I remembered a Howard Zinn story. When asked by his students, who were off to integrate a YMCA in Atlanta, if in fact they did not have the Constitution on their side, he replied, "You absolutely do. The Constitution is clearly on your side. All those cops have is their guns and clubs."

On Wednesday citizens who were more or less peacefully assembled to protest the war attempted to march across the Illinois Central

Rail Road Bridge. They were met by National Guardsmen manning .30-caliber machine guns. I had learned a frightening lesson about National Guardsmen and machine guns in Detroit. The authorities were not kidding around. The city stank of tear gas, and a deep sense of fear spread over downtown.

In the meantime McCarthy supporters could not get telephones installed or even turned on in their hotel rooms and offices. Other than Humphrey and his supporters, candidates were frustrated at every opportunity as they sought transportation or communication. The spirit of Big Brother ruled the town. Gandhi was nowhere to be found.

I was at the amphitheater when the worst moments of violence came. Near the Hilton Hotel on Michigan Avenue, police rushed protesters and pushed them through the big plate-glass window of the Haymarket Lounge. Climbing though the broken window, police proceeded to club people who were drinking in the bar. Sparing two cocktail waitresses dressed like *Playboy* bunnies, cops cleared the lounge and gave Norman Mailer, who was present in the bar, a wonderfully dramatic scene for his book *Miami and the Siege of Chicago*. This seventeen-minute orgy of violence would come to be known officially as a police riot.

I was on the convention floor near the podium that evening when Connecticut senator Abe Ribicoff rose to nominate George McGovern. Commenting on the violence of that afternoon, he said that if McGovern were president, we wouldn't have the Gestapo tactics that we saw on the streets of Chicago. Daley, sitting in the front row of the Illinois delegation just below the podium, rose in a fury, shouting curses at Ribicoff in the most vile and anti-Semitic language. Daley's microphone was off, so it was only later that the general public knew what the mayor had said, but from my position on the floor it was pretty clear that the mayor was using some of the same language he had earlier condemned in the protestors as being "worse than what you would hear in a brothel house."

The next night, the Democrats nominated Hubert Humphrey and went home. When it was over, I had the strongest sense that they had just managed to elect the has-been, Nixon, I had so airily dismissed in the meeting room of the Pfister Hotel in Milwaukee five months earlier. Over the next several weeks, Mayor Daley entertained us with his version of events. He pointed out that "the police are not here to create disorder, they are here to preserve disorder." He could be forgiven for an occasional slip in language, but in the quote that I always believed came out exactly as it was intended, he said, "They have vilified me, they have crucified me; yes, they have even criticized me."

August 1968 was not the finest hour for either Chicago or Mayor Daley, but in the almost three years that I ran the bureau there, I came to see Daley as a kind of homegrown political genius. Given the forces at work in Chicago—the staggering gap between the richest and the poorest, the seething ethnic resentments, the vast influx of rural southern blacks, the deeply rooted grip of organized crime, and a police department that in the best of times was barely under civilian control—Daley did a remarkable job of making it all work. He was a politician through and through, an old-style Democrat. He was not a hypocrite. That was more than could be said for so many others who had chosen his profession.

By the end of August every poll showed that the public was so disgusted with the Democratic National Convention that many voters would either stay home in November or vote for Nixon. George Wallace, the segregationist former governor of Alabama, saw in the situation a great opportunity. With the nation deeply divided, he might win enough of the states still smarting from federal integration actions to deny either major party candidate the 270 electoral votes needed to win the presidency. It was a simple, brilliant, but not original idea.

If he was able to send the election to the House of Representative, each state would have one vote in choosing the president. Democrats controlled twenty-five state delegations, Republicans controlled twenty, and five were divided, two leaning Republican and three leaning Democrat. If all the Democrats stuck together and backed Humphrey, he would be named president by at least one vote. But if some of the southern states won by Wallace were to switch, then Nixon could win. In an even trickier scenario, Wallace could act before the Electoral College met, before the election was sent to the House of Representatives. If Nixon would agree to his conditions, Wallace could throw his electoral votes to Nixon and make Nixon the next president, probably setting back the clock on civil rights by at least a decade and leading to civil disorder of unimaginable magnitude.

Wallace had strong support in the South, among young men and rural voters, and surprisingly strong support among union blue-collar workers in the North and Midwest. In September I went off to Gary, Indiana, to try to gauge Wallace support among unionized steel workers. Without help from polls I had to make some educated guesses about where the workers' loyalty lay, and that turned out to be easier than I thought it would be. Interviewing union bosses, I always got the same answer: "We and our members will support Hubert Humphrey in November." But when I walked through the mills or hung out beside factory gates, I saw Wallace stickers on so many lunch pails that one would have thought he was the union's unanimous choice. In the parking lot, Wallace bumper stickers were everywhere. Humphrey's were not to be seen. I wrote that the Wallace candidacy was a genuine menace.

But after showing frightening strength in the early polls, his strength began to decline as election day approached, in part because he selected retired general Curtis LeMay as his running mate. LeMay was comfortable explaining how hydrogen bombs were just "another weapon" and might be what was needed to end the war in Vietnam. Chillingly, Wallace had promised to win the war in Vietnam in ninety days or pull out. Humphrey named Wallace and LeMay the "Bombsey Twins."

When Nixon won in November, I actually felt heartened. I had been briefly afraid of Wallace, but now his scheme was over. I felt sure that Humphrey, lacking the guts to stand up to Johnson and the hawks in the party, was privately committed to maintaining Johnson's pursuit of the war. I did not like Nixon, but I naïvely believed that he might end it. He had hinted that he would. I recall vividly my sense of despair when, nearly two years later, I sat in a New York bar with my new fiancée and watched as Nixon announced that he had ordered the invasion of Cambodia.

CHAPTER FORTY-SEVEN

With the national political drama taking an intermission, I turned my attention to politics closer to home. Rumors that *LIFE* was failing financially grew in strength and frequency. It was not losing money yet, but the spread between costs and profits was growing narrower each year, adding urgency to the idea that new management might be coming. In keeping with past Time Inc. practices, the election of a new president meant we would likely get a new managing editor. The combination of a poorly performing balance sheet and a new administration in Washington brought to a fevered pitch speculation about our new boss's name. Naturally, everyone had a favorite candidate, not so much because they thought a particular assistant managing editor would be good for the magazine, but because they thought an assistant managing editor with whom they had a good relationship would be good for them.

The other great debate was the editorial direction the magazine would or should take under a new editor. I had been at *LIFE* just over three years, but from the beginning of my short tenure I had heard discussions of how to make it a better, more compelling magazine. I had the strong impression that in its early days, in the 1940s and 1950s, there had been no uncertainty about what *LIFE* was or should be. It had a clear identity, and the people running it knew what it should be. The legendary managing editor Edward K. Thompson, who guided the magazine through its glory days when weekly circulation reached thirteen and a half million copies, knew what he was doing. But we were in a new era, and the old formula wasn't working. There was a pressing need to attract more advertising and increase newsstand sales because they were enormously profitable. A single copy of *LIFE* delivered to a subscriber brought in ten or twelve cents and didn't pay the postage. On the newsstand the same magazine brought in $1.50 or more. In fact, there was nothing wrong with the editorial content of the magazine. People loved it. What was wrong was the business model that relied far too much on underpriced subscriptions to prop up advertising rates that were not competitive with television in reaching mass-market eyeballs.

When a magazine is making money, the editorial people enjoy great freedom and prestige within the organization. Their talent and insights are producing a product that is easy to sell. When a magazine becomes less successful, the business people begin to reach for a larger and larger role in planning, content, and posture. The wishes and prejudices of advertisers become more important.

This was brought home in a most unpleasant way when a major advertiser insisted that we stop showing photos of the international peace symbol because, he said, it was a broken, upside-down cross. It was, he said, blasphemous because it depicted a sacred Christian symbol disgraced and destroyed. In an earlier era, I think the ranting of a John Bircher, even one sitting on a large advertising budget, would have been politely received, laughed at in private, and forgotten about in twenty-four hours, but in 1971 he was taken very seriously. We needed his money. It was very difficult at the height of the Vietnam War to show pictures of what was going on in America and in Vietnam without any of them including the peace symbol. It even appeared on helmets of soldiers in combat.

I was by then a senior editor at the magazine, and I was assigned to research this question and prepare a response. The answer, of course, is that a symbol can stand for anything you want it to stand for. That is what symbols are. Ask a radical Palestinian what the American flag stands for, and then ask a right-wing Republican from Mississippi the same question.

The modern designer of the peace symbol said it represented the semaphore positions for *N* and *D* and stood for nuclear disarmament. He said it also represented him with his arms down and his palms turned up in frustration and despair, a gesture much like Goya's peasant before the firing squad. Some on the extreme political Right and certain Christians had problems with the peace symbol because it was used by people who were against the Vietnam War. They said it was either "the footprint of a chicken" or an ancient symbol of Satanism and Roman cruelty. In fact, the ancient symbol and variations on it had been used to stand for many things in many different cultural contexts, most long forgotten. What the swastika represented for Nazi Germany was and is diametrically opposed to its meaning in Sanskrit and in Hindu mythology. Until the Nazis got hold of it, the swastika was universally regarded as a symbol of auspiciousness and good fortune and remains that today in many Buddhist countries. In New Mexico, as a child, I saw swastikas decorating old hotels dating from the 1920s. They were part of an American Indian motif and also turned up on some old Navajo rugs. So were the people who wanted peace really secret Satanists and Antichrists? Are Hindus and Native Americans crypto-Nazis? I wrote my report and turned it over to the managing editor. I heard back that it had not satisfied our advertiser. Educating a closed mind is very hard.

This sort of thing made me hate any interaction with the business people. My position was prejudiced and counterproductive, but one I could never fully shake. Henry Luce had begun a tradition of separating the business side from the editorial side, and when Hedley Donovan succeeded him, he made it official with something called the Donovan Charter, which stated that the editor in chief was answerable only to the board of directors. The firewall between the business side and the editorial side suited me fine, and I for one would do what I could to help maintain it.

When I worked at the *Tribune* I felt a kind of purity about my work because I imagined that it was free from the influence of greed, business, and self-interest. Knowing too little about the priesthood, perhaps, I thought of journalism as a kind of priesthood of the truth. It sounds grandiose and overblown, but I really felt then that journalists guarded the line between the public good and grasping politicians, unscrupulous businessmen, and crooked cops. We were the good guys and we had to remain pure. This was something of a fantasy, of course. As A. J. Liebling observed, "Freedom of the press is guaranteed only to those who own one."

Still, at the *Tribune* I felt complete freedom to write the truth, and I did. In my first years at *LIFE* I felt that the magazine had the clout and the stature to resist the influence of business and politics, and mostly it did, but as our financial situation changed, that power weakened. This was one of the things that troubled me in the winter of 1968–1969. Another was my future. What would I do if *LIFE* did not last? There were not many places I wanted to work if *LIFE* was gone. I was badly spoiled because the magazine and I seemed then to be a nearly perfect match. Once again, the notion occurred to me that if *LIFE* was gone, and with it my brief and shining career, maybe I'd move back to the country, or at least to a place smaller than New York or Chicago, and pursue a more contemplative life.

Working for *LIFE* I shared in great prestige and great freedom. The magazine was organized almost exactly opposite from the *Tribune*. At the *Trib* you were given assignments and expected to complete them to fill the waiting space. At *LIFE* there was too little space, and one had to compete with a lot of smart and talented people to get in the magazine at all. The result was periods of relative quiet followed by periods of frenzied, exhausting work. When I was onto something good, I could work grinding hours, driving hard to get what was necessary and then score by seeing the story printed. When I had nothing going, I enjoyed the leisure to follow my own instincts while I looked for material. It was hard on the tires, stopping and starting so fast, and it wore out the brakes, but it was never routine and it was never boring—at least not until we were forced to create a hospice for a terminally ill magazine, but that was a few years down the road.

CHAPTER FORTY-EIGHT

The winter of 1968–1969 was a time of waiting. Few things are as corrosive as marking time. It seemed clear that we would soon get a new managing editor, but no one had a lead on whom it would be. The uncertainty created a kind of low-level, free-floating anxiety that tainted everything we did.

In January the New York Jets improbably beat the Baltimore Colts, the eighteen-point favorites, in Super Bowl III. It was a great moment for people who love underdogs and an awful moment for people who bet on favorites. A few days later, Richard Nixon was sworn in as president.

In February the *Saturday Evening Post* ceased publication after 147 years, reminding us all that large-format magazines were vulnerable. The Beatles gave their last public concert, reminding us of nothing much. Sporadic violence flashed frequently in isolated spots around the world. Protestant and Catholic Irish continued to kill each other. In the deep Chicago winter, there was not much to lift one's spirits.

Sally and I could have used some good news, but none came. In fact, as we proceeded toward a pregnancy, our relationship began to fade. Just as a strong marriage became more important than ever, we were drifting apart. We never fought. We rarely argued. We just each lived more and more in our own worlds. I worked, drank, and worried about the future of the magazine and my career. Sally spent more and more time with friends and playing the piano. Then she began to shop more seriously than she had in the past.

When larger and larger bills began arriving from Chicago department stores, I asked her to be more careful with expenditures. She said she would but then ignored the whole matter. Alarmed, I approached Rowan for a raise. It was not a good time to talk about raises, he said. "Use your expense account." A month later, a memo arrived from the business office, formally asking us to hold down on unnecessary expenses, not to fly first class even if it meant waiting for a later flight, and to watch the entertainment. Asking people at *LIFE* to hold back on their expense accounts was like asking a glutton to skip a second dessert. *LIFE* expense accounts were so outrageously used that they produced a whole tradition of jokes.

Charles Bonnay once turned in an expense account in which he reported buying a donkey to carry his camera equipment while on assignment in the Middle East. He listed daily feedings for the donkey, shelter at night, grooming, medical expenses, and all the other costs that might possibly be associated with keeping a donkey in first-class style. At the end of the assignment, he sold the donkey and carefully deducted the price he received from the cost of buying the animal. The sale price was far lower than the purchase price. A frustrated accountant in New York who knew better than to question the whole fabulous story found a nit to pick.

"Charles," he demanded, "this had to be the best-kept donkey in the entire Middle East. How could you sell him for less than you paid?"

"Ah," Charles responded quickly in his French-accented English. "While we were on assignment, the bottom fell out of the burro market!"

In the 1950s John Thorne, one of the stalwarts at *LIFE* from its early days, went to lunch with a colleague. They decided to see how much they could spend on a single meal. There were ground rules. They had to eat or drink everything they ordered. In those innocent days when Johnny Walker Red was sixty cents a drink, they managed to spend $110. When Thorne's expenses reached accounting, a young woman called him.

"Mr. Thorne, I think I found a mistake in your expense account," she said.

"Oh, what?"

"Well, you list $110 for lunch. I'm sure you meant $10.10."

"No," he said. "I really meant $110."

She paused. "Mr. Thorne? What do you do at lunch for $110?"

Without missing a beat, he replied, "What are you doing for lunch today?"

There were dozens of stories. They were funny. They were clever. But most of all, they served to illustrate that writers and photographers at *LIFE* were not to be constrained by accountants. What a sweet victory for all journalists everywhere who forever suffered a thousand little deaths beneath the sharp pencils of bean counters. Sadly, the times were already changing—in favor of the bean counters.

In March 1969 James Earl Ray pled guilty to killing Martin Luther King, but that was essentially old news for our bureau. The previous April we had scrambled to put together a portrait of Ray and his family when the FBI identified him as King's killer. Our story provided the May 3 cover and was one of the most satisfying stories we had done in a long time because we practiced real old-fashioned gumshoe journalism. The moment Ray was named as the killer, we understood that he had been raised and had spent much of his life within our bureau's territory. I managed to interview Ray's brother, who was living in Chicago, while John Pekkanen and Richard Woodbury, two bureau correspondents, went in frenzied search of Ray's history. They turned up old family pictures, police photos of places Ray had robbed, shots of his dysfunctional family—so many photos and so much information that in three days' time we were able to offer our readers a comprehensive look at the two-bit crook who had taken down King. No one talked about "the banality of evil" or Hannah Arendt, but the picture we drew of Ray seemed a case in point of how much evil can flow from a very common person.

Then, before March ended, the Chicago Eight returned to town and were indicted. Entertaining them and socializing with them, a certain segment of Chicago society played out what Tom Wolfe would label "radical chic" in an essay still a year from being written. The guests in those North Shore mansions were happy to enjoy the food, the sex, and the attention offered them by a group of people they planned to send packing "come the revolution."

It was a confusing time, and I found my moorings beginning to shift, the anchor dragging. The official, elected government was vigorously pursuing a deadly, costly, futile war that deeply divided the nation between those who imagined that theirs was "not to reason why / Theirs but to do or die" and those who believed that informed, questioning citizens were essential to a healthy democracy and peace was in the national interest. America was split between people like my father, who was content to let the "smart men in Washington" make the decisions about war and peace, and people like me, who by virtue of access to power and a special opportunity to watch the "smart men" had concluded that political leaders were as morally challenged as any plumber or truck driver (not to take anything away from the latter).

Another aspect of the war was rarely discussed because it was dangerous to talk about it, and that was simply, *Cui bono*? Who benefits? The contractors were making money. My father was piling up retirement money. Military people were gaining the combat experience they needed in order to be promoted. Journalists had an amazing opportunity to cover a serious, ongoing story. The military-industrial complex, the intelligence community, and the various government bureaucracies supporting the war had rarely had it so good. Almost everyone was doing just fine—except, of course, the draftees, potential draftees, their families, and more or less the entire population of Southeast Asia.

The Democratic National Convention and the behavior of the Chicago police made it clear that many of the so-called civil rights Americans imagined they had were actually available only in theory. When a person throws a brick at a cop, he is a felon. When someone sitting in the Hilton Hotel bar gets beaten by an outraged cop, he is a victim denied his civil rights. In Chicago, the city government and the police administration decided they did not have to make any distinction between the brick thrower and the bar patron. The fact that anyone not in the convention hall was regarded as being against the war gave the police carte blanche to practice violence.

So all around me the pillars of what I thought it meant to be an American were bending and peeling, while at home I was faced with an increasingly unhappy woman whom I respected and who was hoping to become pregnant.

In early May the news arrived. Ralph Graves would be *LIFE*'s new managing editor. Of all the possible candidates, Graves was the one I knew the least. He had been an assistant managing editor when I was hired but was soon after promoted to corporate editor, a new position within Time Inc. that was really a holding place until time came for George Hunt to retire. Had the corporation promoted one assistant managing editor over the others, it would have been awkward for those left behind. By discreetly identifying Graves as Hunt's successor early on and moving him into the ranks of corporate management, Hedley Donovan, Time Inc.'s editor in chief, spared the other AMEs from needing to leave to save face. Had I been a more acute observer, I would have seen the plan when Graves was moved upstairs (literally to the thirty-fourth-floor corporate offices), but I missed the meaning. Graves struck me as a man of enormous self-discipline and not a little self-regard. During an editorial meeting, he once stated flatly, "I am an alpha male." He was fond of making reference to classical literature, as in, "Cato was a nag about Carthage," while defending his decision to caption a cover photo of Jane Fonda with the line, "Nag, Nag, Nag." He was punctual. He was decisive. All in all, he was a little too tightly wound for my taste.

Then he took me completely by surprise with an act of enormous courage and brilliant planning. In the June 27, 1969, issue, published almost as soon as he took control of the magazine, *LIFE* featured one of the most remarkable articles ever published by any magazine anywhere: "Faces of the American Dead in Vietnam: One Week's Toll." Page after page of the magazine carried photographs of 242 young Americans, literally boys from next door, killed that week in Vietnam, an average week in the war. The 242 faces carried an impact of a different order of magnitude from the bare, easily dismissed number: 38,000 killed in action so far. By doing what journalism can do in its highest form—revealing painful truths to the people, showing the real cost of a policy—the magazine set off a storm of controversy. Hawks wanted the deaths to remain distant and statistical. Some of the more intellectually challenged members of that breed accused the magazine, and by extension Graves, of treason. Some on the Left and some of the more hysterical peace people groused that the magazine should have done it sooner. But most Americans paging through the magazine were stunned, saddened, and made thoughtful by what they saw. The technique was powerful and original and widely copied in later years.

Anyone familiar with the political mindset within Time Inc. knew that Graves had not published this issue without facing down serious opposition and many warnings about future consequences. Henry Luce had enthusiastically supported the war. Hedley Donovan came slowly to the view that it might not be winnable in any sense that made sense. The editorial staffs of all the Time Inc. magazines were about as divided as the country was between supporters of the war and those who thought it was wrong, so Graves was hardly preaching to the choir.

The question of reporting battlefield carnage has always been troubling, especially to those conducting the war. The Crimean War was the first in which a few war correspondents managed to report to the British public how badly the struggle was being conducted by an officer corps that had largely purchased its commissions. After the abject neglect of the wounded was revealed, and after news of the slaughter of the Light Brigade reached the British public, the prime minister resigned and a new Whig government took over. Politicians have much to fear from a properly functioning press.

Oddly enough, Graves's decision to show the American soldiers killed in Vietnam had a long-forgotten precedent at *LIFE*. Early in World War II, the American press and the Roosevelt government agreed that no photographs of dead American servicemen would be shown. Then Roosevelt decided that Americans were not taking the war seriously enough and encouraged *LIFE* to depart from this policy. The magazine printed a photograph, now classic, of three dead Americans sprawled along a Pacific beach as the surf washed gently against them. It was a shocker, and it had the hoped-for result.

Robert E. Lee, who knew a thing or two about war, is quoted as having said, "It is well that war is so terrible, otherwise we should grow too fond of it." The "terrible" part is where the press often falls short and has the greatest responsibility. It is so easy to love a man or woman in uniform.

In spite of Donovan's efforts to give the passed-over assistant managing editors an out, Roy Rowan decided to leave. I don't know what prompted him to go. He said he thought Ralph should have a free hand without any of his old colleagues looking over his shoulder. I thought it was something deeper and less generous that pushed him along, but Roy was a gentleman. He would never say anything negative about Ralph.

In June Roy flew to Chicago to invite me to leave with him. He wanted to start a boating magazine on Long Island, he said. He would call it *On the Sound*, and he hoped I'd join him in the venture. It was an awkward moment for me. I liked Roy immensely—and respected his judgment in most things, even though he had heavily cut my McCarthy piece—but I had no interest in boating and I did not want to leave *LIFE*. I still harbored dreams of rising to the top of the heap, of someday having a chance to edit the magazine, though it was growing clearer each day that the magazine would likely not survive until someone of my generation could take the helm. "I asked Ralph if I could approach you about this," Roy said over dinner. "He said it was OK."

As we finished eating, I considered what Roy said about Graves allowing him to recruit me. I wondered if Graves had given permission to tempt me away from *LIFE* because he did not want to interfere with an opportunity I might relish or if he regarded me as an expendable member of his staff. I tended to think it was the latter. If I was right, this was not an auspicious beginning with my new boss.

Dinner with Roy left me feeling sad. Roy had pulled me out of Los Angeles and sent me to Chicago when most people would have thought I was too inexperienced to handle the job. He had encouraged me to cover and write about Gene McCarthy even though we had different views of the man. He had been a steady voice guiding our coverage of news and getting that coverage into the magazine. Now he wanted to involve me in a new venture that excited him, and I could not go. I was losing an ally and disappointing a friend.

In July I turned thirty-one, and in the way that only young people can, I started to feel old. There was no further news from New York. The wait and the uncertainty added to my growing unhappiness, already exacerbated by our deteriorating financial situation as Sally spent more and more freely. Then she engaged an expensive psychiatrist, which in other circumstances I would have understood to be a good thing but in the present circumstances just seemed another bill I could not pay. Then she told me that she had been examined by her doctor and found to be perfectly able to become pregnant. As she was not pregnant, the doctor wanted to see me. I found the whole idea alarming. I had a child, which seemed sufficient evidence that I could have another. The invitation to see a doctor revealed the depth of her desire and determination. I was forced now to think seriously and clearly about what we were doing. I began to panic. We were hurtling toward a commitment that I did not want to make and that I felt unable to stop.

Chicago's stifling July heat now closed in around me. The city lies in the middle of a vast, essentially empty plane that is best traversed by air. To feel content in Chicago is to feel nestled into a bustling city, protected from the emptiness all around. To feel discontent in Chicago is to be acutely aware of the isolation and to feel trapped in the middle of that emptiness. As the month dragged on, the distance from Chicago to New York seemed to increase day by day.

On July 20 we got a break from the travails of summer. Sally and I gathered with other Time Inc. people in the back garden of a townhouse where television sets had been placed outdoors so that we could see the moon and watch the moon landing on television. It was an unreal experience, looking at the moon glowing in the eastern sky and trying to imagine that there was at that moment a man walking on its surface. When Neil Armstrong stepped onto the moon and made some garbled pronouncement none of us could quite understand, we cheered. We looked at the moon some more, remarked on what a historic day it was, drank more, and went home. But whatever relief the moon landing afforded from the long string of somber events, it was mostly erased by the accident two days earlier when Senator Edward Kennedy drove his car off the Chappaquiddick bridge and killed Mary Jo Kopechne.

Toward the end of July, a letter came from my mother. She had managed to get tourist visas for herself and Lisa. They were in Saigon with my father.

CHAPTER FORTY-NINE

A wonderful formality practiced by the secretaries at *LIFE* required them to refer to their bosses as "Mr." (there was no Ms., Miss, or Mrs. above the level of department head) and to treat his subordinates with great respect. After all, today's green reporter might be tomorrow's editor in chief. It was in this spirit that Graves's secretary called me early in August to inquire if I might be free to have lunch with Mr. Graves on a certain day the following week. I wasn't just free, I was ecstatic.

The invitation in itself did not mean that I would be invited back to New York, but it would settle the matter that had troubled me since the beginning of the year. Graves would either offer me an editor's slot, fire me, or tell me I was doing a great job in Chicago and to carry on.

On the appointed day I flew to New York and joined Graves and Robert Ajemian, formerly a *Time* magazine political writer and now one of *LIFE*'s assistant managing editors, at a table in the executive dining room in the Time-Life Building. The two men were opposites in almost every way. Graves was physically compact and agile, wore fashionable black-rimmed glasses, and cut his hair longish. Ajemian, a larger man, ambled when he walked; had a large, round head, short, graying hair, and small, delicate hands; and always wore a yellow tie.

In conversation Graves was distracted and eager to dispose of your business. He gave the impression that you had stopped him in the hall as he was making an urgent trip to the bathroom. Ajemian, always sunny, seemed to be amused by the world around him. He laughed easily. He gave you his full attention when in conversation. He was known to be a dangerous poker player, and I came to suspect that he applied those same skills of observation and analysis to everything he did. Despite giving an initial impression of an easygoing person, he was punctilious, doggedly pursuing every possible facet of an idea or event. He was generally pleasant, whereas Graves was harsh. He was exhausting, whereas Graves was merely trying.

Graves asked right off if I thought of myself as a reporter or an editor. The question implied that I had a choice. I responded by saying that I had more ideas for stories than I had time to report. "OK," he said, with great decisiveness. "You're an editor. You'll be working with Ajemian, running the news department." He finished his salad and left.

Ajemian's immigrant parents did well enough in business in Boston to send him to private schools and to Harvard. He served as an officer in the navy in World War II then began his journalism career as a sportswriter for the *Boston Globe*. He continued to see the world through the lens of a sportswriter, viewing politics as another sports event played in different uniforms. Though he had been with *LIFE* for several years, I had never worked with him. He was a stranger, but I sensed we could get along.

As the lunch lengthened into midafternoon, we talked about Graves's new approach to news and how he planned to change the magazine. Graves did not want any "why not" stories, and he didn't want weather stories. He didn't want news stories that were easy for television to cover. He wanted to hold down costs—at all cost. He did not want to cover more stories than we had space to run. He did not want to make expensive assignments for original photography and reporting when we could buy photographs from agencies or freelance photographers. He was probably going to close some of the bureaus around the world and consolidate others. There were a lot of things to be done to lower costs and a lot of things he no longer wanted. It would be up to Ajemian and me to figure out what stories he did want and how to supply those. I felt confident that I could work with Ajemian, even though I had heard people complain that he was too exacting and had trouble pulling the trigger when a decision had to be made.

Time Inc. management was still very WASPish in 1969, dominated by tall men from ivy league and Big Ten schools, but it was moving rapidly toward a transition that within a decade would largely replace the WASP regency with Jewish managers. No one would have felt either comfortable or safe making any sort of anti-Semitic remark, but Ajemian's Armenian heritage was not so well protected. Some of my colleagues, resentful of his success, referred to him as "the rug merchant," an epithet I came to despise as my respect for the man grew from working with him.

Excited by his new assignment, Ajemian wanted to get up to speed immediately. He pressed me to come to New York to begin work as soon as possible. I promised I would. I flew back to Chicago elated about overseeing the news department. It was essentially Rowan's old job, without the title or the authority. That now rested with Ajemian.

Sally was pleased to be returning to New York, but my good news did not go very far in lifting the somber attitude that had descended around her in recent months. She was in no great hurry to leave, and in any case we couldn't move until we had an apartment. We agreed that she would stay in Chicago to close the apartment and arrange the move. I would fly back on weekends.

In a matter of days I was in New York working and pursuing the always difficult task of looking for affordable living space in Manhattan. Our situation was complicated because we needed a bedroom for Cathy and room for Sally's piano. Studio apartments that would have made sense on my salary were too small.

I never knew what the people I worked with earned, but while Time Inc. paid handsomely for the folks at the top, the regular troops, like me, were paid only slightly more than a federal civil servant with commensurate responsibility. There was the expense account, of course, which was good for fancy meals and drinks, but it didn't pay rent or buy clothes. In the northeastern tradition of publishing, many of my colleagues had private money to smooth the way in an expensive city. I worked with a son of Hugh Lofting, who wrote the Dr. Doolittle books, and a son of August Heckscher, the New York City parks commissioner. Another colleague was Adrian Hope, a son of the British ambassador to the United Nations. There were many others whose family wealth was not famous but was substantial. A common arrangement seemed to be that one or another grandparent paid the rent. They were not all private-school rich kids with trust funds, but enough were to nudge the bar upward for an acceptable style of life.

After two weeks of looking at apartments we could not afford or would not occupy, and feeling discouraged, I called Sally to ask if she would consider a place out of the city. We could get a lot more room at a much lower price if I was willing to commute and she was willing to live out of Manhattan. "Not on your life," she said. "You can put your mistress in the suburbs. I'm staying in town." She was kidding, of course—sort of. She seriously had no interest in living anywhere but in Manhattan and she knew I did not have a mistress, but perhaps she sensed that I was about to be blindsided.

On August 15, Woodstock—otherwise known as "three days of peace and music"—began in upstate New York. *LIFE* anticipated the event and laid on heavy coverage. It was just the kind of thing Graves saw as an opportunity for *LIFE* to shine. We had warning, we had a chance to plan, and we could wow our readers with beautiful color photographs of a social phenomenon of our time. I watched jealously from the news department as the human affairs department directed coverage of the concert.

Two days later, August 17, Hurricane Camille hit the Gulf Coast with sustained winds of 190 miles per hour, one of the most powerful and destructive hurricanes ever recorded. Mississippi was devastated, huge ships were blown up onto the land, people were killed, and whole towns were leveled. The middle South sustained heavy damage. Normally I would have ordered up blanket coverage and expected to dominate the front of the magazine, but under Graves's new direction, we did not do weather stories. Acting against my better instincts, I let the event slide. After all, *LIFE* had Woodstock.

Nothing was said about the absence of Camille in any of our editorial meetings. In time I assumed I had properly followed Graves's directions and that he intended to stick with his no-weather-stories decision. Then, a few months later, Graves and Ajemian came back from lunch looking whipped. During a high-powered gathering with editors and advertisers, someone chastised Graves, and by extension Ajemian, for ignoring the hurricane. "I picked up your magazine that week and the week after and the week after that," the advertiser was quoted as having said. "Nothing. You ignored our worst disaster in a generation."

"How did you miss Camille?" Ajemian asked in the time-honored tradition of merde running downhill. "Ralph said no weather stories," I replied. We sent a photographer to Mississippi to shoot an essay on the damage. On the first anniversary of the storm, we ran a series of haunting color photographs: "Camille: A Year Later." We seemed to be making a specialty of addressing things "One Year Later."

Perhaps what had not been understood was that people relied on *LIFE* to reflect the important events in their lives. It wasn't just about news. It was about commemoration, validation, telling their neighbors. We had a relationship with our readers that television did not have. Surely that was worth more than raw numbers in an audience that might or might not be paying attention. Surely being able to hold a great photograph in your hands and savor the moment was something television could not offer. If *LIFE*'s advertising salesmen were making that case to the advertisers, the ad men weren't listening.

I found an apartment in the low Seventies just a few doors in from Central Park West. It was the parlor floor in a brownstone that had recently been renovated by the owner, who lived in the garden apartment. The rent was steep but affordable, and there was room for the piano and a small second bedroom that could double as an office when Cathy wasn't there. I continued to think and to hope that one day Cathy's mother would allow Cathy to live full time with me. I wanted to be prepared if that happened. Hellyn had married a professor of art at the University of Washington soon after she moved with Cathy to Seattle. She herself was teaching art at a small private college. They led busy lives, and I worried that Cathy was not getting the kind of attention she needed. In particular I was not happy with the relationship Cathy had with her stepfather. He was harsh and demanding about ephemeral things, a poor ethnic kid from Chicago who had made good through lots of hard work and some talent. He thought Cathy was overprivileged and wanted to raise her as a "poor kid" because he seemed to think that there was some inherent virtue in being poor. Cathy wasn't a poor kid, and there was nothing he could do about it except show his resentment. We were paying a substantial tuition to send her to the Lakeside School (she was four years behind Bill Gates), and her stepfather was berating her about wearing out her jeans and shoes faster than he thought necessary. Short of a traumatizing legal battle, there was little I could do except visit her often and have her with me during my month-long summer vacation, although I continued to think that a time would come when both Cathy and her mother would conclude that she should be with me.

Sally came to New York and agreed that the apartment was right for us. We signed a lease. The present tenants had a month to move, so I stayed on in my quarters at a residential hotel on Fifth Avenue and Sally returned to Chicago.

In early September, as I wandered the halls just before lunch, a woman from the photography department suggested I join a group of people ordering in from Wolf's Deli. Feeling a bit lonely, I accepted her invitation, gave her my order, and half an hour later sat down with eight or ten people at a long table in an empty conference room to gorge on giant sandwiches. The conversation soon turned to descriptions of summer vacations. I paid little attention until a young woman began to describe her adventures in Greece. I looked down the table and saw a mop of honey-blonde hair, a crisp white-lace blouse—a fresh, innocent-looking, absolutely desirable woman. I listened intently as she described an unpleasant encounter in Athens with two Turkish men. After lunch, not caring to think what I might be doing, I walked down the table to introduce myself.

CHAPTER FIFTY

The stress I felt around this time was enormous, almost overwhelming. Every part of my life was in flux, and I had no reason to be optimistic about the eventual outcome. I was running well into the 300s on the Holmes and Rahe Stress Scale, meaning I was likely to get sick in the near future (though I didn't, not physically at least).

I had succeeded in getting back to New York and would soon be an associate editor of a major national magazine. This was a beginning, not an end. Now I had to demonstrate that I could perform in my new job. It was never enough for me to feel that I was adequate in a job. I could only feel secure if I excelled. I needed a lot of positive feedback, probably more than was healthy and certainly more than is normally available in a competitive corporate environment. I worked hard to get it anyway.

Graves's early decisions for the magazine did not inspire optimism. In fact, they smacked loudly of demise. Virtually all the specific measures he took to improve the economics of the magazine shrank the news department's ability to function. He seemed to believe that the future of *LIFE* lay outside the news department. The result was that he had handed me the department he planned to rely on the least and whose resources he would continue to diminish. It is a cliché, but nevertheless apt: I had been promoted to lieutenant commander on the *Titanic*.

All this stirred a deeply rooted sense of being an outsider that I had suppressed too long and that was now beginning to push back somewhere deep in my psyche. It was a conflict I had endured all my life: the desire to join the group, excel, and be admired versus the desire to remain an outsider, observing, judging, but not part of the gang. I was tormented by the conflict throughout my teen years. I played football successfully in junior high school and in my sophomore year of high school and then left the team, only to return in my senior year to excel, winning a starting spot on the state's all-star team. My coaches were dismayed that I had not stuck with the team in my junior year. I joined the Boy Scouts and became the senior patrol leader in my troop and then dropped out one merit badge short of the Eagle rank. I held offices in the state student-council organization and in the Future Farmers of America and oscillated between being an organization man and a rebel. I graduated first in my class from the police academy, all spit and polish and conformity, then left two years later to roam around Mexico as an alienated student.

The summer in Mexico fully fed the rebel, and for a time that part of me was satisfied, even exhausted. At the newspaper I joined up again, working to perfect my camouflage by copying Fred Bonavita's sartorial style but still feeding the rebel by taking hard shots at the judges and politicians and other members of the local establishment who in my view misused their authority.

Then, whisked out of the Bernalillo County courthouse to a table in Toots Shor's and into the company of the martini-drinking, worldly, gravel-voiced Marion MacPhail, my world was shaken up more than ever. Since that day I had sprinted just to keep up with the arc of my career. Now I was back in New York as an editor. The rebel was stirring again, excited by disappointment and anger that the magazine, and with it my identity and my future, might be taken away. "If it all comes crashing down," I found myself saying too often, "I can always take my ax and go to the mountains."

My marriage was in terrible condition. The more Sally pressed forward with her desire for a child, the more I retreated. If it is possible to become psychosomatically sterile, I probably was. One reason I refused to see the fertility doctor was simply that, if I was broken, I did not want to be fixed. Soon enough I understood that my reluctance to commit to a child was really a failure to commit to the marriage. Had the whole issue come up while we were still in Albuquerque and the marriage was new, I am sure I would have felt differently, but now each day left me feeling more alienated from Sally—from her values, her ambitions, and the path that she would insist upon for our future. When thinking about this, I remembered that Cathy's conception was no accident. Hellyn and I discussed and planned the pregnancy. We entered into the experience as fully informed, freely consenting—albeit naïve—adults. That the marriage failed may be beside the point. When we decided to have Cathy, we believed we were committed to each other.

When I met Sally in Albuquerque, she was conventional, a teacher, but showing great independence socially, an independence born of the confidence one feels when moving from a sophisticated urban culture like Los Angeles to a less sophisticated place like Albuquerque. Her independence was attractive, and it meshed with my inclination to reject convention. Our success—our trip from newspaper to magazine, from Albuquerque to New York, Los Angeles, and Chicago—awakened in her a latent desire to move among the socially prominent, to be conventional but at the upper end of the hierarchy. We were moving past each other. The more rebellious and angry I felt in light of the events in the country and my own psychological baggage, the more she reached for upper-middle-class conformity. Enormous department-store bills were the most immediate symptom of her aspiration. My frustrations and fears were increasingly medicated with alcohol.

Sally listened only to classical music, which I loved, but if I tried to listen to popular music, even good popular music, she derided it as "kids' music." If I smoked cannabis, as I had on occasion when it was offered by friends, she disapproved because it was a "kids' drug." The last straw in this cultural struggle came when she outlawed blue jeans—Levi's—something I had worn all my life. I felt increasingly confined, and she felt increasingly insecure as I pushed back against "respectability." By the time I returned to New York I felt the marriage might not last, but I had no idea how to end it nor was I certain that I should. This was my state of mind the day I strolled along the lunch table to invite Bridget Thomas to meet after work for a drink.

I was not looking for a new wife; I was not looking for a lover, but I was hungry for the company of an attractive woman who did not want anything from me except my company, or at least not anything specific: no babies, no sofas, no personal changes. Bridget had a wonderful life story. As we worked our way through a gin and tonic at a bar near the Time-Life Building, she told me more about her adventures in Greece that summer. I am a good interviewer and moved her along quickly to the deep background stuff.

Her parents, born in Wales, left England with her two older sisters to move to Bermuda in the years just before World War II. Her father, an Episcopal priest, held a position as canon for music at the Cathedral of the Most Holy Trinity in Hamilton. When, soon after the declaration of World War II, he coughed up blood and was diagnosed with tuberculosis, he was summarily ordered out of Bermuda by the bishop. It was a most un-Christian act but necessary to prevent a sharp drop in church attendance by those who might fear infection; it was a sacrifice of the few for the many, Christian charity be damned. Unable to return to England because German submarines were taking a toll on shipping that no parent would accept, unable to get money out of their English bank because of war restrictions, and abandoned financially by the church, her parents sold their valuable furniture, part of a dowry, to raise enough money to get them to Saranac Lake in upstate New York and the tuberculosis sanitarium founded there by Dr. Edward Trudeau.

Without financial resources, confined by bitter Adirondack winters, and isolated by the war, the little family, so recently happy in Bermuda, endured until her father seemed to recover. Apparently healthy after several years of treatment, including sleeping outside in winter and summer, Glenn was named canon for music at St. John the Divine in New York City. They were deliriously happy with this good fortune. Then, on the train returning from New York to Saranac Lake, her father hemorrhaged again. Disheartened, they returned to the sanitarium, where eventually he did recover. The bishop of Albany assigned him to a light-duty post as the parish priest in the small Columbia County village of Kinderhook, New York. Bridget's birth in Albany not long after was at least partly a result of her parents' celebration of his recovery.

She had been a popular high school cheerleader and then went off to Bard College, lived in England, worked for the *London Sunday Times*, and came home after deciding she didn't want to marry an Englishman. She loved Greece more than any place she had ever been. She had recently ended an affair with a married *LIFE* photographer, and she made it clear that she had sworn off married men forever. That decision seemed to include me, but then there she was, sitting across a small table from me, fingering the ends of her long, beautiful hair, looking mighty fine.

At *LIFE* she held an entry-level position as a picture researcher. It was an editorial track from which it was possible to become a reporter and eventually an editor, though in the present climate such advancements were becoming less and less likely. She shared an apartment with two other women on the Upper East Side, but she had a line on a place on the Upper West Side that she could afford and where she hoped to move soon. As she spoke, I noticed that she had the most graceful hands I had even seen. No matter how urgent their task, they moved at a stately pace, with precision and delicacy. Her voice was pleasing and her speech correct, sprinkled with British idioms. She was so essentially female, so utterly attractive, that by the time we had ordered a second drink I was plotting ways to spend more time with her.

We decided to have dinner, of course, and to talk some more—all very innocent, we thought. Just friends from work getting to know each other. When I put her in a cab after lingering over coffee, I felt better about life than I had in a long time. Even though I hardly knew her, the evening left me feeling oddly optimistic, as if I could be happy again.

There were lots of attractive single women at *LIFE*, and a certain number of attractive married women who were known, on occasion, to conduct office affairs. The camaraderie of the place, the working conditions, the hours, and the alcohol all contributed to an atmosphere where intimacy was not just possible, it was often probable. Imagine, for example, a group of people who work together intensely for eight or ten hours; who have been drinking—not excessively but steadily—for five or six of those hours; who are suddenly finished with work at midnight or one or two in the morning, many of them staying in Midtown hotels because the last commuter trains have run or there is no car at the home station. Some people go straight home or straight to a hotel all alone, but for some it was very tempting to have one more drink somewhere, and then who knew what might happen?

There was great discretion about these arrangements. Bragging and gossip were frowned upon. Occasionally, a married man infatuated with a particular woman might generate gossip because women in the office were generally interested in matches being made or being unmade and in the equity or lack of it that was involved.

Still, it was never wise to talk about anyone in a personal way, because the person listening might be involved somehow with the person being spoken about. This was not an uncommon situation in corporate culture in New York City in the late 1960s, but the situation at *LIFE* was about as loose as it was possible for an organization to be without turning into a commune. Henry Luce did not mind. In fact, he had contemplated building dorm rooms into the new Time-Life Building but was dissuaded when his advisers told him that people might never go home. Using camaraderie, voyeurism, sex, and liquor to keep people more or less at their desks round the clock was not limited to journalism and advertising, but it was pioneered there.

CHAPTER FIFTY-ONE

Let it be stipulated that Graves inherited a terrible situation. In the beginning *LIFE* had been glamorous, rich, profligate, creative, and freewheeling—home to a crowd of talented, intelligent people, many of them misfits in ordinary circumstances, but men and women who flourished in the freedom and ferment that *LIFE* provided. For the next thirty years, millions of readers loved the work they produced every week. They loved it so much that at times they fought over who would get to look at the magazine first. Now the bank account was seriously depleted. Television gained ground daily in the race to provide a mass audience at low cost. Graves's job was to get the bills down to something manageable and to shrink the whole enterprise so that if Time Inc. decided to kill *LIFE* magazine, the body would not be so enormous as to poison the rest of the corporation. It was a Gulliver situation—the Lilliputians deciding after some debate to spare the giant because they could not manage such a large corpse.

Graves was perfectly cast for the job. He never fully approved of the informality and loose discipline that characterized *LIFE*. He was too controlled, too rational, and too corporate not to be bothered by the informal working style of many of his contemporaries. This is probably why, at least in part, he was chosen to be the managing editor. He was a tough drill sergeant who could shape up the troops, slim them down, and get the enterprise ready for a last, desperate, life-or-death battle. He began by attacking the very heart of the fun: late closing night.

Each week on Wednesday evening, the current issue of the magazine was put to bed. Throughout the day, pages were laid out and text blocks sketched in to represent the space writers would be allotted to tell the story. Much of the magazine, the back of the book, would have been closed and even printed by this time, but the front of the book—the news pages and the current stories—were never finished until the last moment. The printing presses in Chicago awaited finally approved layouts and copy. Generally, there were one or two late-breaking stories, and the editing and layouts would drag into the late afternoon and evening. Nothing could go out until it was finally approved by the managing editor, after it had been approved by a copyeditor and an assistant managing editor and perhaps negotiated by reporters and writers who often had a point of view about the shape of the story.

When George Hunt was managing editor, this process often extended into the evening, whereupon George and a few editors would retire for drinks and dinner, usually returning around nine at night. George often came back from dinner with new thoughts about the current issue. He would tear up the afternoon's work and start over. Final copy and final layouts were often delayed until near midnight. It was not uncommon for the copy room, the final stage of the editing process, to close at two or even three on Thursday morning.

Wednesday nights were understood to be late nights, and no one involved in the process scheduled anything but work. It was also a time when personal accountability was vague. Commuters generally stayed in town, and people living in the city were not expected home at any given time. Persons involved in a late closing were not expected to work on Thursday until after lunch, although most people came in sooner and were sometimes greeted with an offer of a bloody mary, every office of any size being equipped with a company-supplied liquor cabinet. The costs of this weekly event lay mostly in sizable late fees charged by the printers who were paying overtime wages to union workers. The loss of half a day of work on Thursday for many on the editorial staff was offset by the work they had done the night before.

Hunt justified the practice in the name of quality. The extra expense of a late closing was warranted if he made the magazine a little better in the process. The fact that it happened almost every week raised the obvious question of why inspiration always came late on Wednesday night. Some not very nice people suggested that the drinks at dinner were responsible. The whispered wisdom about Wednesday closing was to "get your copy through George before dinner or you'll be here all night."

Graves made it clear that he intended to end late closings. He would get copy and layouts approved in time so that we could all go home at a reasonable hour, and just to be sure that we did go home, he scheduled

323

his mandatory weekly story conference for nine on Thursday morning, an hour earlier than we normally began work. Sometimes we got home at a reasonable hour, and sometimes we didn't. Graves's desires did not always dominate the process, but regardless of the hour of closing, his Thursday editorial meeting began on time with a crisp, driving Graves demanding to know what we had for him in the coming week.

If there was any change in the quality of the magazine, it was lost on me. The only change we saw, alarmingly, was shrinkage in the number of advertising pages and consequently shrinkage in the editorial space.

While I was getting used to Graves's new management style, my relationship with Bridget seemed to grow day by day without much direction from me. I found myself having lunch with her nearly every day. Many nights we had dinner. In my conscious mind I told myself that I was married to Sally and that Bridget and I were simply friends, but anyone watching the two of us would have easily seen that I was infatuated by her and that she welcomed my attention. We were on a fast track to a relationship and both in denial; she was not going to have another affair with a married man, and I was not going to leave Sally, but going back to Chicago on weekends grew harder and harder.

In September the new apartment was ready, and Sally and I moved in. The place was quite beautiful once everything was arranged. The piano dominated a big living room, and the furniture from Chicago worked even better in a New York brownstone than it had in a railroad flat in Chicago. We had a pleasant view of the back garden and enough height above the sidewalk in front to offer some privacy from the street. The area to the west of us was still problematic. Columbus and Amsterdam Avenues were dense with single-room-occupancy buildings that housed more than a few addicted or disturbed people. Once one reached Broadway, things got a little easier, but the trip across was tense, and Sally found it produced a lot of anxiety when she was alone, even in daylight.

We had barely settled into the new place when one of those events occurred that seem innocuous at the time but in retrospect are life-changing. An old friend of Sally's from Los Angeles came to New York for a few days. Michelle, the daughter of a minor screen actor, had been one of Sally's closest high school friends. She went to UC Berkeley when Sally went to UCLA, but they stayed in touch. Michelle was a large woman with a large presence and a manner both imperious and pretentious. Being married to a physicist on the Berkeley faculty gave her serious social standing in our circle of friends, and she went on and on about how wonderful it was that she and Dick were off to France for a year of teaching and research.

Even before Michelle left town, Sally's envy began to peek through. She wished she could go to France, she said wistfully. New York was nice, but Paris! The desire lingered and then grew into a kind of examination of where her life stood. After a day of two I began to feel that I had failed as a husband. All I could provide was a barely affordable apartment on the West Side and a position as an associate editor at *LIFE* magazine. The more Sally talked about Michelle's wonderful life and her brilliant husband, the more upset I became.

"Why don't you go to Paris?" I said one evening.

"How would I do that?"

"Just get on a plane and go," I said.

"You're being cruel?"

"No, I'm serious. I'm going to be crazy at work for the next few months. Graves is going to drive us all as hard as he can. Go to France. Improve your French, hang out in Paris. I'll send you money. You know people in the Paris bureau. I'm sure you can do things with them." I was referring to Bill and Marlis Ray, whom we knew from Los Angeles, and the Paris bureau chief, Richard Stolley, the dark prince of Time Inc., whom Sally had met a few times at magazine functions.

She considered my offer carefully. "Do you really think it's possible?" she asked.

"Absolutely. I don't have to live high on the hog, and if you aren't shopping I think we can swing it."

"I didn't shop so much."

"Right, but if we apply what you might have spent in stores to you being in Paris, and if I am careful, I think we can manage."

"How long can I stay?"

"I don't know. How long do you want to stay?"

"There isn't much point in going for a few weeks."

"No."

"Can I stay until spring?"

"It's October. You want to stay for six months?"

"Maybe. Yes, I think I do, if I go."

In a shockingly short time the decision was made. She got her ticket, arranged her clothing, and I went with her to Kennedy Airport to see her off. She was thrilled with the prospect of being in Paris for an extended stay. The staff people we knew would provide the seed for a full-fledged social life. The separation would provide some needed space to take stock and understand why our relationship had deteriorated.

This began one of the happiest times in my life. Bridget never officially moved in with me, but she spent every night in the new apartment. I persuaded her, against all the good professional advice she got from colleagues and mentors at work, to give up her job as picture researcher and to become a secretary in the news department. Once she moved, we were together around the clock, which suited me just fine. I had fallen in love in a way that I had not experienced before. It was irrational. Without either of us understanding it, we were in thrall to each other, in the darker sense of that word.

I became extremely protective, awkwardly insisting that my friends accept her as my primary companion while they were still trying to adjust to Sally's absence. Once I understood that the fashionable raincoat Bridget wore was the only coat she had, I took her shopping for a good winter coat. She became, in a matter of weeks, the emotional center of my life. I was prepared to make any sacrifice to be with her. It wasn't long before our relationship began to cause serious gossip around the magazine.

Sally seemed happy in Paris, although it was not long before some helpful person told her that I was seeing Bridget, and that began a period of correspondence in which we explored our differences and resentments and began negotiations for a separation. I continued to send money, and Sally settled into Parisian life with genuine exuberance, alarming a French man or two with her liberated, feminist, American ways. Relaxing at home, I now wore Levi's and listened to Simon and Garfunkel and Isaac Hayes. I didn't give up listening to opera, but I felt free to choose the music that suited my mood.

At work I moved into Rowan's old office. It was quickly reduced in size, in keeping with my lesser status, but I did manage to claim his giant desk, which now crowded my smaller office. It held sentimental value for me, so I lived with the crowding. My staff—the fifteen or so people, researchers and reporters, working in the news department—were all professionals. Most of them needed little supervision once an assignment was made, and I was free to look for stories, respond to queries from the bureaus, brief Ajemian and Graves on our projects, and respond to their requests. I had a first-class operation, and I began to feel confident that I knew how to run it. That assumption was soon tested and proved true.

Joe Eszterhas—soon to be a successful writer of erotic-thriller screen-plays, including *Basic Instinct* starring Sharon Stone, but at the time a reporter for the *Cleveland Plain Dealer*—called to say that he had in his possession a large number of color slides of the massacre at My Lai. Count Eszterhas, as he liked to be known, was acting as an agent for ex-army photographer Ron Haeberle. He wanted two first-class tickets to New York so that he and Haeberle could come to town to conduct a bidding war for the photos.

It took me a few minutes to decide that he was credible. Then I acted quickly. I assured him that *LIFE* would reimburse him for tickets from Cleveland to New York, provided he brought the slides directly to us and allowed us to examine them before anyone else saw them. I insisted they come that day. "Who else has these photos?" I asked.

"The *Plain Dealer* will print some of them tomorrow, but only in black and white," he said.

Seymour Hersh, the McCarthy press secretary whom I had pitied for leaving journalism for politics, was back in business in Washington and had written a long report about a group of American soldiers who, following orders, had rounded up several hundred civilian Vietnamese— old people, children, babies, women, and men—at a place called My Lai and then shot them to death. The article was such an explosive indictment of US military behavior in Vietnam that all the news outlets that Hersh initially approached refused the article. He offered it to small regional newspapers and to major national publications. None would have it. Finally he turned the story over to a small wire service, the Dispatch News Service, which made it available to its members. Thirty of the fifty papers receiving the articles printed it. There was safety in numbers. Never let it be said that being the first to print bad news about your country or its policies is without risk. The Pentagon Papers and Watergate were still in the future, and publishers and editors were understandably cautious. But now the secret was out. Hersh won a Pulitzer Prize the following year for his efforts.

In fairness to the army, it must be pointed out that while many senior officers, including Colin Powell, either ignored the reports they had received about the massacre or actively tried to suppress them, it was army personnel who initially tried to intervene to stop the massacre and later defied orders to talk about it to Congress. By the time Hersh got the story, charges against Lieutenant William Calley, the ultimate scapegoat for the horror, had been quietly filed at Fort Benning, Georgia, in a virtual news blackout.

Reports of the incident roused indignation both among hawks and doves. People who supported the war brushed off the incident as the kind of thing that can happen when men fight. Doves believed the incident revealed the deep immorality and indecency of this particular war. Verbal descriptions of the event were upsetting, but they were nothing compared with high-quality color slides. If the photos were authentic and if we were able to wade through the political barriers to printing them, they would leave no doubt that the event was real and that the victims were human beings.

Eszterhas and Haeberle arrived in my office late in the afternoon. Eszterhas reluctantly surrendered the slides to me, and we laid them out on the light table in my office. I sat down with a magnifying loupe to examine them. They were clear, perfectly exposed, razor sharp, and disgusting. An old woman lay in the edge of a field, her perfectly intact brain resting beside the gaping hole in her skull. Bloody babies lay on top of bloody mothers who had tried to protect them. Terrified women raised their hands in the pitiful, too-familiar gesture of a person trying to fend off bullets. I had to take a break and look away and breathe to regain my composure. There was no doubt in my mind that what I saw had happened on a bright, sunny day in Vietnam.

Eszterhas was irritable and aggressive. He seemed to feel sure that we were going to cheat him in some way. I had to constantly reassure him that we needed to look at the photos and authenticate them before we could hope to place a price on them or even commit to using them. His interest was personal, not journalistic. Haeberle had agreed to an even split of any money they received for the photos.

"Where have these pictures been since they were taken?" I asked. "Why are we just seeing them now?"

"The story just broke," Eszterhas said. "Haeberle read about it and called me and told me he had photos." He was referring to Hersh's story.

"And what was he doing with the photos before that?" I asked.

"He had put together a slide show, about seventy-five slides called *What We Did in Vietnam*. He was on the civic club lunch tour—you know, the Rotary, the Lions, and Kiwanis."

"He went around Cleveland showing these pictures to civic groups?"

"Yeah. Well, it was a whole show," Eszterhas replied. "You know, it started with them in basic training and then some time in Hawaii and then arriving in Nam and going out on operations. This was one of the operations. Then the show ended with them coming back and mustering out."

"Didn't any of the people who saw these think there was something wrong? I mean, dead babies, dead children, dead women, dead old women?"

"I guess," he shrugged.

Haeberle was one of the most passive people I had ever met, and he was completely under the control of the assertive Eszterhas. He was happy to answer any questions, but otherwise he rarely spoke. He told me in a most straightforward, unemotional way what had happened that day. They had gone out and killed a lot of people, and he had taken pictures of the event. He was remarkably unmoved as he described what had taken place.

"How did the troops react to you?" I asked.

"They didn't like me taking pictures. They didn't like what was going on either, but they were told they had to do it. One guy got really upset with me for taking pictures. He said it was bad enough they had to do this, but he thought it was awful that they sent me out to take pictures of them doing it."

Eszterhas fumed quietly as I spoke to Haeberle. He seemed to feel they were being manipulated somehow. I doubted he had ever been in a position of having something many people would pay for. He imagined that there was a way to behave in that situation, he just didn't know what it was. "I have to call *Newsweek*," he announced.

"How much do you want for the photos?"

"Three hundred thousand dollars."

"Look, I'll put you in an office next door. You can use the phone. Do whatever you need to do. I just need an hour or two to show these to my bosses and to the director of photography. This is going to take a little time."

"I'll take this right to *Newsweek*. I know they want these, and they are willing to pay."

"Joe, I promise you they won't pay what we will."

I knew that Dick Pollard was already on the phone to publications in Europe and Asia to determine the resale value of the photos if we bought them outright and if we decided to syndicate them. With Eszterhas temporarily settled in an office, I gathered the photos and took them to Graves's office, where Ajemian met me.

"I have already received a strong suggestion that we buy these at any price and lock them away in a vault," Graves said as I steamed into his office. "Word is out."

This was a warning of the struggle to come. I was simultaneously rattled by the idea that anyone associated with journalism would want the photos suppressed, enraged by the same notion, and fearful that they might prevail. "We have to print these," I said simply.

Graves and Ajemian examined the photographs. They stood back from the light table and looked at each other briefly in silence. They returned to the light table and pulled away again. No one spoke. As worldly as they were, they were shocked. I could see Graves calculating just how far he could go and just how far he should go. "We could run some in black and white," he said finally, as if thinking aloud.

He and Ajemian returned to the light table again and again to reexamine the photos. Other editors hearing of the pictures wandered in for a look. Conversation lagged. I briefed Graves on the origins of the photographs, telling him about Haeberle and Eszterhas and the asking price of $300,000. My anxiety rose as I understood that the final decision to run the photos had not been made.

"The first thing we have to do," Graves said grimly, "is to be absolutely certain these are real and that they represent what we think they represent. How can we do that?"

I called Muriel Hall, the chief of research for the news department, an Oxford-educated Yankee of immense knowledge and integrity. She had helped train me when I arrived at *LIFE* four years earlier. "Muriel, how can we be sure, beyond any doubt, that these My Lai pictures are what we think they are?"

"Let's make up sets of black-and-white prints and send them out to the bureaus. I am sure we can get the names of the men in Calley's unit from the army. We'll find the men and show them the photos and ask them if they are real." It was a simple, brilliant solution, one that should be in every journalism text.

"OK," I said. "Get started identifying the men in Calley's unit and finding out where they are. I'll alert the bureaus to be ready to knock on doors and show the pictures."

"What does Pollard think about the price?" Graves asked.

"He's calling *Paris Match* and *Stern* and the others to see if we can recoup some of the cost in Europe."

"OK," Graves said. "You get the research done and figure out a way to buy these, and I'll work out a way to handle them."

I felt better as I left Graves. I sensed that he was prepared to face down the people who wanted to hide the evidence of an American atrocity. Back in my office I found Eszterhas, who was again demanding that we commit to his price immediately or he was going to shop the photos to *Newsweek*. I reassured him once again that *LIFE* would offer him as good a price as he would get anywhere and that we would do a better job of presenting the pictures than anyone else, but I understood that he was not interested in what happened to the pictures. He was interested in the money.

Around five, I took Haeberle and Eszterhas for drinks at the Ho Ho, a Chinese restaurant and bar downstairs. I persuaded them to let us keep the pictures in our safe overnight. When we got back about an hour later, Pollard called. "You can offer him $125,000 for the pictures," he said. "I think we'll be OK at that price. The Europeans are hot for the stuff."

I decided to make the offer before leaving the two of them for the evening. Eszterhas rejected it out of hand. "We want $300,000. I believe *Newsweek* or another magazine will pay that," he said. "You're not going to steal these pictures."

He was unpleasant in the way that people who are scared and trying not to show it are unpleasant: belligerent and overly confident.

"Joe, if they offer you $300,000, will you give us a chance at a counteroffer?"

"Why don't you just pay that now?"

"I really can't, but if indeed you get a much better offer, maybe we can work something out. You're sure you won't accept $125,000? That's a lot of money."

"No."

Eszterhas seemed unaware of how complex the game was. There were people at Time Inc. and at other publications in the country who did not want the pictures printed at all. They would have been happy for him to take the photos and return to Cleveland. Others wanted the pictures suppressed and were willing to buy them to bury them. Still others did not want a competing magazine to own and print them. Some people thought it was important for the nation to see the photos. There were people, one of them a powerful editor at *LIFE*, who were

331

concerned about the stewardship of the photos. They were afraid that, in the wrong hands, the photos would become crude propaganda. To prevent this occurrence, they were willing to spend money to gain control of the photos. Eszterhas, thinking as a reporter and agent, could only imagine a scenario where the pictures were bought and printed in a "bombshell exposé."

My greatest fear was that, for political and ideological reasons or out of a misguided patriotism, *LIFE* would buy the photos and then let them languish without ever really making a decision one way or the other, a kind of death by indifference. Events in Cleveland and in Paris, Berlin, and London the following morning would resolve all these dilemmas.

With the prints safely locked in Pollard's safe, Bridget and I went to dinner and then home. I could think of nothing but the negotiations. She had not seen the photos, and after I described some of them to her, she decided she didn't want to see them, but she supported my thinking that they should be published, even though *LIFE* was a magazine that went into eight million homes, where millions of children lived.

"You know," I told her, "in a situation like this, my mother hid half a dozen issues of *LIFE* from my sister and me. When the Allies discovered and liberated the Nazi death camps, *LIFE* covered it. Mother said the pictures were too terrible for children. Years later I made a special effort to find those issues and look at the photos."

"And," Bridget said, "was she right?"

"Absolutely. They were ghastly, and they would have upset us. They upset me as an adult, but *LIFE* did the right thing when it put that on the record."

I came to work the next morning filled with anxiety. Pollard called minutes after I arrived. "The European market is gone," he said.

"Why?"

"They copied the photos right out of the *Plain Dealer*. Every tabloid in London has them on the front page."

This was my introduction to the competitive nature of European and British journalism. Papers all over Europe and the United Kingdom simply copied the photos off the pages of the *Plain Dealer* and reprinted them without permission from anyone. The attitude was "Sue me if you can."

When Eszterhas arrived, I told him what had happened. He was dumbfounded. In an act of loyalty, he had given the photos to his paper before leaving for New York, not understanding that he had given them

332

to every paper in the world that was more interested in sensation than in quality, permission, or the niceties of ownership.

Within an hour, Pollard had facsimile copies of a number of the papers. I showed them to Eszterhas. Looking very glum, he said, "Do you still want to buy the pictures?"

"Yes, but the price is $20,000. There is no resale market."

He looked sick. "OK."

He had been so arrogant the day before and so dismissive of our firm offer of $125,000 that I could not resist my next question. "How does it feel to lose $100,000 overnight?" I asked.

He looked at me sharply, but he did not answer.

We wrote Haeberle and Eszterhas a check, and they returned to Cleveland. I heard that Haeberle used his share of the money to put a down payment on a Corvette. Eszterhas got into a big fight with his newspaper and was either fired or quit, depending on who was telling the story. He went to work for *Rolling Stone*, where he wrote an article about selling the My Lai pictures to *LIFE*, and then hit it rich writing screenplays.

With clear ownership of the photos and relieved of the responsibility of being the first to print them, we began an intense effort to complete Muriel Hall's plan for authentication. That became a story in itself. As our correspondents knocked on doors to ask GIs if they recognized the photos, some burst into tears. One pulled the reporter into his house where he confronted his grandmother with the photos and in a shame-filled confession said, "Look, Grandma. This is what we did in Vietnam."

Graves ran the photos in the December 5, 1969, issue. To spare the casual reader and the newsstand browser, he did not put the story on the cover. Inside, the photos ran in color and some in black and white. We did not use the most graphic shots, but the pictures and the explanation that accompanied them left no doubt that the war in Vietnam had lost all moral bearings. The concept of victory through body count, begun under President Johnson, made children, babies, and the elderly— anyone who happened to be available—eligible to become a victory number in the wretched game that President Nixon now pursued in a kind of blind madness that no one could stop.

CHAPTER FIFTY-TWO

"The news department is a rock," Graves said happily, stopping me in the hall. He had taken a chance printing the My Lai story in the face of serious and powerful opposition, remaining steadfast in his belief that it should be part of the record. It was critical that during such a high-wire act he have complete confidence in the validity of his material. The news department provided that. He saw and appreciated what we had done, and I was grateful for his gratitude. Two weeks later he called me in and basically asked me what I wanted from the magazine.

"I'd like to be a senior editor," I said.

"You are a senior editor," he replied, offering his hand.

"That's amazing." I was unable to contain the next thought. "You can just do that, can't you?"

"Yes, I can," he replied, smiling, pleased with himself.

Most of the titles at the magazine seemed banal. "Assistant editor," "associate editor," "reporter," "researcher"—they all seemed common. But "correspondent" and "senior editor" both sounded serious to me, jobs with substance. Not as serious as "editor" or "editor in chief" or "managing editor," of course, but those titles existed in an entirely different world than the one I inhabited. Those ranks were made by the corporation the way making a general requires an act of Congress. Those titles came with stock options and other secret goodies to which mere journalists were not heir. As far as I was concerned, I had reached the top of the heap in my tier. It was like becoming a full-bird colonel at age thirty-one. It was not as good as the producer Frank McCarthy becoming a brigadier at twenty-seven, but good enough. I was delighted.

There was a moment when I wondered if the promotion had come too easily for Graves. Would he, I wondered, have been so quick to elevate me to such an exalted position in the days when *LIFE* was still king of the hill? Did the ease with which he promoted me speak of insouciance in the face of impending doom? Did William Travis promote a dozen men to the rank of general as the Mexican army approached the Alamo? The question was tricky because it played into my tendency to think that the things I achieved were not so valuable once I had them. No matter. The title would become an important part of my resume and provide my mother with bragging rights and a dart to throw at my pompous uncle, R. B. Moore. So much of what we do is rooted in things like that.

It isn't just Hollywood where people change their names to improve their image. Aubrey Moore, my father's older brother, morphed into "R. B." as he became a successful utility executive. Who would fear a man with a poet's name like "Aubrey"? It was not the moniker for a hard-charging executive. "R. B.," on the other hand, was almost *New Yorker* cartoonish in its smack of authority. He lived up to the name. He was smart, aggressive, and often condescending to my father, much to my mother's displeasure. Soon after I was hired by *LIFE*, Mother, in a moment of parental pride, mentioned to him that I had gone to work for *LIFE* magazine. In fact, she said, my name was listed in the masthead, whereupon she retrieved a copy of the magazine and showed him his nephew's name. Rather than feigning pleasure that a member of the family had achieved some recognition, he diminished the accomplishment because it was not one of his own three children.

"Well, so what?" he said dismissively. "There are about a hundred names there."

Mother didn't give way. "Yes," she said, "and Gerald's is one of them."

When the masthead was amended in late December 1969 and my name stood near the top, in very rarified company, I wrote to Mother that she should show R. B. the masthead again and see how he liked it now. She was amused, but she had other things on her mind. She and Lisa and my father were planning a vacation to Laos.

The bifurcated view I had of Vietnam would never be resolved. I saw images daily of killing, burning villages, napalm, and dead and wounded American soldiers. Many of the correspondents and photographers who covered the war were friends or people I knew well enough to be concerned for their safety: photographer Larry Burrows, who in just over a year would die in Laos; Don Moser, the man most responsible for my being at *LIFE* and now Hong Kong bureau chief, spending days on end in the combat zones of Vietnam. On the other hand, I had letters from Mother that included photos of her and my niece in traditional

Vietnamese dress with descriptions of the country that any happy tourist might write. There were occasional references to the war when there was violence in Saigon or if one of their friends found himself in jeopardy. They had made the acquaintance of several young officers, men my age, and valued their company the way older people can value the company of the young. But try as I might, I could not imagine that Mother and Lisa and my father were in the same country I read about every morning.

My father never doubted that the United States would win the war. It was just a matter of time and money. As far as he was concerned, there was no moral confusion, no ambiguity about our aims and methods. As things turned out in the light of history, he and Robert McNamara trod parallel paths from absolute assurance to deep doubt. Mother, correctly believing my father to be the more intelligent partner in the marriage, generally took her cues from him when political questions were concerned. This is not to say that she always agreed with him or believed that "just because he is smarter he is always right." She was a keen observer of people and their motives, a skill that children raised in stressful circumstances often acquire. She was also a more self-consciously moral person than my father, owing, I always believed, to her greater natural empathy. His childhood on a hardscrabble ranch had inured him somewhat to the suffering of himself and others. His view of human nature was Hobbesian and fatalistic and probably close to the truth. Mother was attracted to a more sentimental and optimistic view of human nature, but where the war was concerned she followed my father's lead.

To celebrate my new title, to publicly acknowledge my growing commitment to Bridget, and to escape some of the tension I felt every day, I suggested we go to Mexico for a holiday. I wired Ken Goldthorpe, who had been assistant entertainment editor when I first came to the magazine to work in that department. He was pleasant and a bit odd, the quintessential old salt of a journalist. Even though he was less than ten years my senior, he assumed the posture of a man who had seen it all. The pose was mostly a ploy for telling good stories. I liked him in spite of his avuncular manner because he did not take himself too seriously. He had worked for the *St. Louis Post-Dispatch* and then for *LIFE* in India, England, and France, where he supervised a vast George Hunt project to present a gorgeous and historically accurate account of the Battle of Waterloo on the 150th anniversary of Napoleon's defeat. He was now head of the Mexico City bureau, an office that serviced both *LIFE* magazine and *LIFE en Español*, the Spanish-language version of the magazine. When I called him to tell him that Bridget and I would be in Mexico, he offered to help us with hotels and arranged to have drinks and dinner with us when we arrived.

Our first evening ended early when Bridget discovered that at seventy-three hundred feet of altitude one artisanal Mexican margarita equals three made from bar mix in Manhattan, but the next day, refreshed and only slightly hungover, we flew off to Acapulco, where seven years before I had been a poor student sharing a hotel bathroom with local fishermen and their families.

In those halcyon days I had not noticed the social rank of tourists in that fading old Mexican resort. There were men my age driving new Corvettes along the Costera. They were none of my concern. They lived in a world different from mine. The luxury hotels and high-end restaurants were so completely out of reach that they did not seem real. I was happy just to be on the Pacific Ocean in Mexico and able to join my companions at a tiny sidewalk café every morning to eat huevos rancheros and then to buy a bottle of rum and take a bus to the beach where ice and Coke and limes were cheap and created enough business to keep the beach waiters happy.

But now that I was an "important editor" at a major national magazine, I very much wanted to be hip, not an easy job for someone who usually felt a step behind the really cool people who always knew what to do in a disco. Of course, I also wanted Bridget to think me a man of the world, which increased my sense of insecurity. According to Ken, a woman named Jan would be my answer. She was, he said, the doyenne of Acapulco social life now that Merle Oberon was older (a claim I doubted). I felt sure that in putting ourselves under Jan's care we would pass as cool people.

We arrived at Jan's house to meet a socially thin blonde of indeterminate age who fixed us up with a drink and then sat us down for a quick briefing. "I'm going to tell everyone that you are the entertainment editor at *LIFE*," she said. "No one here gives a shit about news. And," she added, smiling, "you need to get out of those old, dark city clothes and find some resort wear." Soon enough, we were back at our hotel, where I bought Bridget a new swimming suit and found a thin white "resort" shirt for me.

Ken came down a few days later, and for the next week we partied with people who lived at least part of the year in Acapulco, people with whom we had absolutely nothing in common. We saw some very nice houses; wandered in beautiful garden patios; ate interesting hors d'oeuvres, like tripe tacos; and went to some cool discos, where I finally figured out that what people do in discos is drugs, dancing, and fondling. I felt powerful jealousy as the Eurotrash came on strong to Bridget, and I actually interceded a couple of times when brash Americans seemed to be overstepping their bounds, but then it was that sort of atmosphere: nothing was pinned down, everything was on wheels, and almost everyone was literally up for grabs. It was exciting and scary.

We returned to New York a week later, nicely tanned in the middle of winter. At work I found Ajemian beaming. "Your timing is just superb," he said. "You couldn't have done this any better." I was baffled until he explained that my relationship with Bridget had caused endless heated gossip, some of it detrimental. Our colleagues were not concerned about our adultery; at least, that was not their main concern. Rather, they were mightily upset that I had persuaded Bridget, and that she had allowed herself to be persuaded, to give up an editorial job for a secretary's position, all in the name of love.

I was shamefully ignorant and completely unaware of the powerful undercurrents of feminist discontent then flowing just beneath the placid corporate surface, a discontent that would in just seven months be manifested by the August strike and march of women demanding better, more equitable treatment in the workplace. "Don't iron while the strike is hot," Betty Friedan would admonish, to the delight of everyone but the most reactionary males. It was the beginning of the end for the Mad Men, and I would be as surprised as most of my male colleagues when the second wave of feminism broke over New York City.

By taking Bridget to Mexico I had, in the odd semiotics of magazine culture, made her an honest woman. I was now a man making a new relationship, not just a dirty old man exploiting a beautiful young thing. My commitment to Bridget was public, and therefore her professional sacrifice was less onerous.

When Sally returned from Paris in April, Bridget and I moved into a sublet in Hell's Kitchen, on Forty-Sixth Street between Ninth and Tenth Avenues. It was not a great neighborhood. At night, very tall, muscular transvestite prostitutes lined Ninth Avenue like sentinels, but the apartment was special: small, with a working fireplace and a large, almost-secure courtyard outside. The owner had covered the walls with theatrical posters, mostly of the Barrymores, appropriately dramatic for a place on the edge of the theater district.

Sally and I managed to remain friends. There really wasn't much to argue about. I turned over the apartment and all the furniture, everything except my clothes and books, and continued to provide the money I had sent her in France. We still met from time to time to have lunch and to exchange news, but the intimate relationship was over. In the odd way of male-female relationships, I liked Sally better as a friend than I liked her as a wife. Her sharp and often insightful sense of humor was no longer threatening. Her vulnerabilities did not require my personal protection. Her expensive tastes were her own concern. She quickly recruited me as a sort of mentor in the magazine world, and in that role I would eventually help her become established as a founding member of the *People* magazine editorial staff (a dubious honor), though that was all a year or two down the line.

CHAPTER FIFTY-THREE

It was egotistical to think that my sense of responsibility for the well-being of the country—or to put it more plainly, my naïve patriotism—should have any impact at all on the actual course of events in America. It was one of my illusions and one of the conceits of journalists that by writing about ideas and events we could bring about change. Change does come—sometimes—through public discussion, revelation, and reportage, but if and when it comes at all, it comes slowly. To a thirty-one-year-old in 1970, change was glacial: the war in Vietnam and the struggle for racial justice in America, often bordering on civil war, seemed permanent conditions of American life.

My first experience with journalism in Albuquerque spoiled me. A few investigative news reports resulted in substantial improvement to bad situations. This led to the mistaken idea that good reporting can quickly lead to social betterment. Arriving at *LIFE* magazine, I thought that a larger sound system would bring greater accomplishment. If I could affect social conditions in Albuquerque writing for an afternoon daily, then writing for a national weekly magazine should produce major results. The test of this belief was delayed because my personal adjustment in the first few years at *LIFE* was so dizzying that I didn't have time to think about anything larger than professional survival. Now, back in New York, attending editorial meetings on a regular basis and talking with other writers, reporters, and editors working for national publications and network television, I began to see that we were engaged in a highly complex activity that went far beyond discovering and reporting the truth. Our survival depended on our ability to engage the public, to excite and entertain people. The scorekeepers in this effort were, to a distressing extent, our subscription department and advertising staff. Enlightenment and social improvement were mostly incidental to the process.

Early on, I chose to ignore the business side of journalism, to act as if business was irrelevant to the editorial side. I wanted work that was not tainted by commerce. I wanted to think of reporters as secular working priests ministering to the public's well-being. The more I confronted the reality that *LIFE*'s survival was based on profit and loss, the more I resented the marketplace realities that ultimately governed us. Initially, I thought and acted as if I worked for a well-endowed nonprofit foundation rather than a publicly held company whose stock was traded daily on the New York Stock Exchange.

Sometime in the spring of 1970 two bits of reality began to sink into my consciousness: that we were wholly beholden to the marketplace and that what we wrote had only a marginal effect, if any, on the conditions of public life in America. The convergence of these two insights acted like a slow-release toxin on my ambition and enthusiasm. A more worldly person might have known that this is the way things are and therefore have enjoyed some immunity to their effects, but my background was in rural America, where many of our ideas about human behavior and the national purpose were founded in patriotic myths and religious idealism. That did not prepare me well for what I was learning now working as a senior editor at *LIFE* magazine in New York City.

The opportunity to publish the My Lai photographs was an exception that delayed my dissatisfaction. The struggle by powerful people, including some major journalists, to suppress the photos surprised me, but we won that battle. Graves was steadfast, and anyone looking at that story now had a better understanding of what was being done in Asia with American money and lives. The reports we did on Watts, the social dysfunction in Chicago's West Side ghetto, the riots in Detroit, and college students facing the draft all shoved public thinking in the right direction, but the tide of events seemed to be running against us. The good guys were not winning. I was learning the painful secret that successful periodical publication is not so much about leading public opinion as it is about sensing the direction of public opinion and being just slightly ahead of it. "Leadership," someone said cynically, "is finding a parade and getting in front of it."

What? Journalism won't save the world? Publications have to make money to survive. Human beings ignore good advice and turn their backs on cruelty and misbehavior. At some level I knew all these things to be true, but I chose, like a perfectly fallible human being, to ignore them, and that failure ate at me. The sequence of events that spring did not help.

In March a group of young men and women set out to make bombs in a townhouse on West Eleventh Street in Manhattan. They planned to attack, among other targets, Columbia University and a dance for noncommissioned officers at Fort Dix, New Jersey, where they would set off dynamite pipe bombs packed with roofing nails to maim and kill a group of young men and women about their own age, though far less privileged. Being better schooled in political theory than in electrical circuitry, the would-be terrorists set off a bomb accidentally, killing three of their number and wounding two others. They destroyed the townhouse, which belonged to the father of one of them, and played squarely into the hands of their political enemies. They brought the violence of war to Greenwich Village, forty-odd blocks from my office, and tainted Manhattan with a sinister air. For a time, until we knew more about the bombers, we expected more bombs, in places like department stores or theaters.

Less than two months later, on May 4, as I prepared to attend an editorial lunch, John Pekkanen, my replacement as Chicago bureau chief, called to say that he had heard that students at Kent State University in Ohio planned an antiwar protest that day. "I doubt if anything will happen," he said. "But just in case, I hired a student photographer, a kid named John Filo, to cover the event for us."

Before I finished lunch, word came that the Ohio National Guard, carrying live ammunition, had gone to the Kent State campus and, in a bizarre act of confusion and failed discipline, opened fire on the unarmed students, killing four and wounding nine, most of whom had nothing to do with the demonstration. John Filo won a Pulitzer Prize for his photo of a young woman kneeling over a mortally wounded student as she screamed in anguish and shock. Professionally I was grateful that Pekkanen had the foresight to arrange coverage. Once again, the news department would be "a rock." We had the photographs that described the event, and *LIFE* printed them. Personally I was outraged that the National Guard was shooting students, even unruly ones.

Two days later, four million students nationwide went on strike to protest the killings. When a group of people attempted to demonstrate near Wall Street, they were attacked and violently dispersed by construction workers organized by the man Nixon would soon appoint as his labor secretary.

So in the spring of 1970—as Nixon widened the war in Asia by invading Cambodia; as guardsmen shot students; as police killed black students and demonstrators in Augusta, Georgia, and Jackson, Mississippi; and as riots disturbed Miami—our major concern at the magazine was our own survival.

It was hard to get any solid fix on the magazine's exact financial condition. The corporation held that kind of information very close. The golden age of corporate raiders still lay ahead, but management at Time Inc. was already nervously looking over its shoulder, and any solid financial information might be used to undermine the current management. In addition, there was a well-grounded fear that if advertisers came to believe the magazine was failing, they would pull their support, not wanting to waste money on an audience that would soon be gone. Less dangerous but more annoying was the glee that some people in the advertising and publishing world felt at the prospect of the marketplace humbling a proud and aggressive magazine.

I saw Graves making all sorts of changes, initiating all sorts of money-saving efforts, undermining (of necessity, I assumed) the robust news coverage of events we had always enjoyed. We were closing bureaus, dropping subscriptions, and trimming costs anywhere possible. Until that spring I never felt that considerations of cost interfered with our coverage. We had always been willing to pay whatever it took to get the very best picture, quote, insight, or byline. Now I found we were starting to operate like a tabloid, buying photos from any source offering them, looking for stories that would not cost much, and passing over stories that might be expensive. Every week a new edict would arrive further restricting our freedom to work and imposing more controls on the perks we enjoyed (often in lieu of better salaries). Rowan's suggestion in 1968 that I use my expense account more aggressively to compensate for a modest raise would have seemed heresy now. We regularly received memos about expenses, and I had been visited personally by an accounting person who hoped that I could entertain less.

I knew the essential question to be answered: Could Graves cut costs enough to make the magazine break even? There was a possibility (one that I considered more likely every day) that no amount of cutting would be enough, that *LIFE* was simply no longer viable as a business model. There were lots of ifs that came into play, but they were in the nature of all ifs. They were dreams. If we could tremendously increase our circulation so that our numbers compared more favorably with television. If we could cull and substantially shrink our circulation so that we serviced fewer readers but they all lived in affluent zip codes. If we could get subscribers to pay more for their weekly magazine. If we could sell more copies on the newsstand, where each copy represented a huge profit compared with a small loss on each copy sent through the mail. If the price or paper and postage did not increase. If pigs had wings, they could fly.

In fact, I needed to know more about the aerodynamics of pigs in order to plan my immediate future. If *LIFE* survived, I would probably stay, unless the magazine became so distorted by economic stress that working there disqualified me as a serious journalist. There was still a lot to learn, and Time Inc. was a huge, robust company with many opportunities, although the possibility of switching to another Time Inc. publication was not something I savored. Having risen to what I regarded as the dizzying heights of magazine journalism, I would have trouble accepting a lesser job; it would be hard on my ego. I dreaded starting over at another publication, and I doubted that, with the huge, talented staff of *LIFE* suddenly on the market in Manhattan, any of us would be in a strong position to bargain. More and more, I began to think that if it folded, I would move to a less expensive place and attempt to make a living as a freelancer. A quieter life, probably in the country, looked better and better.

A major factor in my thinking was Cathy. I had a feeling from conversations with Hellyn and Cathy that I might gain de facto custody of her in the near future. If that happened, I needed to be in something more spacious than a tiny sublet. The thought of trying to afford a two-bedroom apartment in Manhattan, even a very small one, and a private school for Cathy while getting established in a new job made me shudder. I decided to put the whole matter out of my mind and concentrate on the present, which was good. Bridget seemed content to work with me and to be with me. As desperate as the situation at the magazine sometimes appeared, my life with Bridget was perfect, and more than any other single thing, it sustained me. We worked together all day. We ate together at lunch. We were together in the evening. Our passion was insatiable. I doubt if two people have ever spent more time in each other's company than we did in those first years of our relationship.

As summer approached, I began to feel a strong desire to go back to New Mexico. Somehow my native soil would give me strength. I located an old adobe house for rent in Pojoaque, just north of Santa Fe, and booked it for July. Bridget, Cathy, and I would have a month together there, enjoying the country, swimming, going to the Santa Fe Opera, eating wonderful green-chile dishes in Chimayo. Cathy and Bridget should get acquainted because, I felt certain, they were going to spend a lot of their lives with each other.

Bridget and I met Cathy in Chicago, and we all flew to Albuquerque. We rented a car and drove north to our retreat. I was determined that for a month I would enjoy being in the country without financial worries, without the pressure of a weekly news budget, and away from the city. I would try to forget how temporary my situation might be.

There are lots of wonderful places in New Mexico, but none holds more enchantment for me than a huge triangle marked by Santa Fe in the south, Dulce on the west, and Raton on the east: Kit Carson country, Santa Fe Trail and Philmont Scout Ranch country, Maxwell Land Grant country. It contains the remains of some of America's oldest civilizations, wild animals in astonishing abundance, and country so beautiful it can make you cry.

We arrived midmorning at the late nineteenth-century adobe we had rented. It sat along a dirt road in the southern reaches of my triangle. The house was authentic in every respect. It was built in the original fashion, where form truly followed function. The materials were local. Thick adobe walls supported the weight of heavy log vigas to make a roof capable of holding a foot or two of wet snow. The walls, thirty inches through, created deep window ledges where old geraniums thrived, climbing and coiling in the sun. A well-used corner fireplace, blackened at the edges by piñon smoke, graced every room. Stone floors shone with the polish of a million trips. A cool, shaded portico offered shelter along three walls of the courtyard and gave the place a feeling of security and intimacy. The opportunity to be there for a month with Bridget and Cathy was like holding everything I loved in my arms all at once.

Cathy was nine, almost ten, and in that most charming of all stages of childhood—where the personality is fully engaged in the world but still uncomplicated by all the driving desires and fears and passions that will soon move in to complicate life. And Bridget showed an easy, natural way with children that I found enormously reassuring after watching Sally's awkward and strained efforts to get along with kids. Within a day or two they seemed to be pals, a condition I deeply desired and had always sensed would be the case.

Contrary to the common notion that time accelerates when things are good, July passed in a slow, delicious procession of love and good times. We drove to Chimayo many evenings to eat delicate, freshly made tortillas with green-chile stew. We swam in a huge, cold pool built in the 1930s by a previous owner who had entertained visions of Olympic swimming fame. We found Cathy a kindly flute instructor who played in the Santa Fe Opera orchestra. When it rained, we borrowed a Ford pickup of 1950s vintage to drive to the opera over muddy country roads, feeling thrilled by the wild juxtaposition of an empty desert and a full symphony orchestra. I threw a party for all my old friends in Albuquerque, and most of them were willing to make the eighty-mile drive to hang out on our lawn and eat a meal Bridget and Cathy prepared after hours of long-distance phone instructions from Bridget's sister in New York. Cathy made friends with four burros kept for some reason in a pasture near the house, sometimes playing the flute for them in an exchange that they actually seemed to enjoy. In Santa Fe I briefly met Richard Bradford, who excited a deep jealous depression in me when, two years earlier, he published *Red Sky at Morning*, a wonderful New Mexico coming-of-age novel that drew effortlessly on material I considered mine. It was the same feeling of an opportunity missed or ignored that later overwhelmed me when I read Larry McMurtry's *Lonesome Dove*. Both books touched my heart. They were filled with characters I recognized and attitudes and beliefs that suffused my childhood, all of them too familiar to be noticed until they were highlighted by two skillful writers. They did for me what great visual artists do: they made me see for the first time things I look at every day without really seeing them.

As July played out, I felt an unshakable sadness at the prospect of being without Cathy again, at least until Christmas. Back in New York, the August heat and humidity lay over the city like a fetid gym towel. Each morning as I walked to work past piles of restaurant garbage baking on the streets of the theater district, I remembered the sweet high-mountain air of New Mexico.

Graves, Ajemian, and Wainwright were off to Martha's Vineyard for the month of August. It was understood that August was the preferred month for vacations, and the senior people had dibs. I didn't mind. My birthday fell in July, and that seemed like a good time to be away. Filling in for Ajemian while Kunhardt directed the show, I got to look down the road from the driver's seat, and I liked the view.

Then, on August 26, the Women's Strike for Equality changed things forever at the magazine. I had not heard much about the strike, and when I did hear I didn't think it was anything that ought to concern us, until late in the afternoon when I realized there were no women in the building. "Where have all the women gone?" I asked several equally mystified men until one said they had gone "to the march."

"What march?"

"They are all marching down Fifth Avenue, demanding equal treatment."

Even Bridget was missing. I was mystified. I had not been aware of any particular unhappiness on the part of my women colleagues. I had pushed to have Joan Downs sent to Chicago to join the all-male staff of correspondents. I had done other small things to help female colleagues move ahead, but I was not aware that anyone was especially aggrieved, at least not until that day when the women came streaming back into the building after the march, their faces flushed with excitement and their spirits high.

Afterward, there was a lot of excited talk about the working conditions of women and what, if anything, should be done about them. A group from the news department—three women, two other men, and I—retired after work to the bar at La Fonda del Sol on the ground floor of the Time-Life Building. As we discussed feminist issues, Peter Young, an affable associate editor, announced to the table that he knew of a situation that demanded the attention of concerned women. "You should really go after Volkswagen," he said, addressing the women. "Did you know that they don't even put a lock on the woman's side of the car?"

No one seemed to notice what he had said, leaping instead directly to the question of why Volkswagen would do such a thing. Then, after a second or two, someone said, "The woman's side of the car?" The depth of our benighted state was revealed. Until that moment it was accepted that there was a man's side and a woman's side of a car. That was about to change.

Graves's wife, Eleanor, had been a powerful presence at *LIFE* as head of the "Modern Living" department. When Graves was named managing editor, she was forced to resign to prevent any perceived conflict of interest. That she had to end a very successful career at the magazine because her husband had succeeded so well must have come as a nasty and surprising blow to a woman of great ambition. Her absence did not end her influence. One could easily imagine that a woman of her skill and drive had some opinions about the role of women at the magazine and about the ferment and excitement of women asserting their right to equal work and pay. In the following months, as Graves reorganized the staff to give women more control and responsibility, it was never clear to me when he was acting on his own and when he was carrying out suggestions from home. In any case, the position of women at *LIFE* improved markedly under Graves.

In fairness, it should be noted that women were treated better at *LIFE* than they were in most workplaces at the time. The magazine employed many powerful women—Eleanor Graves, Sally Kirkland, Mary Leatherbee, and Marion MacPhail, among others—and important photographers such as Margaret Bourke-White, Nina Leen, Hansel Mieth, and Ruth Orkin, though they were a minority. Yet there were no women at the top of the company, and certain Time Inc. editors continued to accept as their right certain sexual favors from certain ambitious female members of their staffs. This probably would not change much in the years ahead, despite advances in gender equality.

While I would have denied it, my own behavior with regard to Bridget, when I persuaded her to leave an editorial job for a secretarial position (though, ironically, the secretarial salary was higher), fell short of a feminist ideal. But she agreed with me that experience in the news department would make up for the loss of status. And in any case, we wanted to work together.

CHAPTER FIFTY-FOUR

By the fall of 1970 I fully appreciated what it meant to be an editor. I was expected to find or to conceive articles, shape our coverage to assure that articles were properly reported, and staff and track stories to give the managing editor advance notice of when they would be ready and what they might contain. As the news editor, the task was especially difficult because we were now rarely able to report news as such. Most anything worth reporting would have been on television long before we could go to print.

Arriving at the office one September morning full of praise for a morning television news story, Ajemian called me into his office to fret over the leftovers. "They get it all," he said, shaking his head. "They've got great color and sound, and it is so immediate! You can almost smell it. What can we do with this? Isn't there something in this that we can turn into a story, maybe something important that they missed?"

Graves and Ajemian began to press harder for new angles or a new slant on things already reported. They themselves had no clue. Their clever younger editors were meant to figure this out. But angles and slants can be a problem. They take time to develop and to understand. They quickly leave the arena of news and move into the arena of human interest, an arena where I was expressly forbidden to go.

Most of the events the world witnesses are just what they seem. They can be turned a hundred different ways and looked at from all sides, but in essence they remain what they first appeared to be: "A kiss is just a kiss."

Kurt Vonnegut brilliantly illustrated this when he applied for a position at Time Inc. He was given a news clip and asked to rewrite it in exciting *Sports Illustrated* style. The clipping recounted an afternoon at Belmont when a horse jumped the rail and wandered around the infield for a few minutes. After an hour or so, Vonnegut's interlocutor returned to find the soon-to-be-famous writer gone and a sheet of paper protruding from the typewriter. It read, "The fucking horse jumped the fence." That was the beginning and the end of his career as a Time Inc. writer, and it was an exquisitely accurate account of the event, one that seemed more salient each time I was pressed to find a different angle.

Sitting in my office on the twenty-ninth floor that fall, reading through the five or six newspapers I read every day, scanning reports from bureaus, reading wire copy, and watching television news, I discovered I had become a consumer, not a reporter, of news. I was losing my instincts. Cooped up in an office talking to my New York colleagues every day, reading the same newspapers they read, watching the Exxon skyscraper next door climb slowly, story by story, toward the sky, I suddenly realized how much I missed the sense of the hunt.

"I've got to get out of here and do a real story," I told Bridget. "I'm starting to rot in that office. Every time I have a good idea, Graves declares it not news and gives it to another department. Last week at lunch, for some reason I don't even begin to understand, he looked me straight in the eye and said, 'If you think I'm going to let you and Ajemian run the magazine, you're wrong.' I'm not trying to run the magazine. I'm trying to suggest some good stories. This is getting to be bullshit."

Somewhere I read that, so far that year, 80 policemen had been killed in the line of duty, 18 in random, pointless shootings. There had been 641 cops killed since 1960, and the rate was growing. It may have had something to do with all the rhetoric about "Off the pigs." Then again, it may not have meant anything other than more crazy people with guns and nothing to lose, but the situation had been largely obscured by the terrible violence of Vietnam. I went to Ajemian.

"We need to do something with this," I said. "I'm not sure just how to get a handle on it, but it's a story."

"Who does it really impact?" he asked.

"Mostly cops and their families," I said. "I mean, when a cop gets killed, people feel bad about it, but the real impact is on the family—the wife and kids."

"Maybe that's the angle."

"That is the angle. But I think doing a profile on the family of a murdered cop would be way too sad for *LIFE* magazine. And there are no pictures."

"Yes, but how about a family of a cop who hasn't been killed—a story about how they feel about having a cop in the family?"

"Strikes me as pretty thin, unless the guy is in some super-dangerous kind of police work."

"What about a family of cops? Find a family where every generation has a cop, and ask them if they will let their kids go to the academy. Find an attractive, articulate family, one with a pretty wife, maybe a schoolteacher. Then we can kind of wrap that around an account of the cops who have been killed and maybe get some expert to speculate on why it is happening."

"I want to report this story."

"You work in New York, in this building. What makes you think I'm going to let you go out there and have fun reporting this story?" Ajemian started to laugh.

"I need to get out of town and do some real work," I said, not sharing his mirth.

Ajemian was one of the best reporters of his generation. His ability to get politicians to speak honestly, more or less, and often to reveal themselves against their will was second only to his ability as a sports-writer. I thought he had given up his interest in reporting and writing, but I could see now that he shared with me a sense of being trapped by success in a job far more lucrative and far more boring than reporting.

"You can get by without me for a week," I said.

"I can probably get Ralph to agree because you were a cop. See if you can find a family."

They were in San Francisco, a father and son, third- and fourth-generation San Francisco cops: Mike Dower and Mike Dower Jr. The younger Dower's attractive blonde wife taught school, and his eight-month-old son was probably not going to the academy.

The whole thing was great fun: hanging out with cops, going with them as they worked, learning about San Francisco from their point of view. Mike Sr. was a detective on the fraud squad and a student of human nature. Mike Jr. was an earnest young man who had just been promoted to detective on the vice squad. At the end of a week I returned to New York with a solid story that ran for ten pages with a byline and an editor's note recalling my own days as a cop in Albuquerque. We ran pictures of the eighteen cops randomly killed that year and discussed the phenomenon. When the November 13 issue hit the desk, I felt restored.

It was good work, and it set me to thinking that perhaps I would be happier doing something more basic than editing.

With the success of my cop story still glowing in my mind, Bridget and I went to Kinderhook, the upstate village where her mother and sisters lived, to celebrate Thanksgiving. The country was especially beautiful that fall. No snow had fallen, and the autumn leaves were ankle deep along the streets. The air was sharp and clean. Everywhere we went, a warm fire welcomed us.

"You know," I said to Bridget after an evening with one of her old school friends, "I think I could get used to living like this."

She smiled, knowingly it seemed, but said nothing. Riding the train back to Manhattan, watching the Hudson River out the window, recalling the pleasant holiday, I began to think for the first time that maybe Bridget and I should try to find a small place in the country where we could spend weekends and some of our summer vacation.

The beauty of rural New York had largely escaped me until the train ride up, from Grand Central to Hudson, the old river town between Poughkeepsie and Albany. The New York Central track is close to the river, and for a hundred miles it reveals enchanting scenes that could easily be a slide show of the work of the Hudson River School. The river creates a special feeling in me, and I don't know why. I remember distinctly seeing the Hudson for the first time on my first trip to New York, on the way to the abortive trip to study in Europe. I felt then that I was in the presence of something mystical. Looking up the misty ravines, the distinction between fact and fiction seemed to disappear. I would not have been surprised to see Rip Van Winkle rubbing his eyes, or Ichabod Crane fleeing a headless horseman. Something about the Hudson is mysterious, especially in winter, or maybe I just read too many stories about it as a child. The trip was easier than I thought it would be, and by the time we found the subway in Grand Central it seemed quite possible to make it on a regular basis.

CHAPTER FIFTY-FIVE

"Do you hear anything from upstairs?" Ajemian asked one evening as I sat in front of his big desk trying to brainstorm a lead story for the next issue. It was after six, an hour when we sometimes began the most productive work of the day. Behind him, the late spring sun was setting over New Jersey.

"No. You?"

"I heard we lost around $10 million in 1970 and that ad pages for the coming six months are down. I don't know how true it is, but look at the magazine. Some issues we are down to, what, seventy to eighty pages? It used to run over a hundred."

I knew this was not closely held information, because Ajemian was the last person who would ever share anything when he had been instructed not to. He was better at guarding secrets than anyone I had ever known, and I was something of a gossip. "Where did you hear this?"

"Some of the business guys, at lunch."

"Do you think it's true?"

"Probably, but you know those guys. There's always a lot of rumor and guesswork floating around." He seemed to want to dismiss the information, but he couldn't.

"Do you think they would ever actually fold it?"

"I don't know," he said in exasperation. "The brand has got to be worth a lot. It's the Time-Life Building. How can they change that?"

"I know."

"It is Time-Life Books. It is Time-Life Records. Still, it's business. They might figure out a way to keep it alive in another form, to keep the name alive."

"You mean a zombie magazine? How so?"

"Well, they could make it a monthly. They could make it just special issues. We make a pile on special issues. We make a pile on anything we just sell on the newsstand. Maybe they can give up all the subscribers and just do newsstand issues."

"You think any of this could happen soon?"

"No, no. I don't see how they could fold it soon. It's too big. The cash flow alone is critical, millions in ad revenue every week. We have millions out in subscriber obligations. We have a huge staff. We still have bureaus and real estate. I think we have car ad commitments into early 1972."

Ajemian's restrained optimism did not make me feel especially secure. None of the possible options sounded as if they would require a senior editor for news. It seemed to me that he was saying we had some time but unless something radical came along, that time was limited.

Anxious about my future, I turned to Steve Gelman for advice. He was the most savvy journalist about journalism whom I knew. Raised in Brooklyn, a classmate of Sandy Koufax, a graduate of the Columbia University graduate program in journalism, Gelman had edited *Sport* magazine in the late 1950s and early 1960s. Hired by *LIFE* as an editor in the articles department at about the time I came on board, he had edited my big text pieces, teaching me lessons in the intricacies of structure and tone that simply were not available anywhere else. Far from the adversarial atmosphere that can characterize a relationship between writer and editor, we became friends, partly because I came to deeply respect his skills as an editor and partly because I just liked who he was. Slender, tightly wired, smoking too many Kent cigarettes, and walking in a kind of country lope, Gelman spoke in long, halting sentences over which he seemed to labor even as they emerged from his mouth. There were many articulate people at *LIFE* and many who believed they knew the score, but Gelman's thoughts on things professional seemed to me to be on the mark. When I asked him if I should put my career on hold and go to Columbia for a master's in journalism, he said no. In a kind of vindication of the apprentice theory of journalism that Dan Burrows, my editor at the *Tribune*, had espoused, Gelman said I had already learned from experience most of what the J school could teach. When I asked him how one became a successful independent writer, he replied that one achieved that blessed state when editors called you and invited you to write for them.

Gelman's advice on freelance writing did not make me especially happy. Somehow a writer had to manage to appear in print and present a style and an intellect that would attract editors, but he had to do this by invitation. It seemed a kind of Catch-22. How did one get the invitation that would lead to the invitation? Then Tom Lewis, an editor at Harcourt Brace Jovanovich, called and invited me to lunch, essentially answering my question. He and some of his colleagues had seen the story on the San Francisco cops. He wanted to talk about the possibility of a book.

I was a little like the owner of a new lottery ticket who, long before the numbers are picked, allows himself to imagine what he will do with his winnings. I ran through a scenario where I was asked to write a serious book on "social control." In another version I was sent to investigate the effect of different policing philosophies on crime rates. When I finally met Lewis and heard the pitch, I was disappointed. They wanted me to write an introductory textbook for the police science courses that were increasingly popular in community colleges opening all over America. I had to agree that the casting was good. Recruiting a journalist ex-cop to write an introductory police science text made perfect sense. The money they offered was not great, though I knew it was possible to make large sums of money on a college text if it became the preferred edition. But something larger than money was standing in the way. I still hoped to become a respected author of books on important current topics, and I was afraid that writing a textbook would sully my chances, branding me as a gun for hire and not a serious person. I decided not to decide until I returned from vacation.

In early July I flew to Puerto Rico with Bridget, Cathy, and Bridget's widowed mother, Mary. We spent a month enjoying the beach, listening to news of the Pentagon Papers, and discussing whether writing a textbook would be bad for my career, foreclosing some better opportunity. I spent way too much time trying to decide that simple question and eventually understood that I simply did not want to do the project. After a wonderful month we came home to discover a new Graves edict—a rather minor one, but one that would change everything.

Because of my exalted status at the magazine, I was entitled to five weeks of vacation. This was generally understood to be a month in the summer and a winter week to permit skiing or a retreat from the northeastern cold. Bridget was entitled to only three weeks, and we had for the past two years solved our dilemma of unequal vacations by having Bridget take a week off without pay. The ability for the two of us to go away with Cathy for a full month had grown enormously important to me, beginning with the magical summer month in New Mexico. The month in Puerto Rico was almost as good. Bridget loved those breaks as much as I did. But now, Graves, for some reason I failed to understand, said that no unpaid time would be granted. I felt the policy was aimed at me. In fact, the memo outlining the new policy stopped just short of reading, "editors and their secretaries." Why would anyone object to a person taking a week off without pay in the middle of the summer, and why were there no exceptions, like the need to have a family together once a year?

I was still seething from Graves's high-handed vacation memo when I was told he intended to take the five researchers assigned to the news department and place them under the direction of Josefa Stuart, the new chief of research. Graves's logic was that placing all research resources under one person would create greater efficiency. He also wanted to build a bigger empire for Stuart, who was one of his designated stars in the new plan to create more powerful positions for women. I didn't mind that, but I did mind that I would have to secure Stuart's permission for any research project I might wish to undertake and that the research itself would be overseen by another person with his or her own interests and priorities. I took my case directly to Graves. He reversed the decision, but it was not the end of his efforts to make the news department smaller and reduce our area of responsibility. Each new move eroded my agency, made me more beholden to others, and further undermined my faith in my instincts as a journalist.

I understood that the portion of the magazine devoted to news had to be smaller. If the magazine hoped to survive, it would not be primarily on covering news. We had to get that through our heads. Still, watching my venue shrink and feeling that Graves was drawing lines all around my turf to keep me from breaking out into other areas did not make my life happier or improve my self-regard.

When Graves, after rejecting many suggestions for what I took to be solid news stories, ordered up a cover story to be called "Americans Go Shopping for Cars," I was appalled. I suspected that the advertising department had moved onto our floor. The automakers were always complaining to the advertising salesmen that Detroit spent millions on *LIFE* ads and *LIFE* hardly ever wrote about cars. In better days we largely ignored the complaint. Detroit was important, but they had never influenced editorial policy in any major way, although Roy Rowan, my old boss and mentor, once showed me a little brass plaque on the dashboard of his vintage Mustang and told me that Lee Iacocca insisted he buy the car while he was doing a story on the new Ford sensation. "I was just a correspondent. I couldn't afford a new car, but Lee wouldn't take no for an answer," Rowan said. "I don't think he even gave me a very good discount."

"Americans Go Shopping for Cars" was a story that I would never, ever have suggested. Had I done so, I would have expected to be laughed out of the story conference, but here we were, explaining to America how people in Atlanta were out buying new cars. Perhaps more than any other single event, this convinced me that my good efforts as a journalist and editor were being wasted. There were too many agendas being serviced offstage for me to play the game with any success.

Then, as if he were building a metaphor for *LIFE*'s dilemma, Graves ordered, at considerable cost, an infernal machine to assist in layouts. It was an elaborate child's toy. The process of putting the magazine together involved choosing slides from many scattered on a light table. After a discussion of which selected slides should be seen large and which small, an art director would take the slides and go away to draw the page as he saw it. The drawing, sketch really, would become more and more concrete in subsequent passes until copies of the photos in actual size and dummy type were pasted in to produce a mock-up, a page that looked exactly as it would appear in the magazine, except for color and actual words. Sizes and word counts were included, and when it was approved, the whole business was sent to Chicago to be copied and printed. It was a good system that allowed flexibility and discussion. It was a system that had produced an outstanding picture magazine for thirty-five years. Graves wanted something more efficient.

One day we were ushered into a cramped office where we were confronted by a series of large, gray glass screens. It was explained that, through the use of frames and lenses and wires and projectors, slides could be loaded and shown on the large screen, where an editor could see in color what his page or spread might look like. While we watched, slides were loaded, and the machine began a clumsy, noisy attempt to do mechanically what some years later any simple home computer would do effortlessly using electronics. The wires and lenses and lights and frames, clanking and squeaking, eventually produced a rough facsimile of a magazine spread. It was a Rube Goldberg contraption, pure and simple. Graves was so proud of it that he issued another edict: all pages

357

would be laid out using his machine if it was available. His vision was ahead of its time, but as with *LIFE* magazine itself, the technology was ancient. Watching his machine labor at a job that had been done well for many years without mechanical help, all to report car sales in Atlanta, I began to suspect that my time at *LIFE* might be drawing to a close.

Graves's machine was an annoying distraction, but his next move was an editorial disaster. Clifford Irving, living in sybaritic isolation on the island of Ibiza, decided that he was smart enough to fool a lot of people and make a lot of money by claiming that he had been hired to write the authorized biography of the compulsively secretive Howard Hughes, one of the twentieth century's most fascinating characters. Irving's plan depended on one crucial element—that Hughes, a billionaire with a vast reach that extended even into the White House, would stand aside in silence while Irving wrote and sold an entirely fictitious biography of the man. Irving had convinced himself that Hughes had become such a recluse that he would not even speak out in the face of this monstrous affront. Using forged letters and other specious evidence of his deal with Hughes, Irving convinced editors at McGraw-Hill that he was authorized to write Hughes's biography. McGraw-Hill offered Graves the opportunity to buy in for magazine rights, and he did.

It was not the kind of mistake that just any editor could make. It is the kind of mistake that an editor makes when his normally skeptical nature has been battered by circumstance until he is desperate for a break. It is the kind of mistake a U-boat captain makes when, pursued by a pack of destroyers, he allows himself to be convinced that he can sneak through a narrow, rocky channel to safety. Graves needed something big and spectacular to give the magazine a lift. A biography of one of the most interesting men of the twentieth century might do it.

In what would result in one of the great ironies of journalism, Graves opened the Time Inc. archives to Irving to assist in his research. One day, passing the office where Irving worked, I saw him photographing files sent to New York by Frank McCulloch, a Time Inc. all-star who was the last journalist to interview Hughes. I thought Irving looked furtive. I felt sure of it when he quickly slid the door closed as I made my way down the hall. I dismissed the whole thing. It was not my problem.

From the beginning of the project, Graves held everything about it in great secrecy, even going so far as to have brown wrapping paper taped over the glass windows, seven feet above the floor, in the offices where the project was housed. During this time I began to understand something basic about Graves. His selection as managing editor was far more a function of his hard-ass administrative style than his creativity. He was authoritarian and exclusionary. Rather than bringing many of his editors in on his decision about Hughes, he developed a very small working group and swore them to total secrecy.

Unfortunately, he was living in an organization of journalists. As soon as the brown paper went up on an office window, Tommy Thompson, the six-foot-six-inch entertainment editor-writer, rolled a chair against the wall, climbed up on it, and looked through a crack in the paper. He began reading what he saw on the desk inside the locked office. The whole matter was an open secret from start to sad finish.

Time and *LIFE* had both been deeply intrigued by Hughes and his activities over the years. A corporate interest drove the amount of resources the magazines devoted to knowing about the man and his activities. With Irving in possession of literally thousands of pages of reporting from the Time Inc. archives, he had no trouble producing an initially credible manuscript. When Irving's draft was delivered to Graves, it was quickly compared to McCulloch's files to see if the Hughes quotes were similar in language and usage. Lo and behold!, they were. "This is Hughes," Graves said to the assembled editors. "It sounds just like the stuff Frank got in 1957." Well, yes, because it *was* the stuff Frank got in 1957.

LIFE advertised the soon-to-be-published biography. The magazine practically took a victory lap with McGraw-Hill. Then Hughes came to town to tell everyone it was a big fraud, to file a lawsuit, and to say he wanted it stopped.

We all watched in embarrassment as Irving confessed in January that he had never met Hughes and that he had made up the entire manuscript and the whole fantastic story surrounding it. I felt personally embarrassed because two years earlier we had published memoirs by Nikita Khrushchev, and I had stoutly defended the magazine when a lawyer at my dinner table questioned their authenticity. "How do you know for certain if they are real?" he asked, a little smugly, I thought. He was older than me and due my respect, but I went into a long dissertation about the "huge amount of resources that had gone into confirming their authenticity" and how Time Inc. would never publish anything so important if there was any doubt of its integrity. I could just see the old lawyer in his deep-blue pinstripe vest, gently touching his white hair as he read about Irving and thinking about the rookie editor he had indulged during a dinner discussion about how we know things to be true.

Graves attempted to recover by being forthright and running several stories on the whole matter, including a portrait of Irving's beautiful mistress (thus getting yet another beautiful woman on the cover) and an article on Hughes himself, but by that time my attention was wandering. I felt less and less identification with the magazine. It was as if I had fallen in love, gone on a seven-year honeymoon, and then watched my partner morph into someone unrecognizable to me. I was starting to worry that in order to save *LIFE*, the managers and editors were destroying all the things that made *LIFE* worth saving.

CHAPTER FIFTY-SIX

The rumor began as rumors usually do, with someone saying, "Did you hear they are going to cut the staff by half?" It is hard to keep a secret from a hundred-odd intensely interested journalists. By early February 1972, well-founded rumors that a massive layoff was on the way were sweeping the halls. Some said that half the editorial staff would be gone before summer.

It was an odd time. Some of us were marked for removal, and no one knew who the marked people were. It was a time of fear and a time when the worst in us came out. I found myself actually hoping that certain of my colleagues would be gone when the bloodbath was over. I would not have wished them fired, but if people were going to get the ax anyway, then I had a list I would prefer to see disappear.

"Who is on the list?" I asked Ajemian.

"I can't tell you," he said, in effect admitting that there was a list.

"Can you tell me the logic that underlies the list, other than cutting overhead?"

"Well, you can imagine, can't you? It is no secret that we have a sizable load of dead wood. I mean, you know the same people I know, who come back from lunch and fall asleep on their couch, the people who haven't done much in years. I mean, they are nice people, but in tough times do we really need them?"

"OK, I can think of maybe eight people who fit that category."

"I think Ralph is trying to be very humane in this. Some people have a fortune in profit sharing, and some don't. Some people are close to retirement anyway. Some people have young families."

"Well, it doesn't hurt that the younger people have the smaller salaries."

Ajemian just looked at me and smiled.

"So when is this going to happen?"

"I can't talk about this. I've already told you more than I should."

Bridget and I got out a magazine at home and went through the masthead, trying to guess who would be left and who would be gone. I was never entirely sure that, when the dust settled, I would not be among the missing.

"Don't be silly," Bridget said. "They need you."

"Sometimes I wonder."

"You're just scaring yourself."

When the cuts came, it happened in one day. People were called in and told that they were going to be let go or that it was time to retire. Names came spinning though the halls.

Bridget left her desk and came into my office. "Mary Leatherbee is leaving."

"Mary?"

"Yes, and Marion MacPhail."

"I'm astonished. Marion MacPhail?"

The impact on my morale was complex. Graves's appointment as managing editor, and now the cut, made opportunities for some of my allies to move into important jobs, but it also swept away a whole generation of people who had helped to build and sustain *LIFE* over the past twenty or thirty years. Many of them had been resources for the younger crowd. They were the keepers of traditions and a repository of great *LIFE* magazine stories. They took our history with them as they left. Those of us who survived the cut were relieved that we still had jobs, but we felt a certain survivors' guilt for having avoided being fired.

Traditionally, there had been agreement among the staff that working for *LIFE* was actually fun. We often paused in the middle of a long day or night to note that what we were doing was not drudgery, not repetitious, not repugnant, but actual fun. The fun was not gone, but it was getting rare.

Partly in pursuit of my hope of writing books in a post-*LIFE* life, and partly because Bridget and I liked them, we had cultivated a friendship with Tom Lewis, the Harcourt editor, and his wife, Madeline, after I turned down the textbook offer. The Saturday night after the big cuts, Bridget and I went to their apartment for dinner. Tom had gone to Columbia before and after the army, and he and Madeline were still in their old Morningside Heights quarters at 111th Street and Broadway. We had a nice evening with lots of talk about publishing and speculation about the chances that *LIFE* would survive. At about eleven we left to return to our apartment at Eighty-Ninth Street and West End Avenue, where we landed when we escaped Hell's Kitchen. It was a nice night, and we decided to walk. I had about a hundred dollars in my pocket because I had cashed a check at the magazine before we left Friday night, getting enough money to carry us through the weekend. We walked through the streets below 111th, strolling down West End Avenue. It was deserted. Somewhere in the vicinity of Ninety-Second Street, I looked ahead to see two very muscular young men standing on the corner. As we approached, one of them walked to the curb and waited, in effect creating a gauntlet through which we had to pass. Bridget's grip on my arm tightened, and I tugged just slightly as if to say, "Come on, don't miss a step."

As we neared, the man standing nearest the street stepped toward me, one hand in the pocket of his baggy pants. "Hey, man," he said, "you got five dollars?"

His companion shoved off from the wall where he had been leaning and stood ready. I had had a few drinks with dinner, and I was just loose enough to be casual. In a tone that implied I was surprised by such a silly question, I said, "Do you think that if I had five dollars I would be out here on these unsafe streets? Man, if I had five dollars, I'd be in a fucking cab!"

He laughed at the soundness of my logic and held out his palm. We swiped hands in mutual understanding, and Bridget and I continued our walk home.

"I didn't pee my pants," she said proudly when we were a block away.

It was the worst thing that had happened to us in New York, and it didn't amount to much, but I had watched the murder rate climb each year until it was double what it had been the year I first came to New York. The city was growing darker. The newspapers I read each day were filled with more and more stories of crime. The *New York Post* thrived on the stuff, producing, a few years down the road, the most memorable crime headline of all time: "Headless Body in Topless Bar." Tom Hyman, a fellow editor, came home to find two men burglarizing his apartment. Ann Thurman came home to find two men struggling to load a television set into a truck. She held the truck door for them, not recognizing her own TV as it went into the truck. "They were very polite," she said later.

I understood how much I had accepted the state of affairs when we returned home from work one evening to find one of the yellow steel doors of our apartment house lying on the sidewalk. It was badly distorted, twisted by some sort of powerful illegal entry device, probably a car jack. Without feeling much sense of surprise, I walked to the door and turned it over to see if it bore our apartment number. It didn't. We went upstairs, past an apartment temporarily closed off by a sheet of dirty plywood, and made dinner as usual.

The weekend after our encounter with the two men on West End Avenue, we went to Kinderhook and started looking seriously for a weekend place. It was not because we were suddenly afraid of the city. It was more that everything was kind of sliding slowly downhill and a country place might give us an anchor, a place we could count on. And with Ralph's edict about no unpaid time off, we would have to work out something less grand than our summers in New Mexico and Puerto Rico.

The divorce from Sally was expensive. I was still paying her alimony. I sent Hellyn child support each month for Cathy, and we had decided that Cathy should attend the Lakeside School in Seattle, which was expensive. This left a relatively slender purse for a house, but we were not looking for a mansion. The farther out in the country we went, the lower the prices, which suited me fine.

We looked for property almost every weekend in March and April and found nothing suitable that we could afford. We gave up temporarily, and then, in early May, Bridget's mother called. "I found your house," she said happily.

"You are kidding."

"No, no, I'm not. I just know it is the right house for you. But you have to come up and buy it. It won't last."

It was an old stagecoach stop built in the early 1800s—a tavern, really—that had been rescued and patched up by a handyman from Connecticut. The place was abandoned for a time during the Great Depression, when many upstate counties were depopulated, and it had suffered from that, but many of the unique original details survived. Old pine floors cut from trees four feet thick lay hidden beneath many coats of ugly paint. A post-and-beam frame made of chestnut beams twenty inches thick mostly survived. The floors were so uneven and the boards so warped that we joked that if we spilled something we'd have to chase it all over the house to clean it up, but with lots of hand-hewn details and wobbly window panes it was charming. Fragile, in need of much work, and with winter occupancy questionable, we decided to take it on anyway.

One of the main attractions for me, aside from the age and style of the place, was its location in the steep, heavily wooded Taconic Hills of eastern Columbia County that parallel the Berkshire Hills of western Massachusetts. The country reminded me a little of northern New Mexico. I could reconcile it with a picture I had of someday living in the mountains writing great books.

The house sat near a country road in the middle of a large clearing. Behind the house, an old wooden fence bisected the property, forming one side of what I guessed had been a pen for horses. I noticed that over the years the wind had deposited a mound of topsoil and manure along the fence. It cried out to be planted with something more interesting than native grass. In late May, without really understanding why, I pulled out the grass, made the dirt smooth, and planted hundreds of flower seeds. I wasn't selective. I didn't have much time. I just threw in the seeds: asters, sunflowers, cosmos, nicotiana, pansies, petunias, zinnias—whatever I could find in the rack at the local supermarket. It was a nice feeling to be back in touch with dirt. Then we bought an ancient Ford station wagon.

When Cathy arrived in July, she thought we had gone a little crazy. After a grand old adobe in New Mexico and a luxury apartment on the beach in Puerto Rico, she was now expected to spend her vacation in what must have appeared to her to be the epitome of rural poverty. She saw the place clearly as it was—not as we saw it, completely restored—but she had a good month. She played with Bridget's nieces, and we sat on the lawn at Tanglewood to picnic and listen to wonderful music. I took her fishing in a neighbor's pond, and when the month was over she said that she looked forward to coming back to the country again.

When she returned to Seattle and we began the weekly Sunday-night commute back to the city, I found leaving more and more difficult, but I had serious responsibilities to keep me moving. Ajemian was away for August, and I was sitting in for him again.

In another time, occupying Ajemian's big office with the layout room next door and all the trappings of corporate prestige would have excited my imagination and my ambition. "Oh, the places we'll go!" But with the future of the magazine so unsettled, everything seemed temporary—even the solid wooden furniture, the big desk, and the stocked bookcases. This could all be gone after one large meeting in an auditorium somewhere. It might already be gone, for all I knew. The business guys upstairs were not sharing any information about their plans.

My mood improved in September when the social life of the city began its annual renewal. People were refreshed after a hot summer and vacations. A new season for all the arts was opening. People were having parties to catch up on events after the summer.

Bridget and I arrived at one of these gatherings at a large apartment on Riverside Drive after work on a cool September evening. The place was jammed with magazine writers and editors, and many magazine alumni who had graduated to better things, like Tom Wolfe dressed in his signature white suit, who stood in the kitchen holding a drink, looking very much like an egret.

I had read and admired Nora Ephron's work in *Esquire*, but I had never met her. I was astonished by her height when she approached me with laughing eyes, a big smile, and a question. "Why," she said, looking down at me, "do you part your hair in the middle?"

I was completely confused, because I was not aware that my hair was parted in the middle. In fact, I was rapidly balding. "Oh, you're working on a column about opening lines," I said. She smiled and moved on.

Gloria Steinem, Jimmy Breslin, Nick Pileggi—the *LIFE* crowd— were all there, including Graves, who had one martini and left. Had the building collapsed, nothing of interest would have been written in New York for at least a month or two. Looking around the room, I understood that *LIFE* had indeed been the magic carpet that carried me to New York and to the cognoscenti I admired. In a very real sense, I had arrived at the destination I so ardently desired when sitting in Al Monte's Taos Bar in Albuquerque reading the *Saturday Review* with Fred Bonavita and wondering what it was like to actually know the people who wrote such things.

Then, in another of those rare moments that inform a life, I knew that I had done at *LIFE* magazine what I came to do. It had been a great run. I had met fabulous people both as colleagues and as subjects in stories. I had arrived here in this room, where it was revealed to me that I had accomplished my ambition. The next move was not clear, but I knew there had to be a move. My resolve was strengthened further just days later, when a young man I had mentored in Chicago called and asked if we could have a drink. There was something he wanted to tell me.

Michael Shamberg worked as a stringer for both the *Time* and *LIFE* bureaus and quickly became indispensable. Loy Miller, the *Time* bureau chief, and I were soon in competition to see who would successfully recruit him. When he opted for a job at *Time* magazine, I felt he had made the right choice, given the condition of *LIFE*, but I was disappointed because I had hoped he would become a colleague. We arrived in New York at about the same time, and I had kept in touch. On the phone it sounded like he might want advice. After work, we settled in at the Ho Ho, and Mike startled me by announcing that he was leaving *Time*.

"Why?" I asked.

"I'm working in a video commune, Raindance Foundation," he said. "We are going to start a video wire service."

I listened, fascinated and alarmed by what he told me. He and a number of friends, including his soon-to-be-wife, Megan, were going to cover the Republican National Convention in Miami using video cameras. Video was still a kind of toy, something people used to record family picnics. Television used cameras and shot film. I did not see how the TV people would be able to use video, or why they would want to, but I soon understood that Shamberg and his colleagues were involved with concepts well outside ordinary journalistic thinking, concepts that in three decades would completely disrupt traditional journalism. They correctly saw video as a technology that would have a huge political impact. A few months later, Shamberg published *Guerrilla Video*. I was flattered when I read in the acknowledgments that he credited me with having helped him learn to write.

"Mike, you have a great future here. You could be a managing editor. I think you are making a mistake."

He smiled. "Maybe."

I couldn't convince him to stay. As I thought about it, his decision seemed one of courage and conviction rather than recklessness. If bright younger guys like Shamberg had the courage to walk away from an assured future, then I was being too timid about leaving the less than certain prospects facing *LIFE*.

As it turned out, I lost track of Shamberg until a decade later, when I watched him accept an Academy Award as producer of *The Big Chill*. It was a long way from *Guerrilla Video*. In some respects it was even further from an editor's slot at *Time* magazine.

CHAPTER FIFTY-SEVEN

Now I faced a practical dilemma. If I resigned and moved to the country, I would take my last check and go. If the magazine folded while I was on board, I would leave with a year's salary in severance. I decided it was stupid to walk away from a year's pay. I could hold out a few more months. If the magazine managed to right itself, then I could decide what to do next. If it folded, at least I would have enough money to sustain us while I started over.

Having made the decision to leave, I felt fraudulent just hanging on waiting for the end. I felt like an heir pacing outside a rich father's sickroom, waiting for his inheritance. Where I had dreaded the end of *LIFE*, I now found myself wishing it would come quickly. Going to work became a chore. Making any worthwhile contribution seemed pointless. The trappings of success—the suits, the restaurants, the posh office—all lost their appeal. Something fundamental in my nature, ignored too long, was stirring, pulling me to a simpler, quieter, rural life.

I chose a Thursday while Graves was gone and went to see Ajemian. I was frank with him. "Bob, I just don't think I can stay any longer," I said, half hoping that he would say something like, "Hang in another month or two," thereby revealing the timetable. But he didn't. If he knew the deadline, he would not give it away.

He studied me for a time, thinking. "If you will get your stuff together and be out of here before Ralph gets back on Monday, I'll fire you."

His words landed and caused a violent tangle of emotion. He was offering me the severance check I badly needed, but it meant leaving with a less than honorable discharge. I considered his offer, but only briefly. "I'll be out of the building by Friday night."

He stood and shook my hand. "I have really enjoyed working with you."

"Thanks, Bob. You have been a terrific boss."

"You know," he added, winning my heart forever. "You really ought to be running something big. You could, you know."

I was able to fit all my stuff into a single cardboard box. It would be a few days before I turned in my *LIFE* ID, signed the necessary papers, and collected my last check. Then Bridget, who had resigned a week earlier, and I got into our station wagon and followed the Taconic State Parkway north to Columbia Country and a new life.

I felt very melancholy leaving New York. I knew it was the right thing, but it was going to be tough. I would not be "Gerald Moore from *LIFE* magazine" anymore. The world would react very differently to just plain old "Gerald Moore."

When we pulled up to the house in the country, I got out to walk a bit before unloading the car. The flowers I planted in May were now in a riot of late-summer bloom. Every color imaginable was bursting out of the fencerow, marching off toward the deep-green woods, welcoming me to my new life. I stood looking at them for a few minutes, thinking of how truly beautiful they were and of all the springs that lay ahead when I could plant even more. The sense of sadness I carried from the city left. The air was growing chilly. I decided we should have a fire, our first since we bought the house.

When the fire was blazing and our little sitting room grew cozy, I poured out two drinks and we settled in to watch the flames. We were content to be silent for a time, each lost in our own thoughts. Then Bridget stirred.

"What's your guess?" she said. "Will they fold it?"

"I think the year-end issue in December will be the last."

And it was.

ACKNOWLEDGMENTS

I must thank my agent, Jill Kneerim, and her agency, Kneerim & Williams, for acting well beyond the call of duty on behalf of *LIFE Story*. Jill's faith, good humor, and steadfast efforts brought the book to Elizabeth Hadas, whose clear vision and persistence as my editor and advocate have earned my deepest gratitude.